ADVANCED LEGAL WRITING AND ORAL ADVOCACY: TRIALS, APPEALS, AND MOOT COURT

Michael D. Murray
Valparaiso University School of Law

and

Christy Hallam DeSanctis
The George Washington University Law School

FOUNDATION PRESS
2009

THOMSON REUTERS

© 2009 By THOMSON REUTERS/FOUNDATION PRESS

195 Broadway, 9th Floor
New York, NY 10007
Phone Toll Free 1–877–888–1330
Fax (212) 367–6799
foundation–press.com

Printed in the United States of America

ISBN 978–1–59941–397–6

ABOUT THE AUTHORS

Michael D. Murray is Associate Professor of Law at Valparaiso University School of Law. He has taught at the University of Illinois College of Law from 2002 to 2008, and Saint Louis University School of Law from 1998-2002. He teaches law school and undergraduate courses in Art Law, Civil Procedure, First Amendment and Censorship, International Art and Cultural Heritage, International Civil Liberties: Freedom of Expression, Introduction to Advocacy, Legal Research and Writing, Legal Writing and Analysis, and Professional Responsibility. Professor Murray is the author or coauthor of eighteen books and several law review articles on art law, civil procedure, copyright, freedom of expression, law and the health care professions, legal research and writing, and products liability. His casebook, *Art Law: Cases and Materials* (2004), is one of the most widely adopted casebooks in the field. Professor Murray graduated from Loyola College in Maryland and from Columbia Law School, where he was a Harlan Fiske Stone Scholar. He was a member of a national champion Jessup International Law Moot Court team at Columbia, and Notes Editor of the Columbia Journal of Transnational Law. After law school, he clerked for United States District Judge John F. Nangle of the Eastern District of Missouri and Chair of the Judicial Panel on Multidistrict Litigation. Murray also practiced commercial, intellectual property, and products liability litigation for seven years at Bryan Cave law firm in St. Louis.

Christy H. DeSanctis is Associate Professor of Legal Research and Writing and Director of the Legal Research and Writing Program at the George Washington University Law School. The Program encompasses 1L Legal Research and Writing, and Introduction to Advocacy; the Scholarly Writing and LL.M. Thesis Programs; and an in-house Writing Center. After graduating from NYU School of Law, she clerked for John W. Bissell, the former Chief Judge of the U.S. District Court for the District of New Jersey. Prior to joining the GW faculty, Professor DeSanctis practiced at the Washington, D.C., law firms of Collier Shannon Scott and Steptoe & Johnson. There, she focused on trial and appellate litigation at both the state and federal level, including in the U.S. Supreme Court, and worked on a variety of regulatory and legislative matters before federal agencies and Congress. She also published numerous articles relating to major legislative efforts with which she was directly involved, including terrorism insurance legislation and federal health and financial privacy regulations. Professor DeSanctis began teaching as an adjunct faculty member at GW in 2002; she was appointed to the fulltime faculty and assumed the Directorship of the LRW Program in 2004. In addition to teaching legal research and writing courses, she also teaches Law and Literature. She regularly speaks at conferences on legal writing and rhetoric. Professor DeSanctis also has taught several undergraduate English courses at the University of Maryland, College Park, including: Introduction to the Novel; American Literature after 1865; and Freshman Composition, a persuasive writing course based in part on theories of classical rhetoric. In addition to her J.D., Professor DeSanctis holds a Masters in English language and literature with a minor in rhetoric and composition from the University of Maryland. She is currently at work on a Ph.D. in late nineteenth and early twentieth century American Literature.

DEDICATION

To Denise, Olivia, and Dennis, who make it fun;

To my sisters, Margaret, Mary, Jeannette, Anne, and Laura, who proved to me that the benefits of a teaching career outweigh all the costs.

M.D.M.
St. Louis, MO
March 2009

To Michael B. DeSanctis, as always;

To my friends and family who have put up with me for all of these years.

C.H.D.
Washington, DC
March 2009

ACKNOWLEDGMENTS

This book is a continuation of the LRW Series at Foundation Press that we, the authors, started four years ago. We have had a great deal of assistance from editors and others at Foundation Press over the past eight years. In particular, we would like to thank Robb Westawker, who steered this current interactive book project through the production process at Foundation Press, and Heidi Boe and Bob Temple for their part in making it come to fruition. We continue to thank John Bloomquist, the Publisher of Foundation Press, for five years of helping us through each of the stages of publication, marketing, and sales of our books. And we remember fondly Steve Errick, formerly Editor of Foundation Press, for being the first to latch on to our book proposal and for never giving up on it.

Several other people also are owed our gratitude for their unwavering support of our professional endeavors and participation in the process resulting in this book. Professor Murray would like to single out his research and teaching assistants: Sasha Madlem, Robin Martinez, Tyler Pratt, and Vanessa Sheehan at Valparaiso University School of Law; Lindsay Beyer, Brian George, Aaron Goldberg, and Maurice Holman at the University of Illinois College of Law, and Renee Auderer, Jeannie Bell, Jonathan Blitz, John Challis, and Katalin Raby at Saint Louis University School of Law. We also thank the students who allowed us to use their work as writing examples: Joshua Klasic and Travis Weber at Valparaiso University School of Law; Lindsay Beyer, Jessica Bregant, Michelle Chen, Jim Davis, Jeffrey Ekeberg, Ken Halcom, James Klempir, Suleen Lee, Gerald Meyer, Greg Rubio, Vaishali Shah, Ellen Shiels, Gabriel Siegle, Joshua Watson, and Jim Williams at the University of Illinois College of Law; and Jeannie Bell, Kevin Etzkorn, Josh Knight, Kirsten Moder, Allison Price, Gaylin Rich, Jerrod Sharp, Katherine Weathers, and Cherie Wyatt at Saint Louis University School of Law. Special thanks also are due to Professor Murray's assistants over the last eight years, Kristin Takish at Valparaiso University, and Mary Parsons and Deanna Shumard at the University of Illinois, whose support above and beyond the call of duty is remarkable and much appreciated.

Professor DeSanctis would like to recognize Jessica L. Clark and Kristén E. Murray, for their outstanding assistance running the GW LRW Program in past years, friendship, unabashed humor, and superb insight on how to teach students to write well; Professor Lorri Unumb, my predecessor at GW, for teaching me not only how to teach legal writing but also how to run a great program; and all of the GW Law Dean's Fellows and Writing Fellows from 2004 to 2008 for their energy and unceasing desire to make teaching legal research and citation interesting, rewarding and fun (and the 2004-05 Writing Fellows in particular for their assistance with the Appendix in this text on grammar rules).

The authors thank their legal research and writing colleagues who reviewed and commented on the text: Kenneth Chestek (University of Indiana-Indianapolis School of Law); Jessica Clark (George Washington University); Jane Ginsburg (Columbia Law School); Terri LeClercq (University of Texas School of Law); Pamela Lysaght (University of Detroit Mercy School of Law); Joanna Mossop (Columbia Law School); Kristen Murray (Temple University, Beasley School of Law); Suzanne Rowe (University of Oregon School of Law); Ann Davis Shields (Washington University School of Law); Judith Smith (Columbia Law School); Mark Wojcik (John Marshall Law School); and Cliff Zimmerman (Northwestern University School of Law). This book is the better for their kind and generous review and input.

Professor DeSanctis also thanks the following people: Linda A. Shashoua for her unwavering support in this endeavor and all of my others, as well as her guidance, friendship, and expertise in putting thoughts into both writing (and music!); Michael S. Levine, for his seemily undying friendship (despite my attempts to ignore him) and for sharing with me his thoughts and insights from almost ten years of teaching legal writing; George D. Gopen, for teaching me everything I know about reader and listener expectations; the Hon. John W. Bissell, for the opportunity to work with a true wordsmith; Scott A. Sinder, for teaching me how to write anything in one hour (and a Supreme Court brief in a weekend! (extenuating circumstances)); Pam Chamberlain for her institutional know-how and priceless advice on how the GW program operates; and to all of the past, present and future GW LRW adjunct professors (including, in no particular order: Lisa Goldblatt, Tom Simeone, Ken Kryvoruka, Andrew Steinberg, Josh Braunstein, John Arnett, Andrea Agathoklis, Tim McIlmail, Donna McCaffrey, Scott Castle, Bill Goodrich, Susan Lynch, Erik Barnett, and many others, from whom I have learned and continue to learn an enormous amount about a practice-oriented approach to teaching legal writing). And, oh yes, Michael DeSanctis – you simply cannot be a better writer than he is, hands down (*how* do you so masterfully edit things that you know nothing about?).

PREFACE

This book is a part of Murray and DeSanctis's Legal Research and Writing Series of books at Foundation Press, the latest titles of which are interactive texts providing a print format of the book and an electronic format that is enhanced with pop-up definitions, callout boxes, linked documents and presentations, and internal and external hyperlinks to expand the capacities of the text beyond the four corners of each page.

The three, new, interactive titles in the series are: ***Legal Writing and Analysis***, ***Legal Research Methods***, and ***Advanced Legal Writing and Oral Advocacy: Trials, Appeals, and Moot Court***. These books teach legal method, which consists of the skills necessary to determine legal issues (legal questions that need to be answered) from a given situation or set of facts, to research the law that speaks to these issues, to analyze the law, and to communicate the legal analysis or to advocate a client's position based on the legal analysis. The 1L legal method, legal research and writing, or introduction to advocacy course usually is the first course to teach law students these skills directly and to evaluate a student's progress in learning them.

The Interactive Casebook Series is designed for the current generation of law students whose familiarity and comfort with on-line and computer-based learning creates a demand for teaching resources that take advantage of that familiarity and comfort level. The first two interactive legal research and writing texts will provide a process-based legal methods course book and a legal research text covering all aspects of first year legal analysis, research, and objective legal writing topics. The third text is designed for second semester and upper-division advanced writing courses involving advocacy and oral argument at the trial and appellate levels and in moot court competitions.

Paired with the course books will be electronic, computer-based versions of the texts that add links to on-line databases and internet-based resources and supplement the text with pop-up definitions, graphical and textual explanations and depictions, and presentations to introduce and summarize the material. The electronic versions of the text will be fully searchable and highly portable, and each page can be annotated or highlighted. The table of contents and each of the chapters will contain internal and external navigation links, making them more valuable for use in class and out.

The Interactive texts will employ a layout that departs from the traditional, all-text casebook format through use of callout text boxes, diagrams, and color/border segregated feature sections for hypotheticals, references to scholarly debates, or other useful information for law students. Call-out topics include: Food for Thought; FYI; Major Themes; Make the Connection!; Point-Counterpoint; Do it with Style!; Apply it!; Take Note!; What's that?; and Practice Pointer.

These texts will deliver a process-oriented approach to writing and analysis in objective and adversarial contexts supplemented with product-based analytical tools. The texts will cover objective office memoranda and client letters as well as pretrial motions (motions to dismiss and summary judgment motions), writ petitions, and appellate briefs, and oral argument at the trial and appellate level. The texts are designed by professors with substantial practice experience, employing advanced rhetorical techniques, Explanatory Synthesis, and multiple annotated samples of work product.

CONTENTS

Chapter 1

Adversarial Legal Writing

This text focuses on **advocacy**–or **persuasion**–in legal writing and oral communication. As an attorney, you have an ethical obligation to represent your clients effectively in contested legal matters. A contested matter is any legal matter in which the interests of the parties differ – which means representation during anything from litigation before a court or governmental agency to a purchase and sale transaction, corporate deal, or patent application. Contested matters are the most typical legal situations in which you will be representing a client. In contested matters, you often must communicate with an opponent and a third-party decision-maker, such as a court or an arbitrator, in addition to communicating with your client and your supervisors and colleagues at your law office. The examples and chapters below focus on litigation at the trial level and appellate level, but the considerations raised throughout this section really apply to any contested matter.

This chapter focuses on the **differences between objective legal writing and adversarial legal writing**. Chapter 2 focuses on the general requirements of pretrial motions in court, and Chapter 3 and Chapter 4 zero in on the particular requirements of motions to dismiss and motions for summary judgment. Chapter 5 concentrates on appellate advocacy and the general requirements for appeals and writs, including the topic of standards of review. Chapter 6 considers the structure and content of appellate briefs, and Chapter 7 examines the art of oral advocacy at the pretrial, trial, and appellate levels of litigation. Finally, Chapter 8 looks beyond your first year legal writing experience to moot court and to actual practice situations in which collaborative legal writing is the norm.

I.   PRIMARY DIFFERENCES BETWEEN OBJECTIVE AND ADVERSARIAL LEGAL WRITING

Objectivity always is required to render appropriate legal advice to your colleagues and clients. The office memorandum – the paradigmatic example of objective, informative legal writing – is typically targeted to people on the same side – *i.e.*, people working for a client and presumed to be friendly to the client's position (or at least owe a duty to the client to keep its confidences). Office memoranda in general must reflect a critical appraisal of the client's situation, and not just engage in cheerleading to pump up the team. An internal office memorandum especially must consider the good and bad facts of the case and present the blemishes along with the beauty marks of the client's legal position.

Adversarial legal writing is a different animal. It is not quite *the opposite* of objective writing—because it also must be a truthful presentation of the merits of the client's case. However, adversarial writing turns

PRACTICE POINTER

Lawyers wear several hats in contested matters. As officers of the court, they are bound to uphold the law and promote justice. Accordingly, adversarial legal writing does not engage in fraud or obfuscation about the facts and law concerning the matter—nothing can be gained from lying and cheating except defeat and disbarment. The briefs and memoranda that you file with a court and serve on your opponents thus cannot change the facts or misstate the law. As attorneys and representatives, though, lawyers must also find the pathway to the best outcome for their client. The art (and skill) of persuasion, then, is really about how to present (and represent) the facts and the law in the light most favorable to your client. You should note that the best advocacy doesn't always mean taking the most aggressive position; rather, sometimes the best advocacy involves cooperation and concession.

on *persuasion* and thus *is crafted* so that it supports the client's position and **only** the client's position in the best possible way. A good advocate must not abandon objectivity, but her work product will emphasize or illuminate the strong points of the case and mitigate or diffuse the weaker points. **In other words: adversarial writing takes sides and advocates for one outcome—the outcome favoring the client.**

Indeed, our legal system necessitates this kind of representation. Anglo-American legal tradition and, in particular, the American legal system has as its fundamental underpinning the theory that a judge and jury are better able to do justice and resolve disputes when the parties to the suit each are represented by advocates who present a biased, one-sided argument in favor of their clients. The adversarial system depends on its participants approaching litigation and dispute resolution as a high stakes contest in which their clients can win or lose something that is significant, and in which each of the players in the process is expected to promote their clients' interests and not promote their opponents' interests. There are other models for justice and dispute resolution in the world, but this is the American way.

FYI

How zealous are you supposed to be?
Many lawyers in the United States suffer from a grand misinterpretation of the word "zealously" that used to be part and parcel of the lawyer's Model Code of Professional Responsibility (Canon 7, EC 7-1, and DR 7-101), and was adopted as part of the ethical code of many state bar associations. The intended meaning of the word was "promptly" and "diligently," but many lawyers interpreted it as "fanatically" or "cravenly." As a result, many lawyers took the position that their representation must be extremely contentious, aggressive, and unpleasant. The Model Rules of Professional Conduct that replaced the Model Code of Professional Responsibility have replaced the word "zealously" with more appropriate terms that mean "prompt" and "diligent" (*e.g.*, Model Rule 1.3 and Comment 1 thereto), and you should be advised that the requirement is for you to strengthen and advance your client's position and assert your client's interests above the interests of the other parties, but not to behave like a craven zealot and pursue every advantage to harm and inconvenience the other parties and their attorneys. Never is it your duty to try to hide facts, distort the truth, or obfuscate the law. The skill of advocacy is follow the rules and tell the truth and still advance the client's interests in a contested matter.

II.   STRATEGIES AND GOALS FOR ZEALOUS REPRESENTATION IN AN ADVERSARIAL CONTEXT

A.   In general, follow the "fifteen minute rule"

Supreme Court Justice Ruth Bader Ginsburg has commented that brief writers before the United States Supreme Court make two mistakes: first, they do not write clearly and concisely, and second, they do not write with their audience—the U.S. Supreme Court, with its current composition of judges—in mind.[1] In the words of Justice Ginsburg,

[2] That is a high standard to meet.

---

1   Comments delivered during "A Conversation with Justice Ruth Bader Ginsburg," at the Annual Meeting of the Association of American Law Schools, Washington D.C. (Jan. 8, 2000).

2   Id.

FOOD FOR THOUGHT

Justice Scalia agrees with Justice Ginsburg, and he has commented in his recent book with Bryan Garner that the "overarching objective of a brief is to make the court's job easier. . . . What achieves that objective? Brevity. Simple, straightforward English." Antonin Scalia & Bryan Garner, *Making Your Case: The Art of Persuading Judges* 59 (2008), http://west.thomson.com/productdetail/146377/40646555/productdetail. aspx.

Judges everywhere believe that they have more than enough cases to work on and too much material to read and digest in any given case. They will not tolerate complex, cumbersome, redundant, and overly verbose writing in briefs and memoranda to the court. Justice Ginsburg promised her audience that if a brief writer failed to follow her advice, and she felt bogged down in a work, she would skip back to the summary of argument and forget the rest of the brief, or hand it off to one of her law clerks to digest and encapsulate for her.[3] That kind of reception is not your goal as an advocate. If a justice on the highest court in this country with one of the smallest caseloads of any appellate court believes this, imagine the attitude of the typical judge with hundreds more cases pending on his docket when he receives your complex, prolix work. A judge is not going to suffer through this kind of work for very long.

In response to these attitudes, we advocate following the **Fifteen Minute Rule**:

FIFTEEN MINUTE RULE

Write so that you can prove your argument
to the reader in fifteen minutes.

There is nothing magical about fifteen minutes per se—and no guarantee that you will get even that much attention from a judge. But if you draft and edit your work so that a busy judge can capture the best parts of your entire position and argument on a given motion or appeal in approximately fifteen minutes or less, you will have served your client and the court very well.

---

3 Id.

There are several ways to accomplish this in your writing:

☒ **Front load** your best material in two respects:

- First, include an **introduction** to your brief that tells the court enough facts, law, and argument that you can convince the judge that your client should prevail, all in roughly half a page of text. (If the Local Rules on formatting are so specific that an introductory paragraph is specifically prohibited, then be sure that the first paragraph of your discussion on each major issue does this work for you).

- Second, always **lead with your strongest argument**, unless logic requires otherwise (because factors or elements must be discussed in a certain order, or the particular issues in question require a different order of progression (*e.g.*, A must be proved before B, even though your argument is stronger on B)). This is critically important because if you had the option to lead with an argument, and you did not, the reader almost always will perceive that the argument you chose to lead with *is* what you, the author and advocate, thought was the best argument. The reader further will perceive that any arguments coming second or third are *not* the best arguments, or at least they were perceived by you, the author and advocate, *not* to be your best arguments. You certainly do not want to create that impression when persuasion is your goal.

☒ Use the statement of facts to advocate your position. Here, we do not mean that you should include legal argument in your fact section; rather, we mean that you should consider the statement of facts as another place to advance your client's cause. You should carefully craft your fact section itself (in terms of the order in which you introduce facts, the specific vocabulary you choose, and the overall story that you tell) as a piece of advocacy.

☒ Use meaningful, argumentative **thesis headings** throughout the discussion or argument section.

☒ Draft the discussion or argument section in as **clear, concise, and direct** a manner as is possible.

☒ Use the **conclusion** solely to request relief, not to summarize or rehash your arguments and not to make a new point in support of your case.

These topics all will be discussed at greater length in the next chapter.

B.   Know your audience and write with that audience in mind

Knowing your audience is a basic principle of all legal writing. With objective writing, you will tend to know your immediate audience very well, whether they are your colleagues or your clients, because you will have worked with them for some time, or at least you likely will have access to people who know them well. Often in a litigation context, however, knowledge of your precise audience will be difficult to come by. You may be writing to a judge before whom you have never appeared prior to this case, and with whom no one in your office has had experience. At the appellate level, depending on the shuffle of panels and assignment of cases in your jurisdiction, you may not know your panel very far in advance (not even by the time your appellate briefs are due), and you may never get two of the same judges on a panel more than two or three times in your career.

Simply living with the uncertainty as inevitable kismet is not good enough. You should make calls to people who have tried any number of cases (even one) before a particular judge. Private civil litigators may not have as much exposure as prosecutors, public defenders, and criminal defense attorneys whose case loads often give them a better chance of seeing the same judge repeatedly over the course of several years, so do not neglect them when you are gathering your information. Use on-line resources to read everything that your judge has written in the area of law of your particular case. Westlaw allows you to search the judge field (ju) for opinions written by a particular judge, and Lexis allows you to search the OPINIONBY segment for the same purpose. In appellate courts, even before you find out the exact members of the panel hearing your case, you can read the recent opinions of the court in your area of the law or related areas to try to detect trends, biases, or preferences of the court.

PRACTICE POINTER

Is it the Roberts Court or the Kennedy Court?
The United States Supreme Court typically takes on as a shorthand reference the last name of the current chief justice of the court. As of the time of this writing (spring 2009), the United States Supreme Court is referred to as the "Roberts Court" in honor of Chief Justice John Roberts. But perhaps it should be referred to as the "Kennedy Court" in honor of Associate Justice Anthony Kennedy because in most cases, Kennedy is the swing vote between the four conservative justices and the four more liberal justices on the court. In closely disputed, controversial cases—the kind that are likely to be chosen for the extremely short list of cases that are selected for review by the high court—it is Kennedy's vote that is typically the most decisive. If you are writing a brief or making an argument to the United States Supreme Court, you are in large part making an argument to convince Justice Kennedy to vote your way. It would be a terrible tactical mistake not to know in intimate detail everything that Justice Kennedy ever has written about the area of the law that governs your case and any related areas of law, not just his majority opinions but every concurrence or dissent he ever has written in the applicable area of the law and any other related area. Finding one more point to press, one more case to emphasize, or more public policy discussion to bring to the forefront in your argument based on what you find in Kennedy's opinions may make the difference for your appeal.

Certainly, the sitting members of the United States Supreme Court have the most well documented track record of any judges in the nation. Every opinion, concurrence, and dissent written by the members of the Court is well documented, and the oral arguments before the Court are recorded on audio tape and text, so that the personal style of each justice during the arguments can be reviewed. In spite of this, Justice Ginsburg bemoans that many litigants write and argue as if their client and their friends at the firm were their only audience, and that they simply are preaching to their own choir.[4]

---

4 Comments of Justice Ruth Bader Ginsburg, <u>supra</u> note 1.

C.   Concede facts and give up arguments when it will benefit your client to do so; do not concede when it will not

Please disabuse yourself now of the notion that lawyers should never concede facts or abandon arguments. Absolutely not so. Of course, you always will want to make a conscious decision whether to make a concession or abandon a line of argument, but do keep an open mind as to the possibility (or necessity) of doing so.

The value of a concession depends in part on the stage and nature of the dispute. Early in a contested matter, it may not benefit your client to reveal all the facts your client knows to your opponents until you discover what your opponents know (and their version of the facts). On the other hand, early in the dispute may be a good time to reveal or stipulate to certain facts to save your client the time and energy of responding to onerous discovery requests. Certain concessions simply are against your client's interest no matter what the stage of the dispute. If you are representing an accused party, be especially wary about conceding facts that have any bearing on liability or damages. If you are representing an aggrieved party, be careful about conceding facts that may provide grounds for an affirmative defense by your opponent. In short, your evaluation of the facts must be long-sighted.

In litigation, you always should consider whether abandoning an argument will advance your cause with the court. Do not brief an argument if the chances that it will make you look foolish and obstinate are greater than the chances that any legal decision maker will agree with the argument and rule in your favor. Similarly, your best argument will shine brighter if you do not undermine your overall credibility by advancing indefensible positions. And certainly do not fall into the trap of thinking "the more, the better." The prevailing party is not simply the party with the most arguments. Judges do not make decisions based on the number of arguments you raised, and littering your writing with every argument you can conceive of only risks diluting the force of whatever strong arguments you have in your favor. That said, of course you never want to limit *arbitrarily* the number of arguments you make; rather, you should always be making reasoned, strategic decisions about the positions you put forward and the arguments you raise.

D.   Know the facts and the law, know your case and your opponent's case, and *know your options*

Finally, it should almost go without saying that you cannot help your client if you do not learn the facts of your client's case. And, to know which facts are likely to be important (or "legally significant"), you have to know the law. Naturally, knowing the law and the facts is required if you are going to give advice and represent your client in any way or shape or form. You also should know what you're up against, and this requires knowing your opponent's case as well – and what arguments and facts are against you. A lawyer who does not know the facts and the law sooner or later is destined to take an action that is directly against her client's interests. Knowing the facts and the law also will enable you to know your options. If you do not know the facts or law, you might inadvertently close off one or more of your options and eliminate otherwise perfectly acceptable forms of relief for your client.

The law is **not** one of the disciplines where 90% of the battle is just showing up. You must be prepared for the setting in which you are about to engage your lawyering skills. If it is the motion to dismiss stage, think about what you are doing with the motion or opposing the motion— What does it mean to bring (or defend) this motion? What are you trying to accomplish? What is the effect of this course of action as opposed to others? If it is the summary judgment stage, ask the same questions. What you can and should do at these stages differs, so think about it and make sure you are aware of what you are doing. You may not always win your motions or win the case just by being prepared, but you certainly will lose more motions and cases (and clients) if you are not.

Chapter 2

Pretrial Motions

The "pretrial" phase of a case is, as it sounds, the period between when a case is filed in court and before it goes to trial. During this phase, the parties may raise defenses and investigate the facts in the process of discovery. Importantly, this also is a phase where the parties may ask the court to "do something" on their behalf—*i.e.*, rule on an issue formally brought before the court. Such requests are called "pretrial motions." The parties may move for relief on a wide range of issues, from relatively mundane (but important) requests for extensions of time to more dramatic requests for the final disposition of an issue before the case proceeds to trial. Such "dispositive" motions include motions to dismiss and motions for summary judgment which, if granted, can result not only in a final resolution of one or more issues, but in the dismissal of the entire case in the initial pretrial phase.

I.   STRUCTURE OF PRETRIAL MOTIONS AND MEMORANDA IN SUPPORT

Pretrial motion practice encompasses the back-and-forth of briefs by the parties in this initial phase of litigation. Any party to the litigation may initiate the process by filing a motion with the court that seeks some decision on its part. Whatever the party's status (plaintiff or defendant), the initiator is called the "movant." The party against the motion is the "opponent," and if there are multiple parties in the action, there can be multiple movants and opponents of the motion.

It is important to remember that a motion is a formal document filed with the court requesting the proposed relief. Depending on the nature of the motion and the jurisdiction, this formal document itself may contain all the necessary factual and legal support for the court to rule on it. For example, a motion for an extension of time to answer may simply consist of a single document. However, the more complicated a particular request is, and almost certainly if the movant is seeking dismissal of a claim or claims, the formal motion must be accompanied as well by a brief, or "memorandum in support of the motion,"[1] which contains the legal and factual support for the motion.

Responses, or oppositions, to motions[2] and replies to responses or oppositions typically include all of the factual and legal support in the same document; *i.e.,* typically no one other than the movant files a separate formal memorandum in support or other supporting brief (unless of course the opponent also is cross-moving).

The section below outlines the basic structure of the document that presents the legal arguments of the movant in support of the motion, whether it is included in the motion itself or in a separately filed document. We will refer to this document from now on as the "**memorandum in support**" but, as noted, it may be called something else in the jurisdiction in which you are litigating. We also cover the basic structure for responses or oppositions, which we will call the "**memorandum in opposition**." The third structure outlined below applies to the document that presents the movant's further legal and factual support for its motion in response to the opposition to the motion; we will refer to this simply as the "**reply**."

PRACTICE POINTER

We are presenting the common structure of the documents associated with motions, but it is not the only structure you might employ. As always, you should consult the local rules of your jurisdiction to determine the court's preferred structure or the specific items it expects to see in these documents.

---

1 The requirements, if any, for a motion to be accompanied by a separate "memorandum in support of the motion" will be identified and defined in the local rules of the court where you are litigating. In various jurisdictions, this document may be called "suggestions in support," "points and authorities in support," or "brief in support" of the motion. You must pay attention to the local rules and not become too attached to one particular name for this type of litigation document.

2 Depending on the local rules, the document may be titled "response," "opposition," "memorandum in opposition," "suggestions in response," or "points and authorities in opposition" to the motion.

A.   The structure of the memorandum in support

A typical pretrial memorandum in support, no matter what kind of relief it seeks, will have the following sections:

Caption

Title

Introduction

Statement of Facts

Argument

Conclusion

Each section is discussed in detail below.

B.   The structure of the memorandum in opposition

The structure of the document that opposes the motion is the same:

Caption

Title

Introduction

Statement of Facts

Argument

Conclusion

C.   The structure of the reply

A reply typically uses the following format:

Caption

Title

Introduction

Argument

Conclusion

Here, the movant will omit the statement of facts (because it has already presented its version of the facts in the initial memorandum), unless of course the movant needs to clarify or correct something the opponent put in its version of the facts.

II.   THE CAPTION AND TITLE

The caption identifies the court, the parties, and the docket number for the case. Often the judge's name or initials is listed. How this information is arranged varies from jurisdiction to jurisdiction, but a typical structure is shown in the examples below.

The title also is relatively straightforward—it should introduce the party filing the memorandum and its purpose. For example: Defendant Smith's Memorandum in Support of Motion to Dismiss Plaintiff's Complaint for Lack of Personal Jurisdiction, or Plaintiff Arch Communicator's Memorandum in Support of Motion for Summary Judgment.

Here is an example:

Parties

UNITED STATES DISTRICT COURT
SOUTHERN DISTRICT OF NEW YORK

Caption

GEORGIE DOLLING, a Minor, by his father and next friend, Robert Dolling,

Plaintiff,

v.

ALDEN HALL HISTORICAL SITE, and ELLIOTT STIRLING,

Defendants.

Docket Number with Judge's Initials

No. 97 2343 TRW

Title

DEFENDANTS ALDEN HALL AND STIRLING'S MEMORANDUM IN SUPPORT OF MOTION TO DISMISS FOR FAILURE TO STATE A CLAIM PURSUANT TO FED. R. CIV. P. 12(b)(6)

The Title should be sufficiently detailed to tell the court at a glance who is moving and on what grounds. Usually, you will be moving the court pursuant to a specific rule of procedure or local rule, and it is a good idea to cite the rule in the title.

- *Properly detailed title:* **Plaintiff Van Pelt's Memorandum in Opposition to Defendant Brown's 28 U.S.C. § 1404 Motion to Transfer**

- *But not this:* **Plaintiff's Memorandum in Opposition to Motion to Transfer**

The same principle applies to the reply—at this point the court should be very familiar with the motion, so a properly drafted title to the reply identifies the movant, the opponent, and the motion.

- *Properly detailed title:* **Defendant Brown's Reply to Plaintiff Van Pelt's Opposition to Brown's 28 U.S.C. § 1404 Motion to Transfer**

III.   THE INTRODUCTION

A.   First sentence

The first sentence (or two) of your memorandum—following immediately after the title—in some respects repeats the title of the motion, although it typically contains slightly more detail in its specificity of the parties and the relief sought (that together would make the title itself too long). Think of this lead-in sentence or two as a kind of formal "pre-introduction" to your memorandum. This section is straightforward—you should identify yourself (the movant) and the party against whom the motion is brought. This is a good place to interject your shorthand references for the parties; e.g., "Plaintiff Donuts Manufacturing Conglomerate International ("Donuts") moves this Court pursuant to Fed. R. Civ. P. 12(b)(6) to dismiss the counterclaim of Defendant McKenzie Brackman LLC ("MB") for failure to state a claim upon which relief may be granted." Usually, you will be moving the court under the auspices of a certain rule of procedure, so cite the rule in this pre-introductory sentence. Then state the relief sought, and move on.

This lead-in sentence is not separately titled and typically *precedes* the heading of the next section, the "Introduction."

Opponents do not necessarily have to include this initial sentence. Remember that the opposition follows the motion and memorandum in support, so the court has had the opportunity to become familiar with the motion and has likely read the movant's papers before looking at the opposition papers. If the title of the opposition is sufficiently detailed to identify the party opposing the motion, the movant's name, and the nature of the motion that is opposed, then the opponent does not need to repeat the information and can proceed straight to the Introduction section discussed below. The same, of course, is true for the reply.

B.   The objective and importance of the introduction section

The introduction section has a simple objective, but one that truly takes all of your accumulated skill and experience to accomplish: **You**

must grab the court's attention and try to win the motion in the introduction. Many seasoned litigators will tell you that the introduction is one of the most important sections of the memorandum that follows it. You must place your best facts and the best points of your legal argument before the judge as soon as you can. This means that you should not be cagey in the introduction. Do everything you can to present your best points to the court and win the motion in the introduction. If you can draft an introduction that meets these ends, you will be well on your way to a successful career in litigation.

The movant and opponent obviously have different interests, but the objective to be obtained in the introduction is similar: win the motion. Therefore, the parties will state:

> **Movant:**   Why the motion at hand is necessary, and why I prevail.

> **Opponent:**   Why the motion at hand is improper (untimely, unnecessary, or scandalous), and even if it's not one of the above, why I should prevail.

C.   Drafting the introduction

1.   Movant's Introduction

Movant's Introduction must include:

- **Background facts (from movant's perspective)**
- **Movant's theme or theory of the case and of the motion**
- **Key operative facts upon which the motion turns**
- **Snapshot of the law on the motion**
- **Movant's conclusions (why the client prevails)**

Background Facts: As movant, you must present enough of the background facts to tell the court what is going on, but only facts favorable to your client's position.

Theme: In teaching students how to draft award-winning introductions, especially in dispositive motions, we have found it useful to have students contemplate constructing *one sentence* that captures the essence of the motion or opposition (or even the case as a whole) and why that side should prevail: "This case is about X." Of course, you will have more than one sentence to perform magic in your introduction, but it may be useful to take a step back and think about how you would fill in this blank.

For example, consider the following opening lines to this introduction:

- *Example – Interjecting theme and story of the case*: This lawsuit represents Van Pelt's attempt to spread the blame for her own negligence. Van Pelt's unauthorized modification of Brown's treadmill caused it to malfunction, killing one of Van Pelt's employees. In spite of the fact that the treadmill was in perfect working order when it was delivered to Brown's shipper and when it arrived at Van Pelt's health club as acknowledged by Van Pelt on the shipping receipt, Van Pelt has sued Brown for strict liability for design defect and failure to warn.

FYI

Of course, it should go without saying that the introduction should be *immediately identifiable* as belonging to one side or the other (even if the caption and title were omitted). In the example here, there is no way that the opponent, Van Pelt, could have written it.

The filing of a pretrial motion may provide the first occasion for the court to take notice of a pending lawsuit and open the court file and read about the case. Courts generally do not read complaints or answers as they are filed, and most will wait for a reason to read up on a case before they will invest that kind of time. The filing of a motion provides that reason. The court may start with the motion papers themselves, as these papers may be sitting on top in the court file (a typical system for filing material in a court file is by reverse chronological order with the most recently filed material sitting on top in the file). Even if the filing is done electronically, the motion papers will be among the most interesting things to read in the case file. Therefore, the movant has a strong incentive to present the background of the case early in its memorandum in support as this may be the court's first introduction to the case.

Key Operative Facts and Snapshot of the Law: The next task is to tell the facts that are most important to the motion at hand, and to give a snapshot of the law that applies. **Remember: this is the introduction.** Only tell as much of the law as is necessary to drive home your conclusions, and only discuss the elements of the rule that turn the case in your favor. Drive home the one or two best facts that further your argument.

Conclusions: Lastly, you will plug in your conclusions (which should be obvious from what you wrote leading up to them). Your main conclusion, of course, is that your client must prevail, and the client's position should appear as ironclad as a tank and as righteous as scripture.

If you are going to accomplish all of this in a reasonable amount of space, you should draft the introduction so that each sentence does double-duty, telling key facts and elements of the law, or conclusions and facts and legal principles, all in the same sentence.

DO IT WITH STYLE!

When discussing the law and your legal conclusions in the introduction, you should try to make each sentence perform two or three tasks; give a conclusion and the "because" part— the facts and the principles of the law that lead to the conclusion.

- *Example – Every Sentence Does Double-Duty:* {**conclusion**} Personal jurisdiction over the defendant Brown is improper because the {**legal principles**} Due Process clause requires minimum contacts with the forum state and {**facts**} Brown's two visits to the state were for charity purposes unrelated to any business activity conducted by Brown. {**conclusion**} Brown did not form any substantial connection to Pennsylvania because {**facts**} his two visits to the state were volunteer appearances for fund raising, amounting to less than six hours in the state, and thus were {**legal standards, conclusion**} random and fortuitous contacts. {**conclusion**} The visits were not connected to this lawsuit because {**facts**} the suit arises from Brown's sales of exercise equipment to plaintiff Van Pelt which were {**legal principles, facts, and conclusion**} transacted in Ohio where the sales agreements were signed and the contracts were formed.

There is no requirement to cite authority in an introduction. In fact, if you decide to cite anything at all, it should be extremely limited so that the section remains short and the text flows well.

DO IT WITH STYLE!

Limit your citations to authority in the introduction to the barest minimum. The default rule is not to cite *any* authority in the introduction. Most of the time, you will not have anything you need to cite in the introduction, but a short reference to the one statute, rule, or regulation that governs and controls the outcome, or to the very most important and strongest controlling cases that favor your position (no more than one or two) may be appropriate. This section has to flow, and long form citations clutter it up too much.

- *Example – Limits Citation to Authority:* Personal jurisdiction over defendant Brown is improper because the Due Process clause requires minimum contacts with the forum state and Brown's two visits to the state were for charity purposes unrelated to any business activity conducted by Brown.

- *Bad Example – Far Too Much Citation to Authority*: Personal jurisdiction over defendant Brown is improper because the Due Process clause, U.S. Const. amend. XIV, sec. 1, requires minimum contacts with the forum state, <u>Int'l Boot Co. v. Texas</u>, 323 U.S. 123, 128 (1945); <u>Hanover Trust Co. v. Blatt</u>, 456 U.S. 678, 682 (1967), and Brown's two visits to the state were for charity purposes unrelated to any business activity conducted by Brown. <u>See</u> Affidavit of Derek Brown dated July 14, 2005, ¶ 4 (attached hereto as exhibit 1).

Occasionally, an explanation for why you are bringing the motion is in order.

DO IT WITH STYLE!

Do not apologize for bringing the motion (unless you already have brought two such motions in the case; at that point, you certainly should explain the need for a third). There are certain conventions in legal drafting ("praying" for or "respectfully requesting" relief; "respectfully submitting" your motion) that are proper, formal writing, but they are not intended to be an apology. If you are forced to bring repetitive motions (such as in a discovery context), explain why your opponent forced you to bring the latest motion.

- *Example – Explains Reason for Multiple Motions:* Defendant Brown moves this court to compel the production of the medical reports of two of plaintiff Van Pelt's doctors. This is the third such motion to compel brought by Brown to obtain Van Pelt's complete medical records because Van Pelt persists in refusing to turn over the reports. In Van Pelt's deposition, she made reference to three treating physicians who attended her at Woodstock Hospital—Doctors Linus Pauling, Ludwig Schroeder, and Patty Peppermint. Only Doctor Pauling's report has been disclosed to Brown. Brown is entitled to the reports of all physicians who treated her for the injuries at issue in this matter.

The remaining components of an introduction consist of your **themes**—a theme for the case and a theme for the motion. A properly drafted theme for the case will be a single sentence or short phrase that sums up the client's position on the merits of the case that will resonate with the court and convince it that your client's position has merit and is worthy of careful attention. Think marketing message, not dissertation.

FOOD FOR THOUGHT

Are themes useful? Do marketing messages work? The advertising industry exists to prove that the answer is yes. Try and identify the companies that are associated with these slogans: "It's the real thing." "Just do it." "You're in good hands." "The king of beers." If you identified at least two of these companies just by their slogan, the marketing agencies are doing their job.

Your goal is for the court to start to think of the case as a whole in a light that favors your client. Naturally, the sound bite you draft will resonate more completely if you back it up with background facts that support your theory of the case. For some common themes, see <u>subsection D</u> below.

> **PRACTICE POINTER**
>
> **Interjecting the Theme Using "Sound Bites"**
> Using effective "sound bites" in your introduction helps the reader to latch on to your theme early and they are an effective tool to help the reader retain the information. Sound bites also will be of critical importance when you prepare for oral argument on the motion (if argument is heard). Oral argument is discussed in <u>Chapter 7</u>.

- *Example – Interjecting the Theme of the Case Using Sound-Bites*: {**sound-bite on theme of the case**} This lawsuit represents Van Pelt's attempt to spread the blame for her own negligence. {**supporting facts**} Van Pelt's unauthorized modification of Brown's treadmill caused it to malfunction killing one of Van Pelt's employees. In spite of the fact that the treadmill was in perfect working order when it was delivered to Brown's shipper and when it arrived at Van Pelt's health club as acknowledged by Van Pelt on the shipping receipt, Van Pelt has sued Brown for strict liability for design defect and failure to warn.

A properly drafted theme for the motion will cause the court to be receptive to your arguments and to sympathize with your client's facts and circumstances.

- *Example:* {**theme of the motion**} There is no legal justification for Van Pelt to file this lawsuit in Pennsylvania; rather forcing Brown to litigate in a distant forum is a strategy to seriously inconvenience him. {**supporting facts**} Although the sales agreement between Van Pelt and Brown were signed in Brown's place of business in Ohio, and Van Pelt took delivery of the goods in Ohio through a shipping agent of her choice (Federal Express), Van Pelt sued Brown in Pennsylvania where she resides.

You may even be able to improve this initial statement – *e.g.*, by characterizing it as harassment or an attempt to drive up litigation costs for Brown if, of course, you have the facts to support this claim.

2.   Opponent's Introduction

Opponent's Introduction must include:

- Background   Facts   **(from   opponent's perspective)**
- **Opponent's** theme **or** theory **of the case and of the motion**
- Key operative facts **upon which the motion turns**
- Snapshot of the law **on the motion**
- Opponent's conclusions **(why the client prevails)**

Opponents must take on the motion and the memorandum in support and turn the tables on the movant. As indicated above, the requirements for the introduction are the same for the opponent as they were for the movant. But an opponent may have more choices to make in responding to a motion. If you actually have a decent argument or even the better of the argument on the motion—the facts and the law actually support your side, not the movant's—then you can take the motion head-on, and argue point by point why the movant is erroneous on the facts, the law, or the conclusions. This is probably the most satisfying option.

If, however, the opponent has a difficult position on the merits, you should examine procedural issues regarding the timing of the motion or the propriety of movant's decision to bring this motion at this stage of the case as a whole. If laches have set in—you are in a much worse position now than if this motion had been brought a month ago—then you should argue laches in defense against the motion. If the motion is the second or third in a row by the movant, you certainly should question whether the second or third motion is necessary or whether the movant simply is trying to delay the case and frustrate the opponent. Courts are sensitive to tactical behavior, and if there is clear evidence that the movant is being tactical in a nefarious way, it typically will benefit you to bring this to the court's attention.

D.   More on themes

As noted, both the movant and the opponent should be able to articulate a **theme** for their motion or the case as a whole and try to sell that
theme in the introduction. Stated simply, your theme should be designed
to help the court grasp the facts and equities of the case, but in a way that
favors your client specifically. A theme should be able to be summed up in
one sentence or even a simple tag line—your pitch to the court in a marketing sense. A theme that catches on with the court can help you play up
your strengths and play down your weaknesses. If you succeed in making
a connection with the trial judge, every time she picks up the court file
of your case she hopefully will categorize the case on your terms. Ideally:
"Oh, this is the case where the woman modified the treadmill and killed
her employee and now is trying to spread the blame."

Of course, you should adopt a theme that ties together with the
facts and your legal argument. Do not forget that although you may be
writing an introduction to an initial procedural motion, it could be the
first document the judge and the law clerk looks at in regard to the entire
case, so you want to get them thinking about the case in the correct way
(your client's way).

FOOD FOR THOUGHT

If you fail to supply a theme for your case, the court (or your
opponent) will supply one for you. Judges (particularly trial
court judges) and law clerks who have to brief and prepare
their judges will often work up a theme to differentiate
one case from another. So much the better if it is your
client's theme. It does not do your client much good if
the court privately refers to the case as **"the case where the tall skinny drug
dealer is stabbing his short skinny drug dealer wife in the back"** if your
client is the tall skinny drug dealer. Better for you to insert the theme of
"the case of the recovering addict who is cooperating with the government
against his spouse who was the mastermind of a drug operation."

Themes vary from case to case. Some popular themes and variations on these themes are:

- **You've got to live by your word.** What good is a person (or a
  company) if she cannot live up to her word? Holding people
  to their word is the foundation of contract law.

- **Misuse of power.** Big, aggressive corporation vs. smart, little, under-financed corporation (your client). Big government agency against the little guy (your client).

- **Getting what you deserve.** Getting exactly what you bargained for. Getting what is fair for a victim in your situation. Getting what is right, in spite of what a contract or a rigid legal stipulation says you should get. A case of an innovative, cutting edge competitor (your client) vs. slip-shod, rip-off upstart company.

- **Cheating, taking what you don't deserve.** Overreaching. Unjust enrichment. Taking unfair advantage of a fortuitous situation. Ducking important rules or regulations.

- **Placing blame on the correct party.** Innocent, diligent bystander (your client) vs. careless and highly culpable opponents.

- **Dishonesty.** Deceit. Hiding important facts. Failing to disclose material information. Your opponent lied about many things in the past. This lawsuit is just the latest example.

- **Sloppiness.** Opponents are sloppy. Look how sloppy they are about the facts and authorities in the motion. Look at their own business practices. Their whole case is sloppy—you'll never get the complete, straight story from them.

- **Laches.** Opponents have brought the suit too late—we've changed our position in reliance on their acting one way, and now they sue to go the other way. This motion is the same thing—too little, too late, and we are put in a bad position by their bringing it at this stage of the case.

Be very careful not to pick an offensive theme. Do not start with an "American vs. foreigner" theme unless you like dancing on thin ice. Do not rely on themes such as, "She was just a hysterical woman" or "He was just a typical good old boy," unless you desire to offend the jury and the judge.

Lying also is a theme you have to think twice about, because it is unpopular with judges and juries. Be careful about trying to say, "The other side is bunch of liars. This latest motion is just a new pack of lies" (even if you believe that). Judges and juries do not want to assume that people lie all the time. If you are going to use this theme, you must have concrete evidence of deception on more than one occasion, and still you should tread lightly with the rhetoric you employ.

This advice goes double (or triple, even) for accusations against other lawyers in briefs or oral argument. Do not call another lawyer a liar in front of a judge unless you have ironclad proof of the lie. Even then, be careful and only accuse as far as you need to go. Use non-confrontational language: "His statement simply was not true" instead of "He lied to me." It makes for a very tense and unpleasant situation when attorneys start pointing the finger at each other over their truthfulness. Ad hominem attacks of all kinds are much more likely to turn the court against you rather than help you prevail on the motion.

E.   Length of the introduction

There is no perfect answer to the question: "How long should the introduction be?" Of course, you will be working within a word count or page limit, and that necessarily will dictate the choices you make throughout the document, but still there is no magic answer here. One tip is to consider the length of your argument section. If it takes you only five pages to cover the argument, it would be very strange to have a two-or three-page introduction. A basic rule of thumb is to aim for about half-a-page to one full page, and certainly to think long and hard about any introduction that is longer than a page. Most are at least half a page, but few are longer than one page total (certainly not impossible, but only truly complex cases will warrant it). Although we have been stressing the importance of the introduction, you do not want to overwhelm the reader with information. The introduction is supposed to be an introduction, not the entire memorandum.

PRACTICE POINTER

Most practitioners that we know (including ourselves) draft the introduction as one of the final components, and almost always *after* the argument section has been drafted. Oftentimes it is only after you've presented your full-blown argument that you have the perspective necessary to write the introduction, and sometimes your themes have not crystallized until you have done just that.

F.   Sample introductions

Here are some examples of introductions from … yes, a dog bite case. Hopefully, you will be able to see the strategies at work and the themes that each party has adopted for its side of the case.

The "objective" facts of the case are as follows:

A small boy, Georgie Bolling, was with his father, Robert Bolling, touring an outdoor historic site walking from building to building. They saw one more building further off to the side and headed for it. No fences or rope blocked off the house. There was one sign buried halfway in a snow bank. By the time they got close enough to see what the sign said—"Private Property - Keep Out"— the two were approached by a dog, roaming loose. The dog was friendly and playful. The boy decided to surprise his father by throwing a snowball at him. The father saw it and ducked, and the snowball hit the dog, spraying it with powdery snow. The dog attacked the boy, and had to be dragged off of him. The boy received 120 stitches and multiple bruises in the altercation. The boy and his father sued the historical site and the dog's owner, Elliott Stirling, for damages for the attack. The defendant now moves the court to dismiss the complaint for failure to state a claim.

EXAMPLE 1 – DEFENDANT'S PERSPECTIVE

UNITED STATES DISTRICT COURT
SOUTHERN DISTRICT OF NEW YORK

GEORGIE BOLLING,	)	
	)	
Plaintiff,	)	
	)	
v.	)	No. 05-2345-TRW
	)	
ALDEN HALL HISTORICAL SITE,	)	
and ELLIOTT STIRLING,	)	
	)	
Defendants.	)	

DEFENDANTS' MEMORANDUM IN SUPPORT OF FED. R. CIV. P. 12(b)(6) MOTION TO DISMISS FOR FAILURE TO STATE A CLAIM

Defendants Alden Hall Historical Site ("Alden Hall") and Elliott Stirling ("Stirling") move this Court pursuant to Fed. R. Civ. P. 12(b)(6) to dismiss the complaint brought by Plaintiff Georgie Bolling ("Plaintiff") for failure to state a cause of action upon which relief may be granted.

INTRODUCTION

Plaintiff Bolling's action to recover damages for a dog bite is barred because his unruly behavior provoked the dog's actions. On February 1, 2005, Bolling was trespassing on private property adjacent to the galleries and display areas of the Alden Hall Historical Site museum. Bolling admits to the behavior that resulted in the response by the dog in question, namely that he hit the dog with a snowball and sprayed it with snow. Although Bolling may not have intended to hit the dog, New York law provides that even inadvertent provocation of a dog precludes an action arising from a bite. Here, Defendant Stirling's dog acted fully in accordance with its training as a guard dog and reacted to Bolling's unauthorized presence on its property by subduing him in the wake of the incident with the snowball, which the dog could only have perceived as threatening. In the process, Bolling received lacerations on his arm. Despite admitting to engaging in this behavior, Bolling nevertheless claims that he is entitled to damages not only from Stirling, the dog's owner, but also from Alden Hall, the adjacent property owner. Yet controlling authority of this state dictates that provocation of a dog is a complete bar to recovery and mandates the dismissal of this complaint.

APPLY IT!

The introduction here is direct and forceful, but can you improve on it? Think about the choices defendants made in presenting the information in this way. What, if anything, would you delete? What would you add? This introduction puts all the blame on the injured party who potentially may be a sympathetic character in the story of the incident. The author calls the injured part, "Bolling" rather than plaintiff—this is midway between the depersonalized "plaintiff" and something warm and friendly such as "Georgie." What would you do to make this introduction more effective?

EXAMPLE 2 – PLAINTIFF'S PERSPECTIVE

UNITED STATES DISTRICT COURT
SOUTHERN DISTRICT OF NEW YORK

GEORGIE BOLLING,	)	
	)	
Plaintiff,	)	
	)	
v.	)	No. 05-2345-TRW
	)	
ALDEN HALL HISTORICAL SITE,	)	
and ELLIOTT STIRLING,	)	
	)	
Defendants.	)	

**PLAINTIFF'S RESPONSE TO DEFENDANTS ALDEN HALL AND
STIRLING'S FED. R. CIV. P. 12(b)(6) MOTION TO DISMISS FOR
FAILURE TO STATE A CLAIM**

INTRODUCTION

In their motion to dismiss, Defendants Elliott Stirling ("Stirling") and Alden Hall Historical Site ("Alden Hall") adopt the untenable position that they can give a vicious dog free rein to roam a public place where it might injure small children. Stirling's dog attacked Plaintiff Georgie Bolling ("Georgie") on February 1, 2005, during which Georgie's arm was mangled so extremely that he required 120 stitches. The dog was not "provoked," as that term has been defined by New York case law. Rather, the attack was vicious and disproportionate to the accidental dusting of snow that the dog experienced when it intervened in Georgie and his father's snowball game. The fact that the dog was loose and menacing patrons of the museum as they were traversing public walkways and going about their business touring the museum points directly to the liability of both defendants. The defendants failed to provide proper signage warning of the dog and failed to provide proper boundaries to prevent young patrons such as Georgie from accidentally straying onto private property. Accordingly, the complaint states all the necessary elements required for recovery under the New York "Dog Bite" statute, N.Y. Dog Bite Law § 516, and Defendants' motion to dismiss for failure to state a claim must be denied.

APPLY IT!

Plaintiff's introduction takes the fight back to the defendant. But can you improve on it? Think about the choices plaintiff made in presenting the information in this way. What, if anything, would you delete? What would you add? The authors chose to call the plaintiff "Georgie." That is acceptable because we are led to believe that Georgie is a young boy, certainly under the age of 18. Calling him "Georgie" would be a questionable tactic if Georgie was an adult. The focus of this introduction is on the dog and his "vicious" behavior. "Vicious" is a term from the authorities. If the facts back up this designation of "vicious," it will make it easier for plaintiff to prevail on the motion and in the case as a whole. But a legally significant *false* designation will be very destructive to plaintiff's credibility. What choices would you make to improve this introduction?

IV.   THE STATEMENT OF FACTS

When you were writing office memoranda, you may have been advised that the statement of facts should be "objective," meaning that it should contain no legal conclusions. Technically, the same is true in adversarial legal writing – at least in the sense that the statement of facts should not contain argument on the law. However, you should not underestimate the importance of the statement of facts in the brief writing context. Many lawyers do just that and thus fail to use it properly.

The statement of facts is yet another place where you should drive home your themes or theory of the case and, like all the other aspects of persuasive writing, there certainly is an "art" to drafting an award-winning statement of facts. Probably the worst mistake you can make is to draft a mundane statement facts, reiterating the background facts weakly in a rote, chronological fashion. The statement of facts is not just about telling the court the background, factual circumstances of the case. It is another place for *advocacy*, which at bottom requires that you take a step back and really think about the particular *story* that you want to tell. Under no circumstances should you compose your statement of facts so that a reader cannot tell on whose behalf it is written.

A.   Drafting the statement of facts

1.   Advocacy through narrative reasoning and storytelling

You always should try to advocate you client's case in every section of the motion, and the facts are no exception. Every chance that you get to write a "Background" or "Statement of Facts" section is a chance to tell your client's story—the good (your client), the bad (your opponent), and the ugly (what your opponent did).

The style of "argumentation" that you should employ in the facts section is **narrative reasoning**. Put on your creative writing hat here. You want to tell a story through a succession of narrated events, building facts upon other facts, choosing their order of presentation and your vocabulary intentionally and strategically, such that your presentation clearly adds up to the conclusion that you want your reader to reach. That said, and this is a challenging caveat: you should not state your legal conclusions outright in the fact section. Rather, you must rely on the manner in which you tell the story to do that work for you here. The key to a successful statement of facts is being able to state the same relevant facts as your opponent ought to state, but in a manner that tends to favor your client. You will not succeed by hiding key facts; your opponent will bring them out and you will look the worse for having tried to sweep them under the rug. Instead, talk about the material facts of the case, good and bad, but emphasize the good, and put the bad in terms that mitigate their effect on your client's position.

Easier said than done, to be sure. This is a challenging art to master with proficiency. But there are various techniques for emphasizing good facts and downplaying bad facts.

- ◆ Facts you want to emphasize always will have a greater impact if you phrase them in the active tense.

- ◆ Facts you want to deemphasize sometimes can be mitigated by phrasing them in the passive tense. The passive tense also takes the focus off of the true subject of the sentence (the actor or instigator), and if your client is the actor and instigator and she did something undesirable, use of the passive voice will help draw attention away from the doer of the action.

- ◆ You always should critically evaluate the vocabulary that you use, especially your verbs, adjectives, and adverbs. "Letting someone go" or "laying off someone" is a fairly neutral way of expressing a reduction in force (as is the term "reduction in force"); "firing" someone is not neutral at all, nor is "canning" someone, or "slashing" the workforce. "Coming into contact" with something does not paint much of a mental picture; "smashing into it," however, paints a picture with sound effects.

APPLY IT!

As a short exercise, return to the introductions that we presented above (Examples 1 and 2) in connection with the Bolling dog bite case and consider the word choices we made in presenting our introductory scenarios. Note at least three examples of wording that was chosen intentionally to advocate the client's position.

Consider the following examples that work from a single set of facts, but paint two widely divergent pictures:

- *Example 1 - Common Facts:* Client Jones was going 60 m.p.h. in a 45 m.p.h. zone on his way to his therapist, a doctor of psychology. He was late. The road was wet. A poodle came out from behind a parked car and moved into the road in front of him. Jones swerved, his car slid out of control, and he hit a parked car owned by plaintiff.

- *Plaintiff's Version:* Defendant was late for an appointment with his psychotherapist and was speeding at 60 m.p.h. on rain slick pavement in a 45 m.p.h. zone. A poodle entered into the path of Defendant's speeding car, and Defendant swerved and sent his car spinning out of control. Defendant then smashed his car into the back of plaintiff Smith's parked car.

- *Defendant's Version:* Mr. Jones was proceeding to an important appointment. A dog jumped out in front of him taking him completely by surprise. In an effort to avoid hitting the dog, he turned the wheel quickly but the car slid on the damp pavement and came into contact with the plaintiff's car.

> *Comment: Plaintiff's version makes us think, perhaps, that Jones had psychological issues. Sadly (we believe), there may be some subconscious bias at work in judging someone attending a psychotherapy appointment, as opposed to, say, a dentist appointment. Your own experience (as well as ours) may dissuade you from including the specifics here, but we have done so because it is something **to think about**, a strategic decision that you should make rather than an unthinking one. If you also have facts that suggest that Jones was*

indeed likely to fly off the handle at any moment, how might that influence your decision? If Jones was on his way to an appointment with an anger management counselor — what might be the result? Also notice how Plaintiff emphasizes the speed and the lateness factors. The road sounds danger-ous— slick with rain. The facts about Jones's reaction to the dog all are phrased in the active tense—Jones swerved, he sent the car out of control, he hit the other car. And not just hit it, he smashed into it.

Defendant Jones certainly does not ignore all of the events of that day or pretend that he was somewhere else. His side deals with the same facts, but we hear them in terms that allow us to give Jones a little more credit. Jones gives a plausible reason for his haste. Important, credible people have important appointments. Damp pavement is a much better adjective for wetness than rain-slick. The dog took Jones completely by surprise. What happened next is phrased in the passive tense, taking some of the heat off of Jones. The result is plaintiff's car was hit, but "coming into contact" certainly is not as auditory as "smashing" (with metal and glass flying).

- *Example 2 - Common Facts:* ABC Corp. laid off thirteen work-ers in a reduction in force (RIF). ABC used a business pro-ductivity formula. Six of the workers who were laid off were over the age of 40, four of these were women. Four more who were laid off were minorities, two of whom were women. Mr. Smith, a white male age 37, made the final decision of whom to lay off.

- *Plaintiff's Version:* ABC's most recent RIF was spearheaded by Cliff Smith, a white male. Smith targeted women, minori-ties, and workers whose age was over 40 for ten of his thirteen cuts. When he fired six elderly workers, he made sure four of them were women, and when he singled out four minorities for firing, he made sure half of them were women. Smith used a formula that ensured that these people could be disposed of with the excuse of increasing productivity.

- *Defendant's Version:* ABC was forced by competitive economic factors to lay off thirteen workers. A formula was used based on a worker's years of service, evaluation grades, and amount of contract revenue generated in the last five years. The thirteen lowest performing workers were laid off.

Comment: Isn't "spearheaded" a wonderful word for plaintiff? It is a perfectly common word in daily parlance, but in a fact pattern involving a reduction in force, it (arguably) suggests that Smith carried off someone's head on a spear. Plaintiff's statement of facts is drafted entirely in the active voice, because plaintiff wants the reader to focus on a particular person (Smith) doing these things. The mention of an "excuse" is a polite and formal way of suggesting subterfuge—an artifice. Plaintiff would have liked to have used the word "pretext" or "pretextual" but these are legal conclusions, and legal conclusions do not belong in the statement of facts as discussed in the section below.

Defendant's section is drafted in the passive voice so that the reader does not focus on who did these actions. But whoever they were, they didn't want to do the reduction in force; they were forced to do it. Defendant's fact statement also is short; it suggests that this was a routine procedure, done at dozens of companies across the country each day, and there is not much more to say about it than that.

FOOD FOR THOUGHT

One of our favorite examples of excellence in writing a statement of facts can be found in the briefs to the U.S. Supreme Court in the famous case, *New Jersey. v. T.L.O.*, 469 U.S. 325 (1984), where the parties' statements of fact tell the chronology of events so differently, and using such different vocabulary, that you might be fooled into thinking (as you should be) that two different events took place. The case involved (in essence) the constitutionality of a search of a minor's purse on school grounds. T.L.O.'s attorneys, of course, started with the search itself, and emphasized the rifling through her belongings. The State of New Jersey, in contrast, began with a stricter chronology of events that led up to the search, and whereas T.L.O.'s brief characterized the items found one by one, N.J. summarily characterized the items as "drug paraphernalia." You can review the briefs here.

2.   Legal conclusions vs. factual conclusions

Legal conclusions do not belong in the statement of facts section; in fact, they will stick out like a sore thumb. Judges get exercised about legal conclusions in the facts because when they find them, it looks like the author is trying to cheat, starting her argument too early and in the wrong section. Judges tend to think that statement of facts should be "objective," not argumentative, and you only will irritate them by stating legal conclusions right under their noses in the facts section. Of course, as we have noted, the statement of facts can advance your argument—that is really the whole point we have been trying to communicate above—but you cannot do it in a sloppy, careless manner by stating obvious legal conclusions along with the facts.

In order to carry out the objective of advancing your client's cause in the statement of facts without stating legal conclusions, you must understand the distinction between legal and factual conclusions. Factual conclusions that are logical *inferences* drawn from the facts generally are fine to insert in the statement of facts. Consider the following examples:

Factual Conclusions:

The car ***was going fast*** on the wet road.

The accident happened ***when there still was enough light to see***.

The doctor had ***followed the standard procedures*** at the hospital for learning a new surgical procedure before she attempted to do it herself.

Smith used a formula that ensured that these people could be disposed of with the ***excuse*** of increasing productivity.

What you really need to avoid are legal conclusions:

Legal Conclusions:

The driver was ***reckless*** for driving at that speed.

The accident was **caused** by the defendant.

The doctor was **not negligent** in attempting to perform the procedure she had just learned.

Smith used a formula that ensured that these people could be disposed of under the **pretext** of increasing productivity.

These are all things—characterized as fact—that really depend on the operation of law. A basic tip is to avoid (or use very cautiously) legal terms that you need to explain and prove in your argument section. "Provocation" in the dog bite hypothetical above is a perfect example. It means something specific under the law; it requires a finding. You might be tempted to say in the Bolling example, above, that Bolling "provoked" the dog (and perhaps you are correct under the law). But in the Statement of Facts, you want to write around (or toward) this conclusion. In other words, you want to display the facts that ultimately will produce the conclusion that the dog was or was not provoked, but to simply state that "Bolling obviously provoked the dog" is not sufficient—and a court will be highly suspicious of this attempt to bootstrap.

In short, you should not *need* to state legal conclusions in the statement of facts; if you tell an engaging story and emphasize the right facts and draw appropriate inferences and factual conclusions, every law trained reader will know where you are going and they will fill in the legal conclusions. Even if they do not, they are one page turn away from reading your legal conclusions in the proper place for them—the argument section.

B.   Limits on drafting the facts – style and good taste

There are several rules of style and decorum that apply in this setting.

- ♦ **Do not go overboard with emotion**. It is unprofessional, and will turn the court against you.

Acceptable: After being fired by ABC Corp., plaintiff Smith was forced to take two jobs to support her two daughters. As a single mother living far away from all of her relations, she had no other choice. Smith became ill from stress and exhaustion, and was hospitalized for two days in May 2005 with chest pains and irregular heart beats.

Do not say: Defendant ABC Corp. was not satisfied with destroying plaintiff's dreams of lifetime employment at the company; the company threw this poor, struggling single mother out into the street, abandoning her in her time of need just as her worthless lover had abandoned her seven years earlier. ABC Corp. caused Smith's heart attack and put her in the hospital just as surely as if they had injected her with adrenaline and electrified her chest. They broke her heart, plain and simple.

If you are a plaintiff, give a fair account of the injuries, using compelling terms. Do not overstate the injuries in a blatant attempt to draw sympathy or outrage. Do not give gruesome, gratuitously revolting statements of the facts.

Example: If the broken machinery almost ripped your client's arm off, say so: Plaintiff's arm was caught in the machine and nearly ripped off of his body.

Do not say: The machine acted with murderous efficiency to rip plaintiff from stem to stern.

A fair account of the injuries by a plaintiff is not a stump speech to inflame the listeners. If the facts are particularly heinous or grisly—a sex crime or violent act against a child, for example—tell the story completely, but remember to write it as a professional. Think network evening news, not Jerry Springer (although, sadly, the two formats these days are sometimes indistinguishable). Write it like the New York Times would, not like a "National-Midnight-Star" rag sheet (to borrow a clever name from Second City Television) would. Be clear and compelling, but do not put on a gratuitous tear-jerker or freak show:

Acceptable: Plaintiff Kruger's arm was caught in the machine and nearly ripped off of his body. Kruger described the pain to a paramedic as "excruciating." In a matter of seconds, he lost complete use of his arm.

Do not say: Plaintiff's screams rang out as the machine slowly, horribly tore his flesh. Blood spurted from his arm and coated the machine, dripping down to form a large puddle on the floor. Words cannot describe the sounds of a man having his arm ripped from his body and the scene of gore as the jaws of a murderous machine try to tear a limb from its shoulder.

There may be a fine line sometimes between the grotesque and ridiculous, and that which accurately captures the sympathetic visuals that you are attempting to call to the fore, but do tread lightly on this terrain and ask yourself (always) whether you are intending to write to a court, or to a producer of *Law and Order: SVU.* In other words, by all means be *legitimately* specific, but despite our suggestion to put your creative writing hat on, *do not* be overly dramatic, gory, or gratuitously obscene.

A defendant obviously has no incentive to dwell overly long on plaintiffs' injuries. You should try to downplay these as best as possible and move on quickly.

Example: The machine caused several lacerations to plaintiff's arm resulting in loss of its functionality. However, plaintiff experienced a quick recovery and regained nearly complete functionality of his arm within six weeks of the incident.

◆ **Do not give unnecessary detail** because you will wear the court out. You should not have to spend more than a page or two pages on the statement of facts for the average pretrial motion. (Again, there is no magic formula or page limit. However, consider the overall length of the brief as well as the complexity of the facts).

Good: Defendant Jones was late for an appointment with his psychotherapist and was speeding at 60 m.p.h. on rain slick pavement in a 45 m.p.h. zone. A poodle entered the path of Defendant's speeding car, and Defendant swerved and sent his car spinning out of control. Defendant then smashed his car into the back of plaintiff Smith's parked car.

Not this: Defendant Jones was running approximately eight minutes late for his appointment with his psychotherapist, Dr. Will B. Shrinker. He went speeding along on his way to Dr. Shrinker's office on Mulberry Lane, a mixed business and residential zoned area with a posted 45 m.p.h. speed limit. He was traveling at an average speed of 60 m.p.h. as confirmed by a passive police monitoring unit on Mulberry Lane that Jones passed by; his speed also was generally confirmed by two eye witnesses at the scene, Mrs. Vera Stigmatism and Mr. Esau Nothing, both of whom were on their daily exercise walks. At some point soon after passing by the monitoring unit, a poodle walked out into the path of Defendant's speeding car. Defendant took action immediately. He swerved the car to the left, and sent his car spinning out of control. There is no indication that he was able to regain control of the car. Jones' car spun out of control for more than two seconds, again, as confirmed by Mrs. Stigmatism and Mr. Nothing. Defendant then smashed his car into the back of plaintiff Smith's parked car. No one witnessed the actions of the poodle after Jones swerved away from it, but the poodle was unharmed in the incident.

Do you see the difference? Perhaps an exaggeration, these details may well be interesting to your client, but it is unlikely that they will have any effect on the average pretrial motion. Remember, a motion represents only a tiny part of a much bigger case, and if these details are not relevant for the particular purpose of the motion at hand, leave them out. They will wear out your reader and squander her attention span.

♦ **Do use descriptive terms** for facts, verbs, adjectives, and adverbs borrowed from the case law and authorities to describe the facts (i.e., employ parallelism). For example:

> *Example:* If the facts described in the authorities for proper conduct is "proactive measures to prevent infection," state in the facts that your client "undertook the following proactive measures to prevent infection by viral agents."

> *Do not say:* The client undertook "safety measures," "infection control protocol," or "strenuous action to curb infection."

♦ If, however, the term is a **legal conclusion** – this is important – avoid stating it using the conclusory term. This would be the equivalent of writing a legal conclusion in the facts section. Instead, simply report the action:

> *Example:* If the legal standard requires a finding of lack of provocation, do not simply state that: "Plaintiff did not provoke the dog in any way." This is a legal conclusion. Instead, say: "Plaintiff did not bother the dog, or anger, or threaten, or intimidate, or rile up the dog in any way." Perhaps "plaintiff did not approach the dog" or "made no hostile or threatening movement toward the dog." Even an adjective like "provocative" carries a legal conclusion, so be careful of such words.

> If "immediate notification" of the injury is the operative legal standard, you can probably get away with stating that your client "immediately notified the plaintiff of the injury at 11:23 a.m." But this is a bit conclusory, and it might offend some judges. To be on the safe side, avoid the legal terms of art, but state what happened in explicit terms: "Within four minutes of the incident, defendant informed plaintiff of the injury."

◆ **Do not be redundant**, unless the point that you are making *is* the number of times your opponent did the same bad thing.

C.   Do you cite authority in the statement of facts?

Cites to *legal authority* should by definition be unnecessary in the statement of facts, because you generally should not be making statements about the law in the facts section. But citation to *factual authority* to back up your statements in the statement of facts always is required. Do it whenever you have a document to which to cite, and especially for the first time you mention a specific fact.

> *Example:* Brown's two visits to the state were for charity purposes unrelated to any business activity conducted by Brown. See Affidavit of Derek Brown dated July 14, 2005, ¶ 4 (attached hereto as exhibit 1) ("Brown Aff."). Van Pelt did not attend either of the visits. Complaint ¶¶ 3-5. The charity visits had nothing to do with Brown's sales of exercise equipment to Van Pelt. Brown Aff. ¶ 6. Neither visit lasted longer than three hours, putting the total time that Brown spent in Pennsylvania at less than six hours. Id.[3]

Later, in the **argument section**, you do not need to keep citing back to the authority each time you discuss that fact, *unless* you have a reason to point the court specifically to a piece of factual support (such as if you are **quoting** something that one of the parties said).

D.   In what order do you have to present the facts?

From what we have said already, you should know to choose whichever order is the most compelling for your argument. But we have one piece of advice: *if* chronological order works for your side, use it because it is the easiest to follow. People expect it. It makes them happy. But it is

---

3 As illustrated in the example, id. is a proper shorthand for referring back to the immediately preceding factual authority. Other shorthand phrases should be defined for the benefit of the reader, as shown in the example: Affidavit of Derek Brown dated July 14, 2005, ¶ 4 ("Brown Aff.").

not required. So, if a chronological presentation does nothing for your client, use a topical or thematic presentation of the facts. In a contract case, you might first talk about the contract terms, then how the parties first got together on the deal, pre-negotiation actions, then the negotiation, then the post-contracting activities, **or** you might talk about the three main components of the contract, and how each one was negotiated and performed. In a personal injury case, you might first talk about the accident and the injury (your client's involvement) then about the facts leading up to the injury (the causation facts). In a search and seizure case, if you are representing the party searched, you might start with the allegedly illegal action that brought your client to the forefront. In a patent infringement or unfair trade practices case, you might first talk about your client, its history, its business, then the development of the client's product, then the competitor and its product (which may have been earlier in time). In short, always consider a client-oriented presentation. Always tell the facts with the client's interest and client's point of view in mind.

E.   Sample statements of facts

Consider the following examples:

EXAMPLE 1: INTRODUCTION AND STATEMENT OF FACTS FROM DEFENDANTS' MOTION TO DISMISS IN THE BOLLING V. STIRLING AND ALDEN HALL CASE:

UNITED STATES DISTRICT COURT
SOUTHERN DISTRICT OF NEW YORK

GEORGIE BOLLING,	)	
	)	
Plaintiff,	)	
	)	
v.	)	No. 05-2345-TRW
	)	
ALDEN HALL HISTORICAL SITE,	)	
and ELLIOTT STIRLING,	)	
	)	
Defendants.	)	

DEFENDANTS' MEMORANDUM IN SUPPORT OF MOTION TO DISMISS FOR FAILURE TO STATE A CLAIM

Defendants Alden Hall Historical Site ("Alden Hall") and Elliott Stirling move this Court pursuant to Fed. R. Civ. P. 12(b)(6) to dismiss the complaint brought by Plaintiff Georgie Bolling for failure to state a cause of action upon which relief may be granted.

INTRODUCTION

Plaintiff Bolling's action to recover for a dog bite is barred because he provoked the dog. On February 1, 2005, Bolling was trespassing on private property adjacent to the galleries and display areas of the Alden Hall Historical Site museum. Bolling admits that he engaged in the conduct underlying the confrontation with Stirling's, namely that he hit the dog with a snowball. Although he was not trying to hit the dog with a snowball, New York law provides that inadvertent provocation of a dog precludes an action arising from the dog's bite as surely as intentional provocation. Here, Stirling's dog acted fully in accordance with its training as a guard dog and reacted in its defense by subduing Bolling, which in the process resulted in Bolling receiving lacerations on his arm. Even though Bolling admits to the behavior that provoked the dog's trained reaction, he nevertheless brings this complaint seeking damages not only from Stirling, the dog's owner, but also from Alden Hall, the adjacent property owner. Under controlling authority of this state, even accidental provocation of a dog is a complete bar to recovery and mandates the dismissal of this complaint as against Alden Hall and Stirling.

STATEMENT OF FACTS

On February 1, 2005, Bolling and his father were touring the grounds of Alden Hall. Complaint ¶ 4. Instead of remaining on the tour route, they strayed near Stirling's private residence, a building set off from the rest of the museum buildings. See id. ¶¶ 4-5. Though a posted sign clearly indicated to Bolling that he and his father were standing on private property and should "Keep Out," Bolling claims that the entire sign was not visible and thus that they were unaware of the presence of Stirling's dog. Id. ¶ 6. Bolling and his father ignored the portion of the sign that was visible and proceeded directly toward a building that they knew was private property. Id. ¶ 7. Shortly thereafter, Stirling's dog, Pebbles, greeted the two. Id. ¶ 8. Pebbles did not attack but approached them in a friendly manner. Id. At this point, Bolling

---

EXAMPLE 1 (Continued)

and his father began a snowball fight. Bolling missed a throw at his father and the snowball hit the dog, spraying it with snow. See Affidavit of Elliot Stirling dated June 3, 2005, ¶ 7. The dog reacted to this attack by uninvited guests according to his training as a guard dog and engaged Bolling to subdue him. See id. The restraint necessarily involved pinning the arm of the attacker with the only means available to a dog, his mouth. Id. Bolling apparently struggled with the dog and received several cuts on his arm in the encounter. See Complaint ¶ 9.

The two most important facts in this case, which Bolling must concede, are first that he strayed off the public pathways onto private property and that he did not return to the public path even after seeing the warning sign. See id. ¶¶ 4-5. And, second, that Bolling intended to throw the snowball that ultimately angered the dog by spraying it with snow. See id. ¶¶ 7-8.

APPLY IT!

What kind of story did plaintiff's lawyer tell here? What language was used to make plaintiff seem justified if not sympathetic in what he did? What is the theme of this facts section?

EXAMPLE 2: SAME EXAMPLE, BUT FROM PLAINTIFF'S PERSPECTIVE.

UNITED STATES DISTRICT COURT
SOUTHERN DISTRICT OF NEW YORK

GEORGIE BOLLING,	)	
	)	
Plaintiff,	)	
	)	
v.	)	No. 05-2345-TRW
	)	
ALDEN HALL HISTORICAL SITE,	)	
and ELLIOTT STIRLING,	)	
	)	
Defendants.	)	

PLAINTIFF'S RESPONSE TO DEFENDANTS ALDEN HALL AND STIRLING'S FED. R. CIV. P. 12(b)(6) MOTION TO DISMISS FOR FAILURE TO STATE A CLAIM

INTRODUCTION

Defendants Elliott Stirling and Alden Hall Historical Site ("Alden Hall") have taken the untenable position that they can give a vicious dog free rein to roam a public place where it might injure small children. Stirling's dog's attacked Plaintiff Georgie Bolling ("Georgie") on February 1, 2005, in such a manner that Georgie required 120 stitches to repair his badly

EXAMPLE 2 (Continued)

damaged arm. Moreover, the dog was not "provoked" by Georgie as that term has been defined in New York case law. The attack was vicious and disproportionate to the accidental dusting of snow that the dog experienced when it intervened in Georgie and his father's snowball game. The fact that the dog was loose and menacing patrons of the museum as they attempted to keep to the public walkways and go about their business touring the museum points directly to the liability of both defendants. The defendants failed to provide proper signage warning of a vicious dog and failed to provide proper boundaries to prevent patrons such as Georgie from accidentally straying onto private property. Plaintiff's complaint states all the elements required for recovery under the New York "Dog Bite" statute, N.Y. Dog Bite Law § 516, and defendants' motion to dismiss for failure to state a claim therefore must be denied.

STATEMENT OF FACTS

As stated in the Complaint ¶¶ 4-9, the incident in question here involved a vicious attack by a German Shepard guard dog on a small boy, Georgie Bolling. Georgie and his father were following a tour route and keeping to the public walkways. But these walkways ultimately led them to a building which looked the same as all the other museum buildings. Id. ¶ 4. Nothing demarcated this building and its surroundings from the rest of the public tour area, and no fence or other physical boundaries prevented their path. Id. By the time the two stumbled upon a sign sticking up out of the snow and only partially visible that informed them that they had wandered onto private property, Georgie and his father were already face to face with defendant Stirling's guard dog. Id. ¶ 5. Nothing about the dog appeared threatening at first, so the two proceeded along the public walkway to the house to ask if there was any more to see on the tour. See id. ¶ 6.

Georgie, as a typical seven-year old boy might do, thought it would be amusing to start a friendly snowball game with his father in the yard. See id. ¶ 7. Georgie never intended to involve the dog in the game and aimed his first snowball at his father. See id. The snowball somehow missed its mark, and the dog was accidentally sprayed with light powdery snow. See id. ¶ 8. This accidental dusting with snow is what the defendants characterize as "direct provocation" for a vicious attack. Defendants' Memorandum in Support of Motion to Dismiss at 2, 4.

The guard dog's reaction to the snow dusting he received was completely unexpected and violent: the dog jumped on Georgie and ripped into his arm with vicious force. See Complaint ¶ 9. The cuts inflicted were deep, and the German Shepard had to be dragged off his victim by Georgie's father. Id. Georgie's father managed to pick Georgie up and flee from the scene, chased by the guard dog who continued to menace them. Id. He ran several hundred feet until two museum employees could assist his escape by grabbing and restraining the dog. Id. After Georgie was rushed to the hospital emergency room, Georgie needed 120 stitches to close up the wounds inflicted by the German Shepard. See Affidavit of Walt Paquin dated June 4, 2005, ¶ 3.

APPLY IT!

What kind of story did defendant's lawyer tell here? What language was used to make defendants seem justified if not sympathetic in what he did? What is the theme of this facts section?

V.   ARGUMENT

The argument section of a brief or memoranda of law roughly parallels the discussion section of the office memorandum. But, as you probably already have guessed, it is not drafted in the same manner as the discussion section of an objective, informative legal memorandum. The argument must be as persuasive, well-reasoned, and credible as any office memorandum, but it must be completely one-sided in favor of your client.

"One-sided" obviously is not the same as "untruthful," although many law students and young attorneys often feel that they cannot be anything other than neutral with the law. You may think that the law is what it is, but that does not mean it is concrete and black and white. If a case—one worthy of litigation—were that much of a slam dunk, it would never progress to the phase that we have been discussing in this chapter. You typically will not be litigating over black letter law principles (though, of course, the higher the court you are in, the more you may be arguing over purely legal tenets). Rather, you most often will be litigating *at the margins* of an area of law (often broad margins), which are fluid, changing, and painted in shades of gray. In many cases, it will take all of your skill as an interpreter and analyst of legal sources to take the raw material of the law and find a way to present it such that your client's position looks like the more reasonable, logical, and downright righteous position under the law already established. You are like a painter on a canvas of legal rules that form its parameters.

A.   Goal for the argument section

The argument section has one goal: enabling your the client to win the motion.

As a general matter, the argument section of most briefs is not designed to present an in depth exposition on the general area of law presented by the motion. It is not intended to inform the court of the most interesting and difficult aspects of the specific area of the law that governs the motion. It is not usually meant to educate the court about the pros and cons of a decision on the motion. Though these goals may well be worth having at the appellate stage, at the trial (and, here, pretrial) stage, the number one message you should send is that the only proper outcome is ruling in your client's favor (and that there are many negatives associated with not ruling in your client's favor).   It's persuasion time. Obviously, you should not take this to mean that the goal of the argument section should be to misrepresent or distort the true meaning and effect of the controlling law in your jurisdiction. Nowhere do we advocate misrepresenting the law.   Rather our rule for the argument section is as follows:

> **THE RULE FOR THE ARGUMENT SECTION:**
>
> Advocacy requires a client-oriented, persuasive rendering of the correct legal standards that govern the motion.

Each part of this "rule for the argument" is important and deserves explanation and emphasis.

1.   Client oriented

You must show why your client should prevail using controlling and persuasive legal authorities in a way that supports your arguments. It is a one-sided presentation. You will make the argument that your client should win.

2.   Persuasive

Certainly, no one wins an argument by shouting the loudest. Your skills of legal exposition and creativity will be tested as never before when you have to take on a difficult assignment in a difficult area of law and present the law in such a way that any reader will be able to understand your points and be convinced that your client's position is sound. Naturally, your ultimate goal is to convince one person, the judge, that your position is not just sound, but in fact correct.

3.   Correct legal standards

If we are being redundant, we apologize, but we want to be exceedingly clear that the proper and ethical methodology of an advocate is not to misrepresent the law. You must present a correct interpretation of the law (albeit not necessarily every case that has been handed down in this area, and not every sentence about the rules from every authority in the area). If the law does not support you, either *do not make the argument* (best idea), or present your argument with an explanation that it depends on a change in the law. Never misrepresent the law to a court.

4.   Advice for each side

Movants should follow this advice: **Never bring a motion for which there is no legal support.** If you are the movant, you should not wonder about stretching or distorting the law because you should not bring a motion for which there is no legal support.

If you are the **opponent** and you have a decent argument on the merits, then pursue it first and foremost. But if the movant has done her job correctly, chances are that the law may not support your client's position. You still have a number of choices:

• **Distinguish, distinguish, distinguish**

As we just noted, most cases proceeding to litigation fall at the margins of well-defined legal issues, and typically what determines the outcome are *the facts*. Accordingly, your first instinct as an opponent should be to drive a giant wedge between your case and those that the movant cites in support of her position. You must always think outside the box. Does your opponent state the *legally significant facts*? And, even if so, are her analogies germane? Is she drawing simple, surface level analogies between her case and earlier cases, or do the analogies match the public policies that drive this area of law? For example, assume that a movant claims that a necessary factor of her cause of action is that a particular event occurred in her client's "home." And, movant proceeds to argue that the event occurred on the movant's back (outdoor) patio, which movant argues is part of her home. Might you be able to distinguish the circumstances by claiming that an outdoor patio is not properly part of the "home" as previous courts have defined that term? Absolutely. Honestly, this process of drawing distinctions can be the most challenging but rewarding part of litigating a case.

- **Change the issues, and argue a legal position that you can defend**

No one said you have to stick to the issues that the movant thought important for the motion. If the substance of the motion (the merits) are bad for your client, argue procedural reasons for the denial of motion. In other words, consider whether it is possible for you to argue that the motion is improper, against the rules, untimely, unnecessary, violates laches, and then, and only then, get into the merits. You might argue that the motion is described as or argues XYZ, but the movant really should be bringing PDQ motion or making a PDQ argument, and you proceed to explain that your client wins under a PDQ analysis. This is the method of the skilled litigator, to turn a sow's ear of a motion into a silk purse.

We explained this tactic more thoroughly above in the section on the introduction, and if you get the impression that we really like this option, you are right. This option turns the tables on the movant so that you can set your own playing field, and argue your own points. Not only do you increase your chances of actually winning, but the movant will have to use space in the reply brief addressing your points rather than furthering hers.

- **Be open and discuss the law as it is, but argue for a change**

In every opposition, you will do you best to argue against the Movant's position, and attempt to distinguish Movant's authorities, but if the controlling law is against you, the most forthright and sometimes most effective course to follow is to admit the controlling law is negative and against your client, but argue that the law should be changed or interpreted differently so that your client should prevail. You may not have the opportunity to win this way very often, but you will impress the court a great deal with your candor (and possibly your client with your tenacity). Naturally, the more effort you put into the task of finding primary and secondary persuasive authorities that *actually are* favorable to you client, and support the policies you will assert are furthered by a change in the law, the more likely it is that you will prevail.

Note here that we are talking about a situation where the indistinguishable **controlling** authority in your jurisdiction is against you, or there is no controlling authority and all of the persuasive authority you can find goes against you. If it is merely a situation where there is some good and some troublesome authority, you should not be approaching the court in a defensive posture, but rather doing your best to present the best law to the court, and trying hard to distinguish and downplay any existing negative or potentially harmful authority.

B.   Structure of the argument – TREAT format[4] revisited

The TREAT format applies as equally to the drafting of the argument section of a pretrial brief as it did to the discussion section of an office memorandum. What that means is that you want to craft argumentative Thesis headings (and statements), a Rule section, an Explanation of the authorities that illustrate how the rules work, an Application of the rules to the client's situation that applies the good principles of interpretation illustrated by the authorities and distinguishes the negative principles of interpretation (if any) that might be derived from some of the authorities, and reiterate your Thesis restated as a Conclusion. Because the argument has to further the client's cause in winning the motion, the following considerations apply that may be different from (or come in addition to) those that you were considering when you drafted the discussion section of the office memorandum:

1.   Argumentative thesis headings

One of the reasons that we stress the importance of the introduction is that it presents the critical information in your case to the reader at the very first opportunity, on the first page or pages of your motion. Basically the same principle applies to drafting the headings that will divide up your argument section. Many seasoned litigators and judges to whom we have spoken report that your thesis (major issue and sub-issue) headings should read like a succinct summary of your argument as a whole.

That means that your headings should be useful, informative, and **persuasive** (in other words, argumentative). Even if your reader only

---

4 If you are not familiar with the legal writing structural format **TREAT** (Thesis-Rule-Explanation-Application-Thesis restated) as a refinement of IRAC (Issue-Rule-Application-Conclusion), or if you would like a refresher on how TREAT works, please see Appendix.

skims your document, she will see at a glance each conclusion that you want her to draw.

A good thesis heading not only reveals a conclusion but provides **the "because" part**—the legal principles and facts that lead up to the conclusion. For example, the following are good argumentative Thesis headings:

- **Examples of proper thesis headings in the argument**

    A. Bolling did nothing to provoke the dog prior to the attack because he did not directly attack or threaten the dog as required under New York law.

    B. Bolling was acting peacefully in a place where he had a lawful right to be because he walked on a public sidewalk at Alden Hall without causing any noisy disturbance.

    C. Provocation does not bar Bolling's recovery because the dog's attack on Bolling was vicious and disproportionate to the dusting of snow the Dog received from Bolling.

The following generally are **not** good headings, especially for a persuasive piece of writing:

    A. Lack of Provocation

    B. Bolling was acting peacefully in a place where he had a lawful right to be.

    C. The dog's attack was disproportionate.

These last three examples do not suggest enough of the facts and principles of the law to make the headings useful, and the first of these three does not even tell the author's conclusion about the topic. Do not waste your headings; let them provide a quick summary of your argument if read one right after the other.

2.   Forming a favorable rule for the rule section

The law is not static, and neither does your expression of the law have to be. There are many ways to express legal rules and to characterize how the rules work and how they ought to be interpreted and applied. This section reviews these methods.

TIP 1

There is one hard and fast rule for the rule section of your motion: **you must cite and discuss all applicable constitutional provisions, statutes, or administrative regulations.** If a constitutional, statutory, or administrative provision is on point, it is controlling and must be presented. There is no way around it. You at least must cite it, and with operative language from a constitutional provision, statute, or administrative regulation, you should go so far as to quote the pertinent, applicable language.

Beyond this rule, you actually have many opportunities to express what the law means in a way that favors your client. You certainly should plan to cite and discuss controlling cases that construe (alter, modify, extend, etc.) the statute or rule, and any administrative law authorities (administrative rules and regulations) that interpret and implement the legislation. If the prevailing rule is determined solely or largely by case law, whether in a Common Law rule or as the prevailing interpretation of a constitutional, statutory, or administrative law provision, you must focus on formulating the best rule for your client using the best authorities available.

This is difficult advice to communicate tangibly. We can describe the goal and offer a few pointers, but the actual task of taking a body of undigested law and pulling from it the best authorities and the best language of rule (and its prior factual applications) is no small order. You will have to feel out this ground for yourself at some level, because what is a good use and what is a great use of authorities will necessarily vary from assignment to assignment. Alas, we are at the point where we must admit that what we are asking you to do is challenging. Do not be discouraged; this takes practice. Consider the following short examples:

- *The rule reads:* Plaintiff's choice of forum is a factor in the determination of a transfer of venue motion but it is not a conclusive factor.

> *Example 1 - Favoring transfer:* Plaintiff's choice of forum never has been given conclusive weight in the venue transfer analysis. [CITATIONS]. It merely is one of many factors for the court to consider. [CITATIONS].

> *Example 2 - Opposing transfer:* In determining a transfer of venue motion, the court must give regard to the plaintiff's choice of forum. [CITATIONS]. Each court is mandated to consider the effect of denying plaintiff her choice of forum, and most courts give it priority in the order of discussion of the issues. [CITATIONS].

Both of these characterizations of the rule are entirely accurate, but one tends to favor transfer and the other does not. "Priority" in the second example refers to the fact that in most cases, the issue of protecting plaintiff's choice of forum is discussed first, but the word has positive connotations beyond the simple expression of the order of discussion. (In both examples, it may be necessary to use the prefatory word "<u>see</u>" in front of the citations to authority if you are drawing a direct inference supported by the authorities rather than repeating exactly what the authorities say.)

- *The rules read:* Claimants must demonstrate a likelihood of confusion between the trademark and the allegedly infringing mark. Courts are to use a "reasonable viewer" standard.

> *Example 1 - Favoring claimant:* Plaintiff need only show that there is a likelihood of confusion by a reasonable viewer when the infringing mark is compared to the original trademark. [CITATIONS]. Plaintiff need not prove actual confusion among a particular group of viewers, but only the potential confusion of a "reasonable viewer." [CITATIONS].

> *Example 2 - Opposing claimant:* Plaintiff bears the burden of proving that there is a likelihood of confusion not among a learned consumer or a devoted user of its products, but among a random group of "reasonable

viewers." [CITATIONS]. It is not enough to show that devoted users would recognize the similarity. [CITATIONS].

The characterization of the rule in example 2 sounds much harder to meet. It lays out the same principles of the law as the first example, but it does so in a way that expresses that the burden on the claimant is onerous. This phrasing helps to oppose the claimant.

The following chart should refresh your recollection about how to go about putting together the rule from multiple authorities, performing a "rule synthesis," and putting it into the Rule section of an objective work. Naturally, you should start with any controlling authority.

FORMULATE THE RULE
(Rule Synthesis)

☒ **Start with the highest and most recent controlling authority.**	☒ If you have a statute (or regulation), start with the statute. ☒ If you have a watershed case that is controlling, start with that. ☒ If your best authority is from the court of last resort, take the most recent opinion from that court, and start with that. ☒ If these first three criteria do not apply, start with the most recent actual controlling authority that is on point. ☒ Only if none of the above applies would you consider turning to non-controlling authority—primary or secondary. ☒ Don't expect to use all of your authorities.
☒ **Reconcile differing statements or phrasings of the rule from controlling authorities, and attempt to synthesize the material into one coherent statement of the legal principles that govern the issue.**	☒ Don't change the wording of or paraphrase rules from statutes, administrative rules and regulations, and watershed cases. ☒ Unless a processed applied rule can be written smoothly and effectively in one sentence or phrase, write the rule first with modifications second.
☒ **Write the rule first, interpretative rules second, and exceptions to the rule third.**	☒ Write interpretive sub-rules on elements of the rule in the section or sub-TREAT discussion that discusses that element of the rule. Write exceptions to the sub-rules after you lay out the sub-rules themselves.
☒ **Do not write a rule with inherent contradictions.**	☒ Check for ambiguity in the terms you have used to formulate the rule (even if some of these terms came from the authorities).
☒ **Do accept the <u>remote</u> possibility that two competing rules on the same issue might exist in the same Jurisdiction.**	☒ When this happens, you may have to analyze the facts under both competing sets of rules.

TIP 2

You should always try to find a common, underlying rule of law that governs the issue at hand that can properly be derived from or traced to controlling authority. Examine the ways that the rule has been recited in the various controlling authorities. Then draft the rule section compiling the best words and standards from the authorities in the form of a rule synthesis with terms that tend to favor your client's legal position. You must be fair, but you most often will have leeway to craft the rules in a light that is more favorable to your client than a random selection of principles and interpretive rules found in cases.

The style and formatting advice for how office memoranda should be drafted generally applies here, but remember that the goal in a persuasive document is to present the law in the best possible light for your client. Explore the authorities for the best possible rendition of the legal standards that govern the issue. Rule synthesis may help you avoid a sticky wording of the rule on the issue that shows up in some but not all of the authorities. Naturally, if the rule comes from a statute or administrative rule, you are stuck with the official wording, but you still can look for later interpretive authorities that may have explained the rule in ways that are kinder to the client. Even if you refuse to do a rule synthesis, and decide to present the legal principles seriatim, start with the rules and standards that most favor your client's situation, and finish with those the client has the most problems with, but still can manage to meet.

3. Use *interpretive rules* that support the client's case

Look for interpretive rules and sub-rules that help your client's cause. If the rule is from a statute or administrative rule, these interpretive rulings may be the only friendly rendition of the legal standards that you will find in favor of your client. Do not cite incidental interpretive rules that do not help the client's cause; leave that to your opponent. Only cite interpretive rules that support your client's facts and your theory of the case.

- *Example:* Your client manipulated a photograph of a famous celebrity who was on trial for murder by combining it with the famous photograph of Lee Harvey Oswald holding the mail order rifle that he allegedly used to assassinate President John F. Kennedy so that it appears that the celebrity is holding the famous rifle in the famous Oswald pose. The celebrity sued your client for violation of his right of publicity. One defense is to show that the use is a parody. In your jurisdiction, in order to prove a parody defense, you must show that the original image was transformed in such a way that it is obvious that there are two works present—an original image of the celebrity and a new image that is directly critical of the celebrity.

In your rule section that discusses this parody requirement, you have the choice of using the following interpretive rules for parody that appear in various controlling authorities of the applicable jurisdiction:

Good interpretive rule: "The creator of the new work must add value to the old work."

> *This is good because your client did add "value" to the work through her artistic additions. The new work is clever and comments on the celebrity through use of artistic symbolism.*

Better interpretive rule: "It must be obvious that there are two works evident from examination of the alleged parody—an older image of the celebrity, and a new image with new content, meaning, and expression that is critical of the celebrity. It is not enough if the creator of the images intends to criticize the celebrity if the meaning of the altered image is not evident from looking at the altered image itself."

> This is even better than the above example because it is closer to your client's facts. Your client's work reveals two well-known original images and a third image—the combined image—and it will be obvious to anyone familiar with the two original images that the client's image has achieved new content, meaning, and expression by putting the celebrity into the position of a famous assassin. This effect needs no explanation from your client; it is obvious from looking at her work.

Not good interpretive rules: "The value of the new work may be established by showing that the application of artistic skill transformed the work into a unique new work that does not depend on the celebrity's image for its value. It also may be shown by the fact that the artist is so famous that his work is far more valuable for his having created it than any mundane image of the celebrity created by an unknown artist."

> *Although these interpretive rules would not necessarily be fatal to your client's situation, they are not that helpful. Remember, you have a choice of what interpretive rules to bring out, and the first rule here seems to fit the situation of a painter or sculptor—or even a cartoonist—better than an artist like your client who combines photographs for expressive effect. Would the average person viewing your client's works see the application of valuable artistic skill, or just cleverness? The second rule may not suit your client at all if your client is not a famous artist whose works are of obvious value even to a casual follower of the arts (such as most judges and some jurors). Therefore, you should avoid bringing out both of these interpretive rules in your rule section.*

4.   Use of explanatory synthesis

In the explanation section, you should use explanatory synthesis[5] to explain how the rule works in real life situations in the most compact and powerful manner available. The following chart reveals the principles and methodology of drafting the explanation section and using explanatory synthesis:

---

5 If the term "explanatory synthesis" is completely unfamiliar to you, then please see <u>Appendix</u>.

EXPLAIN THE RULE
(Explanatory Synthesis)

The goal is to explain how the rule is to be interpreted and applied based on how the authorities have applied it in actual concrete factual settings, and on how commentators have interpreted the rule.	❐ You are going beyond what the courts already have said about the rule in interpretive rules found in cases. ❐ You are presenting principles of interpretation that are supported by a careful reading of the cases. ❐ You are doing the work of digesting and synthesizing the cases so the reader doesn't have to.
Case-by-case presentations make the reader do most of the work and they are wasteful of space and time (i.e., the reader's attention span).	❐ Avoid case-by-case presentations even though they are easy to write, and sometimes fun to write. ❐ Avoid case-by-case presentations even though courts use them. ❐ The only time to resort to a case-by-case presentation is when you have one or two cases that are so close to the facts that you want to cover them in great detail, or if you want to distinguish one or two troublesome cases in enough detail to make your point.

GOALS OF THE EXPLANATION SECTION

The Process of Explanatory Synthesis

❒ **Read the cases and look for common facts and common outcomes.**	❒ Group cases by facts. ❒ Divide groups of cases by outcome.
❒ **Review the groups to find the factors or public policies that make the difference in the outcome.**	❒ Reconcile cases that have different outcomes; what policy or theme or factor determined the outcome in these cases. ❒ Reconcile cases that have the same outcome on different facts; what common policy or theme or factors brought about the same outcome on
❒ **Write principles of interpretation that explain your findings.**	❒ Phrase your principles of interpretation in language that mimics interpretive ❒ Often you can use interpretive rules as principles that tie together multiple authorities; there is no requirement that you always have to come up with brand new principles.
❒ **Cite the cases that support your principles of interpretation with parentheticals that provide facts or other information about each case.**	❒ Parentheticals should contain enough information to illustrate how the individual case supports the general principle you have laid out. ❒ Use shorthand and abbreviated phrases to save space.
❒ **When you draft the Application section, apply the principles of interpretation to your own facts; as a general rule, do not apply individual cases to your facts.**	❒ Applying principles to facts will make your analysis more convincing; you you have spelled out the connections to be made between the authorities and then followed through and showed how the principles learned from a study of the authorities determines the outcome of the case at hand. ❒ The exception to this rule is when you have one or two fabulous cases that are worthy of individual attention in the Explanation section; these should be discussed individually in the Application section, whether as support or to distinguish them.

As always, you want to avoid wasting the reader's time in an adversarial matter. Judges will not take the time to read five or more paragraphs of facts from cases that have applied the rule. You only should discuss as much of the facts from the authorities as is necessary to explain your application of the law to the client's facts. Sometimes, and especially with critical and controlling cases, you will need to discuss factual similarities and differences in the text of your argument. Remember, though, that you can use case parentheticals and other devices to shorten the discussion (*e.g.*, conclusory, declarative statements of the critical importance of the authorities, followed by a cite to multiple authorities, or use of the "Compare . . . with . . ." citation method). If you decide it is necessary to expound on the facts of one or more particularly controlling cases, you should do so because these are ***the*** pivotal cases on your topic in the applicable jurisdiction. Still, you should limit yourself to an exposition of those *legally significant* facts to which you are going to draw an analogy or distinction.

The necessity to provide explanation of the authorities that discuss a rule will depend on the procedural versus substantive nature of the rule (see discussion of procedural vs. substantive arguments below), and the importance of the rule to the motion at hand.

5. Movant's anticipation and handling of negative authority

In the process of legal analysis, "good" authorities are those that support your thesis on the law whether or not the outcome of a particular case is the same outcome that you are pursuing for your client. Cases whose outcomes are different from that which you seek for your client may still follow the same interpretation of the law and support your analysis of which factors and policies are important to the adjudication of your client's case; thus, these cases do not necessarily work against you. Negative authorities are those that do not support your interpretation of the law. If the court were to follow the path of negative authorities, your theses would no longer make sense. Therefore, negative authorities must be distinguished by the movant in light of her arguments of which factors, or facts, or policies carry the day on the adjudication of the issue at hand. In this way, movant can quarantine the negative authorities and still advance her theses.

Example: You are arguing that <u>copyright law fair use</u>
analysis requires the court to weigh each of four
factors separately on a case-by-case basis, and that
no one factor is dispositive (not the purpose and
character of the use, nor the commercial nature
of the use, nor the effect of the use on the market
for the original work). Your argument is that the
purpose and character of your client's use was to
comment and on and criticize the original work,
which is a permissible fair use because, although
done for commercial profit, it did not threaten
to usurp the market for the original work. In
this argument, cases whose outcomes were a
find of "no fair use" are not necessarily negative
cases. In fact, you can make good use of such
cases in an explanation section by synthesizing
the "no fair use" cases together and showing what
facts, policies, or factors made these cases fair use
"losers" while your client's circumstances follow
the path of cases that are fair use "winners." The
"no fair use" cases still support your thesis by
revealing what your client's circumstances would
have to look like for your client *not* to have a fair
use. Thus, the "no fair use" cases are not "bad"
cases.

In these circumstances, negative authorities—
"bad" authorities—would be ones that contradict
your legal analysis. A negative authority might
be one that asserts that the commercial nature of
the use outweighs all of the other factors; if the
alleged infringer was out to make a profit when
it copied the original work, the other factors
together or separately cannot outweigh this one
factor and the use is presumptively unfair. This
case must be distinguished or it contradicts your
interpretation of the rules. Either the rogue case
is wrong or your reading of the cases is wrong.
Assuming you did not make an error in your
legal analysis, you should be able to distinguish
the "bad" case without too much difficulty. It

may be dated, or an anomaly, superseded by later
cases; in other words, the case really is not good
law. If this is the case, you need not bring the
case into the discussion unless your opponent is
trying to use the case and you must refute your
opponent's argument. In other instances, the
negative case might be good law, but its holding
is limited to certain kind of fair uses (e.g., just for
alleged fair uses for educational purposes), or for
certain kinds of infringement-fair use disputes
(e.g., just for copying of musical recordings for
looping as background music). Once you point
out why the bad authority is not applicable, you
have quarantined it. This effort is necessary in
movant's opening brief; it is better to put the case
in quarantine first and force your opponent to
try to get it out of quarantine.

If you have a number of good **controlling** authorities, the fact
that there are a number of negative **persuasive** authorities out there is
of little concern to anyone. Occasionally, you, as the movant, will have a
situation where nothing but favorable authority exists on the motion you
are drafting. Enjoy that feeling as long as you can, because it is fleeting.
Just as often, you will have a body of good authorities that favor your client's position and some bad authorities that go against it.

When dealing with unfavorable cases—cases whose outcome goes
against your client, not truly "bad" authorities who contradict your interpretation of the law—one of the toughest jobs of the movant is to decide
how much of the unfavorable authority on the law to anticipate and explain (i.e., synthesize and distinguish) in the opening motion. It is tough
because your space always is limited, and you do not want to do such a
good job raising and discussing unfavorable authorities that you write
your opponent's brief for her.

• **Highlight the good cases**

For present purposes, we will assume first of all that you do have
some controlling authorities whose outcome goes in favor of your position. Always cover your positive controlling authorities first in the ex-

planation section—you do not want to start off in a defensive posture. Then, the best advice we can give is to try to save space at the end of each explanation section to discuss any significant potentially controlling unfavorable authorities. "Significant" means they are close enough to the facts of your situation that you are given pause when you read them, and they are recent enough that you cannot easily argue that the law has changed or progressed from these older sources. It pays to have the first word on any unfavorable potentially controlling authorities, and it is far less likely that you will be educating the other side about cases that they would not otherwise find in their research (and even if the opponent would have missed them, the court probably will not).

If you do not have any controlling authority in favor of your position, then you **must** show why there is no controlling authority that goes directly against your position (or you should not be bringing the motion in the first place). In the explanation section, you first should discuss your positive persuasive authorities, and then distinguish any negative potentially controlling and negative persuasive authorities.

• Distinguish the unfavorable cases

The principles of "explanatory synthesis" discussed above apply with equal force in distinguishing negative and unfavorable authority in the explanation section. If there are several negative cases, try to group them based on common facts and common holding, and discuss them as a group. Thus, you can distinguish the whole group in one fell swoop, and de-emphasize the impact of the number of cases. If there is no way to group them on the basis of facts and holding, you still should try to find a common thread of legal argument or public policy that characterizes them. If you can refute and distinguish the logical underpinning of the cases, you can more easily convince the court that the entire group of cases should be rejected because they all rely on the same logical foundation.

If there is no negative potentially controlling authority, you have more leeway in determining how much negative persuasive authority to anticipate and distinguish. Be careful not to raise and explain too much negative persuasive authority and thus help your opponent write her brief in opposition. The scope of persuasive authority is far ranging, and if you are the kind of diligent and thorough researcher that we hope you will be, you may find yourself reading a lot more negative persuasive authority that your opponent and the court will find or look for. Remember, too, that you will have a reply brief in which to address anything that your opponent finds and puts to good use against you.

So, what kind of persuasive authority should you incorporate? We would limit it to primary persuasive authorities (cases, primarily) that are from the proper jurisdiction.

- **Example:** In a case in the New York Supreme Court for New York County that is governed by New York law, your case is controlled by the decisions of the 1st Department of the Supreme Court, Appellate Division. Cases that are not from the proper hierarchy of judicial authority are not controlling (e.g., cases from the 2nd, 3rd, or 4th Departments of the Supreme Court, Appellate Division), but these may be regarded as highly persuasive.

- **Example:** In a federal question case in the United States District Court for the District of Massachusetts, only decisions from the United States Court of Appeals for the First Circuit control. The decisions of the other United States Courts of Appeals (e.g., from the Second through the Eleventh Circuits and the D.C. and Federal Circuits in between) are not controlling, but should be regarded as highly persuasive.

These authorities are highly persuasive because of the law they apply, and even if they are not even potentially controlling, they can carry the day and deserve your attention to distinguish and explain them.

We would not go out of our way to address other kinds of primary or secondary persuasive authority unless it has an extremely high stature—for example, Wright & Miller on Federal Practice and Procedure, a restatement of the law, a judicial superstar—and the discussion is close enough to your situation to cause you to sweat. A very practical test.

Lastly, let us advise you that if you have nothing with which to distinguish persuasive authority or no explanation that ameliorates the effect of the authority, it is best **not** to raise it at all. You are drawing a lot of attention to a persuasive authority when you anticipate it in your opening brief, and if you only make a half-hearted attempt to distinguish the authority, it will stand out like a beacon for your opponent and the court to notice. Remember, we are talking about a motion and memorandum of law drafted in the adversarial system, and if you do not cover something, it is your opponent's job to raise it and cover it. Always try to distinguish an authority that is more likely than not to be *controlling*, but beyond that, avoid doing your opponent's work for her.

6.   Opponent's handling of negative and unfavorable authority

The opponent has little choice in this matter—you must attempt to distinguish and explain all of the potentially controlling and strong persuasive authority that the movant has thrown at you. It is a terrible error not to address all of the potentially controlling authority in your opposition papers. Beyond that, we would strive to say something positive about the primary persuasive authority upon which movant relies, and do as much as you can to counteract the negative secondary persuasive authority.

C.   How much to "TREAT"? – procedural vs. substantive issues, and counter-arguments

1.   Procedural versus substantive issues

The procedural-substantive (form-substance) distinction is undoubtedly one that you will get a quick hold on in law school and are well familiar with by the time you are reading this chapter. That distinction, however, can help you determine whether to draft a complete TREAT of an individual issue in your motion documents—and especially whether to draft a full blown explanation section to explain the rule on the issue and how it works in various factual situations.

The simplest way to determine whether or not an issue is more procedural than substantive is to see if the governing rule emanates from a court rule of procedure, such as the Federal Rules of Civil Procedure. Generally speaking, ***procedural issues*** deal with topics relating to the propriety of the case being in a court (*e.g.*, subject matter jurisdiction), a person being before the court (personal jurisdiction, service of process, and venue), the content of pleadings and papers and addition or amendment of claims and defenses, timeliness issues (timing of filings and statutory limitations periods), whether complete relief is possible between the parties (joinder of claims or parties, third-party practice), discovery matters, evidence, and whether and how a party gets to do something in the case (including motions, scheduling, stays, trials, and relief from judgment).

In contrast, ***a substantive issue*** involves the parties' rights and defenses on the merits, including claims and causes of action (and the elements of same), affirmative defenses (and the elements of same), damages and remedies, and the actual substantive right to certain relief, such as the substantive law that determines whether a complaint has stated a claim upon which relief may be granted, whether the actual claims or defenses asserted in the parties' pleadings are subject to summary judgment, and whether a party is entitled to a new trial or judgment as a matter of law on one or more of its actual claims.

If you determine that an issue is purely procedural, you may consider the following when deciding how much of a TREAT and explanation to give the issue:

1. If you are citing an authority solely for a legal standard on procedure that it discusses, it is most likely unnecessary to discuss the facts of that authority. Many of the rules on procedure come from statutes and "rules," such as the Federal Rules of Civil Procedure. Aside from that, the facts of a case that states a useful legal standard or interpretive or explanatory rule on a procedural issue may not be particularly important or illustrative to your argument. The summary judgment standard often fits in to this category (though not always).

2. If, however, you are making an argument that procedural rules should be applied in a certain way to the client's facts, then you likely will want to analogize to other cases where the rule was also applied to similar facts, and therefore you will need to draft an explanation section. Often in a motion to dismiss for lack of personal jurisdiction, venue, subject matter jurisdiction, or violation of the statute of limitations, you will need to compare and analogize your client's facts to facts in similar cases in order to make a compelling argument on what is otherwise a purely procedural point.

Courts tend to be somewhat less consistent on purely procedural matters (who gets to do what and when and how) than on substantive determinations. As a result, you often will find cases that come out both ways. This result may be attributed in large part to the appellate standard of review on procedural points, which generally grants a great deal of discretion to the trial court to make whatever procedural decisions it feels appropriate in the case before it. In the face of this body of potentially inconsistent authority, you still must discuss and apply or distinguish all potentially controlling authority on purely procedural points, but any persuasive authorities that go against your client's position on these points generally should be ignored. Cite the good persuasive authority on procedure and leave the rest out. Of course, if the "bad" persuasive authority is a powerhouse (some super-judge, a great treatise such as Wright & Miller, etc.), then you still might take the time to explain it away, but it is not required. Maybe wait and see if your opponent tries to make a to-do about it.

2.   Anticipating counter-arguments

Anticipation of an opponent's defenses and counter-arguments on a motion is something that every movant must contend with, although movants have a choice. An opponent *must* respond to the movant's arguments one way or the other. But devoting an entire TREAT section to laying out and refuting an opponent's (potential) counter-argument is a substantial investment of precious space in your motion, and you should be wary of attempting this maneuver unless you know that the opponent's counter-argument is very likely to come up.

In general, the same principles apply here that determine when to cite and distinguish negative authority: if the opponent's argument is fairly obvious and the negative authorities are almost certainly going to be found by your opponent, then it is a good idea to try to have the first word and spin the argument your way. If the opponent's argument is not particularly strong, or the authorities are fairly obscure and not easily found and interpreted, then you have much less incentive to take them up in the first instance.

The core of the problem is that you do not want to do your opponent's work for her. You do not want to so fully develop and discuss a contrary argument that your opponent will easily take up your discussion and do a good job briefing the counter-argument in her opposition brief. Your discussion and counter-analysis on the topic may provide more fodder for her brief than anything the opponent could develop in support of the argument on her own. Thus, if you are fairly certain that your opponent will not even think of an argument or will present it in a most unconvincing way, do not discuss the issues and points of the contrary argument ahead of time. Of course, if your opponent is a top-flight lawyer who will not miss the issues and arguments that are present in the case, then you should feel free to do as thorough a counter-analysis as you can afford to, in light of the available space for the argument.

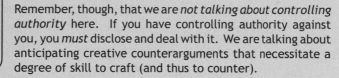

FYI

Remember, though, that we are *not talking about controlling authority* here. If you have controlling authority against you, you *must* disclose and deal with it. We are talking about anticipating creative counterarguments that necessitate a degree of skill to craft (and thus to counter).

One additional piece of advice: do not set up a straw man argument and attribute it to the opponent in one breath just so that you can tear it to pieces in the next. Do not try to reduce a rational argument to a ridiculous and frivolous position that no one would actually assert. Straw man arguments are a cheap rhetorical device that will never carry much weight with the court, and instead risk making you look ridiculous. Give fair credit to a serious counter-argument and then do the best job you can to refute it.

However, when you have decided to anticipate and refute a serious potential counter-argument, you should still limit your citations to negative authority in your counter-analysis. Although we are being a bit redundant here, this piece of advice is worth repeating and remembering. When you are spinning out an argument that belongs to your opponent, you should never present it with all the cases you found in support of that argument. If there are potentially controlling (or persuasive) authorities, by all means discuss and distinguish the most recent ones. If it is an argument that will rely only on persuasive authorities, discuss a few of the weakest, most easily refuted persuasive authorities. In other words, make the house look so shabby that even your opponent will be embarrassed to live in it.

D.   How many issues should you "TREAT" in a given motion?

Once again, we must stress that we are discussing here *an art.* The answer to any question that asks how much or how many is necessarily dependent on the individual problem you were assigned and the substance of the motion that relates to the problem. A single motion may present several issues to brief, some procedural and others substantive, each of which might deserve its own TREAT, and the rule that governs each issue may have multiple elements in dispute, each of which deserves its own sub-TREAT. Your ability to identify the issues from the problem (the facts) that were told to you, and your ability to unpack these issues and add new issues based on your research into the law that applies to the problem, is the key ability that your entire law school education is attempting to develop. So: there is no easy answer to this question.

But the following example is illustrative of the process. A motion to dismiss for lack of personal jurisdiction under Fed. R. Civ. P. 12(b)(2) might assert that defendant has no minimum contacts with the jurisdiction and no "hook" or nexus with the jurisdiction under the state "Long Arm" statute. The various TREATs necessary to answer the question might be broken down as follows:

ARGUMENT

Rule Section – this **procedural** rule does not require a full TREAT. The second sentence merely is a roadmap or "umbrella" section for the rest of the motion.

Fed R. Civ. P. 12(b)(2) provides: " . . ."
This action must be dismissed because plaintiff cannot obtain personal jurisdiction over defendant in this forum under either the state Long Arm statute, and any attempted exercise of jurisdiction would violate the requirements of the Due Process clause of the United States Constitution.

Thesis on first substantive Issue

I. PLAINTIFF FAILS TO SHOW DEFENDANT'S CONNECTION TO THE FORUM UNDER THE WISCONSIN "LONG ARM" STATUTE BECAUSE DEFENDANT DID NOT MAKE A CONTRACT OR TRANSACT BUSINESS IN THE STATE.

Rule Section – this is a substantive rule, so a full TREAT with sub-TREATs is necessary.

A federal court sitting in diversity must evaluate the propriety of the exercise of personal jurisdiction over the defendant under both the local state "Long Arm" statute and the requirements of the Due Process clause of the United States Constitution. <u>Tough v. Easy</u>, 123 F.3d 456, 458 (7th Cir. 1998). The Wisconsin "Long Arm" statute, Wis. Stat. § 1000.01 ("Long Arm Statute"), provides for service of process and the exercise of jurisdiction over an out-of-state defendant when the defendant has performed one or more of the following acts in the State of Wisconsin:

  (a) made a contract in the state;
  (b) conducted business in the state;. . .

Sub-Thesis regarding second substantive Issue

A. Defendant did not make a contract in Wisconsin because the sales orders between the parties were entered into in Illinois.

Sub-Rule, Explanation, Application and Thesis-Conclusion on second Issue.

This is a sub-TREAT of the first prong of the Long Arm Statute

In order to satisfy the "making of a contract" prong of the Long Arm Statute, plaintiff must show that defendant . . .

Making a contract means . . . <u>Parker v. Brothers</u>, 567 N.W.2d 987, 989 (Wis. 1973) (sales order issued from Illinois so contract was made in Illinois); <u>Clifford v. Eisle</u>, . . .

In the instant case, the contract was executed in and intended to be performed in Illinois. Defendant did not . . .

Therefore, plaintiff fails to satisfy the first prong of the Long Arm Statute.

Sub-Thesis regarding third substantive Issue

B. Defendant did not transact business in Wisconsin because transaction of business requires a party's physical presence, and mere communication of business information by electronic media is insufficient.

Sub-Rule, Explanation, Application and Thesis-Conclusion on third Issue. This is a sub-TREAT of the second prong of the Long Arm Statute

In order to satisfy the "transaction of business" prong of the Long Arm Statute, plaintiff must show that defendant . . .

Transaction of business includes . . . <u>Trivial v. Pursuit Co.</u>, 897 N.W.2d 487, 488 (Wis. 1993) (yearly visits to distributors in Wisconsin was transaction of business in Wisconsin); <u>Alfred v. Wayne</u>, . . .

Defendant was not doing business in Wisconsin because defendant never stepped foot in Wisconsin and only communicated over the Internet and through telephone conversations. . . .

Therefore, plaintiff fails to satisfy the second prong of the Long Arm Statute. Because plaintiff cannot show defendant's nexus with the forum under either prong of the statute, this action must be dismissed.

Thesis regarding fourth substantive Issue

II. EXERCISE OF JURISDICTION OVER THE DEFENDANT VIOLATES THE "MINIMUM CONTACTS" REQUIREMENT OF THE DUE PROCESS CLAUSE.

Rule, Explanation, Application and Thesis-Conclusion on fourth Issue

Even if jurisdiction were proper under the Wisconsin Long Arm Statute, plaintiff still cannot show that jurisdiction would be proper under the Due Process clause of the United States Constitution . . .

Due process requires a showing of minimum contacts . . .

In the instant case, defendant has never stepped foot in Wisconsin, and . . .

Therefore, the exercise of personal jurisdiction over defendant would violate the Due Process clause, and this action must be dismissed for lack of personal jurisdiction.

VI.   THE CONCLUSION SECTION

Do not fall into the common trap of confusing the introduction and conclusion of a persuasive piece of writing. Sadly (for some of us), a legal brief is not a mystery novel, and you generally do not want to fall into the habit of saving the best for last. Ideally, you could accomplish both brief-writing and mystery-novel-writing. A reader who is utterly entranced by your rhetoric and the suspense of the introduction might read your brief to the end and find herself faced with a strong, satisfying summation that not only reemphasizes the points raised in the brief but caps them off with a zinger to send the happy reader on her happy reader way. However, in reality, your reader will not necessarily get to your last page. Therefore, a strong beginning is much more important than a strong ending. Focus your efforts there.

What, then, is left for the conclusion of a pretrial motion document? Basically, all you need to do is to tell the court exactly what action you want it to take, and then sign your name. The following are examples **of perfectly good conclusions to pretrial motions:**

Example 1:

CONCLUSION

For the reasons stated here, this Court should dismiss plaintiff's Petition for failure to state a claim upon which relief can be granted.

Example 2:

CONCLUSION

For the reasons stated above, plaintiff Jones respectfully requests the Court to deny defendant Smith's motion to dismiss or in the alternative, to stay this action.

Powerful stuff? Perhaps not what you envisioned. But in a persuasive piece, such as a brief on a motion, this is really all that is required (and all the court typically wants to see).

That said, you might have more to ask of the court, so the conclusion conceivably could be more complicated (and interesting). Consider the following conclusion of a motion for preliminary injunction in a trademark infringement case:

Example 3:

CONCLUSION

For the reasons stated above, plaintiff respectfully requests the Court to:

(a) issue an order temporarily enjoining defendant and all of its agents, employees, and contractors from the creation, display, distribution, and sale of the "Bart Simpson" mark T-shirts and products described in ¶¶ 6-9 of the Complaint;

(b) issue an order temporarily enjoining defendant and all of its agents, employees, and contractors from all advertising involving the "Bart Simpson" mark described and defined in ¶¶ 6-7 of the Complaint, and specifically requiring defendant to cancel, suspend, and withdraw all print ads described in ¶ 10 of the Complaint, all radio promotions described in ¶ 11 of the Complaint, and all web pages of the internet web site at http://www.gocrazy-folks.com displaying or describing "Bart Simpson" T-shirts and products described in ¶ 12 of the Complaint;

(c) issue an order temporarily enjoining defendant from the creation, display, distribution, sale, and advertising of any other and additional works (including derivative works) displaying or using the "Bart Simpson" mark described and defined in ¶¶ 6-7 of the Complaint.

VII.   FORMATTING A TRIAL LEVEL BRIEF

Very often a court's local rules will require a certain kind of formatting for a brief, and you always, always should follow what the local rules dictate. In the absence of such rules, however, we recommend the following, a basic and generally acceptable format for brief-writing:

A.   The caption, title, all headings, the signature block, and all footnotes are single-spaced. Everything else is double-spaced.

B.   All text should be in the same font style, e.g., Times New Roman, CG Times, Courier, or other professional font. Footnote text should be the same size as the regular text, or no more than one point smaller than the regular text; i.e., if the regular text is 12 point, the footnote text should be 12 point or 11 point, but no smaller.

C.   One inch margins on all four sides.

D.   Page numbers should be at the bottom center of each page from page 2 to the end.

E.   Major headings for divisions of the brief are in bold, all caps, centered, and underlined. For example:

INTRODUCTION
STATEMENT OF FACTS
ARGUMENT
CONCLUSION

F.   Major headings for the Argument are in bold, all caps, and preceded by an uppercase Roman number (I, II, III, etc.), which begin at the left margin. The text of the heading is indented one tab from the Roman number.

G.   Secondary headings in the Argument are in bold, underlined, lowercase (or title case – initial letter of each significant word capitalized), preceded by an uppercase letter (A, B, C, etc.), and are indented one tab from the left margin. The text is indented so as to match up to the first letter of the secondary heading (beginning the paragraph).

H.   Tertiary headings are in bold, lowercase or title case, not underlined, preceded by an Arabic number (1, 2, 3, etc.), and are indented two tabs (generally ten spaces). The text is indented from the number.

I.   Quaternary headings are in lowercase, underlined, not bolded, preceded by a lowercase letter (a, b, c, etc.), and are indented fifteen spaces, with the text indented from the letter.

J.   Further headings are lowercase, preceded alternatively by lowercase Roman numbers (i, ii, iii, etc.), or Arabic numbers in parentheses ((1), (2), (3), etc.), or other numbering of your own devising, and indented five additional spaces per level. Bolding alternate headings will help to distinguish them one from another.

What we have just narrated looks like this:

PROGRESSION OF HEADINGS FOR PRETRIAL MOTION:

<u>ARGUMENT</u>

I.   **PLAINTIFF FAILS TO ALLEGE A CAUSE OF ACTION FOR FRAUDULENT MISREPRESENTATION.**

Plaintiff Jones set out to format his brief. He started with a "Roman numeral I heading" . . .

    A.   <u>**Plaintiff fails to allege that the representation was material.**</u>

Then, Jones wrote a secondary "heading A" . . .

        1.   **The representation did not impact either part of the contract implementation plan.**

This was followed by a tertiary "heading 1" . . .

            a.   <u>Part I of the plan was completed.</u>

The next heading was a quaternary "heading a" . . .

                i.   **The time table for Part I was met.**

For some reason he added another level – a "heading i" . . .

                    (1)   Groundbreaking occurred on schedule.

Strangest of all was his last heading: a "heading (1)." Jones was heading into uncharted territory . . .

If you need to go further, what you do is up to you. Additional levels are almost never necessary, but if you get a little crazy, you have a basic format to refer to.

VIII.   STYLE ISSUES OF MOTIONS

A.   Tone and formality

A motion and its supporting documents absolutely must be formal in tone because your audience usually is a judge or other legal decision maker (arbitrator, mediator, rule-making committee, etc.), and she rarely will be impressed with levity or informality in writing. The same general rules regarding formality and tone that apply in the case of office memoranda also apply and with additional force in the case of court briefs (which are different from those that we have used when writing this book, precisely for the purposes of informality). By way of review, these rules are:

1.   Do not use slang.

2.   Do not use colloquialisms.

3.   Avoid first-person and second person references – I, my, you, your, etc. A party asserts arguments or makes motions, not the attorneys, no matter if you are referring to your own side or the opposition.

4.   Avoid slash constructions (Bob was a teacher/researcher) unless that is the actual word, phrase, or address that you are quoting or referring to.

5.   Do not use contractions.

6.   It is fine to use shorthand words and abbreviations of parties, institutions and agencies, acts and statutes, once you have correctly identified them in your work.

> *Example:* The Securities Exchange Commission ("SEC") refused to apply the provisions of the Securities Act of 1933 ("'33 Act") to the post-sale use of the Section 14 red herring prospectus ("prospectus") by McDonnell Douglas Corporation ("MDC"). The SEC said that MDC

> satisfied the requirements of the '33 Act by
> providing an updated prospectus to each buyer.

7.   Do not use symbols (&, @, #) unless the symbol is part of a rule, statute, or an email address; e.g., 14 U.S.C. § 123, 13 Lab. L. Ann. ¶ 3-307, <u>goldmanr@slu.edu</u>.

8.   Avoid the use of humor. *This is not to say leave out all vivid, descriptive, and even clever language from your writing!* Clever language used sparingly can be effective and is acceptable. You can turn a clever phrase, but do it to make a point, to drive something home, to make an impression that might last a bit longer; never do it just to be funny.

9.   As with the statement of facts, do not show anger or other excessive emotion in your argument. No one wants to read a lawyer's vicious sniping at the other side, or a long, sorrowful recitation of the equities of the situation. It is not professional. You might lose your cool in person in the heat of argument, but you should not do it in writing. This is not to say be bland, dull, and never get assertive or forceful about your position. You can be forthright! You can be direct! You can show that you feel strongly about the equities! But not by bleeding your sympathy and sorrow all over the page or burning the very words off the paper with scorching prose.

B.   Footnotes

Footnotes are a luxury in court briefs; some lawyers and judges embrace them, others have no tolerance. In short: do not abuse the privilege. Footnotes may be single-spaced and appear in slightly smaller font size. As a result, you can fit more in them per square inch than regular text. But avoid devilish temptations and use them correctly.

Often there are local rules which force you to use footnotes in very limited ways: for example, some local rules provide that no legal argument can be asserted in footnotes and no legal authority may be cited or discussed in footnotes. Even if these rules are not operative in your case, *you should never put a significant part of your argument in footnotes.* Why?

1.   It might look bad

The courts (and many writing instructors) create page limits for a reason: they do not want to read excessive material. If you cheat them by loading up a page count with huge footnotes, they could resent it.

2.   Some people swear they never read footnotes

There is a vast difference of opinion on this matter, but some readers purposefully avoid footnotes. If you put something important in a footnote, it might be lost to these people forever.

3.   Footnotes are a nuisance

Even if the judge or other reader does read footnotes, if you constantly pull her attention away from the regular text and down into footnotes she might be irritated (or at the very least perplexed).

So, what do you use footnotes for?

1.   Side issues that deserve brief attention

If you have a minor, non-dispositive issue, not related to other issues (a stepping-stone issue or sub-issue), and you think it should be raised and discussed, but you are certain that it does not deserve its own TREATment, then you probably should raise and discuss it briefly in a footnote. Again, err on the side of *not* relegating (especially potentially important) issues to footnotes until you have the confidence won from years of experience.

2.   Additional facts of some interest to the analysis

In the argument section, you might consider raising additional facts that have some interest value to the analysis, but which were not raised in the statement of facts. A proper citation to support for the facts is necessary. As suggested by our warnings above, you should never relegate key facts upon which the case might turn to footnotes. We also point out that this is really only an option for the argument or discussion section, because you certainly should avoid using footnotes in the statement of facts (if you are tempted, then the fact is probably not necessary).

3.   Tertiary legal support for the argument

This is an area rife for abuse, so tread lightly. If you have a bit of persuasive primary or secondary authority that helps the cause but is not a show-stopper, and there is no critical reason for it to be discussed in the regular text, you might raise it in a footnote. In order not to appear to be violating the page limitation, you should use this option not more than two or three times in any motion document. In addition. never use a footnote as a place to squeeze important controlling authority or any other vital part of the support for your argument. Do not use footnotes as a place to create or continue a string-cite of redundant authority—these are abuses of the page limit that will only serve to anger your reader.

C.   Parentheticals

The rules on the use of parentheticals in adversarial legal writing generally are the same as with office memoranda. You can use them as a helpful way of presenting factual and secondary (or tertiary) legal information in shorthand form, *if the information is properly presented* (and that's a big "if"). Some readers tell us that they are inclined to ignore parentheticals in the same way that they are inclined to ignore footnotes, and certainly that may be the case. But that should be less of a warning *not* to use parentheticals than an admonition that you need to use them correctly.

The whole process of explanatory synthesis is designed to impress upon you the importance of the task of clearly illustrating rules. What you write in the parentheticals that illustrate the legal propositions you have laid out absolutely must be sufficient to get your point across. You may want (or need) to highlight certain factual circumstances in the cases you have analyzed and synthesized that led you to articulate the rule or interpretive principle in the precise way that you have fashioned. Here is the place for case parentheticals – *they are a buttress to your points* through clear, careful, and properly detailed illustration.

By way of summary, in an explanation section, you must construct clear, concise parentheticals that illustrate how your cases support the principles you are proposing. In a rule section, parentheticals also may be employed in citations to indicate additional, pertinent information about the authorities you cite.

Beyond these uses in citations and explanatory syntheses, do not attempt to use parentheticals simply as a space saving device. They do not substitute for a proper explanation of information from the facts or holding of a case when this information cannot be summarized in a few words or a short phrase. In addition, they should not be used as a way of presenting facts or other information in a brief without regard to the niceties of grammar, and thereby saving space

- *Questionable uses:*   Parody requires transformation which creates new content, meaning or expression (parodies add: text, transforming images, commentary, ridicule, messages) so that the new work is shown to comment on the original and not supersede the objects of the original (parodies avoid drudgery of coming up with something fresh). <u>Smith</u>, 12 F.3d at 34; <u>Jones</u>, 11 F.3d at 567; <u>Hardy</u>, 123 F.2d at 45.

IX.   FINISHING THE PRETRIAL MOTION MEMORANDUM

A.   Cite-checking

Cite-checking is an absolute ***must*** for anything you submit to a court. If you cite a case that is bad law, your opponent is afforded a great opportunity to embarrass you in front of the court, and you and your client will look very bad. If you are not fortunate enough to work in a place where someone else checks your citations before you submit your work product to a court (or your boss), then you absolutely must familiarize yourself with the cite-checking services available on Westlaw or Lexis.

B. Proofreading

Some of you may be allergic to proofreading your own work. We feel your pain, but our true advice is to take an antihistamine and do the proofreading. The appearance of your work will affect what the reader thinks of it (and you as a lawyer), whether consciously or unconsciously. Sloppy writing equals sloppy research equals sloppy lawyering equals sloppy lawyer with a sloppy case destined to lose. You do not want to create such a negative perception for you, your client, and perhaps even your law firm. It is important to take the time to proofread.

In most law schools, this function must be performed by each student on her own (in part because law professors want to teach you the skill, in part because law school is a credit-bearing enterprise in which each person earns her own degree). In practice, however, it is always a good idea to get someone that did not work on the matter in question to proofread your final work. This may not always be possible, and for that reason alone you should become your own proofreader.

It can be tough to read your own work even just for grammar and punctuation because the mind has a way of playing tricks on you and will automatically supply what is supposed to be there or read over what's in error. One tip if you find yourself proofreaderless is to read your own work backwards, because you will tend not to supply what's missing or overlook what's there if you are reading out of order. Reversing the reading forces you to read each word and each sentence slowly, and you will catch a lot more typographical and spelling and citation errors at this speed. This can be a painful chore, but the results are excellent. Another method is to read the work out loud to yourself (or to have someone else read it out loud to you). Not only will you catch some errors in this way, you also are likely to find awkward passages and words that do not flow easily which you can then go back and rework to improve your phrasing.

In addition, please note that using the **spell-checker** on your word processing program is not always sufficient. Your spell-checker is not going to catch "form" when you meant "from," "statue" when you meant "statute," "pubic" when you meant "public." It will not know that you meant to put "your" not "you," or "there" not "their." A spell-checker also might suggest changes to legal words that you actually spelled correctly; it may tell you to use "tortuous" when you actually mean "tortious" (in relation to a tort). Spell-checkers have their limits, and their limits require you to get used to proofreading your own work.

C.   Edit, edit, edit

A much repeated adage in writing is that, "There is no such thing as good writing; only good rewriting." The first drafts of your memoranda will not be perfect. You must allow yourself the time to correct mistakes, clear up rough patches that destroy the flow of the work, tighten up the sentences, and improve the wording.

Moreover, editing often is needed just to get the memorandum within the prescribed page limits. Page limits are not just for legal writing classes. Every court in which we've practiced has had page (or word) limitations.

Of course, beyond page limits is the general rule that a pretrial motion (or any legal brief) should be direct and to the point. Terse writing is more effective. Flabby writing makes the reader spend more time than she wants on your brief. This is a sin committed more often by the so called "premiere" law firms, because they allow their attorneys the time to crank out huge documents, and they have clients that can afford to pay the legal fees racked up when an attorney writes a massive volume of material in a brief. Do not perpetuate this trend. If you can say it very well in five or six pages, do not turn in fifteen.

The skill of what to cut out and what to leave in is the sum and substance of legal advocacy and legal writing. Naturally, the same criteria as to what to put in your brief apply when you are considering what you should take out. The practice of this skill truly is a lifetime devotion.

X.   SAMPLE PRETRIAL MOTIONS MEMORANDA

If this is your first time reading through a text from Murray and DeSanctis's Legal Research and Writing Series, our approach to sample briefs and memoranda is as follows: we provide multiple samples because we want you to understand that there is no model, no perfect example, no single correct way to produce work that is competent, lawyerly, and effective for its purposes in the law. We choose good samples of above average legal writing—each one most likely would receive an "A" grade in our classes—but none is perfect.

The first two samples at the end of each chapter will be annotated with our comments and questions for the reader—the interactive electronic edition of this book shows the text of the annotations. We annotated the samples to point out noteworthy parts of these sample briefs and to help you identify the parts that are done particularly well and the parts that could use some improvement. **Any additional sample briefs and memoranda offered at the end of a chapter will be unannotated so that you can see the brief in full without interruption, but we encourage you to read each sample carefully and critically, expecting that the author did some things well but other things poorly.** Our plea (or prayer for relief, if you will) is that you not try to copy one or more of these samples. Rather, you should study them and try to learn from them techniques and strategies that can improve your writing that you create in your own voice.[6]

---

6 Note, too, that we have provided samples of pretrial motions memoranda in this chapter that are not motions to dismiss or motions for summary judgment. Samples of these types of pretrial motions memoranda are provided in Chapter 3 and Chapter 4 of this book respectively.

Sample 1 – Memorandum in Support of Motion to Transfer Venue

IN THE SUPERIOR COURT OF CALIFORNIA
IN AND FOR THE COUNTY OF SAN FRANCISCO

JEFFREY KOONS and	)	
PETER MAX, d/b/a	)	
NEWSFLASH CREATIVE	)	
MEDIA,	)	
	)	
Plaintiff,	)	No. 03-C-9345
v.	)	Judge Lillian K.
	)	Sing
	)	
ARNOLD SCHWARZENEGGER,	)	
	)	
Defendant.	)	

DEFENDANT'S MEMORANDUM IN SUPPORT OF MOTION TO CHANGE VENUE

Defendant Arnold Schwarzenegger moves
this Court pursuant to Cal. Civ. Proc. Code. §
396a (1933), and Cal. Civ. Proc. Code. § 397
(1872) to transfer venue from the Superior
Court of California, County of San Francisco
to the Superior Court of California, County of
Los Angeles.

INTRODUCTION

On August 7, 2003, in response to
defendant's announcement that he would run for

governor, plaintiffs began the production and sale of T-shirts bearing defendant's likeness. Such actions were without defendant's consent, and have caused significant damage to his persona and rights of publicity. Under the controlling authority of this state a change of venue is proper, "when the convenience of witnesses and the ends of justice would be promoted by the change." Cal. Civ. Proc. Code. § 397. Defendant has named three witnesses whose convenience would be promoted by transfer to Los Angeles County, while plaintiffs have named none. The ends of justice would be promoted by saving such witnesses time and money. The ends of justice would further be promoted by holding the trial in the location where defendant developed his fame, and where the bulk of his evidence lies. Ultimately, justice requires a change of venue, due to the responsibility of defendant to the people of California.

STATEMENT OF FACTS

On August 6, 2003, defendant Arnold Schwarzenegger announced his bid for

governor of California in the recall
election (Complaint, ¶ 4). The very next
day, plaintiffs Jeffrey Koons and Peter Max
(Newsflash Media) began to produce and sell
T-shirts bearing pictures of Schwarzenegger,
either from his bodybuilding, or acting
work (Complaint, ¶ 5). These T-shirts are
sold for $15, and were produced without
Schwarzenegger's permission. All of the
T-shirts bear the name "Newsflash" in large
letters, and in prominent positions along with
phrases referencing defendant's career and
heritage (Exhibit 1). When Schwarzenegger
learned of the T-shirts on December 1, 2003,
he sent a letter to Newsflash, requesting that
they cease and desist <u>in the production and</u>
<u>sale of the T-shirts (Exhibit 2).</u>

Despite being governor, defendant resides
in Los Angeles County full time, along with all
of his witnesses, and documents which evidence
the injuries he is sustaining (Schwarzenegger
Dec., ¶ 1). While he occasionally travels
to Sacramento, Schwarzenegger conducts most
of his crucial duties as governor from Los

Angeles. Furthermore, the greatest and
most damaging injuries to his persona and
publicity rights from the plaintiffs' actions
are occurring in Los Angeles county, where
his fame was developed over many years
(Schwarzenegger Dec., ¶ 3).

California is in the middle of the worst
budget crisis in state history, making any
travel exceedingly difficult for Schwarzenegger
(Schwarzenegger Dec., ¶ 4). Furthermore,
plaintiffs' frequently do business in Los
Angeles, and there is no difference in civil
case time from filing to disposition between
the Superior Court of Los Angeles County and
the Superior Court of San Francisco County
(Skiptracer Dec. ¶ 7,8,9).

ARGUMENT

I.   **ARNOLD SCHWARZENEGGER IS ENTITLED TO A
     CHANGE OF VENUE FROM THE SUPERIOR COURT
     OF CALIFORNIA, COUNTY OF SAN FRANCISCO TO
     THE SUPERIOR COURT OF CALIFORNIA, COUNTY
     OF LOS ANGELES FOR THE CONVENIENCE OF
     WITNESSES, AND THE ENDS OF JUSTICE.**

A motion for a change of venue may be
made if the case should for some "cause

be transferred." Cal. Civ. Proc. Code. §
396a. The standards for when venue may be
transferred <u>include</u> "(c) When the convenience
of witnesses and the ends of justice would
be promoted by the change." Cal. Civ. Proc.
Code. § 397.

A change of venue to promote the
convenience of witnesses and the ends of
justice is in the sound discretion of the
trial court. <u>Ayres v. Wright</u>, 205 <u>Cal.</u> 201,
201 (1928).

A.   **<u>The convenience of witnesses would
be promoted by a transfer to the
Superior Court of California, County
of Los Angeles because the only
named witnesses reside there.</u>**

Where the movant shows that the
convenience of witnesses will be served by the
transfer, and the opposition can only show
that none will be inconvenienced, the motion
to change venue must be granted. <u>Rothschild
v. Superior Court, City and County of San
Francisco</u>, 216 <u>Cal. App. 2d.</u> 778, 780 (1st
Dist. 1963).

The rule that experts are not to be

considered in determining convenience of witnesses does not apply to one who has direct knowledge of relevant facts. Id. at 779. Additionally, the convenience of a party or of an employee of a party may be considered under special circumstances. Id. at 780.

When movant has shown that the convenience of witnesses will be promoted, and the opposing party has failed to put forth any evidence to the contrary, a change of venue will be ordered. Compare Pearson v. Superior Court, City and County of San Francisco, 199 Cal. App. 2d. 69, 78 (1st Dist. 1962) (defendant named 11 witnesses convenience promoted, plaintiff none), and Rothschild, 216 Cal. App. 2d. at 780 (movant showed two witnesses convenience from transfer, including doctor, opposition showed no inconvenience), with People v. Spring Val. Co., 109 Cal. App. 2d 656, 667 (1st Dist. 1952) (no transfer where opposing party showed equal inconvenience).

The plaintiffs in this case have not named a single witness that would be

inconvenienced by a change of venue to Los
Angeles County, while defendant has named
<u>three to benefit</u>. While the opposition might
claim these witnesses cannot be considered as
employees of defendant, they are hardly his
employees in the traditional sense. Agents,
managers, and accountants are more akin to
independent contractors, and therefore can
properly be considered for the convenience of
witnesses. Additionally, such witnesses are
experts as to damages incurred to publicity
rights, and the convenience of experts with
a direct knowledge of the relevant facts
may be considered. The case law further
recognizes that the convenience of parties
and their employees may be considered under
special circumstances. Given defendant's
urgent duties in Los Angeles, this is a
special situation. Furthermore, as defendant
developed his fame in Los Angeles, and as it
is the principle place of his injuries, there
are likely to be many more witnesses called
from that locale.

The convenience of witnesses would be

promoted by a transfer to the Superior Court
of California, County of Los Angeles because
the only named witnesses reside there.

   B.   **The ends of justice would be served
         by transferring venue to the
         Superior Court of California, County
         of Los Angeles because of the time
         and money that would be saved.**

   To determine whether the ends of justice
are promoted by a change in venue, the court
can rely not only on facts in affidavits, but
also on any reasonable inference arising
therefrom. Harden v. Skinner & Hammond, 130
Cal. App. 2d. 750, 755 (1st Dist. 1955). The
time and expense of witnesses that will be
spared can itself be evidence that the ends of
justice will be promoted. Pearson, 199 Cal.
App. 2d. at 77. The location and availability
of evidence may also be considered when
determining the promotion of the justice.
Barclay v. Supreme Lodge of Fraternal
Brotherhood, 34 Cal. App. 426, 430 (1st Dist.
1917).

   If a change of venue will save time
and money, then it will promote the ends of

justice.   Compare Harden, 130 Cal. App. 2d.
at 755 (court inferred travel time, money
saved, access to evidence, granted transfer),
and Barclay, 34 Cal. App. at 430 (motion
granted when time, money saved due to evidence
location), with Minatta v. Crook, 166 Cal.
App. 2d. 750, 756 (2d Dist. 1959) (action
to recover freight charges, transfer denied
because would create waste of time, money,
justice not promoted).A motion to change
venue should be granted when the center of
gravity of the case lies in the proposed
forum.   Compare Viacom Int'l, Inc. v. Melvin
Simon Productions, Inc., 774 F. Supp. 858, 868
(S.D.N.Y. 1995) (transfer granted where bulk
of evidence, events occurred in location), and
S.C. Johnson & Son, Inc. v. Gillette Co., 571
F. Supp. 1185, 1188 (N.D. Ill. 1983) (granted
where bulk of patent infringing activity
occurred in venue), with Willingham v. Pecora,
44 Cal. App. 2d. 289, 295 (4th Dist. 1941)
(court looked at totality of circumstances
in personal injury suit, ends not served by
transfer).

Justice necessitates in this case, that the motion for change of venue be granted. First, because the only named witnesses would save time and money, while the plaintiffs frequent Los Angeles and have named no witnesses. Second, because all of the defendant's evidence of the injuries he has sustained reside with him in Los Angeles. Third, the center of gravity of this case lies in Los Angeles. Los Angeles is where defendant built his fame and persona, and it is where he is sustaining enormous injuries at the hands of the plaintiffs. Fourth, and most importantly, the demands on the governor are enormous, as he is faced with the greatest budget crisis in the history of the state. His time is precious, and a loss of his time, is a waste of the time and money of every citizen of the state. Justice demands a change of venue to the Superior Court of California, County of Los Angeles.

The ends of justice would be served by transferring venue to the Superior Court of California, County of Los Angeles because of the time and money that would be saved.

CONCLUSION

For the reasons stated herein, this Court should grant defendant' motion for a change of venue.

Sample 2 – Memorandum in Opposition to Motion to Transfer Venue

IN THE SUPERIOR COURT OF CALIFORNIA
IN AND FOR THE COUNTY OF SAN FRANCISCO

```
JEFFREY KOONS and        )
PETER MAX,               )
d/b/a NEWSFLASH          )
CREATIVE MEDIA,          )
                         )
           Plaintiff, )      No. 03-C-9345
    v.                   )      Judge Lillian K.
                         )      Sing
                         )
ARNOLD SCHWARZENEGGER,    )
                         )
        Defendant. )
```

MEMORANDUM IN OPPOSITION TO DEFENDANT'S MOTION TO CHANGE VENUE

INTRODUCTION

Arnold Schwarzenegger's ("Movant") frivolous motion to change venue is wholly without merit, and can only be part of his

campaign to intimidate Jeffrey Koons and
Peter Max ("Plaintiffs") and scare these
great artists into silence. Ignoring decades
of precedent holding that the Court may not
consider the convenience of litigants or the
employees of litigants, Movant asks the Court
consider his own convenience and that of his
agent, personal manager, and accountant. Even
if the Court considered such witnesses, Movant
cannot prove that the convenience of witnesses
and the ends of justice require a change of
venue. Because this motion lacks legal and
factual support, it must be denied.

STATEMENT OF FACTS

On August 5, 2003, Movant, a bodybuilder-
cum-movie star, announced his candidacy for
Governor of California. Complaint, ¶ 4.
The next day, Plaintiffs, exercising their
right to express themselves on newsworthy
political events, created and began selling
shirts bearing Movant's likeness which offered
commentary on Movant's entry into politics.
Id. ¶¶ 5-7. On December 1, 2003, two weeks
after Movant was inaugurated as Governor

of California, Movant ordered Plaintiffs to cease exercising their rights or face a lawsuit. <u>Id.</u> ¶ 9. Plaintiffs refused to be bullied into giving up their rights and sought the protection of San Francisco County Superior Court. <u>Id.</u> ¶ 10. Now, even though he concedes that Plaintiffs chose a proper court, Movant asserts that the convenience of witnesses and the ends of justice require a transfer to Los Angeles County. Defendant's Motion to Change Venue 1. <u>Movant travels "a great deal" and has "traveled to San Francisco" as Governor. Declaration of Arnold Schwarzenegger ("Schwarzenegger") ¶ 4.</u> Movant conducts official state business long-distance from Los Angeles and works in temporary offices when "forced" to be in Sacramento. <u>Id.</u> ¶ 2. Movant's witnesses reside in Los Angeles and, Movant asserts, are not "amenable" to San Francisco. <u>Id.</u> ¶ 3. <u>Plaintiffs, famous artists whose art is sold in galleries statewide, live and work in San Francisco. See Declaration of Scott Skiptracer ("Skiptracer") ¶¶ 4-6.</u>

ARGUMENT

I. **MOVANT HAS NOT SHOWN THAT HIS OWN CONVENIENCE WOULD BE PROMOTED BY A CHANGE OF VENUE.**

> <u>If it appears</u>...that the..court location where the action...is commenced is not the proper...location for the trial, the court where the action..is commenced... shall...transfer it to the proper... location.

Cal. Civ. Proc. Code § 396a(b). "The court may, on motion, change the place of trial... (c) when the convenience of witnesses and the ends of justice would be promoted by the change." Cal. Civ. Proc. Code § 397. The burden rests on the moving party to prove that both the convenience of witnesses and the ends of justice will be promoted by a relocation. <u>Hamilton v. Superior Court</u>, 37 <u>Cal. App.</u> 3d 418, 424 (1st Dist. 1974). The affidavits in support of the motion must set forth (1) the names of each witness, (2) the nature of the testimony expected from each, and (3) reasons why the attendance of each at trial would be inconvenient. <u>Peiser v. Mettler</u>, 50 Cal. 2d 594, 607 (1958).

It is well established in California
that the convenience of a litigant is not a
factor to be considered in a change of venue
motion under § 397(c). E.g., id. at 612; Wrin
v. Ohlandt, 213 Cal. 158, 160 (1931); Chaffin
Construction Co. v. Maleville Bros., 155 Cal.
App. 2d 660, 663 (1st Dist. 1957). However,
courts may consider the convenience of a
litigant when travel might be fatal for such a
litigant. Simonian v. Simonian, 97 Cal. App.
2d 68 (1st Dist. 1950).

Movant, a former bodybuilder, has offered
no evidence that he is not in top shape, so
he must be asking this Court to create a new
exception just for him. Yet, he has presented
no compelling justification for taking that
dramatic step: the Simonian exception reflects
the principle that every litigant has a right
to his day in court, and Movant does not claim
that venue in San Francisco would deprive him
of that right. Therefore, the Court should
not consider the convenience of Movant.

However, even if the Court should
consider Movant's convenience, Movant has not

shown that venue in San Francisco would be inconvenient. Since Movant travels "a great deal," Schwarzenegger ¶ 4, it is difficult to conceive why a trial in San Francisco would be a dramatic disruption. <u>A man as fabulously</u> <u>wealthy as Movant cannot plausibly claim that</u> <u>travel to San Francisco for trial would be a</u> <u>financial hardship.</u> Movant goes to Sacramento only when "forced" to be there, <u>id.</u> ¶ 2, so clearly he is capable of conducting official state business from a distance. He offers no reason why it would be more difficult to conduct state business from San Francisco (which is just eighty miles from Sacramento) rather than Los Angeles (which is over 500 miles from Sacramento). Indeed, since Movant is able to conduct state business from temporary offices when not in Los Angeles, <u>id.</u>, it is unclear why he could not do the same during this suit. Movant simply has failed to show that trial in San Francisco would be inconvenient for him.

II.   MOVANT HAS NOT SHOWN THAT THE CONVENIENCE OF OTHER NAMED PERSONS WOULD BE PROMOTED BY A CHANGE OF VENUE.

California courts long have held that the convenience of the employees of a litigant cannot be considered in a change of venue motion under § 397(c). E.g., <u>Rothschild v. Superior Court</u>, 216 Cal. App. 2d 778, 779 (1st Dist. 1963); <u>Carnation Co. v. El Rey Cheese Co.</u>, 92 Cal. App. 2d 726, 728 (1st Dist. 1949). "It is a matter of common knowledge that many actors *employ* managers and personal representatives." <u>Meyers v. Nolan</u>, 18 Cal. App. 2d 319, 322-323 (2nd Dist. 1936) (emphasis added).

Movant names three witnesses in his affidavit: his agent, personal manager, and accountant. The former two should be considered employees under <u>Meyers</u>. However, even without <u>Meyers</u>, all three should be considered employees because the nature of Movant's relationship with them are virtually identical to the employer-employee relationship. First, <u>Movant's wealth and fame is vast enough to be considered an industry</u>

unto itself. Second, agents, managers, and accountants provide services to actors subject to the actor's direction. Third, actors dictate the scope and extent of the services provided by an agent, manager, and accountant. Therefore, they should be regarded as employees and, as such, disregarded for the purposes of this motion.

However, if the Court did consider convenience of Movant's employees, Movant has not shown that their convenience would be promoted by a change of venue. The convenience of a witness in attending trial, not their place of residence, is the salient consideration. Willingham v. Pecora, 44 Cal. App. 2d 289, 293 (4th Dist. 1941). The moving party must stand on the strength of his own showing rather than the weakness of the opposition. Chaffin, 155 Cal. App. 2d at 664.

When movants do not comply with Peiser's affidavit requirements, Courts deny their motion. See, e.g., Chaffin, 155 Cal. App. 2d at 663 (movant did not describe testimony expected from witnesses); Corfee v. Southern

California Edison Co., 202 Cal. App. 2d 473,
478 (2nd Dist. 1962) (movant failed to reveal
why change would be more convenient). The
decision whether to change venue often hinges
upon whether witnesses will suffer substantial
financial hardship. See Richfield Hotel
Management Inc. v. Superior Court, 22 Cal.
App. 4th 222, 227 (1st Dist. 1994) (witnesses
were low wage workers for whom transportation
was inaccessible and significantly expensive);
Silva v. Superior Court, 119 Cal. App. 3d
301, 306 (1st Dist. 1981) (attending trial
would significantly impair father's ability to
support six children). If movant shows that
the current venue inconveniences all witnesses,
and movee offers no contrary evidence, courts
may grant the motion. See Rothschild, 216
Cal. App. 2d at 780 (movant showed convenience
of witness would be promoted by change, movee
showed only equal convenience in both venues);
Pearson v. Superior Court, 199 Cal. App. 2d
69, 79 (1st Dist. 1962) (movant presented
unchallenged evidence that convenience of
witnesses would be promoted).

Movant's affidavits are fatally insufficient. He does not describe the testimony his witnesses will offer, so it is impossible to know if their testimony will be cumulative, material, or relevant. Beyond the mere conclusion that witnesses are not "amenable" to San Francisco, Movant cannot give any reason why attending trial in San Francisco is inconvenient, or a financial strain, for any person named in his affidavit. The inference must be that, for the employees of the rich and famous Movant, trial in San Francisco presents no hardship at all. Even assuming that Movant had shown convenience, the fact that Plaintiffs live and work in San Francisco is contrary evidence sufficient to justify denying the motion. Thus, Movant has not shown a change of venue would promote the witnesses' convenience.

Similarly, he cannot show that a change of venue would serve the ends of justice. The ends of justice are promoted by saving witnesses time and expense, and by avoiding delay and expense in court proceedings.

<u>Pearson</u>, 199 Cal. App. 2d at 77. The most Movant can claim is that his witnesses, documents, and exhibits are currently in Los Angeles, Schwarzenegger ¶ 3, and that the case disposition rate in Los Angeles is the same as in San Francisco. Skiptracer ¶ 8. Conspicuously absent is any claim that production of evidence in San Francisco would be any more difficult than in Los Angeles. Similarly absent is any evidence that witnesses would save any time or expense. Naturally, Movant does not even attempt to explain how transferring this suit to Los Angeles could serve the ends of justice when it would be resolved in San Francisco just as swiftly. Movant has <u>failed quite miserably</u> to provide this Court with any cognizable reason to grant his motion to change venue.

CONCLUSION

For the foregoing reasons, this Court should deny Defendant's motion to change venue.

Sample 3 – Memorandum in Support of Motion to Transfer Venue

```
        IN THE SUPERIOR COURT OF CALIFORNIA
      IN AND FOR THE COUNTY OF SAN FRANCISCO
```

```
JEFFREY KOONS and        )
PETER MAX, d/b/a         )
NEWSFLASH CREATIVE       )
MEDIA,                   )
                         )
          Plaintiff,     )    No. 03-C-9345
     v.                  )    Judge Lillian K.
                         )    Sing
                         )
ARNOLD SCHWARZENEGGER,    )
                         )
          Defendant.     )
```

MEMORANDUM IN SUPPORT OF MOTION TO CHANGE VENUE

Defendant Arnold Schwarzenegger moves this court pursuant to California Code of Civil Procedure § 396a for a change of venue to transfer the action brought by plaintiffs Jeffery Koons and Peter Max d/b/a Newsflash Creative Media to the Superior Court of California in the County of Los Angeles.

INTRODUCTION

Plaintiffs, without any permission, created t-shirts bearing the image of Mr.

Schwarzenegger. (Complaint, ¶¶ 5,9). When Mr. Schwarzenegger asked them to stop production, they sued, claiming the t-shirts were of great public interest. The suit is brought in an improper place. As the governor of a troubled state, Mr. Schwarzenegger and his witnesses conduct most of their business from Los Angeles. Their presence is needed there; therefore, they would not be able to fully participate in the trial if it is held in San Francisco. Under controlling authority of this state, an action can be transferred for the convenience of the witnesses and for the ends of justice to be promoted.

The day after Mr. Schwarzenegger announced he would run for the office of Governor of California, Plaintiffs began selling t-shirts bearing his image. See Exhibit 1; Complaint ¶ 5. They claimed they were reporting newsworthy information when all they were doing was taking old movie images and selling them for profit. See Exhibit 1; Complaint ¶ 6. Mr. Schwarzenegger sent a letter to Plaintiffs requesting that they cease all productions

and sales.   See Exhibit 2; Complaint ¶ 9.
Instead of complying, Plaintiffs sued Mr.
Schwarzenegger.   Memorandum at ¶ 4.

Mr. Schwarzenegger and his witnesses
(his staff) live and work out of Los Angeles.
(Declaration of Arnold Schwarzenegger, dated
Dec. 29, 2003 at ¶¶ 2-3). The state, one of the
largest in the nation, is in the middle of a
huge budget crisis, and Mr. Schwarzenegger and
his staff cannot leave their duties repeatedly
to travel to San Francisco for the purposes
of this lawsuit.   ("AS Dec.").   Plaintiffs
have sufficient personal and business ties to
Los Angeles.   Declaration of Scott Skiptrace
Skiptracer, dated Jan. 12, 2004 at ¶¶ 5-6.
They display their art work in galleries
in Los Angeles, and they have been spotted
selling t-shirts there as well.   ("SS Dec.").
There is no significant difference in trial
time between the two counties.   ("SS Dec.").

ARGUMENT

I.   **THE TRIAL SHOULD BE TRANSFERRED FOR THE CONVENIENCE OF THE WITNESSES AND FOR THE ENDS OF JUSTICE TO BE PROMOTED.**

The California Code of Civil Procedure 397 provides:

> The court may, on motion, change the place of trial in the following cases:
> a.   When the court designated in the complaint is not the proper court.
> b.   When there is reason to believe that an   impartial trial cannot be had therein.
> c.   When the convenience of the witnesses and the ends of justice would be promoted by the change.
> d.   When from any cause there is no judge of the court qualified to act.
> e.   When a proceeding for dissolution of marriage has been filed...

Civ. Proc. Code § 397 (Deering 2004).

Mr. Schwarzenegger has filed this motion to transfer based on subdivision (c) of the statute. California Code of Civil Procedure § 396a(b) provides that a defendant can move to transfer a case if it appears that the

court where the it is filed is not the proper
location for the case. Cal. Proc. Code §
396a (Deering 2004). In order to uphold this
claim, Mr. Schwarzenegger must prove both
parts of § 397(c) and prove that there is no
showing to the contrary. County of Orange
v. The Superior Court of the City and County
of San Francisco, 73 Cal. App. 4th 1189, 1192
(1st Dist. 1999). The burden is on the moving
party. Richfield Hotel Management, Inc. v. The
Superior Court of San Mateo County, 22 Cal.
App. 4th 222, 227 (1st Dist. 1994).

**A.   Mr. Schwarzenegger and his witnesses
would find it convenient to
participate in the trial only if it
was moved to Los Angeles County.**

The convenience of the party or his
employees is not normally looked at absent a
special or unusual circumstance or hardship.
Compare Rothschild v. The Superior Court of
The City and County of San Francisco, 216
Cal. App. 2d 778 (1st Dist. 1963) (passenger's
injury was a special circumstance that called
for a change of venue), and Richfield, 22 Cal.
App. 4th 222, 224 (hardships of employees who

were witnesses in the trial were considered in changing the venue), with Harden v. Skinner and Hammond, 130 Cal. App. 2d 750, 756 (1st Dist. 1955) (conditions of the party and his employees were not taken into account because no hardships or special circumstances were shown).

The convenience of witnesses is shown by the fact that the residence of all the witnesses is in the county to which the transfer of the cause is requested. Richfield, 22 Cal. App. 4th 222, 224 (witnesses resided in Visalia and found it inconvenient to travel to San Mateo County); Harden, 130 Cal. App. 2d 750, 753 (over 90 of the witnesses resided in Santa Clara County so judge granted the motion); Ventura School District v. The Superior Court of Los Angeles County, 92 Cal. App. 4th 811, 816 (2nd Dist. 2001) (court said that district may be entitled to change venue to the location of the witnesses).

The current case is similar to that of Richfield and Harden and other cases where the convenience of the party and the witnesses was

considered. Mr. Schwarzenegger has special
circumstances that require the trial to be
held in Los Angeles. As the governor of a
large state, his responsibilities are his
first priority. He cannot take the countless
hours away from his work that the trial would
require. Furthermore, the employees of Mr.
Schwarzenegger - his agent, his personal
manager, and his accountant and financial
planner - reside in Los Angeles. They are the
witnesses to his personal affairs, promotions,
and publicity. Since Plaintiffs have not shown
that their witnesses reside in San Francisco
County, the majority of the witnesses for the
trial are in Los Angeles. As employees of a
governor and famous movie actor, they too have
many duties. They do not have the time to
travel back and forth for the purposes of this
case. Their special circumstances must also
be considered. For these reasons, the trial
should be transferred to Los Angeles.

B.   The ends of justice would only be promoted if the trial was held in Los Angeles County.

There does not need to be direct evidence that the ends of justice will be served; the court can rely on facts presented or make any reasonable and relevant inferences from them. Kennedy/Jenks Consultants, Inc. v. The Superior Court of Contra Costa County, 80 Cal. App. 4th 948, 965 (1st Dist. 2000) (if there was no reason to hold the case in Contra Costa County, the ends of justice would only be promoted by transferring it to the appropriate county); County of Orange, 73 Cal. App. 4th 1189 (since some injuries occurred in the County of Orange, justice would be promoted by transferring the case), Harden, 130 Cal. App. 2d 750, 755 (court inferred that justice would be promoted because facts showed that witnesses would be accessible for immediate recall if case was transferred).

The ends of justice is promoted by moving the trial closer to the residence of the witnesses, avoiding delay and expense in court proceedings, and saving witnesses' time and

money. Richfield, 22 Cal. App. 4th 222, 227
(transfer granted because all witnesses lived
in one area and it was expensive to travel);
Pearson v. The Superior Court of the City and
County of San Francisco, 199 Cal. App. 2d 69,
77 (1st Dist. 1962)(wife's witnesses would be
benefited if trial was moved and husband failed
to name any witnesses); Harden, 130 Cal. App.
2d 750, 755 (by moving the trial closer, there
was obvious savings in the witnesses' time and
expenses that would have occurred if they had
to travel).

The case at hand is similar to the cases
cited above. While there is no direct evidence
that the ends of justice will be promoted
by the change in venue, it can be inferred
from the circumstances. As in Kennedy/Jenks
Consultants, there is no reason to hold the
trial in San Francisco. Plaintiffs conduct a
significant portion of their t-shirt business
in Los Angeles. They have been seen selling
t-shirts at sporting events, and others are
sold by "runners" who carry t-shirts to
various tourist spots. The most important on-

going injuries from Plaintiff's actions are occurring in Los Angeles County.

Furthermore, Mr. Schwarzenegger is the governor of a state that is in the middle of the worst budget crisis in its history. It is clearly seen that he cannot abandon his responsibilities to go to San Francisco for the purposes of this lawsuit.

As seen in <u>Harden</u> and <u>Richfield</u>, the witnesses time and expenses would be saved by moving the trial. The witnesses all have tremendous responsibilities that need immediate attention. If the trial is moved to Los Angeles, they can take care of their work and participate in the trial. They have the most knowledge of Mr. Schwarzenegger's affairs and are vital to the outcome.

The plaintiffs have not stated any names of their witnesses. Since they sell their t-shirts throughout the state and have many art contacts in Los Angeles, they would not be inconvenienced by a change in the location. Mr. Schwarzenegger does not have this benefit.

Therefore, the ends of justice can only be promoted if the trial is transferred to Los Angeles.

CONCLUSION

For the reasons stated above, defendant Schwarzenegger respectfully requests the Court to grant the Motion to Transfer.

Chapter 3

Motions to Dismiss

This chapter covers one of the more common types of pretrial motions in civil cases: motions to dismiss. Though certain kinds of motions to dismiss may be brought at various stages in the course of litigation, they most commonly are filed very early in the pretrial proceedings, after the complaint has been filed but before defendant has filed any other motion or pleading, including an answer. In a nutshell, a motion to dismiss posits that one or more or all of the claims raised by plaintiff in its complaint must be discharged from the case.

If all of the claims asserted in the complaint are discharged, then the case itself is dismissed. A plaintiff may appeal the dismissal to a higher court; otherwise, he must start over with a new complaint, or refile in a different forum (if the forum was the reason for the dismissal), assuming that the statute of limitations has not run out or that his claims are "saved" for filing by some other procedural provision. If fewer than all of the claims are dismissed, the litigation continues as to the remaining claims. Plaintiff either has to forego the dismissed claims or try to amend the complaint to reassert the claims for relief in a new and hopefully non-objectionable form. Otherwise, plaintiff has to wait for a final judgment on the remaining claims and then appeal the dismissal of the initial claims at that time.

I.   FEDERAL RULE OF CIVIL PROCEDURE 12(b)

In federal court, a motion to dismiss is governed by <u>Fed. R. Civ. P. 12(b)</u> and its various subsections. There are analogous rules that operate in state courts, but for present purposes we are only going to focus on motions to dismiss in federal court litigation.

As noted, a defendant files a motion to dismiss under this rule early in the litigation. The motion essentially is a defendant's initial answer to the complaint, styled as a motion and typically accompanied by a brief or memorandum of law, along the lines of those that we discussed in the previous chapter. A defendant certainly is not required to file a motion to dismiss and, indeed, grounds for such motion do not exist in every case.

As you might suspect, motions to dismiss are not limited to defendants but, rather, may be filed by any party against whom a claim has been asserted. Accordingly, a plaintiff can file a motion to dismiss a counterclaim, a third-party defendant can file a motion to dismiss a third-party claim, or any party can file a motion to dismiss a cross-claim asserted by a co-defendant or co-plaintiff on the same side of the "v."

Rule 12(b) governs all of these situations. There are several grounds on which such a motion can be brought (discussed below). One important common thread of each ground is that Rule 12(b) motions attack allegations in the complaint and often assume those allegations to be true for purposes of testing the sufficiency or propriety of the allegations via the motion. Remember that we are talking here about a phase of litigation that is pre-discovery. Accordingly, all the defendant and court should have to work with are facts and allegations presented on the face of a <u>complaint</u> (presumably a "well-pleaded" complaint).

FYI

Although Rule 12(b) does not state so specifically, motions challenging the justiciability of a claim based on, e.g., ripeness, mootness, or a political question, typically are brought under Rule 12(b)(1), the theory being that these defects go the heart of a federal court's ability to hear a cause of action.

II.   LACK OF JURISDICTION OVER THE SUBJECT MATTER - RULE 12(b)(1)

<u>Fed. R. Civ. P. 12(b)(1)</u> governs motions to dismiss for lack of subject matter jurisdiction. As you may recall from Civil Procedure, federal courts are courts of limited jurisdiction, meaning that they are not authorized to hear any and all claims that a plaintiff may have against another party. A motion to dismiss under 12(b)(1) asserts just that: the court does not have the authority to hear the dispute because:

- there is no diversity between the parties, or an insufficient amount in controversy under <u>28 U.S.C. § 1332</u>; or

- there is no federal question presented by the complaint under <u>28 U.S.C. § 1331</u>; or

- the subject matter of the action belongs in a specific federal forum (e.g., a bankruptcy action that should have been brought in a United States Bankruptcy Court).

PRACTICE POINTER

As noted, a motion to dismiss often takes the allegations in the complaint at face value. In a 12(b)(1) motion, however, oftentimes the problem is that the complaint erroneously alleges facts and makes improper factual and legal conclusions in support of subject matter jurisdiction. In these circumstances, the movant must challenge and refute these erroneous grounds by bringing out the "correct" facts and conclusions regarding subject matter jurisdiction. In other words, in such instances, the movant cannot assume the facts pleaded in the complaint to be true for purposes of the motion; indeed, it would be a fatal error to do so.

If new operative facts regarding subject matter jurisdiction are alleged in the motion, then a party may request an extension of time to address the new facts, and perhaps even seek limited discovery. There is no guaranty that a party will be afforded the time or granted the right to take discovery on subject matter jurisdiction. In addition, if a Rule 12(b)(1) motion is pled in conjunction with a <u>Rule 12(b)(6)</u> motion (see below), and new facts are alleged, the court has the option of converting the proceedings to a summary judgment motion under <u>Fed. R. Civ. P. 56</u>, in which case the opportunity for discovery will be afforded to parties.

III. MOTION TO DISMISS FOR LACK OF JURISDICTION OVER THE PERSON - RULE 12(b)(2)

A <u>Rule 12(b)(2)</u> motion argues that the court has no jurisdiction over the person of the defendant(s) (or the subject matter "thing," the "res" of the case) because:

- the defendant is not present in the jurisdiction (doesn't reside there, isn't subject to service of process there, and cannot be found there in person or through a proper agent);

- the property in question (the "res") is not within jurisdictional limits;

- the defendant is not properly haled into the court under the applicable state Long Arm statute (the Long Arm statute of the state where the court is located); or

- the defendant cannot properly or reasonably be haled into the court under the Due Process Clause of the U.S. Constitution, and the related doctrines of "minimum contacts" and "traditional notions of fair play and substantial justice."

PRACTICE POINTER

The plaintiff, of course, typically will have alleged facts in support of personal jurisdiction over the defendant in the complaint; however, these facts cannot always be presumed true or complete. Oftentimes, the defendant will have different or additional information bearing on the issue of personal jurisdiction. In such cases, it is incumbent on the defendant to assert and prove the "correct" facts regarding personal jurisdiction in the motion to dismiss. In other words, the movant should strike the phrase "presume the facts alleged in the complaint to be true for purposes of the motion" from any 12(b)(2) litigation document template.

The appropriate way for the movant to introduce new jurisdictional facts is to allege them in the motion supported by an attached affidavit or declaration filed under penalty of perjury from a knowledgeable person (usually your client). Both sides have the right to ask for limited discovery regarding jurisdictional facts. Neither side is guaranteed the right, but a court will be hard-pressed not to grant limited discovery in most cases, especially if both sides request it, or if the movant introduces and attempts to prove new jurisdictional facts in its motion, and the opponent claims that it needs to explore them. The court also might entertain a fact-finding hearing on personal jurisdiction, after which it will determine whether the exercise of personal jurisdiction is indeed proper. The testimony of witnesses and documents and other items that tend to prove such facts might be taken into evidence at such a hearing. Although these hearings can prove expensive for such an early stage in a case, motions asserting lack of personal jurisdiction are always worth bringing if legitimate. Importantly, any defects in personal jurisdiction will be waived if not asserted (and reasserted even if the initial motion to dismiss is denied). In other words, unlike with subject matter jurisdiction, a party can consent to personal jurisdiction in a particular forum even where jurisdiction does not lie. Thus, it is important that a party seeking to challenge personal jurisdiction object to it immediately and continue to preserve its objection for purposes of appeal later.

IV. MOTION TO DISMISS FOR IMPROPER VENUE - RULE 12(b)(3)

Fed. R. Civ. P. 12(b)(3) is the vehicle for arguing that venue is improper, which may be the case because:

- it fails to satisfy the requirements of 28 U.S.C. § 1391 or the applicable venue statute;

- there was a forum selection clause that required the case to be brought in a different venue; or

- plaintiff is mistaken in its facts alleged in support of its choice of venue.

If a motion to dismiss for lack of venue is granted, the plaintiff still can pick up the pieces and file the suit in an appropriate venue, as long as the statute of limitations has not run or plaintiff's claims are saved by some other procedural rule.

A 12(b)(3) motion commonly is brought in conjunction with motions under 28 U.S.C. §§ 1404 and 1406. A section 1404 motion seeks transfer to a more convenient venue—more convenient to the defendant, to be sure, but justified either because of a forum selection clause or under a forum non conveniens argument. A § 1406 motion argues that if the court finds that venue is improper, the court can transfer the case to an appropriate venue, rather than dismissing the suit outright.

PRACTICE POINTER

As with a Rule 12(b)(2) motion, the movant **cannot** presume the facts alleged in the complaint in support of venue to be true for purposes of the motion; it would be fatal to do so. The appropriate way to introduce new and "correct" venue facts is to allege them in the motion supported by an attached affidavit or declaration under penalty of perjury from a knowledgeable person. Both sides have the right to ask for discovery regarding venue facts, but neither side is guaranteed the right to such discovery.

V.   MOTION TO DISMISS FOR INSUFFICIENCY OF PROCESS OR SERVICE OF PROCESS - RULE 12(b)(4) and 12(b)(5)

Fed. R. Civ. P. 12(b)(4) and 12(b)(5) govern motions to dismiss based on a perceived problem with the manner in which the court papers were prepared or served. A deficiency in "process" means that something allegedly is wrong with the papers themselves—there is erroneous, insufficient, or incomplete information in the summons, complaint, or return of service. A defect in "service of process" means that the way the papers were served or the person upon whom they were served is improper. Examples include service by publication when personal service was required, or service on a five-year-old friend of the son of the defendant rather than on the defendant, or service on a receptionist in the building lobby and not on a proper officer or agent of a corporate defendant.

FOOD FOR THOUGHT

A party filing a motion to dismiss for improper process or service of process rarely succeeds in obtaining a full dismissal. The vast majority of the time, the court will just grant the plaintiff additional time for service and issue an additional summons so that the plaintiff can perform service correctly. If delay is your primary goal, then you might have particular incentive to file this kind of motion, but be aware that modern rules often shift the costs of opposing the motion or the cost of additional service of process back onto the movant if the motion is found to be erroneous.

VI.   MOTION TO DISMISS FOR FAILURE TO STATE A CLAIM UPON WHICH RELIEF MAY BE GRANTED - RULE 12(b)(6)

We like to think of motions filed under <u>Fed. R. Civ. P. 12(b)(6)</u> to be the real show-stoppers of Rule 12, and our own experience litigating suggests that winning a motion on 12(b)(6) grounds can be quite exhilarating, indeed. Rule 12(b)(6) motions sometimes are confused by junior attorneys with motions for summary judgment, but only because they have the same effect: complete dismissal of a claim (or whole complaint). The paradigm 12(b)(6) motion argues that even if everything plaintiff alleges is true, under the law applicable to the case, the plaintiff still cannot recover against the defendant. Finally, a pretrial motion you really can sink your teeth into.

There are essentially two variants of the 12(b)(6) motion to dismiss. The "weaker" version alleges that the allegations in the complaint do not make out a *prima facie* case. For example, in a negligence case, perhaps the plaintiff has failed to allege that the defendant owed the plaintiff a duty of care. As duty is a necessary element of the tort of negligence, a claim that fails to allege facts indicating a duty should fail on its face. The main problem with this "weaker" version is that the remedy is often simply a matter of the plaintiff's filing an amended complaint. If the plaintiff can allege facts sufficient to make out the duty element, then the defect is really a drafting one, and most courts will allow the plaintiff to amend.

The "stronger" version of a 12(b)(6) motion is the real show-stopper. This is the motion that assumes all facts pleaded in the complaint to be true and correct for purposes of the motion. Yet, the defendant's claim is that, even taking the facts as they are alleged, the result does not amount to a valid cause of action under the relevant law.

To take an extreme example, presume that your client, a police officer, has been served with a motion claiming damages because your client stuck his tongue out at the plaintiff. The plaintiff presents in the complaint a detailed narrative describing how your client walked up to him on a public street and, in front of other people, stuck his tongue straight out at the plaintiff. In your motion to dismiss, you want to assert that even if these allegations are true (and you are not saying that they are, but for present purposes you will assume them to be), the plaintiff has no legally cognizable cause of action against your client, i.e., that behavior simply does not rise to the level of an claim upon which relief may be granted.

These motions are difficult to win, because the defendant is seeking a dispositive ruling pre-discovery, before any additional facts are known. By the same token, if you can win a motion to dismiss before your client has to undergo the often expensive and time-consuming process of discovery, you will have one happy client on your hands.

If additional, even limited, fact-finding is necessary, the court is very likely to convert the motion to a Fed. R. Civ. P. 56 motion for summary judgment. In that case, the court generally will grant an extension of time to the party opposing the motion so as to allow it time to gather facts in opposition to the movant's arguments. Discovery may be granted to either or both sides, and delay of the proceedings will result. (Similarly, the court might simply deny the motion to dismiss and encourage the movant to refile it as a summary judgment motion once discovery has been completed).

TAKE NOTE!

Note that you really only want to assume "that all facts pleaded in the complaint are true and correct **for purposes of the motion.**" You need not and should not assume the complaint and its claims to be true and correct for any other purpose, and you certainly do not want to create the impression (true or not) that you are admitting to the facts as alleged. So, be careful to use the proper wording of the presumption.

VII.   BASIC FORMAT OF MOTIONS TO DISMISS AND OPPOSITIONS TO THE SAME

As always, you want to check the local rules of your jurisdiction to be sure that you are following any formal requirements for a motion to dismiss. As a general matter, motions to dismiss contain the same elements that we discussed in <u>Chapter 2</u>.

CAPTION

TITLE

INTRODUCTION

STATEMENT OF FACTS

ARGUMENT

CONCLUSION

The title identifies the motion before the court, and we recommend that you reiterate it (sometimes with additional information about the parties and the motion) in a first sentence or two that precedes the introduction.

The Introduction, as always, is the most critical section, and you need to draft a short, persuasive summary of your argument. Discuss the facts, law, and legal conclusions that tell the court why you should win.

Unless you are writing a 12(b)(6) motion, you should draft the Statement of Facts with your client's particular position in mind. On a motion to dismiss for lack of subject matter jurisdiction, personal jurisdiction, or venue, you can introduce and discuss new facts supporting your position. Factual conclusions are permitted, but you should draw the necessary jurisdictional or venue-related legal conclusions in your argument section, not in the fact section. Be wary of creating a "swearing match" on the jurisdictional facts.

In a 12(b)(6) motion, however, you must presume the plaintiff's complaint to be true for purposes of the motion, so you are limited in what you can do with the facts. Of course you should consider reordering and rewording the plaintiff's rendition of the facts, but be careful not to change or challenge the actual facts or introduce new ones unless you are prepared to face a quick denial of the motion or conversion of the proceedings to a drawn-out, expensive summary judgment motion context.

The Argument (or Discussion) is drafted in the usual way as discussed in Chapter 21. The Conclusion also is the same—strive for just one sentence telling the court what you want it to do.

The opposition to a motion to dismiss follows the same format. Of course, the opponent should attempt to refute any new facts alleged, and rebut any legal arguments raised against the complaint and choice of forum. Dig in your heels here—it's your complaint, and your choice of forum. In addition, do not feel that you have to let the movant set the playing field, and that your only option is to respond to the motion point by point in the order presented. Instead, you always want to raise your best points in opposition first, followed by the next best and so on. If you have additional points that support your complaint that the movant did not address, be sure to include them. Try to make your opponent sweat through its reply brief.

VIII.   SAMPLE MOTIONS TO DISMISS

In this section are four sample memoranda in support of or in opposition to motions to dismiss. We have provided multiple samples because we want you to understand that there is no model, no perfect example, no single correct way to produce work that is competent, lawyerly, and effective for its purposes in the law. We choose good samples of above average legal writing—each one most likely would receive an "A" grade in our classes—but none is perfect.

The first two samples are annotated with our comments and questions for the reader—the interactive electronic edition of this book shows the text of the annotations. We annotated the samples to point out noteworthy parts of these sample briefs and to help you identify the parts that are done particularly well and the parts that could use some improvement. The additional sample memoranda offered at the end this chapter are unannotated so that you can see the memoranda in full without interruption, but we encourage you to read each sample carefully and critically, expecting that the author did some things well but other things poorly. Our plea is that you not try to copy one or more of these samples. Rather, you should study them and try to learn from them techniques and strategies that can improve your writing that you create in your own voice.

Sample 1 - Memorandum in Support of Motion to Dismiss

UNITED STATES DISTRICT COURT
CENTRAL DISTRICT OF CALIFORNIA
SOUTHERN DIVISION

GLOBAL STUDIOS,	)	
	)	
Plaintiff,	)	
v.	)	No. SA CV 01-
	)	9999 AHS
	)	
KINGSTON UNIVERSITY	)	
ELECTRONIC FREEDOM	)	
FRONTIER, LARRY MULLEN,	)	
LISA ROGERS, MEGHAN	)	
MORELY, and CHRIS	)	
HANSEN,	)	
	)	
Defendants.	)	

MEMORANDUM IN SUPPORT OF DEFENDANTS' MOTION TO DISMISS FOR LACK OF PERSONAL JURISDICTION

Defendants Kingston University Electronic Freedom Frontier, Larry Mullen, Lisa Rogers, Meghan Morely, and Chris Hansen (collectively referred to as "KUEFF") move this Court pursuant to Fed. R. Civ. P. 12(b)(2), to dismiss this action for lack of personal jurisdiction.

INTRODUCTION

The complaint in this case represents an attempt by Plaintiff, Global Studios, to abolish the constitutional right of defendant, KUEFF from posting newsworthy information on its website concerning the CSS/DeCSS controversy. Global Studios apparently believes that a news organization cannot report on DVD duplication without being subject to suit in California.

KUEFF moves to dismiss the suit for lack of personal jurisdiction. None of its members has been to California since the organization was founded, and fewer than one percent of the hits on the website have been from users located in California. No commercial activity takes place on the website, and the level of interactivity is miniscule. The organization has not purposefully availed itself of the privilege of conducting activities in California. In addition, it would be unreasonable to require four college students to defend themselves in a location across the country against a wealthy corporation like

Global Studios. Accordingly, KUEFF's contacts with California do not satisfy the "minimum contacts" and "fair and substantial justice" required by the California Long-Arm statute, Cal. Civ. Proc. Code § 410.10 (West 2001), and the state and federal constitutional "due process" standards, Cal. Const. art. 1, § 7; U.S. Const. amend. XIV.

STATEMENT OF FACTS

DeCSS is software that can be downloaded and used to unscramble the protection program known as Content Scramble System (CSS) so DVDs can then be duplicated. Since March 2001, Kingston University in Troy, New York, has hosted a web site of a nonprofit student organization known as Kingston University Electronic Freedom Frontier (KUEFF). <u>See</u> Declaration of Tracy Sensor dated Jan. 4, 2002, at ¶ 2 ("T.S. Dec."). The organization regularly posts news on its web site regarding issues of free speech on the Internet. <u>See</u> Declaration of Larry Mullen dated Jan. 8, 2002, at ¶ 2 ("L.M. Dec."). KUEFF's personnel and everything associated with its activities are located in New York. See L.M. Dec. at ¶ 4.

In September 2001, the organization began
reporting on the CSS/DeCSS controversy. See
T.S. Dec. at ¶ 3. The names and addresses
of several web sites that provide DeCSS for
downloading were mentioned in passing. See
T.S. Dec. at ¶ 3. None of the addresses were
hyperlinked. See L.M. Dec. at ¶ 3. KUEFF did
nothing to encourage readers in California to
visit these sites or download the software.
See Complaint, Exhibit 1 ("Exhibit 1").

The organization's only contact with
people in California has been through emails,
the majority of which consist of information
about KUEFF and news previously reported on
the web site. See L.M. Dec. at ¶ 6. There is
evidence of only two donations being made
via email, one by an attorney representing
the plaintiff and another by the plaintiff's
witness. See Declaration of Zachary Schulman
dated Jan. 7, 2002, at ¶ 5; Declaration of
Melanie Smead dated Jan. 12, 2002, at ¶ 5
("M.S. Dec"). No contracts or sales have been

made with anyone in California. There is no evidence that any hits from California led to installation of DeCSS. M.S. Dec. at ¶ 3.

ARGUMENT

I. THE ACTION MUST BE DISMISSED FOR LACK OF PERSONAL JURISDICTION

Fed. R. Civ. P. 12(b)(2) provides that the defendant may make a motion to dismiss for "lack of jurisdiction over the person." This case has been brought before the United States District Court, Central District California. Therefore, the personal jurisdiction laws of California are applied.

The California Long Arm provision, Cal. Civ. Proc. Code § 410.10, states, "a court of this state may exercise jurisdiction on any basis not inconsistent with the Constitution of this state or of the United States." According to Cal. Const. art. 1, § 7 and U.S. Const. amend. XIV, "a person may not be deprived of life, liberty, or property without due process of the law."

Due process requires that a defendant, if

not present in the state, "have certain minimum
contacts with it such that the maintenance
of the suit does not offend traditional
notions of fair play and substantial justice."
Cybersell, Inc. v. Cybersell, Inc., 130 F.3d
414, 415 (9th Cir. 1997) (citing International
Shoe Co. v. Washington, 326 U.S. 310, 316
(1945)). ,

Personal jurisdiction may be founded
on either general jurisdiction or specific
jurisdiction. Panavision Int'l, L.P. v.
Toeppen, 141 F.3d 1316, 1320 (9th Cir. 1998).
General jurisdiction exists when a defendant
is domiciled in the forum state or when the
defendant's activities there are "substantial"
or "continuous and systematic." Panavision,
141 F.3d at 1320 (citing Helicopteros
Nacionales de Colombia, S.A. v. Hall, 466 U.S.
408, 414-16 (1984)).

Nothing in the complaint suggests that
general jurisdiction is being asserted.
Therefore, this motion will address the
absence of specific jurisdiction over the
defendants.

A. The Court does not have specific jurisdiction over KUEFF under the California Long-Arm statute.

Courts use a three-part test to determine whether specific jurisdiction should be exercised:

> (1) The nonresident defendant must do some act or consummate some transaction with the forum or perform some act by which he purposefully avails himself of the privilege of conducting activities in the forum, thereby invoking benefits and protections of its laws; (2) the claim must be one which arises out of or results from the defendant's forum-related activities; and (3) exercise of jurisdiction must be reasonable.

Panavision, 141 F.3d at 1320.

1. KUEFF did not purposefully avail itself.

Under the "sliding scale" approach, the likelihood that personal jurisdiction will be exercised is proportionate to the nature and quality of commercial activity conducted over the Internet. See Cybersell, 130 F.3d at 419 (citing Zippo Mfg. Co. v. Zippo Dot Com, Inc., 952 F. Supp. 1119, 1124 (W.D. Pa. 1997)).

At opposite ends of the scale are
"passive" and "active" web sites; the middle
consists of "interactive" sites where the user
can exchange information with the defendant
site. Callaway Golf Corp. v. Royal Canadian
Golf Ass'n, 125 F. Supp. 2d 1194, 1200 (C.D.
Cal. 2000).

Specific jurisdiction primarily is
exercised over "interactive" web sites when
products, not advertisements or promotions,
are sold. Compare S. Morantz v. Hang & Shine
Ultrasonics, Inc., 79 F. Supp. 2d 537, 539
(E.D. Pa. 1999) (applying federal Due Process
clause) (sale of promotional materials
to forum residents via its web site too
"fortuitous and random" to warrant exercise of
jurisdiction), with Stomp, Inc. v. NeatO, LLC,
61 F. Supp. 2d 1074, 1077 (C.D. Cal. 1999)
(specific jurisdiction appropriate over web
site dedicated to sale of products on-line).
Courts have refused to recognize contacts
manufactured by the plaintiff. Millennium
Enterprises, Inc. v. Millennium Music, L.P.,
33 F. Supp. 2d 907, 911 (D. Or. 1999) (no

personal jurisdiction where the only sales in California motivated by the plaintiff's interest in the lawsuit).

KUEFF operates a relatively "interactive" web site that allows users to email directly to the organization. However, unlike the site in <u>Stomp</u> that was established for the purpose of transacting Internet sales, KUEFF's site does not offer products for purchase. The only commercial activity on KUEFF's site has consisted of donations that were more akin to promotional transactions than product sales. And even if deemed substantial commercial activity, the donations may be disregarded as having been manufactured by the plaintiff.

<u>Under the "effects test," personal jurisdiction in a tort case is predicated on (1) intentional actions that are (2) expressly aimed at the forum state, and (3) cause harm, the brunt of which is suffered—and which the defendant knows is likely to be suffered—in the forum state. Callaway, 125 F. Supp. 2d at 1200.</u>

Believing a corporate defendant might be located in California or "foreseeing" an article might cause harm in California does not satisfy the "effects test." Compare Callaway, 125 F. Supp. 2d at 1200 (no personal jurisdiction where defendant did not know plaintiff had its principal place of business in California and was unaware the effects would be felt in California), with Pavlovich v. Superior Court, 109 Cal. Rptr. 2d 909, 918 (Ct. App. 6th Dist. 2001), *petition for review granted*, 36 P.3d 625 (Cal. Dec. 12, 2001) ("effects test" satisfied where defendant knowingly and intentionally caused harm in California).

The "effects test" should not apply to a strict liability intellectual property case because plaintiff never will have to prove that the defendants intentionally caused harm in California. However, assuming the effects test does apply, the plaintiff fails to meet the three prongs. The only intentional action committed by KUEFF was news reporting. Unlike Pavlovich, KUEFF had no idea their site would be used as a directory to DeCSS sites, nor did they know Global Studios would suffer in California.

2. **Global Studios claim arises out of KUEFF's forum-related activities.**

KUEFF does not contest the assertion that to the extent plaintiff has been injured by defendant's commercial activity on its web site, plaintiff would not have suffered the alleged injuries "but for" defendant's activity. KUEFF does not contest the assertion that the cause of action alleged by plaintiff, if valid, arises out of KUEFF's forum-related activities.

3. **Exercising personal jurisdiction over KUEFF in California would be unreasonable.**

* * *

CONCLUSION

In light of the above, KUEFF respectfully requests the court to dismiss the complaint for lack of personal jurisdiction.

Sample 2 - Memorandum in Opposition to Motion to Dismiss

```
UNITED STATES DISTRICT COURT
CENTRAL DISTRICT OF CALIFORNIA
SOUTHERN DIVISION
```

```
GLOBAL STUDIOS,            )
                           )
           Plaintiff,      )
                           )    No. SA CV 01-
                           )    9999 AHS
                           )
      v.                   )
                           )
KINGSTON UNIVERSITY        )
ELECTRONIC FREEDOM         )
FRONTIER, LARRY MULLEN,    )
LISA ROGERS, MEGHAN        )
MORELY, and CHRIS          )
HANSEN,                    )
                           )
           Defendants.     )
```

**PLAINTIFF'S MEMORANDUM IN OPPOSITION TO
DEFENDANTS' FED. R. CIV. P. 12(b)(2) MOTION
TO DISMISS FOR LACK OF PERSONAL JURISDICTION**

[comment]

INTRODUCTION

Defendants assert that they can
enable the theft of Plaintiff's property
in California, Plaintiff's home state, yet
evade responsibility for the resulting damage
because their contacts with that forum were

directed over the Internet. Plaintiff serves
the public by writing motion pictures to
Digital Versatile Disks (DVDs). Defendants,
through their website, provide access to
a means by which Plaintiff's copyrighted
material may be stripped from those DVDs.
Through maintenance of a continuously
accessible website, direction of explicit
emails intended to and actually causing injury
to Plaintiff, and solicitation and receipt of
donations to support their cause, Defendants
have purposefully availed themselves of
the privileges of conducting activities in
California. Plaintiff's suit arises from
these contacts, and reasonableness dictates
that Plaintiff's and California's interests
in attaining jurisdiction over Defendants be
obliged. Therefore, assertion of jurisdiction
meets the due process requirements of both the
California and United States Constitutions and
comports with the California Long-Arm statute.

STATEMENT OF FACTS

The viability of Plaintiff's business
hinges on the protection of its copyrighted

material stored on DVDs, which is provided
by a computer program known as Content
Scramble System ("CSS"). See Complaint, ¶¶ 10-
11. Defendants provide access to a computer
program known as DeCSS, the only function of
which is to decrypt CSS and allow the pirating
of material stored on DVDs. See Complaint, ¶¶
10-13. Plaintiff filed a complaint with this
Court to restrain Defendants from undermining
its copyrights and ruining its business. See
generally Complaint.

Plaintiff operates its business in
California. See Complaint, ¶ 1. Although
Defendants have no physical presence in that
state, their website is easily accessible to
California residents through the Internet, as
evidenced by the eighty-five hits the site has
received from California viewers. Declaration
of Tracy Sensor dated Jan. 4, 2002, at ¶ 5
("Sensor Dec."). Bolded headings featured on
Defendants' website include "Contact us,"
followed by an invitation to "Subscribe to
the newsletter by email, [and] exchange
information," and "Donations," followed by

a request for credit card information and an assurance that the donations are tax-deductible. <u>See</u> Complaint, Exhibit 1. The first heading has resulted in seven emails from California residents and fifteen reply emails from Defendants, at least two of which accommodated requests for information regarding how DeCSS can be obtained. Declaration of Larry Mullen dated Jan. 8, 2002, at ¶ 6 ("Mullen Dec."). The second heading has induced donations from at least two California residents. Mullen Dec. at ¶ 7. Furthermore, on at least thirty occasions, California residents have downloaded usable copies of DeCSS using only the information on Defendants' website. Declaration of Melanie Smead dated Jan. 12, 2002, at ¶ 3 ("Smead Dec."); Declaration of Zachary Schulman dated Jan. 7, 2002, at ¶ 3 ("Schulman Dec.").

ARGUMENT

<u>Defendants bring a motion to dismiss Plaintiff's action for "lack of jurisdiction over the person" under Fed. R. Civ. P. 12(b)(2).</u>

I. THE CALIFORNIA LONG-ARM STATUTE CONVEYS PERSONAL JURISDICTION OVER DEFENDANTS.

Cal. Civ. Proc. Code sec. 410.10 provides that "A court of this state may exercise jurisdiction on any basis not inconsistent with the Constitution of this state or of the United States." The due process clause of each constitution prohibits the state from "depriving any person of life, liberty, or property, without due process of law." Cal. Const. art. 1, sec. 7; U.S. Const. amend. XIV. Thus, the limits of the state long-arm statute are co-extensive with the limits of federal due process. See Panavision Int. L.P. v. Toeppen, 114 F.3d 1316, 1320 (9th Cir. 1998).

Federal due process permits personal jurisdiction over a defendant in any state with which the defendant has certain minimum contacts, which can be established through contacts that give rise to specific or general jurisdiction. See Helicopteros Nacionales de Columbia, S.A. v. Hall, 466 U.S. 408, 414 (1984). In the present case, Plaintiff claims only specific jurisdiction.

The 9th Circuit applies a three-prong test to establish specific jurisdiction:

> Specific jurisdiction exists if (1) the defendant has performed some act or consummated some transaction within the forum or otherwise purposefully availed himself of the privileges of conducting activities in the forum, thereby invoking the benefits and protections of state law, (2) the claim arises out of or results from the defendant's forum-related activities, and (3) the exercise of jurisdiction is reasonable.

See Bancroft, 223 F.3d at 1086; Cybersell, Inc. v. Cybersell, Inc, 130 F.3d 414, 416 (9th Cir. 1997). This memorandum in opposition will address each basis for specific jurisdiction in the order presented above.

A. **Defendants purposefully availed themselves of the privileges of conducting activities in California.**

When a defendant conducts business over the Internet, purposeful availment is established by measuring the quality and nature of the commercial activity conducted by the defendant on a sliding scale to determine if minimum contacts exist. See Cybersell, 130

F.3d at 419; <u>Zippo Mfg. Co. v. Zippo Dot Com,</u>
<u>Inc.</u>, 952 F. Supp. 1119, 1124 (W.D. Pa. 1997).

    <u>In addition to the mere capacity for</u>
<u>interactivity of a defendant's website,</u>
<u>actual transactions between the defendant</u>
<u>and residents of the forum are required to</u>
<u>establish purposeful availment.</u> <u>Compare</u>
<u>Digital Control, Inc. v. Boretronics, Inc.</u>,
161 F. Supp. 2d 1183, 1187 (W.D. Wash. 2001)
(regardless of nature of website, purposeful
availment requires decision to enter into
transactions with forum residents), <u>with</u>
<u>Tech Heads, Inc. v. Desktop Serv. Ctr.</u>, 105
F. Supp. 2d 1142, 1150-51 (D. Ore. 2000)
(transaction with forum resident through
website was critical to establishing
purposeful availment). Solicitation and
receipt of donations through a website is
sufficient to constitute actual transactions
with forum residents. <u>See</u> <u>Heroes, Inc. v.</u>
<u>Heroes Found.</u>, 958 F. Supp. 1, 5 (D.D.C.
1996) (finding such transactions critical to
establishing purposeful availment).

    It is the quality, not the quantity of

transactions that is relevant. Thus, even one or two transactions may suffice for purposes of establishing jurisdiction, and even if the transactions were initiated by the plaintiff. See Tech Heads, 105 F. Supp. 2d at 1150 (finding jurisdiction when defendant's contacts with forum included one Internet transaction); Stomp, Inc. v. Neato, L.L.C., 61 F. Supp. 2d 1074, 1078 (C.D. Cal. 1999) (finding jurisdiction when defendant's contacts with forum were limited to two sales induced by plaintiff).

Although typically reserved for tort cases, the "effects test" has been used as an alternative method to establish purposeful availment in some intellectual property actions, especially where the defendant's action is akin to a tort. Compare Panavision, 141 F.3d at 1321-22 (effects test appropriate because defendant's registration of plaintiff's trademarks as domain name was akin to a tort), with Cybersell, 130 F.3d at 420 (effects test inapplicable because defendant's posting of a passive website not akin to a tort). Purposeful availment is established through the effects test by showing that a defendant's foreign act was expressly aimed at and had effect in the forum state. See Calder v. Jones, 465 U.S. 783, 791 (1984); Bancroft, 223 F.3d at 1087. Because jurisdiction cannot be predicated on acts with merely foreseeable consequences, the express aiming element requires that the defendant engage in wrongful conduct aimed at entities known to the defendant to be forum residents. Id.

Plaintiffs have two opportunities to prove purposeful availment: either the effects test or the sliding scale analysis will suffice, and if one test is satisfied, the court need not consider the other. See Cybersell, 130 F.3d at 417 (effects test inapplicable, inquiry moved on to sliding scale analysis); Tech Heads, 105 F. Supp. 2d at 1148 (effects test applied but not met, minimum contacts shown by sliding scale test); Bancroft, 223 F.3d at 1088 (purposeful availment analysis ceased when effects test was met).

In the present case, the motion picture

industry is the exclusive major proponent
of the DVD format. Thus, Defendants have
expressly targeted Plaintiff, as a member of
that industry, by providing access to DeCSS.
Defendant's activity, like that at issue in
Panavision, 141 F.3d at 1321-22, is tort-like,
causing an injury to Plaintiff in California;
thus, the "effects test" is applicable.
Moreover, because Defendants' activity has
injured Plaintiff in California by enabling at
least thirty downloads of DeCSS in that forum,
the effects test is satisfied here.

Even without the effects test, however,
Defendants' minimum contacts with California
can be demonstrated with a sliding scale
analysis. Defendants' activity was facilitated
by their website, the interactive nature
of which is indicated by the invitations
to subscribe to a newsletter, exchange
information, and make donations. The emails
regarding how to obtain DeCSS sent to known
California residents, and the online receipt
of donations (privileged as exemptions under
California law) from residents, provide the

actual transactions with the forum required to show purposeful availment.

B.   **Plaintiff's claim arises out of Defendants' forum-related activities.**

As Plaintiff's suit would not have arisen but for Defendant's contacts with California, this prong is satisfied. See Bancroft, 223 F.3d at 1088; Panavision, 141 F.3d at 1322.

C.   **Assertion of specific jurisdiction over Defendants is reasonable.**

* * *

CONCLUSION

For the reasons stated above, Plaintiff respectfully requests the court to deny Defendants' motion to dismiss for lack of personal jurisdiction.

Sample 3 - Memorandum in Support of Motion to Dismiss

SUPREME COURT OF THE STATE OF NEW YORK
COUNTY OF NEW YORK

ERNO NUSSENZWEIG,
 	
        Plaintiff,
 	
  -against-
 	
PHILIP-LORCA DICORCIA,
et al.
 	
        Defendant.
	Index No. 108446/05

DEFENDANT'S MEMORANDUM IN SUPPORT OF MOTION TO DISMISS FOR FAILURE TO STATE A CLAIM

Defendant Philip-Lorca diCorcia moves this Court pursuant to N.Y. C.P.L.R. 3211(a)(7) to dismiss the complaint brought by Plaintiff Erno Nussenzweig for failure to state a cause of action upon which relief may be granted.

INTRODUCTION

Retired diamond merchant Erno Nussenzweig, Plaintiff, seeks to stifle the artistry of Defendant Philip-Lorca diCorcia and earn a payment in excess of two million dollars just for walking down a busy New York street. Defendant diCorcia's artistic photographs capture the vibrant character of the varied inhabitants of New York City and as such their subject matter is of significant public interest. Furthermore, Plaintiff Nussenzweig's one appearance in the hundreds of photographs diCorcia produced is incidental at best. This incidental use in the service of a greater public interest does not fulfill the purely advertising or trade purpose which is required for an action under N.Y. Civ. Rights Law § 51. Plaintiff's erroneous complaint must therefore be dismissed.

STATEMENT OF FACTS

diCorcia, in the pursuit of his art, set up unobtrusive lighting equipment that would illuminate members of the public as they stepped on a plainly marked spot on the ground. See Complaint, ¶ 10. This lighting, as seen through diCorcia's lens, glorified and exalted the common man, showing the humanity of the city's diverse public. Id. ¶ 10;

diCorcia's "Head No. 13" – Photograph of Erno
Nussenzweig (Exhibit 1). Nussenzweig was among
the hundreds of New Yorkers to strut across
diCorcia's stage. Complaint, ¶ 3. diCorcia
did not hassle the busy pedestrians by
seeking consent. Id. ¶¶ 3, 18, 19. diCorcia,
a resident of New York County himself, then
offered his works for sale back to the
community through Pace/Macgill, Inc. and other
agents. Id. ¶¶ 5-7, 17. The works were also
displayed in gallery shows and published in
a catalogue of diCorcia's work. Id. ¶ 15.
Nussenzweig, a resident of New Jersey, became
aware of diCorcia's success and subsequently
brought an action under N.Y. Civ. Rights Law
§§ 50, 51 in the Supreme Court of the State of
New York, County of New York. Id. ¶¶ 13, 21.

ARGUMENT

I.   **THE COMPLAINT MUST BE DISMISSED FOR
     FAILURE TO STATE A CAUSE OF ACTION
     BECAUSE DEFENDANT'S USE OF PLAINTIFF'S
     PICTURE WAS NOT FOR ADVERTISING OR TRADE
     PURPOSES.**

     N.Y. C.P.L.R. 3211(a)(7) (McKinney 2006)
provides that an action may be dismissed

if "the pleading fails to state a cause of action."

Plaintiff Nussenzweig alleges diCorcia violated N.Y. Civ. Rights Law §§ 50, 51 (McKinney 2006). The first of these sections is a criminal statute, and does not mention a private action. Id. § 50. The other requires that:

> Any person whose name, portrait, picture or voice is used within this state for advertising purposes or for the purposes of trade without the written consent first obtained . . . may maintain an equitable action in the supreme court of this state against the person, firm or corporations so using his name, portrait, picture or voice to prevent and restrain the use thereof.

Id. § 51. (emphasis added)

New York State and Federal courts ruling on this law have repeatedly held that advertising or trade purposes are to be strictly limited and do not include publications of matters of public interest. See Finger v. Omni Publ'ns Int'l, 566 N.E.2d 141, 143 (N.Y. 1990); De Gregorio v. CBS,

Inc., 473 N.Y.S.2d 922, 925 (Sup. Ct. N.Y.
Cty. 1984); Mysinka v. Conde Nast Publ'ns,
Inc., 386 F. Supp. 2d 409, 418 (S.D.N.Y.
2005). Additionally, New York State and
Federal courts have ruled that in order to
avoid impinging on freedom of speech and of
the press, incidental usage does not amount
to a violation of the Civil Rights Statute.
See De Gregorio, 473 N.Y.S.2d at 924; Preston
v. Martin Bregman Prod.'s, Inc., 765 F. Supp.
116, 120 (S.D.N.Y. 1991); Groden v. Random
House, 61 F.3d 1045, 1049 (2d Cir. 1995).

**A.   diCorcia's photography of
Nussenzweig served a public
interest, and so does not constitute
an advertising or trade purpose.**

N.Y. Civ. Rights Law § 51 prohibits
unauthorized use of a person's name, portrait,
or picture for narrowly interpreted advertising
or trade purposes. Finger, 566 N.E.2d at 143.
Courts consistently refuse to include matters
of public interest in the definition of an
advertising or trade purpose. Id. Nor does the
fact that the defendants earn a profit from the
use "alter their right to depict matters of

public interest." De Gregorio, 473 N.Y.S.2d at 925. See also Myskina, 386 F. Supp. 2d at 418.

What constitutes a public interest has been interpreted broadly by the courts in a number of different mediums. Compare Finger, 566 N.E.2d at 142 (dismissal granted where picture of six children published in magazine in conjunction with article on fertility was found to be of legitimate public interest), with De Gregorio, 473 N.Y.S.2d at 924 (summary judgment granted to defendant where video of plaintiff construction worker walking with another woman down a public street shown in a story on romance was a subject of public interest), and Myskina, 386 F. Supp. 2d at 419 (summary judgment granted for defendant where picture of plaintiff tennis player illustrating a biographical magazine article was a matter of public interest). Although the subject of interest and medium vary, and the plaintiffs range from a famous athlete to a common man on the street, the rule is broad enough to include all these situations. Plaintiff may contend that his picture was not

used in conjunction with any article, and so
cannot be considered a newsworthy publication,
however, it is well established that
photographs may be newsworthy on their own as
well as in connection with an article. See
Myskina, 386 F. Supp. 2d at 419; Davis v. High
Soc'y Magazine, 90 A.D.2d 374 (1982); Ann-
Margret v. High Soc'y Magazine, Inc. 498 F.
Supp. 401, 405 (S.D.N.Y. 1980). Plaintiff may
also contend that the photograph is somehow
offensive to him; this does nothing to create
a cause of action when the photograph is a
matter of public interest. See DeGregorio, 473
N.Y.S.2d at 924; Myskina, 386 F. Supp. at 419;
Creel v. Crown Publishers, Inc., 496 N.Y.S.2d
219 at 220 (App. Div. 1985).

diCorcia photographed the common
passersby in New York to illustrate the
diverse population that can be seen on the
public streets. Given the broad and liberal
interpretation applied to the public interest
exception, diCorcia's glorification of the
common pedestrian, someone a wide variety of
people could possibly identify with, must

certainly serve the public interest. To
construe otherwise would be a grave injury to
the arts and the freedoms of speech and the
press. diCorcia's use was for a valid public
interest and does not amount to advertising
and trade usage, and therefore Nussenzweig has
not stated a cause of action under N.Y. Civ.
Rights Law § 51.

**B.   diCorcia did not violate
Nussenzweig's Civil Rights because
diCorcia's use of one photograph
in a series of hundreds is merely
incidental.**

New York courts recognize that an
incidental use "cannot form the basis for
liability under Sections 50 and 51 of the
New York Civil Rights Law." De Gregorio, 473
N.Y.S.2d at 923. Even if use is made without
consent for a commercial purpose, the law does
not prohibit incidental usage. Groden, 61 F.3d
at 1049.

Like the public interest exception,
incidental use is not limited by medium,
and has been applied in a variety of cases.
Compare De Gregorio, 473 N.Y.S.wd at 923

(summary judgment granted to defendant where five-second appearance of plaintiff walking down the street with a woman in a ten-minute broadcast was held to be incidental); <u>with</u> <u>Preston</u>, 765 F. Supp. at 119 (complaint dismissed where plaintiff prostitute appeared soliciting for nine seconds in opening scene of a full-length motion picture); <u>and</u> <u>Groden</u>, 61 F.3d at 1050 (complaint dismissed where plaintiff author's name and picture appeared briefly in an advertisement for a book disagreeing with him). The common thread between theses cases is one of quantity, in each instance the plaintiff's "contribution" to the work was minor or brief.

Although plaintiff will no doubt contend that he makes up the entirety of the displayed photograph, his own complaint states that he was only one of hundreds of people photographed for the project. Exhibit 1 implies that his picture is at least one of thirteen actually printed. Anyone walking down the street could have theoretically been included in the project, and indeed many of them were. The art

was not targeted at Nussenzweig in particular,
but at the population in general. Incidental
use of Nussenzweig in one picture of a series
highlighting the millions of pedestrians in
New York does not violate his Civil Rights,
and plaintiff once again fails to state a
claim under N.Y. Civ. Rights Law § 51.

CONCLUSION

For the reasons stated above, this Court
should dismiss plaintiff's petition for
failure to state a claim upon which relief can
be granted.

Sample 4 - Memorandum in Opposition to Motion to Dismiss

SUPREME COURT OF THE STATE OF NEW YORK
COUNTY OF NEW YORK

ERNO NUSSENZWEIG,
 	
        Plaintiff,
 	
  -against-
 	
PHILIP-LORCA DICORCIA,
et al.
 	
        Defendant.
	Index No. 108446/05

**PLAINTIFF'S MEMORANDUM IN OPPOSITION TO
DEFENDANT DICORCIA'S N.Y. C.P.L.R. 3211(a)(7)
MOTION TO DISMISS FOR FAILURE TO STATE A
CAUSE OF ACTION**

INTRODUCTION

Defendant asserts that it is his right to lie in wait off a public street for unsuspecting private citizens, to photograph whichever unlucky pedestrians step into his sights, and then to publish, display, and sell the photos for a profit. Plaintiff, a victim of these activities, found himself dragged from his quiet life and subjected to unwanted public display as a result of having unwittingly walked onto Defendant's stage. As alleged, Defendant secretly photographed Plaintiff, then published and sold the unaltered photos without Plaintiff's permission at a commercial gallery and other locations around the state of New York, although the actual extent of Defendant's commercial activity is as yet unknown. Despite Defendant's assertion that his actions are privileged, the uncontested allegations in Plaintiff's complaint state a clear cause of action under N.Y. Civ. Rights Law §§ 50, 51 (McKinney 2006) and, therefore, Defendant's motion to dismiss for failure to state a cause of action should be denied.

STATEMENT OF FACTS

Plaintiff, in the course of his normal activities, was walking among the throngs who daily travel the streets of New York City when he was secretly photographed by Defendant. Complaint ¶ 3. Though altogether unknown to Plaintiff at the time, Defendant had placed on the sidewalk a mark and had rigged lights

to illuminate the spot. *Id.* Defendant,
his trap laid, then positioned himself
strategically, at a distance and beyond the
observation of the casual pedestrian, from
where he photographed pedestrians, including
Plaintiff, who walked across the illuminated
spot on the sidewalk. *Id.* ¶ 10. Having thus
acquired Plaintiff's photograph but having
failed to obtain his consent, *see id.* ¶ 3,
Defendant proceeded to exhibit, display, and
sell some of the pictures, including the image
of Plaintiff in Exhibit 1, at defendant Pace/
McGill, Inc.'s gallery and at other places
throughout the state, although as yet there
has been no declaration or accounting of
Defendant's sales or profits from the photos.
Id. ¶ 17. Moreover, Defendant has stated
clearly that the taking and selling of these
photos was calculated and that he intends to
continue. *Id.* ¶ 15. Damage to Plaintiff,
including emotional distress and mental
anguish, from these actions is significant and
ongoing. *Id.* ¶ 22. Plaintiff, therefore,
filed a complaint in this court pursuant to
N.Y. Civ. Rights Law §§ 50, 51. *See generally*

Complaint.

ARGUMENT

Defendant's motion to dismiss under N.Y. C.P.L.R. 3211 (a)(7) asserts that Plaintiff's complaint fails to state a cause of action under N.Y. Civ. Rights Law §§ 50, 51 on grounds that Defendant did not use Plaintiff's photo "for advertising purposes or for purposes of trade."

I.   DEFENDANT'S USE OF PLAINTIFF'S PHOTOGRAPHS IS FOR "PURPOSES OF TRADE" BECAUSE HE SELLS THE PHOTOGRAPHS IN FURTHERANCE OF HIS BUSINESS AND BECAUSE THE USE IS NOT PRIVILEGED AS AN ARTISTIC EXPRESSION.

N.Y. Civ. Rights Law § 51 states, in applicable part, that "[a]ny person whose name, portrait, or picture is used . . . for advertising purposes or for purposes of trade," has a cause of action against the person so using. New York courts have held this provision to apply, subject to privilege, where a defendant has sold the photograph in furtherance of his trade. *Arrington v. New York Times Co.,* 434 N.E.2d 1319, 1323 (N.Y.

1982). Notably for the instant matter, courts have found that a use which otherwise would meet this definition may be exempt as protected speech if it is found to be a work of art. *Simeonov v. Tiegs,* 602 N.Y.S.2d 1014, 1018 (Civ. Ct. N.Y. County 1993).

A. **Defendant's use of the photographs meets the definition of "purposes of trade" because he sells them for commercial gain.**

Under New York Civil Rights law, uses are for "purposes of trade" where there is evidence that the defendant has sold the photographs and where that sale is done commercially, or as a part of defendant's business. *Arrington,* 434 N.E.2d at 1323; *Holmes v. Underwood & Underwood, Inc.,* 233 N.Y.S. 153, 155 (App. Div. 1st Dep't 1929). Courts have crafted a number of privileges to which this rule is subject, including where the use is considered "newsworthy" or a matter of public interest, *Stephano v. News Group Publications, Inc.,* 474 N.E.2d 580, 584 (N.Y. 1984), and where the use is found incidental to the commercial use, *Groden v. Random House,*

Inc., 61 F.3d 1045, 1049 (2d Cir. 1995).

Where the defendant fails to assert a
recognized privilege for his use, a finding that
his activities included selling the photos
in the course of his business or commercial
activity will be dispositive, placing the use
squarely within the New York courts' definition
of "purposes of trade." *Compare Murray v.
New York Magazine Co.,* 267 N.E.2d 256, 257-
258 (N.Y. 1971) (sale by photographer who took
photo of a private citizen at public parade
and sold it for publication in news article
on the event privileged by First Amendment as
matter of public interest), *with Arrington,*
434 N.E.2d at 1321-1323 (where photographer
surreptitiously took picture of random,
unsuspecting member of public then sold to a
newspaper who published picture alongside an
article the newspaper's actions were found
privileged as public interest, but sales by
photographer were found to be for "purposes
of trade"), *and Barrows v. Rozansky,* 489
N.Y.S.2d 481, 484 (App. Div. 1st Dep't 1985)
(defendant's sale of pictures of plaintiff,

his former girlfriend, to a newspaper in the
midst of a public scandal regarding her arrest
held to be for "purposes of trade" where sale
was for "his own personal and commercial
gain").

Application of this rule to the instant
case reveals the Defendant's use was for
the "purposes of trade" as defined under New
York law. The facts as alleged regarding
Defendant's use of Plaintiff's photographs
are most readily analogous to that of the
photographer in *Arrington*. There, as here,
the defendant secretly took photographs of a
random member of the public and sold them for
a commercial gain. Although the question of
whether or not Defendant is a professional
photographer would be one for trial, it is
clear that he sold Plaintiff's pictures at
a commercial gallery, among other places.
Therefore, subject to the consideration
below of his claim to an artistic expression
privilege, Defendant's use of the photos
is clearly within the "purposes of trade"
requirement of N.Y. Civ. Rights Law § 51 as

defined by controlling case law.

> **B.   Defendant's use of the photographs is not privileged as an artistic expression because the work sold is not transformative of the photograph taken.**

Defendant urges the court to extend to his work the artistic expression privilege which allows an otherwise commercial use of a plaintiff's photo to be exempt from the statutory provision under a First Amendment protection if the work is determined to be a work of art. *Altbach v. Kulon*, 754 N.Y.S.2d 655, 712 (App. Div. 3d Dep't 2003). To qualify for this exception, the work sold should add something to, or be "transformative" of, the original. *Comedy III Productions, Inc. v. Gary Saderup, Inc.,* 21 P.3d 797, 808 (Cal. 2001). Where a photo is found to be a work of art for purposes of this privilege, the artist may sell "at least a limited number of copies" without consent. *Simeonov,* 602 N.Y.S.2d at 1018.

A survey of applicable case law shows that a finding that the work in question

is "transformative" of the original, as
contemplated by the California Supreme Court,
see Comedy III, 21 P.3d at 808, is necessary
for a defendant to successfully claim an
artistic expression privilege to the "purposes
of trade" requirement under N.Y. Civ. Rights
Law §§ 50, 51. *See Altbach,* 754 N.Y.S.2d at
712 (artist's use of plaintiff's photo, which
consisted of placing it on a flyer next to
artist's caricature of plaintiff, privileged
as parodic art); *Simeonov,* 602 N.Y.S.2d at
1015, 1017 (artist's plaster casting of famous
model's face held to be a work of art and
therefore privileged); *Hoepker v. Kruger,*
200 F. Supp. 2d 340, 342, 350 (2d Cir. 2002)
(artist's use of plaintiff's photo image,
cropping and superimposing the original
on artist's own work, held sufficiently
transformative to qualify under artistic
expression privilege).

The cases cited above dominate the
jurisprudence defining the artistic expression
privilege under N.Y. Civ. Rights Law §§ 50,
51, and their impact on Defendant's motion is

clear. Defendant's use, which did nothing
to transform the original image, is readily
distinguished from the cases above. The
image of Plaintiff in Exhibit 1 is a simple
photograph taken under illumination as he
walked along the street. Defendant has
apparently made no changes at all, much less
any which might make this photo a work of art
under New York law. The photograph taken
of Plaintiff as he walked unluckily into
Defendant's light is the same image Defendant
did and does sell commercially. Defendant's
work, therefore, is not transformative as
judicially required for a defendant to succeed
in an assertion of the artistic expression
privilege.

CONCLUSION

For the reasons stated herein, Plaintiff
respectfully requests the court to deny
Defendant's motion to dismiss for failure to
state a cause of action.

Chapter 4

Motions for Summary Judgment

A motion for summary judgment is the ultimate pretrial dispositive motion in a civil case. Such a motion generally is filed after discovery is complete, *i.e.*, after all the evidence is uncovered in the case. A motion for summary judgment challenges the opponent's claims or defenses (plaintiff's claims or defendant's affirmative defenses or counterclaims) on both the law and the facts. It states that the facts are such that no trial is necessary: judgment is appropriate right here, right now. The touchstone phrase that you will see invoked in the standard for a motion for summary judgment is "no genuine issue of material fact," but it often takes working repeatedly with this standard and the relevant caselaw to truly understand what each of those terms means as applied to a given set of legal and factual circumstances.

I.   FEDERAL RULE OF CIVIL PROCEDURE 56(c)

Federal Rule of Civil Procedure 56(c) governs summary judgment motions in federal court. It states in relevant part:

> The judgment sought shall be rendered forthwith if the pleadings, depositions, answers to interrogatories, and admissions on file, together with the affidavits, if any, show that *there is no genuine issue as to any material fact* and that the moving party is entitled to a judgment *as a matter of law.* A summary judgment, interlocutory in character, may be rendered on the issue of liability alone although there is a genuine issue as to the amount of damages (emphasis added).

Several aspects of this complicated rule deserve closer attention.

A.   Material facts

The key to the consideration of whether each legal issue in a case is appropriate for summary judgment comes in the analysis of whether the issue can be resolved solely as *a matter of law*—meaning without the need for findings by the trier of fact. Thus, while the parties may not agree on every single fact in the case, the movant must show that no *material* facts remain in dispute. Material facts are those that affect or potentially affect the outcome of the case (or the issue at hand) on the merits.

> • *Example:* In litigation involving the performance of a contract to create a metal sculpture, in which defendant asserts that he lacked the mental capacity to understand the terms of the contract because of his intoxication on the day of the contracting, the parties may disagree over the metal content of the sculpture—did it contain titanium or not?—but this fact would not affect a motion for summary judgment on defendant's defenses to the contract. In contrast, the movant could not maintain that there remained a disagreement over the number of drinks defendant had before he signed the contract, or what his blood alcohol level was on that day, because those facts potentially would affect the analysis of his defenses on the merits.

In other words, if a remaining factual dispute does not affect the outcome (no matter who is right on the facts, the outcome from those facts would be the same), then the dispute need not defeat summary judgment. Conversely, summary judgment is inappropriate if any fact material to the outcome of the issue remains in controversy—because those issues must be left to the trier of fact to resolve (the jury in a jury trial, or the judge in a bench trial).

> • *Example:* Assume that the common law marriage requirement in your state is "cohabitation for over a year." The plaintiff argues that the couple lived together for four years, while defendant argues that it was really only two years because during the first two years, the couple only lived together on weekends. Obviously, there still is a factual dispute here, but is it a *material* one? No. *Both* versions satisfy the one-year requirement. Accordingly, there is no need for

a trial to resolve whether it was two or four years, and summary judgment is warranted.

B.   Genuine dispute

In addition, a remaining dispute over a material fact must be *genuine* for summary judgment to defeated. That means that a party's assertion of the facts (or the meaning of the facts) must be plausible and defensible. The nonmoving party cannot defeat summary judgment simply by articulating an outlandish version or interpretation of the facts that is wholly unsupported by the evidence. Similarly, the nonmoving party's position on the facts cannot be directly inconsistent with the position it asserted before litigation was initiated or directly contrary to the position asserted earlier in the same litigation. In other words, a party should not be allowed to defeat summary judgment simply by contradicting everything the party said earlier in the case.

Note that the rule speaks of "pleadings, depositions, answers to interrogatories, and admissions on file, together with the affidavits," as proof of the facts demonstrating "no genuine issue as to any material fact." Thus, the court will consider the *complete record* on the facts (produced in discovery) to determine if there is a genuine dispute. This means that a party cannot change its story simply for purposes of defeating a motion for summary judgment. It should go without saying that the affidavits and declarations offered at the summary judgment stage must be asserted in good faith, and the swearing witness must be competent (have first-hand information of the facts and be able to testify to the same at trial). If a judge thinks that you and your client are cooking up affidavits just to confuse the facts and to defeat summary judgment through false factual disputes, you and your client can be sanctioned.

C.   Who bears the burden of proof?

Initially, the party moving for summary judgment bears the burden of showing that there is no genuine dispute as to any material fact, and that he or she is entitled to judgment as a matter of law. Once that burden is met, however, the burden shifts to the opponent, the nonmoving party, to produce concrete evidence to show that there is a genuine material factual dispute or that judgment is not proper as a matter of law. In other words, if the movant presents a properly supported motion with affidavits or declarations demonstrating that there is no dispute, the opponent cannot simply rest on its pleadings and the arguments of its counsel, but must come forth with affidavits and declarations and factual support of its own to show a genuine dispute as to material facts. (Of course, if the burden is not met at the outset by the moving party, summary judgment is not appropriate.)

D.   Judgment must be appropriate as a matter of law

Finally, the court must be able to determine from the undisputed facts that judgment is appropriate as a matter of law. Thus, although the movant may meet her burden as to the facts, the motion cannot be granted unless the movant shows that the law supports a decision in her favor. In addition, even where *both parties* agree that the facts are such that no trial is necessary, as in the case of cross-motions for summary judgment, the court still is the ultimate arbiter of the law and must agree that a pre-trial decision can be rendered in favor of one of the parties. The court may disagree with the parties and determine that a trial is warranted—because there remain genuine issues of material fact, because insufficient evidence has been adduced, or because the law is not clear enough to make a decision before trial.

FYI

Occasionally, a court may request that the parties file cross-motions on some or all of the issues in the case, or the parties may agree to stipulate to a set of facts and submit the case or issues in the case on cross-motions for summary judgment. As indicated, the filing of cross-motions is no guarantee that one of the motions will be granted if the court thinks there are not enough facts in the record to make a determination on the issues.

II. STRUCTURE AND FORMAT OF A SUMMARY JUDGMENT MOTION AND OPPOSITION

Like other pretrial motions, a summary judgment motion generally follows this format:

<u>**INTRODUCTION**</u>

<u>**STATEMENT OF FACTS**</u>

<u>**ARGUMENT**</u>

<u>**CONCLUSION**</u>

Many courts also require a separate "statement of undisputed facts" (a separate document from the brief and one that is not presented in the narrative form that the traditional statement of facts section will be). As always, check your local rules. The local rules for the United States District Court for the District of Columbia, for example, require that motions for summary judgment are accompanied by such a statement, with references to the parts the record relied on to support the statement. And oppositions must include a separate concise statement that sets forth all of the material facts as to which the opponent contends there is a genuine issue necessary to be litigated. See <u>Local Civil Rule 56.1</u>. Some "legal form" websites include sample "statements of undisputed facts" (for example, see: **http://www.lectlaw.com/forms/f020.htm**).

 **PRACTICE POINTER**

For a sample statement of undisputed facts in an Eastern District of California case, consider the following: **http://www.waldorfcritics.org/active/articles/lawsuit/162%20StatementUndisputed.pdf**.

For a sample *response* to a statement of undisputed facts (in an opposition brief) in a Southern District of Florida case, see the following**: http://docs.justia.com/cases/federal/district-courts/florida/flsdce/0:2006cv60905/25280/50/0.pdf**

These examples are provided by way of information only (we did not write them). Moreover, you *must* consider the local rules in the jurisdiction in which you are litigating to ensure that your own version is what the court is seeking.

As noted, a statement of undisputed facts generally is a document filed in addition to a brief. But the brief itself will contain a narrative factual statement, of the kind we have been discussing in this volume. There, both parties must make strategic choices about which facts to present, in what order, and in what form. While you cannot change the logical meaning of the stipulated facts or conceal facts that are established in the record, you do have a choice about which facts to highlight and which to downplay (depending on which side you are on). Thus, you need to think strategically about the order and placement of your facts, and whether you employ the active or passive voice in presenting them. As always, there is no room here for emotional, argumentative, conclusory rhetoric in the statement of facts of a summary judgment motion. Save that for your discussion of the law and the equities in the case. In fact, if you go too far in drafting a statement of facts section that sounds magnificently favorable to your client, you may defeat the whole purpose of summary judgment by making it sound like there is a factual dispute in the case.

We have alluded here to what you should **not** do to try to defeat summary judgment: do not try to manufacture affidavits for purposes of supporting or defeating a motion for summary judgment. Do not attempt to change factual positions 180 degrees in mid-stream. Do not go back on what you have been stating as the facts and the law since the case began. But do not sit on your complaint and rest on the arguments of counsel and expect the court to give you the benefit of a doubt. If your opponent has made a credible case, then prove a genuine material factual dispute, and refute your opponent's legal arguments. This is one motion where the court will not do your thinking for you.

III.   SAMPLE MOTIONS

In this section are four sample memoranda in support of or in opposition to motions for summary judgment. The first two are annotated and the remaining two are not. As in previous chapters, we have provided multiple samples because we want you to understand that there is no model, no perfect example, no single correct way to produce work that is competent, lawyerly, and effective for its purposes in the law. We choose good samples of above average legal writing—good, but certainly not perfect. You should read each sample carefully and critically, expecting that the author did some things well but other things poorly. You should not try to copy one or more of these samples. Instead, learn from them and apply what you learn in your own writing that you create in your own voice.

Sample 1 – Memorandum in Support of Motion for Summary Judgment

```
            UNITED STATES DISTRICT COURT
            CENTRAL DISTRICT OF CALIFORNIA
                 SOUTHERN DIVISION


GLOBAL STUDIOS,            )
                           )
          Plaintiff,       )
                           )     No. SA CV 01-9999
                           )     AHS
     v.                    )
                           )
KINGSTON UNIVERSITY        )
ELECTRONIC FREEDOM         )
FRONTIER, LARRY MULLEN,    )
LISA ROGERS, MEGHAN        )
MORELY, and CHRIS          )
HANSEN,                    )
                           )
          Defendants.      )
```

MEMORANDUM IN SUPPORT OF DEFENDANTS' MOTION FOR SUMMARY JUDGMENT

```
     Defendants move this Court pursuant to

Fed. R. Civ. P. 56(c) for summary judgment in

favor of Defendants on Plaintiff's complaint.
```

INTRODUCTION

As evidenced by the filing of its
original complaint, Plaintiff asserts that
it is entitled to obstruct the flow of
information and ideas from Defendants to the
public merely because it does not condone
the message of Defendants' communications.
Plaintiff's attempt to suppress Defendants'
First Amendment right to free speech thus
compels this motion. Plaintiff engages in the
motion picture industry by translating motion
pictures to digital versatile disks (DVDs).
Defendants are members of a student group that
operates an informational website featuring an
online student newspaper. Along with several
other unrelated stories, Defendants recently
reported news and information regarding the
debate over the use of DeCSS, a computer
program that allows users to copy DVD movies.
To provide a complete report to the public,
Defendants referred to, in plain text without
the prefix "www.", the names of a small number
of DeCSS-provider sites. Defendants did not
create DeCSS, nor did they post DeCSS, or

provide a hyperlink to any website containing
DeCSS, on their website. Defendants' right to
report news and information on their website
regarding the DeCSS debate is guaranteed by
the First Amendment to the United States
Constitution. Although the Government
has a substantial interest in protecting
copyrights from unauthorized circumvention,
the Digital Millennium Copyright Act
("DMCA") is not narrowly tailored to serve
this interest because it imposes overbroad
speech restrictions that do not withstand
constitutional scrutiny. Even if the DMCA
is not overbroad, it is unconstitutional as
applied to Defendants to the extent that
it prevents them from reporting news and
information in plain text on their website.

STATEMENT OF FACTS

Plaintiff operates in the motion picture
industry by producing and selling motion
pictures on the DVD format, which are encoded
by a program called Content System Scramble
("CSS"). Stipulation of Facts ("Stip."), ¶
1, 7. Defendants are members of a student

organization that publishes an informational website containing an online newspaper. Id. ¶¶ 2, 9. In this newspaper, Defendants regularly report technology-related stories and events. See Complaint, Exhibit 1. One story reported by Defendants was the debate over the use of DeCSS, a program which bypasses CSS and allows users to copy DVDs. Stip. ¶¶ 8, 10.

In the process of reporting the DeCSS debate, Defendants referred, in plain text, to the names of a small number of websites where DeCSS reportedly was available. See Complaint, Exhibit 1. At no time was the object code or source code for DeCSS available on any part of Defendants' website. Stip. ¶ 12. Furthermore, none of the references to reported DeCSS provider sites included the prefix "www." nor were any of them hotlinked or hyperlinked to those sites. Id. ¶¶ 11, 12.

ARGUMENT

1.   LEGAL STANDARDS FOR SUMMARY JUDGMENT.

When a federal court decides a case involving a federal question, federal procedural law is applied. See Benny v. Pipes, 799 F.2d 489, 493 (9th Cir. 1986). Under Rule 56(c) of the Fed. R. Civ. P., summary judgment is permitted if there is "no genuine issue as to any material fact, and the moving party is entitled to judgment as a matter of law." See Anderson v. Liberty Lobby, Inc., 477 U.S. 242, 247-48 (1986); Fazio v. City and County of San Francisco, 125 F.3d 1328, 1331 (9th Cir. 1997). The moving party bears the initial burden of demonstrating the absence of a genuine issue of material fact for trial by showing that there is a lack of evidence to support the non-moving party's case. See Matsushita Elec. Indus. Co. v. Zenith Radio Corp., 475 U.S. 574, 587 (1986). Once the moving party has met its initial burden, the non-moving party must introduce significant probative evidence tending to support the complaint. See Celotex Corp. v. Catrett, 477 U.S. 317, 323 (1986).

In the present case, Plaintiff and Defendants have stipulated to all the material facts, and Defendants are entitled to summary judgment as a matter of law.

In 17 U.S.C. § 1201(a)(2)(A) (1998), the DMCA provides that:

> No person shall manufacture, import, offer to the public, provide, or otherwise traffic in any technology, product, service, device, component, or part thereof, that is primarily designed or produced for the purpose of circumventing a technological measure that effectively controls access to a work protected under this title.

17 U.S.C. § 1201(b)(1)(A) differs slightly from § 1201(a)(2)(A), but in the instant case the distinction is irrelevant because only the sections' shared language is at issue.

II.   THE DMCA DOES NOT SURVIVE A FACIAL CHALLENGE BECAUSE IT IS UNCONSTITUTIONALLY OVERBROAD.

The First Amendment to the United States Constitution states that "Congress shall make no law . . . abridging the freedom of

speech or of the press." U.S. Const. amend.
I. First Amendment protection of speech does
not turn on the popularity or social utility
of the ideas and beliefs which it conveys.
See New York Times Co. v. Sullivan, 376 U.S.
254, 270 (1964). The freedom of the press is
a fundamental personal right that extends
to every medium which acts as a vehicle of
information. See Branzburg v. Hayes, 408 U.S.
665, 703 (1972). The Internet is one such
medium, constituting a vast public forum
entitled to full First Amendment protection.
See Reno v. A.C.L.U., 521 U.S. 844, 868-70
(1997).

The Internet is rapidly evolving into
a universal newspaper. See Religious Tech.
Ctr v. Lerma, 908 F. Supp. 1353 (E.D. Va.
1995). Newspapers constitute important
forums for the dissemination of information
and expression of opinions and are devoted
entirely to expressive activity. See San Diego
Comm. Against Registration and the Draft v.
Governing Bd. of Grossmont Union High School
Dist., 790 F.2d 1471, 1476 (9th Cir. 1985).

When speech restrictions supporting government interests and First Amendment freedoms collide, the risk of non-persuasion rests with the government and not the speaker. See United States v. Playboy Ent. Group, Inc., 529 U.S. 803, 818 (2000). The appropriate level of constitutional scrutiny to be applied to a statute is determined by whether the speech restrictions it imposes are content-based or content-neutral. See City of Erie v. Pap's A.M., 529 U.S. 277, 289 (2000); Turner Broad. Sys., Inc. v. F.C.C., 512 U.S. 622, 642 (1994). A statute is overbroad under the First Amendment if it causes substantially impermissible applications relative to the law's legitimate sweep. See New York v. Ferber, 458 U.S. 747, 771 (1982).

A.   **The DMCA imposes content-based restrictions on speech, which are unconstitutional because they do not satisfy the strict scrutiny standard.**

Content-based restrictions on speech are aimed at stifling speech on account of the message it conveys. See Turner 512 U.S. at 642. A restriction is content-neutral if it is justified without reference to the content of speech. See Hill v. Colorado, 530 U.S. 703, 720 (2000).

In the First Amendment context, the government's purpose for regulating expressive activity is the controlling consideration in determining if the regulation is content-based or neutral. Compare Boos v. Barry, 485 U.S. 312, 321 (1988) (ban on use of signs to criticize foreign government within certain distance of embassy was attempt to regulate direct impact of message on listeners and was content based), with Renton v. Playtime Theatres, Inc., 475 U.S. 41, 48 (1986) (restriction on placement of adult theater aimed at controlling secondary effects of theater on neighborhood was justified without reference to content of theater's speech).

Content-based restrictions are presumptively unconstitutional. See Free Speech Coalition v. Reno, 198 F.3d 1083, 1091 (9th Cir. 1999); Crawford v. Lungren, 96 F.3d 380, 384 (9th Cir. 1996). To defeat this presumption, content-based restrictions

must meet a standard of strict scrutiny, which
requires that they be narrowly tailored to
serve a compelling government interest and
employ the least restrictive means possible to
serve that interest. See Playboy, 529 U.S. at
813; Sable Communications of California, Inc.
v. F.C.C., 492 U.S. 115, 126 (1989).

Statutes placing content-based
restrictions on speech conveyed through
the Internet, although serving substantial
government interests, have been susceptible to
overbreadth defects and routinely are struck
down. See Reno, 521 U.S. at 875 (content-based
federal statute prohibiting communication of
indecent material to minors through Internet
unduly burdened protected speech of adults and
was overbroad); Free Speech Coalition v. Reno,
198 F.3d 1083, 1095 (9th Cir. 1999) (statute
failed strict scrutiny because it prohibited
protected expression of non-minors and thus
was not narrowly tailored).

If a less restrictive means of meeting
the government's interest could be at least
as effective in serving that interest, the

restriction in question does not satisfy strict scrutiny. See Playboy, 529 U.S. at 815 (statute invalidated because targeted blocking of sexually explicit material was less restrictive means of serving government's interest); Sable, 492 U.S. at 130-31 (feasibility of technological means to control minors' access to sexually explicit phone messages provided less restrictive means of serving government's interest).

The anti-trafficking provisions of the DMCA at issue in the present case were recently analyzed in Corley v. Universal City Studios, Inc., 273 F.3d 429 (2nd Cir. 2001). In that case, the court held that the DMCA was content-neutral, and that it was not unconstitutional because it passed intermediate scrutiny. Id. at 456-58. Corley's interpretation of the DMCA was erroneous.

Like the defendants in Corley, Defendants in the present case report information to the public regarding the DeCSS debate. The right to communicate this information is ensured by the First Amendment and is not contingent upon government approval. However, the DMCA inhibits this right by restricting Defendants on account of the government's disagreement with its message. The DMCA seeks to prevent Defendants' speech solely because Defendants are talking about DeCSS as opposed to any other non-encryption related computer program. Thus, the DMCA is content-based, and Plaintiff cannot overcome the presumption against the constitutionality of content-based restrictions. As was conceded in Corley, the government has alternative means of serving its interest in preventing unauthorized access to copyrighted materials, which are less speech-restrictive than the blanket prohibitions of the DMCA. Id. at 455. Thus, similar to the statutes in Reno and Free Speech Coalition, the DMCA impermissibly hampers a substantial amount of protected speech and is overbroad.

B. **Even if the DMCA is content-neutral, it does not constitute a reasonable time, place, or manner restriction and is thus unconstitutional.**

A time, place, or manner restriction of speech is constitutional if it is content neutral, is narrowly tailored to serve a significant government interest, and leaves open ample alternative channels for communication of the information. See Ward v. Rock Against Racism, 491 U.S. 781, 799 (1989); Alameda Books, Inc. v. City of Los Angeles, 222 F.3d 719, 722 (9th Cir. 2000). This analysis of time, place, or manner restrictions varies little, if at all, from an analysis driven by the intermediate scrutiny standard announced in United States v. O'Brien, 391 U.S. 367, 376 (1968). See Clark v. Cmty. for Creative Non-Violence, 468 U.S. 288, 299 (1984).

A restriction meets the intermediate scrutiny standard if it furthers a substantial government interest unrelated to the suppression of free expression, and the incidental restriction on speech is no greater than is essential to further that interest. See O'Brien, 391 U.S. at 376. Interpreting the last element of this analysis, courts have allowed an incidental restriction on speech only to the extent that it does not burden substantially more speech than is necessary

to further the relevant government interest.
See Turner, 512 U.S. at 662; Ward, 491 U.S. at
799.

The intermediate level of scrutiny is
not satisfied if the regulation provides
only ineffective or remote support for the
government's purpose. See Lorillard Tobacco
Co. v. Reiley, 533 U.S. 525 (2001) (statute
forbidding placement of any advertisement for
tobacco products lower than five feet from floor
did not sufficiently serve government interest
of preventing minors from using tobacco);
Bolger v. Youngs Drug Products Corp., 463 U.S.
60 (1983) (statute prohibiting unsolicited
mailing of contraceptive advertisements
did not satisfy intermediate scrutiny test
merely because such mailings were potentially
offensive).

Restrictions are not narrowly tailored
for purposes of intermediate scrutiny if they
fail to leave open ample alternative channels
of communication of the information. Compare
Young v. Am. Mini Theaters, Inc. 427 U.S.
50, 54 (1976) (restriction on place where

adult films could be displayed was upheld because it did not ban the form of expression altogether), with Schad v. Mount Ephraim, 452 U.S. 61, 70 (1981) (purported content-neutral restriction struck down because it imposed total ban on adult theaters).

In the present case, the government has a substantial interest in preventing unauthorized access to copyrighted materials. However, the DMCA is not narrowly tailored to serving that interest because it leaves open no reasonable alternative means for Defendants to communicate their message. The DMCA closes off to Defendants the entire medium of expression offered by the Internet, and in so doing burdens substantially more speech than is necessary to serve the government's interest. As was mentioned above, the DMCA prohibits every means by which Defendants might communicate their message through that medium.

The trial court in Corley was aware of the likelihood that the DMCA burdens substantially more speech than is necessary to serve the government's interest, so the court modified the O'Brien standard to limit the DMCA's linking prohibition. See Corley, 273 F.3d at 456. The trial court's concern with the overbreadth of the DMCA also is evident in its discussion of the legislative history of the DMCA, as there was disagreement in the history over whether the House Commerce Committee's version of the statute, which was written to cure substantial overbreadth defects in the original version, adequately balanced copyright protection with First Amendment rights. See H.R. Rep. No. 105-586 (additional views of Reps. Klug and Boucher). This judicial and Congressional concern further indicates demonstrates the overbreadth of the DMCA.

III. EVEN IF THE DMCA IS NOT FACIALLY OVERBROAD, IT IS UNCONSTITUTIONAL AS APPLIED TO PLAINTIFF.

Trafficking in circumvention devices on the Internet may take the form of linking. See Corley, 273 F.3d at 456; DVD Copy Control Ass'n v. McLaughlin, No. CV 786804, 2000 WL 48512 at *4 (Cal. Super. Ct. Jan. 18, 2000).

Linking is defined as the programming of a
particular point on a screen to transfer the
user to another web page when the point,
called a hyperlink, is clicked. See Universal
City Studios, Inc. v. Remeirdes, 111 F. Supp.
2d 321, 324 (S.D.N.Y. 1998), aff'd sub nom
Corley, 273 F.3d at 456.

The DeCSS debate underpinning the present
case has surfaced in court before, and there
is disagreement on how to interpret the First
Amendment rights of persons linking to DeCSS-
provider sites. Compare McLaughlin, 2000 WL
48512 at *4 (links are the mainstay of the
Internet, and a website owner cannot be held
liable for the content of the sites to which
it links), and DVD Copy Control Ass'n v.
Bunner, 113 Cal. Rptr. 2d 338, 340 (Ct. App.
6th Dist. 2001) (review granted) (injunction
prohibiting posting, and linking by inference,
of DeCSS on website violated defendant's First
Amendment rights), with Corley, 273 F.3d at
456 (linking prohibition is justified because
it pertains only to non-speech component of
hyperlink).

The court in <u>Corley</u>, analyzing this issue
in the context of the DMCA, held that linking
to DeCSS provider sites constituted offering
DeCSS to the public or providing or otherwise
trafficking in DeCSS in violation of the DMCA.
<u>See</u> <u>Corley</u>, 273 F.3d at 455-58. However,
<u>Corley</u> is distinguishable from the present
case in two fundamental respects. First, the
holding of <u>Corley</u> relied upon that court's
finding that the statute was content-neutral
because the DMCA regulates only the non-
speech, functional component of hyperlinks.
<u>Id</u>. at 456-58.

In contrast, the website maintained by
Defendants in the present case contains only
plain, non-hyperlinked textual references to
the names of a small number of DeCSS-provider
sites. This plain text contains no functional
component. If a viewer were to click on one
of these references, nothing would happen.
Furthermore, Defendants chose not to attach
the prefix "www." to the names of the DeCSS-
provider sites. Thus, even if a visitor to
Defendants' website were to "cut and paste"

one of the these names into the URL text
box and then instruct the computer to find
the site, the viewer would be transported
nowhere. It can be inferred that the lack of
functionality of plain text was the source
of the Corley court's apparent unwillingness
to extend its linking prohibition to a plain
text, non-hyperlinked list of DeCSS-provider
sites. See David A. Peteys, The Freedom to
Link?, 25 Seattle U. L. Rev. 287, 334 (2001).

The second distinction between Corley
and the present case is that the defendants
in Corley, by posting DeCSS on their own
website and then creating several links to
DeCSS-provider sites (an act of self-styled
"electronic civil disobedience"), acted for
the express purpose of disseminating DeCSS.
See Corley, 273 F.3d at 442. By contrast, the
Defendants in the instant case used plain text
from which the prefix "www." was excluded. This
confirms that Defendants' intent in using these
references was merely to convey information
as part of their report on the DeCSS debate,
and was not to encourage the dissemination of

DeCSS.

Further weakening the precedential value of <u>Corley</u> is that court's initial pronouncement that, due to the novelty of applying First Amendment law in the digital age, the court was subscribing to an evolutionary approach, favoring a narrow holding to allow the law to mature on a case-by-case basis. <u>Id</u>. at 445. These fundamental distinctions between <u>Corley</u> and the present case, along with the express admonition of that court that its holding be treated narrowly, evidence the fact that the DMCA cannot be extended to cover the activity of Defendants in the present case.

CONCLUSION

For the reasons stated above, Defendants respectfully request the Court to grant their motion for summary judgment on Plaintiff's complaint.

Sample 2 – Memorandum in Opposition to Motion for Summary Judgment

```
UNITED STATES DISTRICT COURT
CENTRAL DISTRICT OF CALIFORNIA
SOUTHERN DIVISION
```

GLOBAL STUDIOS,   )
)
        Plaintiff,   )
)   No. SA CV 01-9999
)   AHS
    v.   )
)
KINGSTON UNIVERSITY   )
ELECTRONIC FREEDOM   )
FRONTIER, LARRY MULLEN,   )
LISA ROGERS, MEGHAN   )
MORELY, and CHRIS   )
HANSEN,   )
)
        Defendants.   )

PLAINTIFF'S MEMORANDUM IN OPPOSITION TO DEFENDANTS' MOTION FOR SUMMARY JUDGMENT

Plaintiff Global Studios, in opposition to Defendants' Motion for Summary Judgment, states as follows:

INTRODUCTION

Defendants are members of an organization dedicated to circumventing technological access control measures and promoting piracy on the

World Wide Web. The organization, masking its illegal activity in free speech rhetoric, wants the court to believe Internet trafficking cannot constitutionally be punished. However, the Defendants' web site provides hackers with instantaneous access to instruments like DeCSS that are used to bypass CSS, copy the content of DVDs, and play the duplicates on unlicensed devices. By prohibiting trafficking, the Digital Millennium Copyright Act ("DMCA") is targeting the "functional" aspect of speech and is not burdening more speech than necessary. The prohibitions are the least restrictive means of advancing the government's interest in preventing DVD duplication and copyright infringement. If hacker sites are not prevented from linking users to this software, the motion picture, music, and publishing industry will be in grave danger. Defendants' Motion for Summary Judgment should not be granted as a matter of law.

STATEMENT OF FACTS

Defendants operate a web site "dedicated to maintaining a free and open electronic frontier." Complaint, Exhibit 1. The organization is funded through donations by hackers and people looking to circumvent various copyright laws. Declaration of Melanie Smead dated Jan. 12, 2002, ¶ 4 ("M.S. Dec"). Defendants' site provides a directory of web addresses where DeCSS is downloadable. See Stipulation of Facts ¶ 9 ("Stip."). The addresses are listed so a user instantaneously can access the decryption sites by pasting the addresses into the locator box of an Internet browser and adding the prefix www. See Stip. ¶ 5. All references to these sites have been made with knowledge of their content. See Stip. ¶ 10. In fact, through several e-mail conversations, members of the defendants' organization directed hackers to sites where the software was located. Complaint, Exhibit 1. DeCSS allows pirates to copy the content of DVDs and to distribute the duplicates throughout the world without making payments to the lawful owners, like Global Studios. <u>See</u> <u>Stip</u> ¶ 8.

ARGUMENT

I.   SUMMARY JUDGMENT STANDARD

When federal law applies, a federal court will apply federal procedural law. <u>New SD,</u> <u>Inc. v. Rockwell Int'l Corp.</u>, 79 F.3d 953, 955 (9th Cir. 1996). Under Fed. R. Civ. P. 56(c), summary judgment is appropriate only if there is no genuine issue of material fact and the moving party is entitled to judgment as a matter of law. <u>Anderson v. Liberty Lobby,</u> <u>Inc.,</u> 477 U.S. 242, 247 (1986). The moving party bears the burden of demonstrating the absence of a genuine issue of material fact. <u>Celotex Corp. v. Catrett</u>, 477 U.S. 317, 323 (1986). All evidence must be construed in the light most favorable to the non-moving party. <u>Gardner v. Nike, Inc.</u>, 279 F.3d 774, 777 (9th Cir. 2002).

<u>This burden will not be satisfied by the</u> <u>mere existence of a scintilla of evidence in</u> <u>support of the movant's position; there must</u>

be evidence on which the jury could reasonably find for the movant. Anderson, 477 U.S. at 266. If the movant has met its burden, the non-moving party must then set forth facts showing that there is a genuine issue for trial. Fed. R. Civ. P. 56(e). A genuine issue exists when the evidence is such that a reasonable jury could find for the non-movant. K. Villiariamo v. Aloha Island Air, Inc., 281 F.3d 1054, 1060 (9th Cir. 2002).

Plaintiff and the Defendants have entered into a stipulation of facts; however, there are genuine issues of fact that remain in this matter on which reasonable minds can differ. As a result, Defendants are not entitled to summary judgment as a matter of law.

II. DEFENDANTS' MOTION FOR SUMMARY JUDGMENT SHOULD BE DENIED BECAUSE THE DMCA IS CONSTITUTIONAL ON ITS FACE

According to U.S. Const. amend. I, "Congress shall make no law . . . abridging the freedom of speech, or of the press." One of the "trafficking" provisions of the DMCA, 17 U.S.C. § 1201(a)(2) (1998), states:

> No person shall . . . offer to the
> public, provide, or otherwise traffic
> in any technology, product, service,
> device, component, or part thereof,
> that— (A) is primarily designed
> or produced for the purpose of
> circumventing a technological measure
> that effectively controls access to a
> work protected under this title.

In addition, 17 U.S.C. § 1201(b)(1)
(1998), provides:

> No person shall . . . offer to the
> public, provide, or otherwise traffic
> in any technology, product, service,
> device, component, or part thereof,
> that—(A) is primarily designed
> or produced for the purpose of
> circumventing protection afforded by a
> technological measure that effectively
> protects a right of a copyright owner
> under this title in a work or a portion
> thereof.

The courts have a duty to insulate
all individuals from the "chilling effect"
upon First Amendment freedoms generated by
vagueness and overbreadth. <u>Walker v. City of
Birmingham</u>, 388 U.S. 307, 345 (1967).

<u>This memorandum briefly will discuss</u>
<u>Defendants' likely claim that their web</u>
<u>site is a newspaper, and then proceed to an</u>

analysis of the constitutionality of the DMCA provisions. Plaintiff concedes that the Internet is a public forum. Planned Parenthood of the Columbia/Williamette Inc. v. Am. Coalition of Life Activists, 244 F.3d 1007, 1019 (9th Cir. 2000). A "newspaper" is a medium for the dissemination of news of passing events printed and distributed at short but regular intervals. United States v. Kelly, 328 F.2d 227, 234 (6th Cir. 1964). A newspaper contains a broad range of news on all subjects and activities and is not limited to any specific subject matter. 17 U.S.C.A. § 202.3 6(f)(2) (2002). Defendants' web site does not meet this definition because it reports exclusively on Internet free speech issues.

Even if considered a newspaper, Defendants' web site would not be entitled to heightened protection from the provisions of the DMCA. Laws of general application do not offend the First Amendment simply because their enforcement against the press has incidental effects on its ability to report

the news. Cohen v. Cowles Media Co., 501 U.S.
663, 669 (1991). The press may not publish
copyrighted material without obeying the
copyright laws; it has no special privilege to
invade the rights and liberties of others. Id.

A.   **Sections 1201 (a)(2) and (b)(1)
of the DMCA are content-neutral
regulations that are constitutional
on their face.**

Restrictions targeting the "functional"
aspect of expressive activity are "content-
neutral." United States v. O'Brien, 391 U.S.
367, 377 (1968). The principle inquiry in
determining content-neutrality is whether the
government has adopted regulation of speech
because of disagreement with the message it
conveys. Ward v. Rock Against Racism, 491 U.S.
781, 791 (1989). The purpose of a content-
neutral restriction can be justified without
reference to the content of the message;
however, the mere assertion of a content-
neutral purpose may not be enough to save a
law which, on its face, discriminates based
on content. Turner Broadcasting Sys., Inc. v.
F.C.C., 512 U.S. 622, 643 (1994).

Expressive activity, whether oral or written or symbolized by conduct, may be subject to reasonable time, place, and manner restrictions. <u>Clark v. Cmty. for Creative Non-Violence</u>, 468 U.S. 288, 293 (1984). Such restrictions are permissible so long as they are content-neutral, are narrowly tailored to serve a significant government interest, and leave open ample alternative channels of communication. <u>Madsen v. Women's Health Center</u>, 512 U.S. 753, 791 (1994).

A content-neutral regulation of expressive conduct that burdens speech incidentally will be sustained if it furthers an important governmental interest that is unrelated to the suppression of free expression and the incidental restriction on alleged First Amendment freedoms is no greater than is essential to the furtherance of that interest. <u>O'Brien</u>, 391 U.S. at 377.

To satisfy this intermediate scrutiny standard, a regulation need not be the least speech-restrictive means of advancing the government's interests. <u>Turner Broadcasting</u>

Sys., Inc., 512 U.S. at 642-43. The means
chosen just cannot burden substantially
more speech than necessary to further the
government's legitimate interest. Id. at 662.

Courts find that a regulation is content-
neutral when people can determine whether the
regulation applies to them without looking
at the content of the speech. Compare Sable
Communications v. F.C.C., 492 U.S. 115, 119
(1989) (determining prohibition on indecent
interstate commercial telephone messages to
be content-specific because applicability
necessarily depended on content), with
Ward, 491 U.S. at 791 (1989) (determining
sound amplification guideline to be content-
neutral because application turned only on
noise level), and Clark, 468 U.S. at 294
(prohibition on sleeping in Lafayette park was
content-neutral because no message content was
precluded).

Whether time, place, or manner
restrictions meet the requirement of narrow
tailoring depends on how effectively the
government interest would be achieved

in their absence. <u>See</u> <u>United States v.</u>
<u>Albertini</u>, 472 U.S. 675, 689 (1985) (finding
legislation making it unlawful for person
to reenter military base after being barred
narrowly tailored where purpose of protecting
government property would be achieved less
effectively in its absence); <u>Clark</u>, 468 U.S.
at 297 (finding prohibition on sleeping in
Lafayette Park no greater than necessary
based on park's exposure to harm without
the restriction). However, courts will not
permit regulations that prevent a person
from all reasonable or effective methods of
communicating a particular message. <u>See</u> <u>Frisby</u>
<u>v. Schultz</u>, 487 U.S. 474, 483 (1988) (finding
ordinance banning picketing in front of a
residence constitutional because it allowed
other means of communication such as telephone
or mail contact); <u>Grayned v. City of Rockford</u>,
408 U.S. 104, 111-12 (1972) (provisions that
forbid noisy or diversionary activity that
disrupts normal school activity left open
ample alternative of peaceful picketing).

A burden on speech is no greater than

essential under the O'Brien standard so long
as the provisions are proportionally related
to the end the legislation was designed to
serve. See Council of Los Angeles v. Taxpayers
of Vincent, 466 U.S. 789, 808-810 (1984)
(complete prohibition of all signs on public
property was necessary because the targeted
"evil," visual blight, rendered each sign
"evil"); Turner Broadcasting Sys., 520 U.S. at
215-16 (modest effects on free speech in the
telecommunications industry permissible where
burden imposed by the must-carry provisions
was congruent to the benefits they afford).

The Supreme Court recognizes that the
time, place, and manner test is essentially no
different than the O'Brien test, which applies
to regulations that incidentally burden
speech. See Madsen, 512 U.S. at 791 (1994)
(recognizing that the difference between the
standards is too subtle for the Court to
describe, yet acknowledging the O'Brien test
is stricter); Ward, 491 U.S. at 798 (conceding
that there is little, if any, difference
between the tests).

<u>The DMCA "trafficking" provisions are</u>
<u>content-neutral on their face because they</u>
<u>can be justified without regard to the content</u>
<u>of the trafficker's speech.</u> Congress's purpose
in enacting these provisions was to counter
the threat of devices that enable pirates to
reproduce and distribute DVDs at no cost. <u>See</u>
H.R. Rep. No. 105-551. pt. 2, at 25 (1998). In
other words, the content of the trafficker's
message was irrelevant to the government's
purpose. Congress has a significant interest in
protecting the motion picture industry from
copyright infringement. The growth of DeCSS
on the Internet creates copyright problems,
reduces DVD sales, and counters the utility of
CSS.

Whether the regulations are assessed
under the time, place, and manner test or the
<u>O'Brien</u> test makes little difference here.
The statute is constitutional under both.
Preventing copyright infringement is done most
effectively by targeting people providing
circumvention devices. Absent the DMCA, the
government's interest would not be effectively

achieved. The restrictions at issue in
this case thus are like the one at issue in
Clark. Not only are they content-neutral and
independent of any specific message content,
but they are no greater than necessary to
achive the government's purpose. See Clark,
468 U.S. at 294, 297. In addition, ample
alternatives for effective communication exist,
which is an important factor in upholding
constitutionality. See Frisby, 487 U.S. at
483; Grayned, 408 U.S. at 111-12. Those
who wish to promote DeCSS may speak in the
print media, on the radio, or in many other
contexts. They just cannot offer the DeCSS
to the public. Each provision of the statute
is directed at protecting the motion picture
industry, which in light of developments such
as the Internet and "Napster," has become
such a substantial and compelling government
interest that any incidental burdens on speech
created by the DMCA are likely to be minimal
in relation to this interest.

B. **Even if the regulations are content-based, they still are constitutional.**

Even if the DMCA is a content based restriction, it still passes muster under the First Amendment. Under the strict scrutiny test, content-based restrictions on speech are permissible if they serve compelling state interests by the least restrictive means available. Sable Communications, 492 U.S. at 126.

When an alternative is available that would effectively further the government's interest without being so burdensome on speech, a content-based restriction is unconstitutionally overbroad. Compare Reno v. A.C.L.U., 521 U.S. 844, 879 (1997) (finding unconstitutional legislation prohibiting "patently offensive" communications from transmission through interactive computer service to minors because exceptions for messages with educational value could be made), and Sable Communications, 492 U.S. at 128 (finding unconstitutional a prohibition of indecent dial-a-porn messages because credit card and scrambling rules represented a "feasible and effective" way to serve the government's compelling interest in protecting children), with Denver Area Educ. Telecomm. Consortium, Inc. v. F.C.C., 518 U.S. 727, 747 (1996) (upholding constitutionality of provision permitting cable operator to prohibit patently offensive or indecent materials because effective alternatives would require an all-out ban to advance the government's interest in protecting children).

Here, the regulations proscribed by the DMCA are the least restrictive means to protect the motion picture industry from copyright infringement. The Defendants may propose exceptions for educational purposes. While a protection scheme with educational exceptions would be less restrictive, it would be ineffective in furthering the government interest in protecting the motion picture industry. The majority of people who obtain DeCSS are not going to use it for educational purposes, but many would be happy to pretend that their piracy was undertaken for these purposes. By allowing such exceptions, the courts would be opening the gates for DVD duplication, defeating the purpose of regulation. <u>Unlike those in Sable Communications, the alternatives here are not feasible and effective.</u>

* * *

<u>CONCLUSION</u>

For the reasons stated above, Global Studios respectfully requests that the Court deny Defendants' motion for summary judgment.

Sample 3 – Memorandum in Support of Motion for Summary Judgment

```
       UNITED STATES DISTRICT COURT
       SOUTHERN DISTRICT OF NEW YORK
            SOUTHERN DIVISION
```

```
ABRAHAM BAUM,              )
                          )
          Plaintiff,      )
                          )
     v.                   )      NO. 09-CIV-123
                          )      (PKL)
                          )
NEW YORK MEDIA            )
HOLDINGS, LLC, D/B/A      )
NEW YORK MAGAZINE,        )
                          )
          Defendant.      )
```

MEMORANDUM IN SUPPORT OF DEFENDANT'S MOTION FOR SUMMARY JUDGMENT

Defendant New York Media Holdings, LLC ("NYMH") moves this court pursuant to Fed. R. Civ. P. 56 for summary judgment in favor of NYMH on Plaintiff Baum's ("Baum") complaint.

INTRODUCTION

Baum's complaint attempts to suppress NYMH's right to freedom of press and speech under the First Amendment of the United States Constitution. NYMH publishes New York

Magazine ("Magazine"), a widely read and successful publication that features pertinent and newsworthy stories for the benefit of the public.

NYMH did not violate Baum's privacy rights under N.Y. Civ. Rights Law §§ 50, 51 (McKinney 2005) because the First Amendment protects the use of a person's image without their consent when used in a newsworthy story of public interest. New York courts consistently recognize that pictures illustrating a newsworthy story fall within this protection.

Additionally, NYMH did not violate Baum's privacy rights under the New York statutes when it used his photograph for two subscription advertisements because such use was incidental to any advertising or trade purpose. The subscription advertisements merely used the cover page that included Baum's photograph to illustrate the substance and quality of the Magazine's articles. The New York statutes are interpreted very narrowly in recognition of the important role media and freedom of the

press under the First Amendment play in our
society. Summary judgment for NYMH should be
granted.

STATEMENT OF FACTS

In November 2008, Baum was walking on a
public sidewalk in New York City. Stipulation
of Facts ("Stip."), ¶ 4. A photographer-
employee of the Magazine snapped a photograph
of Baum outside of the diamond and gem shop
that Baum owns. Stip. ¶ 4. After editorial
board meetings at the Magazine, Baum's
picture was chosen to run with a story on the
current state of the economy and its effect
on the different businesses of New York City,
including diamond businesses, such as the one
owned by Baum. Stip. ¶¶ 1, 5.

Baum is an Orthodox Hasidic Jew who holds
certain deep religious convictions about the
use of his photograph. Stip. ¶ 11. Baum also
is the owner of Abraham Baum Fine Diamonds and
Gem Cutting, and his photograph was used as
representative of the city's diamond and gem
shops. Stip. ¶ 1. Subsequently, the December

9, 2008, issue of the Magazine featured Baum's photograph on the cover as part of the economic story. Stip. ¶ 5. The Magazine is a media publication of general and widespread circulation that is read by tens of thousands of people in and outside of New York City. Stip. ¶ 9.

After the December 9, 2008, issue was circulated, the Magazine selected that issue's cover page along with other cover pages to represent the valuable substance of the Magazine's articles in a subscription page advertisement. Stip. ¶ 6. Two such advertisements that included the December 9, 2008 cover page were published on December 29, 2008, and on January 5, 2009. Stip. ¶ 6.

ARGUMENT

I.   SUMMARY JUDGMENT STANDARDS

Diversity of jurisdiction cases in federal court apply federal procedural law. Gasperini v. Center for Humanities, Inc., 518 U.S. 415, 426 (1996). Fed. R. Civ. P. 56 states, "A party claiming relief may move

... for summary judgment on all or part of the claim." Fed. R. Civ. P. 56(a). Summary judgment is proper when there is no genuine issue as to any material fact and the moving party is entitled to judgment as a matter of law. <u>Celotex Corp. v. Catrett</u>, 477 U.S. 317, 323 (1986). Only disputes over facts that might affect the outcome of the suit will preclude the entry of summary judgment. <u>Anderson v. Liberty Lobby, Inc.</u>, 477 U.S. 242, 248 (1986). In the present case, the parties have stipulated to the underlying material facts and there is no genuine issue to any of those facts.

This memorandum will illustrate that the first use of Baum's photograph is protected under the First Amendment as newsworthy. It will also demonstrate the second and third uses of his photograph are protected under the First Amendment as incidental uses to any advertising or trade purposes. For these reasons, NYMH is entitled to summary judgment as a matter of law based on the facts of this case.

II.   THE FIRST AMENDMENT NECESSITATES A NARROW CONSTRUCTION OF N.Y. CIV. RIGHTS LAW §§ 50, 51 IN FAVOR OF NYMH

Section 51 of the New York Civil Rights Law, which incorporates the provisions of Section 50, states,

> Any person whose name, portrait, picture or voice is used within this state for advertising purposes or for the purposes of trade without the written consent first obtained ... may maintain an equitable action ... against the person, firm or corporation so using his name, portrait, picture or voice ...

N.Y. Civ. Rights Law § 51.

It is recognized that N.Y. Civ. Rights Law §§ 50, 51 provides both publicity and privacy rights to individuals. Time, Inc. v. Hill, 385 U.S. 374, 380-382 (1967). Privacy rights are concerned with a private individual's right to be left alone. Flores v. Mosler Safe Co., 164 N.E.2d 853, 854 (N.Y. 1959). However, when read in conjunction with the First Amendment, the New York statutes are narrowly interpreted. Messenger v. Gruner + Jahr Printing and Publg., 727 N.E.2d 549,

552 (N.Y. 2000). The applicable part of the
First Amendment states, "Congress shall make
no law ... abridging the freedom of speech,
or press;...." U.S. Const. amend. I. Courts
recognize that, "A broadly defined freedom of
press assures the maintenance of our political
system and an open society", Time, Inc., 385
U.S. at 389, and also that, "The court will
construe a statute [narrowly] to avoid serious
constitutional problems ...." Rogers v.
Grimaldi, 875 F.2d 994, 998 (2d Cir. 1989).

In addition to freedom of press, the
First Amendment also guarantees the free
exercise of religion. U.S. Const. amend.
I. The Supreme Court has recognized the
protection of certain non-conforming beliefs
of minority religious groups under the First
Amendment. See W. Va. St. Bd. of Educ. v.
Barnette, 319 U.S. 624, 642 (1943) (Jehovah's
Witnesses students did not have to recite
pledge of allegiance when their religious
views were against such practice). However,
freedom of press and speech is essential to
our democratic form of government and acts as

a cementing foundation of our society. See id.
at 641-43; Time, Inc., 385 U.S. at 389.   There
is no precedent applying the free exercise
clause as a limitation on the freedom of the
press to print newsworthy information. In
Time, Inc. the court explained,

> Exposure of the self to others in
> varying degrees is concomitant of life
> in a civilized community. The risk of
> this exposure is an essential incident
> of life which places a primary value on
> freedom of speech and press.

385 U.S. at 388.

As stated above, the New York privacy
statutes are to be narrowly construed in
recognition of First Amendment concerns.
Additionally, although Baum objects to the use
of his photograph because of his religious
beliefs, such objections must give way to
the free press considerations of the First
Amendment.

III. NYMH DID NOT VIOLATE BAUM'S PRIVACY RIGHTS UNDER N.Y. CIV. RIGHTS LAW §§ 50, 51 WHEN IT PUBLISHED HIS PHOTOGRAPH ON ITS FRONT PAGE BECAUSE FIRST AMENDMENT CONCERNS OVERRIDE ANY SUCH RIGHTS WHEN A MEDIA OUTLET PUBLISHES A NEWSWORTHY STORY

New York courts consistently recognize the First Amendment and the importance of a free press when deciding privacy rights cases. An individual who does not consent to the use of their name, portrait, picture or voice in a journalistic article does not have a privacy right cause of action when that article is found to be newsworthy. See Messenger, 727 N.E.2d at 554 (no cause of action when minor child's parents did not consent to magazine's use of her photographs, story on underage sex was newsworthy); Finger v. Omni Publications Intl., 566 N.E.2d 141, 144 (N.Y. 1990) (no cause of action when family did not consent to use of its photograph with a story on fertilization, story was newsworthy); Arrington v. N.Y. Times Co., 434 N.E.2d 1319, 1322 (N.Y. 1982) (no cause of action when African American man did not consent to use of his photograph with a story on the rise of the "black middle class", story was newsworthy).

Newsworthy stories include actual events, political happenings, social trends, and any subject of public interest. <u>Messenger</u>, 727 N.E.2d at 552. Courts have been reluctant to decide what is newsworthy and the press is given discretion to decide what is of genuine public concern. <u>Gaeta v. New York News, Inc.</u>, 465 N.E.2d 802, 805 (N.Y. 1984)

Even when an individual is not a principal in a newsworthy story and does not consent to the use of her photograph, it is well established that such use is protected under the First Amendment. <u>See</u> <u>Messenger</u>, 727 N.E.2d at 553-554 (photo use protected when girl's photo was used in connection with underage sex story, she was not the subject of story); <u>Arrington</u>, 434 N.E.2d at 1322-1323 (newspaper's use of photo taken of man on public sidewalk and used to illustrate "black middle class" story was protected use even though subject of photo was not featured in story and did not consent to use); <u>Stephano v. News Group Publications, Inc.</u>, 474 N.E.2d 580, 585 (N.Y 1984) (photo's use was protected

where photo of model was used to illustrate
new fashion trends, and model was not
specifically featured in article and did not
consent to use).

In the present case, the Magazine's
article on the economy is newsworthy. As
explained above, courts consistently find
newsworthy stories fall within a wide range of
subjects and the article in question, about the
city's economy, fits within that classification.
Additionally, the use of Baum's picture was
illustrative of the article since he owns a
business of the type that was the subject
of the article. The courts find such use, in
connection with a newsworthy story, protected
under the First Amendment. The Magazine's use
of Baum's photograph on its front page is
protected under the First Amendment and did
not violate his privacy rights.

IV.   NYMH DID NOT VIOLATE BAUM'S PRIVACY RIGHTS UNDER N.Y. CIV. RIGHTS LAW §§ 50, 51 WHEN THE MAGAZINE USED HIS PHOTOGRAPH IN TWO SUBSCRIPTION PAGE ADVERTISEMENTS SINCE THIS USE WAS INCIDENTAL TO ANY ADVERTISING OR TRADE PURPOSE

Baum asserts that NYMH further violated his privacy rights when the Magazine used his photograph in two subscription page advertisements. However, courts have found that such use is protected under the First Amendment as an incidental use to any advertising or trade purposes. Velez v. VV Publg. Corp., 524 N.Y.S.2d 186, 189 (App. Div. 1st Dept. 1988). Photographs within and on magazine cover pages that are used as part of subscription advertisements are merely used to illustrate the content of the magazine and are not considered an advertising use under the privacy statutes. See Lerman v. Flynt Distributing Co., 745 F.2d 123, 130-131 (2nd Cir. 1984) (naked photograph with plaintiff's name on subscription page advertisement, incidental to original article, no violation); Velez, 524 N.Y.S.2d at 189 (individual's picture on front page, later reprinted on subscription advertisement, not a violation);

Booth v. Curtis Publg. Co., 223 N.Y.S.2d 737,
744 (App. Div. 1st Dept. 1962) (reproduction
of actress's photo from article in one of
defendant's magazines to solicit business in
advertisement in two others of defendant's
magazines did not violate civil rights
statutes).

The incidental use exception does not
extend to the commercialization of a person
through a form distinct from dissemination
of news or information; however, transformed
images have been found to be an incidental use.
See Velez, 524 N.Y.S.2d at 189 (reproduction
of front page photograph on subscription
advertisement included plaintiff's full name
with addition of cartoon balloon asking
"what's your address?" was held to be
incidental, satiric expression); Namath v.
Sports Illustrated, 371 N.Y.S.2d 10, 11 (App.
Div. 1st Dept. 1975), *aff'd*, 382 N.E.2d 584
(N.Y. 1976) (photo was cropped from rest of
original cover page and used on subscription
advertisement with addition of phrases such
as "How to get close to Joe Namath" was

incidental use); <u>Booth</u>, 223 N.Y.S.2d at 746
(entire photograph that appeared with original
article in Holiday magazine republished
without article in two different publications
to promote Holiday magazine was incidental
use).

In the case at hand, Baum's photograph
was used on two subscription advertisements
that illustrated the quality of the Magazine's
articles. Such use was incidental to any
advertising or trade purposes. Additionally,
the third use of Baum's photograph which
transformed his image is also recognized
as an incidental use. Like <u>Velez</u>, the
transformed photograph of Baum in the second
subscription advertisement featured his name
and is meant to be a satire of the Magazine.
This is especially evident when viewing the
transformed image in its entire context,
placed below the December 9, 2008, cover page.
Additionally, like <u>Namath</u>, Baum's transformed
image is cropped and taken from its original
use but it is still a part of the subscription
advertisement and an incidental use. NYMH's

use of Baum's photographs in subscription page advertisements were incidental, even if used for advertising purposes, and thus did not violate his privacy rights under the New York statutes.

CONCLUSION

For the reasons stated above, NYMH respectfully requests the Court to grant its motion for summary judgment.

Sample 4 – Memorandum in Opposition to Motion for Summary Judgment

```
UNITED STATES DISTRICT COURT
SOUTHERN DISTRICT OF NEW YORK
SOUTHERN DIVISION
```

ABRAHAM BAUM,	)	
	)	
Plaintiff,	)	
	)	
v.	)	NO. 09-CIV-123
	)	(PKL)
	)	
NEW YORK MEDIA	)	
HOLDINGS, LLC,D/B/A	)	
NEW YORK MAGAZINE,	)	
	)	
Defendant.	)	

**PLAINTIFF'S MEMORANDUM IN OPPOSITION TO
DEFENDANT NEW YORK MEDIA HOLDINGS' FED. R.
CIV. P. 56 MOTION FOR SUMMARY JUDGMENT**

INTRODUCTION

New York Media Holdings (NYMH) is a large media corporation specializing in selling its publications throughout the United States. NYMH serves the most aggressive media market in the world, and has shown it does so with ruthless efficiency.

Plaintiff, Abraham Baum ("Baum") is a

member of the Klausenberg sect of Judaism, which was nearly wiped out during the Holocaust. As an Orthodox Hasidic Jew, he holds a deep religious conviction that the use of his image for open display in public places violates his beliefs. Under the guise of "newsworthy" speech, NYMH would lead one to believe that displaying images and derogatory caricatures of individuals like Baum are essential to its efforts to report current events; rather, it is essential to its bottom line. Permitting this exploitation to continue unabated would be a grave injustice to Abraham Baum and religious minorities everywhere.

Although the First Amendment does protect some speech, the right is not absolute. The exploitation of religious minorities by the mass media is not newsworthy, and should not be allowed to stand unchecked. The New York Statute is expressly intended to prevent such nonconsensual use, and protect an individual's right to privacy, especially when that right is protecting the sanctity of one's religion. Therefore, NYMH's motion for summary judgment should be denied.

STATEMENT OF FACTS

Baum was leaving his place of business
sometime in November 2008, when a photographer
employed by NYMH snapped a photograph of
Baum. See Stipulation of Facts ¶ 4 ("Stip.").
Without Baum's knowledge or consent, that
image became the cover of the December 9,
2008, issue of the Magazine. Stip. ¶ 5. As
an Orthodox Hasidic Jew and a member of the
nearly extinct Klausenberg sect, Baum has
deep religious conviction against the use of
his image in public and certainly not for
commercial or promotional purposes. Stip. ¶
11. Baum communicated his objections to NYMH
directly and explained the sacred religious
foundations of his objections to NYMH's use of
his image. Stip. ¶¶ 6, 13. NYMH did not take
his objections seriously and in fact ignored
them.

After the initial publication of Baum's
photograph, and again without consent, NYMH
created a caricature in Baum's likeness. Stip.

¶ 7. The caricature was then extensively used in advertisements displayed throughout the five boroughs of New York, including placement on buses and in the New York City Subway System. Stip. ¶ 10. In addition to being published on the December issue's cover, the photograph was included in a later advertisement for the Magazine. Complaint, Exhibit 2. By naming their cartoon "Abe", NYMH clearly intended the caricature to be a comedic version of Baum. Complaint, Exhibit 4.

Despite Baum's wishes to have use of the photographs and caricatures stopped, NYMH continued the exploitation in their advertisements. Stip. ¶ 13. This continued use, in Baum's view, is an unacceptable violation of the Second Commandment prohibition against creation and use of graven images. Stip. ¶ 11. NYMH's motion for summary judgment should be denied because as a matter of law, a reasonable jury could, and indeed should find in favor of Baum.

ARGUMENT

I. **NYMH'S MOTION FOR SUMMARY JUDGMENT
    SHOULD BE DENIED BECAUSE IN DRAWING ALL
    INFERENCES IN FAVOR OF BAUM, A REASONABLE
    JURY SHOULD FIND AGAINST NYMH.**

A defending party may move for summary
judgment at any time during the claim. Fed
R. Civ. P. 56(b). Under the Erie doctrine,
federal courts sitting in diversity apply
state substantive law and federal procedural
law. Gasperini v. Ctr. for Humanities, Inc.,
518 U.S. 415, 416 (1996). A case should be
summarily judged if there is no genuine issue
of material fact left in the case, and thereby
the moving party is entitled a judgment as
a matter of law. Anderson v. Liberty Lobby,
Inc., 477 U.S. 242, 247 (1986). "Summary
judgment is appropriate when, after drawing
all reasonable inferences in favor of the
party against whom summary judgment is sought,
no reasonable trier of fact could find in
favor of the nonmoving party." Lund's, Inc.
v. Chemical Bank, 870 F.2d 840, 844 (2d Cir.
1989).

Parties have entered into a stipulation

of facts; thus there is no issue of fact
disputed. This memo will discuss NYMH's
failure to comply with New York Civil Rights
Law, and show that its use of Baum's image
in the creation of a cartoon was not an
incidental use. Additionally, NYMH violated
the well established public policy behind the
New York Civil Rights Law, and the U.S. and
New York Constitutions. In light of the facts
presented, and in drawing all inferences in
favor of Baum, it is clear that a reasonable
jury could find for him.

II. **NYMH'S MOTION FOR SUMMARY JUDGMENT
     SHOULD BE DENIED BECAUSE THE PUBLICATION
     OF BAUM'S IMAGE WAS WITHOUT CONSENT,
     VIOLATING OF NEW YORK CIV. RIGHTS LAW §
     51.**

     Under New York law, it is impermissible
for someone's picture to be used for
advertising purposes without her express
consent. N.Y. Civ. Rights Laws § 51 (2005).
Civil Rights Law § 51 authorizes injunctive
relief and damages if defendant acts knowingly
in violation of the statute. Id. A picture is
used for advertising purposes if it appears
in a publication, which, understood in its

entirety, is a solicitation for patronage of a particular service. <u>Beverly v. Choices Women's Med. Ctr., Inc.</u>, 587 N.E.2d 275, 278 (N.Y. 1991). A newsworthy exemption exists; however, it applies only if the use of the image is directly related to the news story for which it is connected. <u>Arrington v. New York Times Co.</u>, 434 N.E.2d 1319, 1322 (N.Y. 1982).

The "newsworthiness exemption" applies to the use of images to illustrate news articles only when the picture used has a real and substantial relationship to the article. <u>See</u> <u>Murray v. New York Mag. Co.</u>, 267 N.E.2d 256, 258 (N.Y. 1971) (nonconsensual photograph not a violation of § 51 because its publication was directly related to the story accompanying it); <u>Arrington</u>, 434 N.E.2d at 1322 (plaintiff unable to bring claim because his picture accompanied article about which he was a main feature).

NYMH never obtained consent, written or otherwise as required by New York law. Furthermore, there is no logical relation between Baum's face and the news story to which NYMH has linked it. Baum is not in the business of self-promotion, and he in no way represents the diamond industry of New York City. The use was not newsworthy, as it bore no relationship to the story for which it was associated with, and as such NYMH should be held liable under New York Civil Rights law §51.

III. NYMH'S MOTION FOR SUMMARY JUDGMENT SHOULD BE DENIED BECAUSE IT USED BAUM'S PHOTOGRAPH AS AN INTEGRAL PART OF ITS ADVERTISEMENTS, AND IT CANNOT BE SEEN AS AN "INCIDENTAL" USE.

Incidental use of an image or likeness in commercial speech is not sufficient to trigger liability under Civil Rights Law § 51. See Preston v. Martin Bregman Prod., Inc., 765 F. Supp. 116, 119 (S.D.N.Y. 1991); Ladany v. William Morrow & Co., 465 F. Supp. 870, 881 (S.D.N.Y. 1978). However, publications using an image without consent for blatant commercial purposes violate Civil Rights Law § 51. Stephano v. News Group Pubs. Inc., 474 N.E.2d 580, 583 (N.Y. 1984). The courts will weigh the circumstances surrounding the use of the image, the extent it was used, and the character of the use to determine if it was primarily an advertisement rather than a use incidental to a higher first amendment expressive purpose. Netzer v. Continuity Graphic Assoc., Inc., 963 F. Supp. 1308, 1325-26 (S.D.N.Y. 1997). See Preston, 765 F. Supp. at 119 (defendant not liable because plaintiff's image shown for only 9 seconds in full length movie); Ladany, 465 F. Supp. at 881 (plaintiff not entitled to recovery under New York Civil Rights Law because he was mentioned in only 13 of a 458 pages book dealing with Munich Olympics massacre). If a picture is used without consent, and its use is central to the publications commercial message, it is a violation of New York law. Beverly, 587 N.E.2d at 278 (Health clinic's unauthorized use of doctor's picture in promotional calendar was considered an advertisement in violation of § 51).

Baum's cartoon likeness "Abe" in advertisements in defendant's Magazine and in billboards and subway placards smeared across New York City is not incidental;

rather it is central to the advertisement. The image is used as an explicit solicitation for new subscriptions to the Magazine. The derogatory nature of the caricature is extremely insensitive and is indicative of NYMH's intentions to use Baum's image for its own commercial gain. The cartoon does not represent anything regarding the diamond trade, as NYMH alleges. His caricatured image makes up a vital part of NYMH's advertisements. NYMH clearly showed its intent to make Baum into a commercially exploitable image—a cartoon spokesperson for the Magazine—and thus NYMH's motion for summary judgment should be denied.

IV.   THE COURT SHOULD DENY NYMH'S MOTION FOR SUMMARY JUDGMENT BECAUSE IT'S USE OF BAUM'S IMAGE REPRESENTS A VIOLATION OF HIS RELIGION AND OF ESTABLISHED PUBLIC POLICY.

The First Amendment of the United States Constitution states inter alia that Congress shall not make any laws abridging the freedom of the press. U.S. Const. amend. I. The United States Supreme Court has held that commercial speech is afforded less protection than other protected speech. Central Hudson Gas & Elec.

Corp. v. Public Serv. Commn. of New York, 447
U.S. 557, 563 (1980). The Court also has held
that in the United States, individuals cannot
be compelled to compromise their religious
beliefs in order to conform to society's norms
and desires. W. Va. State Bd. of Educ. v.
Barnette, 319 U.S. 624, 642 (1943).

The New York State Constitution provides
that: "Every citizen may... publish his...
sentiments on all subjects, *being responsible
for the abuse of that right*; and no law
shall be passed to restrain ... the press".
N.Y. Const. art. 1, § 8 (emphasis added).
Both documents explicitly protect religious
activities as well. See U.S. Const. amend. I;
N.Y. Const. art. 1, § 3.

The New York Court of Appeals has
noted that "[t]he richness and strength of
our society lies ... in its hospitality to
religious diversity ... the high value our
State places on supporting and protecting
such diversity and in prohibiting invidious
discrimination based on religious choice."
New York City Transit Auth. v. State Exec.

Dept., Div. of Human Rights, 674 N.E.2d 305, 310 (N.Y. 1996). New York Civil Rights Law § 51 was passed in recognition of there being no common law right of privacy in New York, and to create a remedy for individuals whose pictures were used in blatant commercial speech. *Stephano*, 474 N.E.2d at 583. The statute was passed in order to protect against the exploitation of a person's image. *See* *Beverly*, 587 N.E.2d at 279. Ordinary citizens are protected from commercial exploitation, as are persons with professional reputations. *Id.*

An individual may not be compelled by society to compromise their religious beliefs. *W. Va. State Bd. of Educ.*, 319 U.S. at 642 (Jehovah's witnesses cannot be forced to salute the American flag prior to school, as it violated their religious beliefs). The U.S. Court of Appeals for the 1st Circuit has held that it was permissible for the government to ban advertisements that are demeaning or disparaging to a religious group. *Ridley v. Massachusetts Bay Transp. Auth.*, 390 F.3d 65, 71 (1st Cir. 2004) (court forced removal of billboard public location because it was demeaning and disparaging to devout Catholics). Individuals whose image is used on a commercial billboard without consent will have a claim under § 51. <u>Felice v. Delporte</u>, 524 N.Y.S.2d 919, 920 (App. Div. 4th Dept. 1988) (plaintiff's image placed on billboard without her consent; defendants liable).

Baum's image was included amongst famous New Yorkers Nathan Lane, Bobby Flay and Carlita Clausberg, all well known individuals that have made financial gains off of self-promotion. The same cannot be said about Baum. The use of his image creates the illusion that he willingly submitted to, if not sought out this attention. This could not be further from the truth, as his religion precludes any use of his image for public display let alone commercial gain. Abraham Baum is not the face of the diamond district, he is not synonymous with the diamond trade in New York City, and as such his photo was not remotely related to any economic situation that may be facing the industry. An ordinary citizen, one who in

no way can be considered a "public figure",
who clings to his privacy, and who devoutly
practices his religious beliefs, does not
deserve to have his image exploited under the
guise of "newsworthy" speech.

The finder of fact needs to evaluate
the circumstances that NYMH, against Baum's
objections, continued to use Baum's image and
further created an offensive cartoon of him
named "Abe." The cartoon that was created
represents a gross disregard for Baum's
religious principles. The nonconsensual
publication and the continued use of Baum's
image is a clear violation of New York law.
The use of Baum's photograph throughout
the five boroughs of the City, and on buses
and subways, is not unlike the persuasive
authority in Felice. As the 1st Circuit has
shown, it is not unreasonable to halt a
demeaning and derogatory advertisement, like
NYMH's.

The extensive use of Baum's photo
violates the well settled public policy behind
N.Y. Civil Rights Law § 51, N.Y. Const.

art. 1 §§ 3, and 8 and the First Amendment
of the U.S. Constitution. The facts of the
case should be reviewed by a jury. For these
reasons, NYMH's motion for summary judgment
should be denied.

CONCLUSION

In light of the above, Abraham Baum
respectfully requests that the court deny
New York Media Holdings' motion for summary
judgment.

Chapter 5

Appellate Advocacy: Appeals, Writs, and Standards of Review

This chapter presents an overview of appeals and appellate advocacy. It examines the appellate process, types of appeals and appellate writs, the timing of the various types of appeals, and the concept of standard of review. Lastly, it discusses the procedures for the compilation and use of the record on appeal.

I.   INTRODUCTION TO THE APPELLATE PROCESS

As you likely already know by now, an appeal is the action taken by the non-prevailing or aggrieved litigant in litigation or another adversarial matter. An appeal is made to a higher level court, usually a court of appeals or the court of last resort, but sometimes a trial level court can hear an appeal from an administrative agency, arbitral body, or a lower level trial court (for example, a federal bankruptcy court, federal tax court, or a state associate circuit court or magistrate court). The non-prevailing party takes an appeal when it believes that errors were committed during the course of the litigation by the judge(s), and sometimes by the jury. The errors assigned might involve the interpretation of the governing law, the application of the law to the facts, the finding of facts, or a procedural ruling before or during trial. A non-prevailing party typically (and rightfully) will look for any legitimate way possible to reverse the determination against it.

A.   It is hard to win on appeal.

It is important to note at the outset that no matter what court you are in, and absent truly egregious errors, it is very difficult to win on appeal. The majority of appeals fail, and in some jurisdictions, the vast majority of them do. Why? Because it is difficult to convince a higher court that the determination made by a judicial body is simply "wrong." In other words, "I disagree with that outcome!" is generally not going to save the day because the premise underlying any judicial determination is that there was indeed a disagreement in the first place: the two sides did not agree on the merits of their legal situation to the point that they were willing to litigate against each other, and short of a settlement, one side or the other was going to lose. Therefore, the first job of an advocate in a situation presenting a potential appeal is to counsel your client that the deck is stacked against her: the majority of appeals fail, and statistically there is much better than a 50-50 chance that hers will fail as well. In some appellate courts and in many kinds of appeals the odds may be 75% to 90% against the appeal succeeding. You still should review the potential errors that might be asserted in the appeal and see if there are grounds to reverse the lower court that make the risk worth taking. Here, the "standard of review" is critically important, and you should therefore consider carefully our discussion of that topic below.

B.   Quality is much better than quantity.

When evaluating the possible errors committed by the lower court, quality is far more important than quantity. In other words, you

---

PRACTICE POINTER

Shotgun or Scattershot Briefs

It is an all too common practice on appeal, especially in criminal cases, for the non-prevailing party's attorney to throw as much mud (errors) against the wall as she can, hoping against hope that something—anything—might "stick." These briefs—referred to as shotgun or scattershot briefs, or simply as briefs of desperation—have little or no chance of success in most cases. First of all, appellate courts resent having to take up and address so many errors. Second, the sheer number of errors hides any truly meritorious errors you might have raised. You have, in effect, planted a forest to obscure any truly meritorious trees that might be present. Last, this tactic communicates desperation rather than confidence in any of your errors and arguments on appeal. So, please heed our advice and reject this approach to appellate practice. Pick and choose a small number of errors so that you can assert them confidently and effectively and give your client the best chance of success.

---

will do much better if there is one unforgivable error you can point to, rather than a dozen somewhat troublesome points of dispute that you can highlight. Appellate courts are sensitive to the tactic of litigators that announce a "parade of horribles" and stuff their briefs with as many assertions of error as they can think of, hoping that one will stick and cause the case to be overturned. This tactic is only one of desperation, not of effective advocacy. Not insignificantly, a vast quantity of "also ran" errors or legal arguments on the errors can dilute the effectiveness of any of the better allegations and arguments you may have. So, the second piece of advice we will give is to limit yourself to the most important and egregious errors and arguments in support of reversal.

II.   TYPES OF APPEALS AND APPELLATE WRITS

A.   Appeal after a final judgment

The normal channel of appeal is initiated from a final judgment entered in the lower court. 28 U.S.C. § 1291; Fed. R. App. P. 4. Everyone has the right to take this kind of appeal, once. Timing is critical: the appeal must be made within a certain period of time after the final judgment in the case is "entered," and entered can mean "issued" (signed by the trial judge) or entered on the docket, so be sure to check and be absolutely certain what it means in your jurisdiction. If you are late, the appeals court is deprived of jurisdiction. See United States v. Robinson, 361 U.S. 220 (1960) ; Fed. R. App. P. 3, Advisory Committee Notes to 1967 adoption. The court cannot simply excuse your mistake.

The "notice of appeal" required to be filed by Fed. R. App. P. 3 and 4 is important. It triggers the appeal and identifies what exactly it is that you are appealing from—a summary judgment or other order disposing of some issues and claims earlier in the case, a verdict and judgment after trial, the granting or denial of a post-trial motion, or all or some of the above. It is not necessarily sufficient or accurate simply to state that you appeal from the final judgment in the case.

Although each litigant in federal court is entitled to one appeal as of right, it still must be noted that few of these appeals succeed. You may get in the door easily enough, but you may soon be walking out that same door empty-handed. As noted, there are ways to try to improve your odds: pick your appeals carefully, only challenge the most important errors, and only raise the strongest legal arguments in support of reversal. Beyond that, follow the advice on the drafting of briefs and the planning, preparation for, and execution of oral argument that will be discussed in the next two chapters.

B.   Interlocutory appeals

The next type of appeal in order of frequency (going down the scale to remedies that are less frequently available) is the interlocutory appeal, which in federal court is governed by 28 U.S.C. § 1292. "Interlocutory" means that the appeal happens *prior to a final judgment in the case*. A "final judgment" is one that disposes of ***all*** claims of ***all*** the parties in the case, damages included. That can take a while, especially in a multi-party,

---

PRACTICE POINTER

There are a handful of interim decisions that are immediately appealable even though the case itself has not been disposed of. For example, the granting of a preliminary injunction is immediately appealable, a "collateral order" denying a defendant immunity from suit may be immediately appealable, as are many other interim decisions. You always must check the relevant rules of procedure to inform yourself concerning your client's particular situation.

---

multi-claim case, and litigants do not necessarily want to go that far and spend that much money just to have someone take an appeal from the final judgment and show that certain interlocutory decisions were wrong. So, if a legal issue is resolved by the trial court in the middle of a case, not as part of the final disposition of all of the claims and defenses, and that determination of the issue will or may have a tremendous effect on one party's or both parties' prosecution of the case from that point forward, one or more parties might ask the trial court: "May we please find out what the appellate court thinks about this issue before we go further in this case?"

Both sides may have an interest in taking an interlocutory appeal. While the side that lost the point might feel totally handcuffed by the decision, the other side might think they got a good ruling but are not sure it will hold up on the appeal from a final judgment in the case, thus creating the potential that any judgment in the case will be overturned later on. A reversed judgment and a new trial (after an already lengthy one has ended) likely is not be a good use of the client's litigation budget. So, although it is unusual for the party that prevailed on the point to join in the request for an interlocutory appeal, it is certainly not unheard of (similarly, the prevailing party might simply fail to oppose the request very strenuously).

All the party or parties can do is ask. Whether you get an inter-locutory appeal may depend as much on the personality and background experiences of the trial judge (both in private practice and on the bench) as it does on your authority supporting the request. Some trial judges are neutral to the request, or they at least respect the argument that a lot of time and money could be wasted if the appeal is not granted. Other trial judges hate delay, or have been disappointed in the past by an interlocu-tory appeal that dragged one of her cases out for years and years, making the judge decidedly unfriendly to the request.

In any event, even if the trial judge approves the request and certi-fies the point of law for interlocutory appeal, the appeals court still can say, "No," under Fed. R. App. P. 5. This happens less often than a trial judge's actually agreeing to an interlocutory appeal, so once you are over the hurdle of the trial court's certification, the court of appeals part of the process should not cause you to lose too much more sleep.

C.   Extraordinary writs – writs of mandamus, writs of prohibition

The most extraordinary way to obtain review of a lower court's determination is to petition the appeals court to issue a prerogative writ quashing or reversing the lower court's action. The writs most commonly requested in general civil practice are the writs of mandamus and writs of prohibition. They are called "extraordinary" because it is an extraordinary

FYI

Extraordinary Writs

In addition to the writs of mandamus and writs of prohibition described in this section, there are other extraordinary writs including the Writ of Habeas Corpus, demanding the production of some person from captivity or confinement; the Writ of Quo Warranto, addressed to quash a continuing exercise of unlawful authority; and the Writ of Certiorari, which literally refers to a higher court's order to a lower court to produce a certified copy of the record in a case for review of the proceedings, but has come to refer to any higher court's, but especially the United State's Supreme Court's, exercise of discretionary jurisdiction to review the determinations of a lower court or adjudicatory body.

event when one of these requests is granted. The action of the lower court must be extraordinarily bad, the evidence of the errors and the legal support used to make the challenge must be extraordinarily strong, and the appellate court must be extraordinarily moved by your petition to entertain the writ. It is a grave task to chastise the actions of a lower court judge in this way, and the writ will not lightly be granted.

There is no specific time frame in which to bring a request for the writ—you can make the petition "as needed" in a case whenever the court performs an unlawful act or exceeds its powers in an unlawful manner. You should of course resist the temptation to request a writ except when faced with the most egregious mistakes of a judge. The judge you challenge will be aware of your request for the issuance of the writ and may take this challenge to her judicial action as a personal attack on her abilities and good judgment. This perception is unfortunate for at least two reasons: the chilling effect of the desire not to step on the judge's toes probably keeps attorneys from filing a petition for a writ in cases where the issuance of the writ truly is warranted, and when an attorney is driven to make the request in good faith, there is a very real possibility that the attorney's future relationship with the judge who was "brought up on a writ" may suffer in the instant case or others, whether or not the writ is actually issued.

"Mandamus," which literally can be translated as, "we command," is directed to a judge who has undertaken an illegal action or failed to take a required action, or has taken away rights of a party in an unlawful way. See Black's Law Dictionary 866 (5th ed. 1979); Bryan A. Garner, A Dictionary of Modern Legal Usage 546 (2d ed. 1995) David Mellinkoff, Mellinkoff's Dictionary of American Legal Usage 395-96 (1992). It essentially is directed to cure an abuse of judicial power—a refusal to do the right thing for a party, or an insistence of doing the wrong thing. The writ, if granted, commands the inferior judge to restore the rights, perform the required duty, do the right thing, or undo the unlawful act.

"Prohibition" is directed to a judge who has exceeded his or her lawful authority and jurisdiction. Traditionally, it was intended to stop a judge from usurping jurisdiction (i.e., control) over an action or a party or the subject matter of a suit that was beyond the court's jurisdiction. Black's Law Dictionary at 1091 ; Garner, supra at 700-01; Mellinkoff, supra at 513.

In different jurisdictions, the meaning of the two writs has become blurred, see, e.g., Fed. R. App. P. 21(a)(1); Ill. S. Ct. Rule 381, or it may be more precise to say that the terms sometimes are used as if they were interchangeable. "Prohibition" might be used to cure a number of abuses in one jurisdiction, but in another jurisdiction the same abuses would be cured by "mandamus." As always, you must research the law and local practice of your jurisdiction to determine which writ is appropriate. At present, the differences between the two writs largely are academic.

Because these two writs are extraordinary, a litigant requires very good justification for the granting of the writ. You must strive to find the clearest authority that says what the judge did is absolutely wrong ***and*** is reversible error. The best authority to cite is a case from the immediately higher appellate court or the highest court of the applicable jurisdiction in which the court issues a writ of mandamus or prohibition to curb the **same** conduct at issue in your case. Next best is an opinion from one of these courts granting the writ in a similar situation. Next best after that is an opinion describing the conduct as reversible error. If you have to go outside your own line of judicial authority for support, generally speaking, the chances that the writ will be issued are much diminished. If you can come up with four or five examples from other appellate courts where the writ was issued to quash the same action when taken by judges in different jurisdictions, you may squeak by, but citation to controlling authority is far superior.

Under the Federal Rules of Appellate Procedure, Rule 21, the writ process involves the following process:

- The aggrieved litigant in the United States District Court petitions the appropriate United States Court of Appeals to issue the writ.

- If the Court of Appeals does not believe the petition is meritorious, it will deny the writ, with or without detailed explanation.

- But if the Court of Appeals believes that the petition has merit, it will order the nominal respondent—the **district court judge**—to respond. While this is the technical form, the true substance is that the opponent of the petitioner responds in the judge's stead and raises the arguments in support of the judge's action that the judge presumably would raise. The district court judge theoretically could file her own response.

- After this round of briefing, if the appeals court still agrees with the petitioner's charges, it will issue the writ.

- If the petitioner fails and the writ is denied at the initial stage or the second stage, the petitioner can continue up the appellate chain of command until all avenues for appeal are exhausted. For example, in the U.S. Court of Appeals, you can petition the U.S. Supreme Court for a Writ of Certiorari, U.S. S. Ct. Rules 10, 11, or for a Writ of Mandamus, U.S. S. Ct. Rule 20.

To be sure, some jurisdictions do not regard these writs with as much disfavor as others. In some state court systems, writs of prohibition and mandamus are sought and granted more often than in the federal courts. The writs still are regarded as *extraordinary*, but they are not as infrequent as a solar eclipse, which is a fairly accurate description of the frequency of the issuance of writs of mandamus in most United States Courts of Appeals.

III.   STANDARD OF REVIEW

Even before your appeal is pending before a court of appeals, one of the most important concepts to consider is the standard of review that the higher court will exercise when evaluating your various allegations of error and grounds for reversal. The "standard of review" is basically just as it sounds: what is the standard that the higher court will apply to assess the lower court's decision? As noted above, you are generally in deep waters if your reason for appealing a decision is simply that you (or your client) doesn't like it. Litigation necessarily involves winners and losers, and the mere fact that you lost doesn't mean you necessarily have appealable issues.

We like to think of the standard of review as a telescopic *lens* or *window* through which you are assessing what has happened in the lower court. How wide the lens is— literally how much room the higher court has to view (and thus review) what happened before—depends on the nature of the issue on appeal. The available lenses come with different diameters, and how far open a lens is in a given case goes to the issue of **deference.** What the appellate court must always ask itself is "how much deference do we need to give the determination that we are asked to review?" Stated otherwise, how wide is our lens of review – or, how much credit do we have to give to the appealed decision based on the mere fact that it exists. Is it sufficient that we simply would have reached a different conclusion, or is there some additional weight that we must give to the fact that some judicial body has preceded us in making a determination? Appropriate standards of review may allow for no deference (a wide open lens), a great deal of deference (a partially open lens), or an incredible amount of deference (a very small window through which the decision below is viewed).

It should go without saying that the appropriate standard of review can have a tremendous impact on the chances of success of an appeal, and thus that the standard itself is something the parties may argue about. The difference between an issue on appeal case that is governed by a *de novo* standard, for example, which requires essentially no deference to the court below, as opposed to an issue governed by a "clearly erroneous" standard, which is a great deal of deference (but not total), is the difference between an appeal that may have a decent chance and one that may have a snowball's chance in hell. Thus, the issue of the appropriate standard of review must be examined before you take the appeal, and you should counsel your client about the chances for success based on your evaluation of the proper standard of review.

The standard of review is determined by the type of issue that is being asserted on appeal. In that there may be several issues raised in any given appeal, there may be several applicable standards of review that must be anticipated in evaluating and briefing the arguments on appeal. The standards discussed in this chapter generally apply in many jurisdictions, but you must research the law of your own jurisdiction to be sure, because standards do change from jurisdiction to jurisdiction.

The types of issues that might arise on appeal and their corresponding standards of review are as follows:

A.   Determinations of law – *"de novo"* standard of review

The lens is wide open. If you are appealing from a lower court's determination of a *pure issue of law*—what the law is or what the law means, the elements or legal standards that apply, the actual law that applies under a conflict of laws analysis, and other questions of law—then the standard of review is *de novo. De novo* review means that the court of appeals decides the issue anew, as if the lower court had never even taken it up. This clearly is the best standard of review for an appellant, because it means that the court of appeals gets to revisit the issue from start to finish and make its own determination of what the answer should be (as if it were the first court to adjudicate it). So, no deference to the lower court's determination is required.

An appellant can make the same legal arguments in favor of its interpretation of the law that were made to and rejected by the lower court. Naturally, if the arguments failed once, you should go back to the research table and satisfy yourself that you are presenting the strongest possible argument on the law. Point out the specific areas where the lower court's reasoning and analysis went astray. It will do no good to remind the appeals court that they get to take a fresh look at the issue if you present the same failed arguments and do nothing to rebut the lower court's reasoning in the matter.

B.   Determinations of fact – "clearly erroneous" standard of review

The lens is nearly closed (although a slight opening remains). On the opposite end of the spectrum from *de novo* review is the standard of review that applies to review of the findings of fact. For jury trials, the Seventh Amendment of the United States Constitution specifically protects a jury verdict from an all-on attack by an appellate court: "no fact tried by a jury shall be otherwise re-examined in any court of the United States, than according to the rules of the common law." U.S. Const. amend. VII,

This standard of review requires a showing that the findings are not reasonable and are completely against the evidence even when viewed in a light that most favors the jury verdict. <u>See</u>, <u>e.g.</u>, <u>Bykowicz v. Pulte Home Corp.</u>, 950 F.2d 1046, 1050 (5th Cir. 1992); <u>United States v. Dozal-Bencomo</u>, 952 F.2d 1246, 1250 (10th Cir. 1991). If any reasonable inferences can be drawn from the evidence to support the jury's findings, the jury's decision will be upheld. <u>See</u> <u>Bykowicz</u>, 950 F.2d at 1050; <u>Dozal-Bencomo</u>, 952 F.2d at 1250.

In a very real and practical sense, there are good reasons for this standard: if a litigant could readily overturn a jury's findings, it would deny his opponent the right to a trial by jury and replace it with trial by appellate court, in which the litigant would be armed only with a transcript of the testimony of the witnesses (and boxes of exhibits). The second reason is that the appellate court truly cannot sit in the same position as the jury in watching the witnesses and evidence and be as able to evaluate their credibility from moment to moment in the course of their testimony. Nothing at the present level of technology and procedures for the creation of the record can duplicate the benefits of actually being present at a trial. Thus, the appeals court will rarely if ever substitute their impressions and evaluations of the evidence for the jury's impressions based solely on the appellate court's cold reading of the trial transcript and review of the documents and exhibits, divorced as it is from the actual introduction and use of this evidence at trial. The appellant will almost never succeed in challenging the jury's findings under this legal standard, and an appeal will almost always be a waste of the client's time and money.

Is the standard the same when the trial was a bench trial? Technically, yes. If what's being appealed are finding of fact, then the standard is still **"clearly erroneous,"** meaning that the court's factual findings will not be set aside unless they are "clearly" off the mark. That means that it is not enough that the appellate court would have reached a different outcome (as with a *de novo* standard). Rather, the question is whether the fact finder (here, the court) was unreasonable in its own determination. The standard (like above) gives due regard to the trial court's opportunity to judge the credibility of witnesses. <u>Fed. R. Civ. P. 52(a)</u>; <u>United States</u>

v. Oregon State Med. Assoc., 343 U.S. 326, 332 (1952). This, again, provides a great deal of deference, which is warranted because of the inability of the appeals court to sit in the place of the trial judge (to assess the credibility of the witnesses on the stand and the impact and value of each piece of evidence as it was introduced and used in the proceedings).

The *only difference* between a bench trial and a jury trial is that it can be more difficult to determine which questions were ones of fact versus which were ones of law. A bench trial may somewhat obscure these important distinctions and be more likely to leave you in the realm of the "mixed" questions discussed below.

C.   Mixed questions of law and fact

The lens is partially open, although the size of the opening is in dispute. The real trouble comes with "mixed" questions of law and fact—should they be treated like a determination of law, and given little or no deference under a *de novo* standard, or are they more like a determination of fact, and given a great deal of deference under a clearly erroneous standard? This is a tough area, to be sure. If the issue is a finding of historical fact, such as "Defendant was driving at a rate of 55 miles an hour," it is governed by the clearly erroneous standard. But if there is a factual conclusion *as well as* an application of the law to the facts so as to make a legal determination, such as "Defendant's driving at 55 miles per hour on a wet road was reckless," then the issue is more complicated. The court in this example had to make both a legal determination of the applicable legal standard (recklessness), and a factual determination of the defendant's rate of speed (55 m.p.h.) and the condition of the road, in order to make the ultimate determination of whether the legal standard was satisfied by the facts found by the court (defendant was reckless when he drove at 55 m.p.h. on the wet road). It is the incorporation of these factual and legal determinations to make the ultimate determination challenged on appeal that creates the controversy.

Courts are split on what is more factual and what is more legal, so a litigant must research the standards in her own jurisdiction to evaluate the particular problem and be ready to present arguments to demand a favorable standard. *There is room for advocacy in this area.* If the courts of appeals in the jurisdiction tend to resolve these issues in favor of a finding that a *de novo* standard of review applies, appellant should strive to draft her issues presented so that they sound like issues of law or mixed issues of law and fact, so that they can enjoy the benefits of a *de novo* standard. But if these mixed law and fact determinations are treated like fact determinations, the appellant must be prepared for an uphill climb and must counsel her client accordingly.

D.   Review of trial court's rulings on proceedings before and during the trial – "abuse of discretion"

The lens is almost closed.   A trial court makes a great deal of determinations in the course of a litigation, any one of which might cause discomfort to one side or the other and might be challenged on appeal. The trial court might have to decide whether an amendment to the pleadings will be allowed, whether one party will receive an extension of time, whether certain types of discovery may be had or whether certain categories of information will be subject to discovery. All such decisions are reviewed under an "abuse of discretion" standard, meaning that unless the trial court wholly abused its authority when it made a determination or failed to make one, the ruling will stand.

Still, the breadth of the discretion afforded to the trial court will vary from issue to issue, and from jurisdiction to jurisdiction. If the matter is one that clearly relates to the operation and proper administration of the court, such as granting an extension of time or allowing additional pages beyond the page limits imposed by local rules for motions, the matter will not be overturned even if the court of appeals thinks the trial judge's decision was ill advised. The trial judge has the right to be wrong on these determinations. On the other hand, if the determination has a more profound impact on the outcome and merits of the case, such as the denial of an amendment to the complaint or the denial of the right to conduct additional discovery after new evidence has been uncovered in a case, then the trial court is afforded less discretion, and the decision will more readily be overturned on appeal. As you can tell, these are all complicated questions.

On the other hand, a trial court's demonstrated ignorance of the applicable legal standards for the decision or of available options for the decision may more readily be interpreted as an abuse of discretion or the failure to exercise discretion, and thus be overturned on appeal. Finally, just because the trial court *appeared* to exercise discretion in a matter does not mean that the court had any discretion to exercise under the applicable legal standards, and so the purported exercise of discretion in and of itself may be an abuse. Careful research and analysis of the authorities in the local jurisdiction on the particular issue that is being challenged are required before an appellant can properly define the discretion afforded and determine whether it may have been abused.

E.   Trial court's evidentiary determinations – "abuse of discretion" still applies, but the discretion is more limited

The lens is nearly closed (although a slightly larger opening remains). A trial court's determinations regarding the admissibility and exclusion of evidence and witnesses also is subject to an abuse of discretion standard, United States v. Abel, 469 U.S. 45, 54-55 (1984), but in light of the fact that these decisions are so closely tied to the litigants' ability to prove their case or establish their defenses, the discretion afforded is scrutinized more carefully by the appeals court and tends to be more limited than other determinations made in the course of a trial. See, e.g., United States v. 68.94 Acres, 918 F.2d 389, 392, 395-96 (3rd Cir. 1990). If the trial court applied the wrong legal evidentiary standard or if the court makes an erroneous application of the proper standard to the evidence in the case, the appeals court may find that the trial court abused its discretion and overturn the decision. See id. The appeals court does not completely second guess the trial court as it might in *de novo* review, but it will substitute its judgment for the trial court on legal and mixed law and fact determinations where "a substantial right of the party" is clearly affected by the determination. Id. at 396.

If the trial court merely excludes evidence or witnesses that were not listed in pretrial materials, or were not disclosed to the opponent at the proper time in the litigation, or are otherwise offered in violation of a local rule or pretrial order, these evidentiary rulings will generally be held to be within the "broad discretion" of the trial court and affirmed. See id. at 396-97; Jansen v. Aaron Process Equip. Co., 149 F.3d 603, 609 (7th Cir. 1998).

IV.   THE RECORD ON APPEAL

An integral part of the appeals process involves the compilation (and reference) to the record of the proceedings in the court below, commonly referred to as the "record on appeal." The record on appeal actually can mean three different things:

(1)   the district court's record, comprising everything that was filed in the district court, plus the trial transcript and docket entries ("district court record");

(2)   the record actually transmitted to the court of appeals, which consists of some but not all of the district court record ("transmitted record"); or

(3)   a further distilled version of the transmitted record provided by the parties to the court of appeals in the form of a joint appendix or record excerpts ("excerpted record").

The transmitted record is prepared or supervised (monitored) in its preparation by the parties. Primary responsibility lies with the appellant, but either side has an interest in the process. The court of appeals ideally would prefer that the parties get along enough to compile and submit one *joint appendix* of the proceedings below. That is not always possible, however, and either side may feel the need to present its own version of the record (or submit additional portions not submitted by the other side). If these competing versions wind up playing a critical part in the court of appeals' review, it will have to sort out the mess and make a determination of what is the actual record.

A.   What is the "real record" on appeal – district court record or transmitted record?

Prior to 1967, there was no question that the transmitted record was the "real" record; nothing else mattered. If you left something out of the transmitted record that you later decided you wanted to use, you were stuck, and the support for the argument you wanted to make was lost to you. A revision of the Federal Rules of Appellate Procedure, specifically Rule 10, sought to eliminate this trap by providing that the entire district court record constituted the record on appeal regardless of what was transmitted to the court of appeals. In other words, as a matter of law the district court's record now constitutes the record on appeal.

As a matter of reality, however, the court of appeals will rarely look beyond the transmitted record. Unless you properly supplement the transmitted record (see below), it likely will help you little to argue that the court of appeals may consider something in the district court record that you forgot to include in the transmitted record. The court of appeals is likely to dismiss such an argument with a terse remark about how a party waives or abandons any argument that it fails to support by including the relevant parts of the district court's record in the transmitted record. As a practical matter, the transmitted record becomes the real record on appeal.

B.   Supplementing the transmitted record

That said, if a party realizes that it inadvertently omitted something from the transmitted record, it certainly may (and should) move to supplement the transmitted record. If the court of appeals has not yet considered the case on its merits, the court is likely to grant such a motion. Thus, the district court record still remains a reservoir from which the parties may select items for inclusion in the transmitted record throughout most of the appeal.

C.   What the transmitted record contains

The transmitted record on appeal contains three types of materials selected by the parties:

(1)   the court reporter's transcript of the trial, which includes the parties' statements and oral arguments and objections, the judge's statements and rulings and instructions to the jury, the testimony of the witnesses, and the record of the admission of evidence in the case;

(2)   the pleadings, motions, and other filings from the clerk's office case file; and

(3) the actual exhibits.

The district clerk's certified copy of docket entries is also part of the transmitted record, but the district court clerk sends that up as soon as the notice of appeal is filed, so that counsel have nothing further to do with it. The court of appeals may order additions to the district court record for materials that were considered by the district court but not included in its record.

D.   Appellant's and appellee's duties regarding the record

Appellant's primary duty with respect to the record is to "monitor" its preparation; appellee's duty is to make sure nothing is left out that can support the trial court's decision. While the appellant has an incentive to make sure the record gets done on time (i.e., appellant must order the transcript and see to it that the file was sent), the appellant really only needs to be sure to get the parts of the record sent up that can support an argument that the trial court erred. Because appellee needs *all* the material that could support the trial court's decision, it must pay careful attention to what is being sent up.

Chapter 6

Appellate Briefs

I.   THE IMPORTANCE OF ADVOCACY IN WRITING IN THE APPELLATE CONTEXT

The appeals process calls for the highest degree of advocacy in writing. As discussed in the previous chapter, most appeals involve an up-hill fight, and in many cases the chances of success are dismal. To have a fighting chance, an advocate must pay close attention to the drafting and editing of her briefs.

Oral argument is a wonderful exercise, and we will devote an entire chapter to the examination of the skills and preparation needed to make the most of your time at the podium. But we must point out that of the many appellate court judges we have talked to or heard speak on this topic, the vast majority of these jurists find the briefs filed by the parties to play a greater role than the oral arguments in helping the judges make up their minds as to who should prevail in an appeal. All judges report that oral arguments are helpful, and occasionally these fifteen to thirty minute sessions of intense discussion and questioning of the issues can turn a judge around or convince a fence-sitter to jump to one side or the other. But no one discounts the critical importance of good appellate briefs.

Appellate courts have to look at cases from two perspectives: the rights and equities of the parties before them on the appeal and the effect that their ruling will have on the body of law in the area and on all future litigants in their jurisdiction. Advocates must be sensitive to these dual pressures and not over-emphasize the individual rights and equities of their clients to the exclusion of the bigger picture and the impact of these same arguments on future parties. Policy arguments play a greater role in advocacy the higher you go up the appellate chain because a court of last resort has the power to make the ultimate determination of the public policy that will be embodied in the case law of the jurisdiction. Appellate courts at any level will inquire into the implications of the arguments raised by the parties at oral argument, but you can set the stage for the argument by briefing these policy issues in your appellate briefs.

II.   WHAT BRIEFS ARE ALLOWED?

In an interlocutory appeal or regular appeal pursuant to <u>Fed. R. App. P. 28(a)</u>, <u>(b)</u>, and <u>(c)</u> , the parties to the appeal are allowed the following briefs:

- Appellant's brief,[1]

- Appellee's brief,[2] and

- Appellant's reply brief[3] (optional).

With cross appeals, the party who appealed first is considered the appellant. Fed. R. App. P. 28(h). If both parties appealed on the same day, the plaintiff is treated as the appellant unless the parties otherwise agree or the court otherwise orders. <u>Id.</u> In a cross-appeal, the appellee's brief combines an answer to the first appeal with appellee's opening arguments on the cross appeal. <u>Id. </u> The second section of the brief that asserts appellee's cross appeal should not contain arguments that are properly addressed to the opponent's arguments on its appeal—these arguments should be kept in the answering part of the brief. Otherwise, it confuses the issues. Appellant then combines in one brief its answer to appellee's cross appeal and any reply on appellant's appeal. <u>Id. </u> , <u>Rule 28(c)</u>. Appellee concludes, if it chooses, with a reply to appellant's answering brief on the cross appeal. <u>Id.</u>

Extraordinary writs require a petition for the writ, and an answer that may be filed by some or all of the respondents, if the court of appeals orders respondents to answer. Fed. R. App. P. 21. Nothing in Rule 21 pro-

---

1   In different jurisdictions, this brief might be called Appellant's Opening Brief, or Petitioner's Brief, or Petitioner's Brief on the Merits.
2   In different jurisdictions, this might be called Appellant's Answering Brief, or Appellant's Response, or Appellant's Brief in Response, or Respondent's Brief, or Respondent's Brief on the Merits.
3   In different jurisdictions, this might be called Petitioner's Reply Brief.

vides for a reply brief. <u>Id.</u> The petition serves the function of an opening brief by an appellant, although the internal structure is more like a trial level brief, as discussed in the next section.

III.   STRUCTURE OF APPELLATE BRIEFS AND APPELLATE WRITS

A.   Structure of writs of mandamus and prohibition

A petition for a writ is organized like a trial-level brief, with one critical addition: you must clearly state the grounds for the issuance of the writ up front in the introduction or, better yet, create a brand new section that will precede the introduction called "**Grounds for the Issuance of the Writ**." Sometimes the general rules of procedure or the local rules of the court require additional sections to be drafted. <u>See</u> <u>Fed. R. App. P. 21(a)(2)(B)</u>; <u>Ill. S. Ct. R. 381</u>; <u>Mo. S. Ct. R. 94.03</u>.

Do not pull any punches here. You are not going to succeed if you hide the grounds for the issuance of the writ in the argument section. You need to get the court's attention early and show why the writ must be issued, using primary controlling authority. If that kind of authority does not exist, your chances of getting the writ issued are virtually nonexistent, but do your best with what you have to work with.

B.   Structure of interlocutory appellate briefs

Interlocutory appellate briefs are organized the same way as the briefs in a regular appeal after final judgment. Of course, in the statement of the case or proceedings below sections, you should point out that the trial court certified the issue you are appealing for interlocutory appeal. Other than that, the briefs will look the same.

C.   Structure of appellate briefs in the U.S. Supreme Court

The local rules of the court in which you are practicing will specify what sections you will need to include in your briefs. As an indicative example of these requirements, we will discuss each of the sections of the brief that are required by the United States Supreme Court Rules in the order required by those rules. <u>Rule 24.1 of the U.S. Supreme Court Rules</u> requires the following sections of a brief and it requires them to be presented in this order:

- **Caption**

- **Questions Presented for Review (or Issues Presented, Points of Error, Points Relied On, Points on Review)**

- **Parties to the Proceeding**

- **Table of Contents**

- **Table of Authorities**

- **Opinions and Judgments Entered in the Case (or Opinions Below)**

- **Statement of Jurisdiction**

- **Constitutional, Treaty, Statutory, and Administrative Law Provisions**

- **Statement of the Case (or Statement of Facts and Proceedings Below)**

- **Summary of the Argument**

- **Argument**

- **Conclusion**

- **Appendices (or Addenda)**

The rules of other appellate courts might require you to draft other sections, such as:

- **Standard of Review**

- **Statement of Facts (if not included in the Statement of the Case above)**

Each of these sections deserves closer attention, as follows:

1.   Caption (on the Cover)

Appellate briefs are bound, meaning they have a stiff, card-stock cover and backing. The caption appears on the cover, and it generally takes up the entire cover of each appellate brief. The caption names the court, the docket number, the parties, the party submitting the brief, and the title of the brief. Typically the caption also will identify the court from which the appeal is taken and sometimes the name of the judge below, and the identity of the attorneys that produced the brief.

Drafting a caption should not be too much trouble. If you have never seen what the formatting of this information looks like in your jurisdiction, get your hands on a sample brief from a colleague or go to the court and ask to see some briefs that are on file. Briefs can be found on the Internet in a form that reveals the true appearance of the caption, such as the portable document format (.pdf) produced by Adobe Acrobat®. A typical format is shown in the following example:

**IN THE
UNITED STATES COURT OF APPEALS
FOR THE FOURTEENTH CIRCUIT**

No. 99-234

BRANCH LOUISIAN OF THE UNITED CHURCH OF
CHRIST THE SAVIOR,

Plaintiff-Appellant,

— *against*—

METROPOLITAN SCHOOL DISTRICT OF GOTHAM,
STATE OF NEW KENT,

Defendant-Appellant

Appeal from the United States District Court for the Central District of New Kent
Hon. Learned Foot, Judge

BRIEF FOR APPELLANT

Mary Patricia Silverberg
D. Heimlich Maneuver
Large Law Firm LLP
25 Commerce Street
Industry, TX 87878
Counsel for Appellant

2.   Questions Presented for Review (or Issues Presented, Points of Error, Points Relied On, Points for Review)

As you can see from our heading here, the terms that are used to identify this section vary greatly from jurisdiction to jurisdiction. The basic idea is to lay out in one section all of the issues or points of error that are asserted by the appellant or petitioner so that the appellate court easily can see all of the issues that will need to be resolved in the appeal. It is important to list every issue or error that will be discussed in the brief because failure to do so may be interpreted as a waiver of the unlisted arguments, and the court may disregard any issue or argument regarding an issue that is not presented in this section.

a.   Questions presented in an intermediate level appellate court

There are two basic methods for drafting the questions presented section in an intermediate level appellate court, and the local rules or case law of the court where the appeal lies will instruct you in which method to employ. The first is the "Notice" method, and the second is the "Complete Disclosure" method. The Notice method is most commonly used. It requires a description of the issue or error **in the form of a question** that mentions the specific error of the court below and the legal standards that show why it was an error. The Complete Disclosure method largely is the same, but you must add a summary of every argument regarding this issue or error that you intend to present in the brief. If you fail to summarize each legal theory and argument in a Complete Disclosure jurisdiction, you run the risk of the appellate court's ignoring the arguments you failed to list. Compare the two methods in the following examples:

Notice method: Whether the trial court erred in denying Garcia's motion for summary judgment on liability because the evidence cannot support a finding of recklessness under the <u>Dolan</u> standards?

Complete Disclosure: Whether the trial court erred in denying Garcia's motion for summary judgment on liability because the <u>Dolan</u> standards require proof that Garcia acted with careless disregard for the safety of others and the evidence shows that Garcia undertook the unloading of Fernandez's equipment in a prudent manner, Garcia used the standard methods of unloading approved by the Teamsters' Union and the National Transportation Authority, Garcia postponed the unloading for four hours because Garcia determined that the weather conditions were not safe for unloading, and Garcia undertook to unload the equipment only at the insistence of Fernandez's agent and foreman?

If the Complete Disclosure method looks awkward and overkilled, it is. **Do not use the Complete Disclosure method for your issues presented or questions presented section unless you are compelled to do so by the local rules of the court.**

The phrasing of the questions presented should be neutral, not biased in favor of your client. Do not interject argument and accusations into the issues. An appellate court does not want to read a statement laced with rhetoric that drives the parties apart from a consensus on the issues on appeal. The court would rather see a statement of the issues that both sides can agree upon so that the appellee does not have to draft a competing set of issues for review. <u>See, e.g.</u>, <u>Fed. R. Civ. P. 28(b)</u>. When appellant and appellee do not agree, this makes the court's job harder because it will have to determine what separate issues are raised that will need to be resolved in the appeal.

As discussed in the previous chapter, if the standard of review is a standard other than *de novo* review, you should weave this into the statement of the issue. For example, using the Complete Disclosure method, if the standard of review for the point of error you are drafting is "abuse of discretion," you might phrase the issue as:

> Whether the trial court abused its discretion when it denied Nunez the right to amend its petition, because under Fed. R. Civ. P. 15, leave to amend shall be freely granted when justice so requires, the amendment was required because of new facts and evidence produced to plaintiff just five days before it moved to amend the petition, and there would have been no prejudice to defendant if the amendment were to be allowed?

If the point of error is a pure issue of law, you might use the Notice method to state that the court erred as follows:

> Whether the trial court erred in its determination that New Hampshire law applied to the contract because the parties chose Rhode Island law in a valid, enforceable forum selection clause?

b.   Questions presented in a court of last resort

If you are phrasing a question presented for a court of last resort, you should draft the question so that the individual parties' names are obscured and their roles or the class of persons or entities that they represent are presented instead of the individual parties' names. This method brings to the fore the public policy implications of the dispute for the court to resolve, and reminds the court that it is not just the petitioner and the respondent who will be feeling the effects of their ruling, but all persons in similar situations. Courts of last resort are particularly sensitive to public policy concerns because they will be determining the law and establishing policy for the entire jurisdiction to follow. Consider the following examples:

> Example: I.   Whether a public school district violates a religious organization's First Amendment free speech rights by refusing to post information regarding creationism on the school district's web site created to further the educational mission of the school district?

II.   Whether a public school district violates the First Amendment's Establishment Clause by sponsoring a religious organization's web page on the school district's web site created to increase the educational opportunities for students on topics within the curriculum?

Not this: I.   Whether Metropolitan Kent School District violated Branch Louisian Church's First Amendment free speech rights by refusing to post information regarding creationism on the Metropolitan Kent School District's web site created to further the educational mission of the school district?

II.   Whether Metropolitan Kent School District would violate the First Amendment's Establishment Clause by sponsoring Branch Louisian Church's web page on the Metropolitan Kent School District's web site created to increase the educational opportunities for students on topics within the curriculum?

Note that the first two examples are phrased in the present tense. This reinforces the relevance of the issue for the court—it is a current, troublesome issue for people in similar situations as the petitioner and the respondent. The last two examples were forced to be phrased in the past tense and future tense respectively, in the one case because the party already undertook the action from which the suit arises, and in the other case because the party had not taken the action and now seeks to be heard on what would have happened if it had.

3.   Parties to the Proceeding

The rules of the U.S. Supreme Court and other courts require a section that lists all parties to the proceedings in the court whose judgment is sought to be reviewed. If all the parties happen to be listed in the caption, <u>i.e.</u>, there were few enough parties to list all their names in the caption, then the rules of the Supreme Court state that this section is unnecessary. S. Ct. Rule 24.1(b). Parent companies and non-wholly owned subsidiaries may have to be listed, too, as per <u>S. Ct. Rule 29.1</u>.

4.   Table of Contents

You have seen tables of contents before, and there is little that is unusual about a table drafted for an appellate brief. Although each individual entry in the table is single-spaced, the entries are separated from each other by two spaces, as shown in the example below. When you provide page references for the argument section, be sure to list in their entirety each of your major and minor headings and subheadings in the argument section. In this way, your table of contents can be a useful outline of your entire argument for the busy judge to look at before or during oral argument. For example:

TABLE OF CONTENTS

---

5.   Table of Authorities

This is a list in **alphabetical order** of each of the authorities you cite in the brief. A typical way to organize the table is to list cases first, then constitutional and statutory provisions, then rules and administrative law, then treatises and other secondary authorities.

You should italicize or underline the case names (whichever form you are using in the rest of your brief) because you are making a citation to a case in a court document. Jump cites (pinpoint cites, pin cites) to the internal pages of the authorities that you will refer to are **not** included. As a rule of thumb, if you cite a case on more than four pages of your brief, you may write *passim* instead of writing all of the page numbers where the case is cited (unless the rules of the court require something else). The page numbers are right justified and preceded by a string of periods. In some word processing programs such as Word Perfect this is referred to as "flush right with dot leaders."

The local rules of the appellate court may ask you to separate the authorities you are using into categories; for example: United States Supreme Court Cases; United States Court of Appeals Cases; United States District Court Cases; State Cases; Constitutions, Statutes and Administrative Regulations; Legislative History Documents; Treatises, Books, and Law Review Articles; Other Authorities. **Alphabetize** the entries in each category. A table of authorities that complies with this rule might look like the following:

TABLE OF AUTHORITIES

United States Supreme Court Cases:

Adams v. Baker, 434 U.S. 456 (1976) 13, 15

Attila v. Romans, 671 U.S. 789 (2005) ....*passim*

Rotten v. Vicious, 668 U.S. 123 (2004) 10

United States Court of Appeals Cases:

Able v. Incapable, 786 F.2d 234 (7th Cir. 1989)..............................23, 24, 27

Farnsworth v. Williston, 678 F.2d 45 (2d Cir. 1972)..6

Goldfarb v. Silverfarb, 333 F.3d 12 (11th Cir. 2005)..............................6, 8, 22

Even in the absence of a local rule, it makes sense to separate your authorities into cases; constitutions, statutes, legislative history, and administrative regulations; treatises, books, and law review articles; and miscellaneous authorities, as depicted in the following:

TABLE OF AUTHORITIES

6.   Opinions and Orders Entered in the Case (or Opinions Below)

In the rules of some courts, such as the Rules of the United States Supreme Court, a section is required that lists the citations of the opinions and orders from courts or administrative agencies from which the appeal arises. Not a very complicated section, but it is necessary nonetheless. If you do not have a full citation for the opinion or judgment, cite as much information as the record gives you and follow citation rules for the citation of slip opinions. At a minimum, you should be able to describe the opinion or judgment and cite the names of the parties, the docket number, the court, and the date of the decision. For example:

OPINIONS AND ORDERS ENTERED IN THE CASE

Order granting summary judgment in favor of defendant Jones and against plaintiff Smith. *Smith v. Jones*, No. 04-CIV-245-DNL (E.D. Cal. Jan. 14, 2005).

Opinion reversing the above order, and remanding the case to the district court for trial. *Jones v. Smith*, No. 05-258-EM (9th Cir. Aug. 24, 2005).

7.   Statement of Jurisdiction

The Statement of Jurisdiction is a brief section explaining the jurisdictional basis for the case being in the court where it is set. For example:

STATEMENT OF JURISDICTION

This Court has jurisdiction over the subject matter of this case because it is an appeal from the final judgment of the trial court entered on January 12, 2005. 28 U.S.C. § 1291; Fed. R. App. P. 4.

8.   Constitutional, Treaty, Statutory, and Administrative Law Provisions

Some court rules, including the rules of the U.S. Supreme Court, require a section that quotes the applicable constitutional, treaty, statutory, and administrative law provisions that are implicated by the problem. If the text is short—less than two pages—quote each provision verbatim in this section. If they are lengthy, cite the provision, quote the pertinent language, and then set out the full text in an appendix to the brief, as provided in S. Ct. Rule 24.1(f) .

9.   Statement of the Case (Including Statement of Facts and Proceedings Below)

In many courts, the **Proceedings Below** section is a summary of the proceedings of the case since the time it was filed to the present. You give only the highlights, such as the date of pleadings and amendments to pleadings, major dispositive motions that were granted or denied, and an explanation of how the case got to the appeals court. This section is not intended to be very argumentative, and it should be kept short. Avoid the temptation to take pot shots at the trial court judge when recounting the history of the case—you will have plenty of opportunity to point out errors in other sections of the brief.

You can draft the **Proceedings Below** so that it supports your argument by highlighting language used in the courts below, and by trying to summarize and hone down the opinions of the lower courts in such a way that you easily can trounce these opinions in the argument section if you are an appellant or petitioner, or buttress these opinions if you are a respondent. Several of the briefs we have included as sample briefs in this book have excerpted the opinion of the lower court. The skill in choosing what language and what items to highlight in this section parallels the skill you must employ in choosing what facts to highlight in the statement of facts.

In the United States Supreme Court, the rules contemplate that the **Statement of the Case** section will encompass **both** a **statement of the pertinent facts** of the case and a **statement of the proceedings below** with citations to the record or joint appendix to support the information in both sections. The facts part of this section should be drafted as a statement of facts as described in the next section, and you would draft both parts (**Statement of Facts and Proceedings Below**) under the single heading of **Statement of the Case** with sub-headings to indicate where the **Statement of Facts** section ends and **Proceedings Below** section begins.

10.   Statement of Facts

The statement of facts presents a summary of the historical facts of the case that led up to the date that the case was filed. Since the facts are very important in any appeal, you should take the time to draft them in such a way that your client's position looks strong, by using crisp, active language and strong nouns, adjectives, and adverbs, and by giving appropriate detail to facts that support and sustain your arguments, and limiting the discussion of relevant facts that are detrimental to your arguments. Certainly, there is no need to raise and discuss facts that you believe are irrelevant to the issues on appeal from both your client's and your opponent's perspective, unless you are going to take the time in the argument to demonstrate why certain negative facts are irrelevant. The authors of the **sample briefs** at the end of this chapter have attempted to accomplish these goals with varying degrees of success. Read these samples critically, and note our annotations.

a.   Persuasive facts vs. argument

Two principles are at war in drafting the statement of facts. First, the court of appeals would like you to state just the relevant facts, with no argument or innuendo. See Fed. R. App. P. 28(a)(4); Local Rules of the U.S. Ct. App. 7th Cir., Rule 28(d)(1); Il. S. Ct. R. 341(e)(6). Indeed, the local rules of the court of appeals may strictly limit the amount of argument or "bias" that you can interject into the facts. E.g., Local Rules of the U.S. Ct. App. 7th Cir., Rule 28(d)(1); Il. S. Ct. R. 341(e)(6). Even if the local rules do not prohibit argument or comment on the facts, it is advisable to avoid argumentative language and to eliminate any legal conclusions in the facts.

Factual Conclusions:

The truck ***was going fast*** when it approached the curve.

The driver had trouble steering **because** the truck began to rock and sway.

The trailer became detached from the tractor **because** the connector pin was sheared off.

Legal Conclusions:

The truck driver was **reckless** for driving at that speed.

The truck driver **caused** the trailer to become detached by his **driving too fast** in the curve.

He **caused** the truck to become **too unstable to control.**

The driver was **negligent** in attempting to take the turn at that speed.

However, the second principle is that a good advocate wants a statement of facts that will persuade the judges to rule in the lawyer's favor as soon as they finish reading the facts. Satisfying both ends requires careful attention to accuracy and advocacy.

b.   Accuracy

Accuracy is paramount. You cannot win by misstating facts. If your statement sounds persuasive but your opponent identifies errors or pokes holes in what you told the court, your chances of success will be severely damaged. If evidence is contested, do not recite it as if it were a fact. Give a fair account of the testimony and supporting exhibits, and if you can show why other testimony should be believed or not believed, do so, but do not present one side's witnesses as the only story that was told.

One important part of the requirement of accuracy is to draw only the most logical and most reasonable inferences from the facts in the record.

- *Example:*   If a commission called for a sculpture to
be created in two weeks time, and the facts
indicate that the artist completed the work
in one week, it would be completely safe to
point out that the artist did the work "in half
the time anticipated by the parties in their
contract." It would not necessarily be fair to
say that the artist did the work "quickly," and
it certainly would not be fair to infer that the
artist "rushed" the job. "Rushing" implies a
state of mind, and nothing in the facts we
have revealed shows the artist's state of mind.
Performing a commission in half the allotted
time is not automatically rushing; you do not
have enough facts to make that inference.
Perhaps the artist routinely does these works
in a single day, and one week is a luxurious
amount of time.

If the work turned out to be unacceptable to
the client—the client found it to be "ugly" and
"unappealing"—you could state that "the artist
only used half of the allotted time to produce
the sculpture, and wound up producing a
work that was ugly and unappealing to the
client." You could not draw the inference
that the artist was "sloppy" or "careless" in
producing the work, and certainly could not
infer that the artist was "negligent" or "reckless"
by producing the work in half the allotted
time. Aside from the problem that these are
legal conclusions, you do not have enough
facts about the artist, her state of mind, her
expertise, her prior work production methods,
and a host of other factual information that
would affect that inference. All you can say is
that she produced the work in half the allotted
time, and the work was unacceptable to the
client because the client found it to be ugly and
unappealing.

Missing information from the record necessarily will limit the kind of inferences you logically can draw. Do not get caught up in a spirit of advocacy and fill in details that affect the logical limits of the facts in the record.

• *Example:*   If the record states that the commission required the sculpture to be 50% titanium, and tests show that it is less than 50% titanium, you could draw the inference that the sculpture produced "does not meet the terms of the contract," or "does not contain the percentage of titanium that the parties specified in the contract." You cannot automatically draw the inference that the artist "breached the contract." Breach, a legal conclusion, depends on a host of factors relating to performance. The artist may have a lawful excuse or justification for his performance. You cannot state that the artist "purposefully" or "intentionally" left titanium out of the sculpture. You simply do not know what the artist's state of mind was. You only can state exactly what the facts state: "The artist produced a sculpture that did not contain the percentage of titanium that was specified in the parties' agreement."

If you find out additional facts, you might be able to draw other inferences. If you discover that the price of titanium doubled the day after the commission was signed, you now can state that "the price of titanium doubled the day after the commission was signed, and one week later, the artist delivered a work that did not contain the percentage of titanium specified by the parties in their contract." You still cannot infer that the artist "breached" or "purposefully" or "intentionally" left titanium out of the sculpture.

c. Highlighting good facts and downplaying bad facts

You can balance the separate duties of accuracy and advocacy with more subtle but still effective methods. The same set of facts can be drafted differently in ways that better support the client's position and hinder the opponent's. Fed. R. App. P. 28 requires that you present the facts relevant to the issues on appeal. That standard offers considerable latitude in choosing *what* to recite. You can report both favorable and unfavorable facts on a given point, while still presenting the facts in the best possible light for your client.

You can highlight facts with the amount of detail you present, the sequence in which you present them, and your own careful choice of words. Instead of using neutral words, slant the facts with language that carries overtones. Avoid the passive tense and use strong engaging verbs and descriptive nouns and adjectives in sections that discuss facts favorable to your client, and do the opposite in sections containing facts unfavorable to your client.

- *Example 1 - Common Facts:* Client Jones was going 60 m.p.h. in a 45 m.p.h. zone on his way to his therapist, a doctor of psychology. He was late. The road was wet. A poodle came out from behind a parked car and moved into the road in front of him. Jones swerved, his car slid out of control, and he hit a parked car owned by plaintiff.

  Appellant's Version: Defendant was late for an appointment with his psycho-therapist and was speeding at 60 m.p.h. on rain slick pavement in a 45 m.p.h. zone. A poodle walked into the path of Defendant's speeding car, and Defendant swerved and sent his car spinning out of control. Defendant then smashed his car into the back of plaintiff Smith's parked car.

  Appellee's Version: Mr. Jones was proceeding to an important appointment. A dog jumped out in front of him taking him completely by surprise. In an effort to avoid hitting the dog, he turned the wheel quickly but the car slid on the damp pavement and came into contact with the plaintiff's car.

- ***Example 2 - Common Facts:*** ABC Corp. laid off thirteen workers in a reduction in force (RIF). ABC used a business productivity formula. Six of the workers who were laid off were over the age of 40, four of these were women. Four more who were laid off were minorities, two of whom were women. Mr. Smith, a white male age 37, made the final decision of whom to lay off.

Appellant's Version: ABC's most recent RIF was spearheaded by Cliff Smith, a white male. Smith targeted women, minorities, and workers whose age was over 40 for ten of his thirteen cuts. When he fired six elderly workers, he made sure four of them were women, and when he singled out four minorities for firing, he made sure half of them were women. Smith used a formula that ensured that these people could be disposed of with the excuse of increasing productivity.

Appellee's Version: ABC was forced by competitive economic factors to lay off thirteen workers. A formula was used based on a worker's years of service, evaluation grades, and amount of contract revenue generated in the last five years. The thirteen lowest performing workers were laid off.

d.   Level of detail

Although the level of detail is one way to highlight important and helpful facts, you can go overboard with too much detail. In a fact intensive appeal, it sometimes is hard to mention all the facts in the statement of facts because it would produce a facts section that is the same length as the argument. In general, ask yourself whether every detail in your recital of the facts is needed. Trial lawyers writing or editing briefs on appeal are especially prone to include facts that seemed important at trial but have little or nothing to do with the issues on appeal. Try to get these weeded out before you send it to the court.

- ***Good:***   Defendant Jones was late for an appointment with his psycho-therapist and was speeding at 60 m.p.h. on rain slick pavement in a 45 m.p.h. zone. A poodle walked into the path of Defendant's speeding car, and Defendant swerved and sent his car spinning out of control. Defendant then smashed his car into the back of plaintiff Smith's parked car.

- **Not this:**   Defendant Jones was running approximately eight minutes late for his appointment with his psycho-therapist, Dr. Will Shrinker. He went speeding along on his way to Dr. Shrinker's office on Mulberry Lane, a mixed business and residential street with a 45 m.p.h. speed limit. He was traveling at an average speed of 60 m.p.h. as confirmed by a passive police monitoring unit on Mulberry Lane that Jones passed by; his speed also was generally confirmed by two eye witnesses at the scene, Mrs. Vera Stigmatism and Mr. Esau Nothing. At some point soon after passing by the monitoring unit, a poodle walked out into the path of Defendant's speeding car. Defendant took action immediately. He swerved the car to the left, and sent his car spinning out of control. There is no indication that he was able to regain control of the car. Jones' car spun out of control for more than two seconds, again, as confirmed by Mrs. Stigmatism and Mr. Nothing. Defendant then smashed his car into the back of plaintiff Smith's parked car. No one witnessed the actions of the poodle after Jones swerved away from it, but the poodle was unharmed in the incident.

The details in the second example above may be interesting, but it is unlikely that they will have any effect on the appeal unless this interchange of the car sliding on the wet road and the collision with the parked car is the only incident from which the appeal arises. If this incident is a tiny part of a much bigger case, and if these details are not relevant for the particular purpose of proving a point of error charged to the lower court, then leave them out. They will wear out your reader and squander her attention span.

e.   Divide facts with subheadings

When you have a lot of facts that need to be presented, internal subheadings and topical groupings can help to divide up the facts into more manageable and digestible chunks. Subheadings allow you to focus on separate issues in the facts, presenting only the facts that go with that issue. This paragraph should remind you that you need not present the facts in strict chronological order if that order does little to highlight the important facts of your client's case.

f.   Citations to the record

Every fact must be referenced by citation to the record. The appeals court is likely to ignore any facts that are not supported by a citation to the record. Rule 24 of the Supreme Court Rules provides for a cite to the joint appendix, e.g., App. 12, or to the record, e.g., Record 12. Some practitioners place the citations inside parentheses but the rules do not require this method.

- **Examples:**   The contract was signed on August 13, 2005 (Record 132, ¶ 12).

    Jones testified that he called the police at 10:00 a.m., App. 12, but the police dispatcher records indicate that the call from Jones was received at 10:42 a.m. Plaintiff's Ex. 44, App. 14, ¶ 4.

Other appellate court rules may allow you to shorten the citation to the record to (R. pg. #) or (R-pg. #) as in (R.23) or (R-23), and citations to the joint appendix as (J.A. pg. #) or (JA-pg. #) as in (J.A. 133) or (JA-133).

g.   Party names

Describe parties consistently throughout the facts. Do not switch from calling your client "the tenant," to "plaintiff," to "Sam Smith Slaughterhouse Company." Fed. R. App. P. 28(d) and most appellate judges we have talked to discourage the use of such generic labels as "appellant" and "appellee." Some brief writers believe that it is it acceptable to use the designations used in the trial court (plaintiff, defendant), but we do not agree that this practice promotes the necessary clarity and individuality that you are seeking to achieve in your brief. The authors believe that using the actual names of the parties is the best practice: "McMannis," "Allied Widgets," "Governor Black." Next best is to use descriptive terms, such as "the employer," "the driver," "the taxpayer," "the ship," and so forth.

h. Abbreviations and acronyms

Use abbreviations and acronyms cautiously. You and your client may understand an acronym identifying a party, an agency, a group, a set of laws or regulations, or other items described in the facts, but using abbreviations or acronyms that are not self-explanatory to the court is like using a secret code that taxes the ability and patience of the judges. Most judges know that ACLU refers to the American Civil Liberties Union and RICO refers to the Racketeer Influenced and Corrupt Organizations Act, but how many judges know that FIFRA refers to the Federal Insecticide, Fungicide, and Rodenticide Act or COBRA refers to the Comprehensive Omnibus Budget Reconciliation Act? Be kind to your readers and define all abbreviations and acronyms up front and use them consistently throughout your brief.

i. Tell your client's story

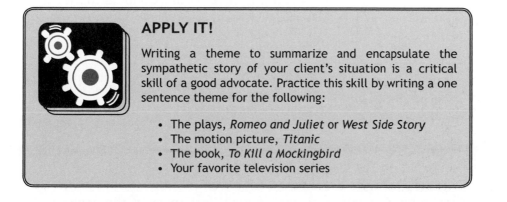

APPLY IT!

Writing a theme to summarize and encapsulate the sympathetic story of your client's situation is a critical skill of a good advocate. Practice this skill by writing a one sentence theme for the following:

- The plays, *Romeo and Juliet* or *West Side Story*
- The motion picture, *Titanic*
- The book, *To Kill a Mockingbird*
- Your favorite television series

The best possible statement of facts tells a story in which your client is a character, the plot is a straight-forward recounting in lay person's terms of what happened to your client and the opponent and other characters, and the conflict and resolution (if any) is one that shows why your client must win. The moral of the story is the theme of your case, and it should be able to be stated in a single sentence no matter how long it takes you to boil the case down to a single sentence theme. As with most good stories, the reader (the court) should be pulled into it so that they care what happens to the main character (your client) and are eager to know what happens next until they get to the end of the story. Critically evaluate the stories told by the authors of the **sample briefs** at the end of this chapter and decide for yourselves what stories seem the most effective.

11.　Standard of Review

In some jurisdictions, the court of appeals' local rules require you to draft a short section laying out what you have determined to be the appropriate standard of review for each issue that is raised on appeal, and stating your legal support for that determination. <u>E.g.</u>, <u>Alaska R. App. P. 212(c)(1)(h)</u>; <u>Haw. R. App. P. 28(b)(5)</u>. In other courts, you will state the standard of review for each point after you list the point in the issues presented section or incorporate the discussion into the argument section, <u>see</u> <u>Fed. R. App. P. 28(a)(6)</u>; <u>Ariz. R. Civ. App. P. 13(a)(6)</u>; <u>Ga. Ct. App. R. 27(a)(3)</u>, <u>27(b)(2)</u>, so there will be no separate standard of review section.

If the standard of review is obvious, limit the discussion to one sentence for each point of error, and cite one or two powerful authorities that conclusively state the standard. If there is some doubt as to the standard (which might be the case with mixed issues of law and fact), present a short argument with citations to relevant and analogous authority to argue in favor of the standard that benefits your client. Even in this latter situation, you should limit the argument to one or two pages except in the most unusual and complicated of circumstances.

12.　Summary of Argument

Federal appellate courts, including the United States Supreme Court, require a separate section entitled "**Summary of the Argument**" that precedes the argument section. <u>Fed. R. App. P. 28(a)(5)</u>; <u>S. Ct. Rule 24.1(h)</u>. The drafters of the rule have precluded litigants from simply stringing their argument headings together into roughly connected paragraphs, so avoid the temptation. Instead, make a clear and succinct presentation of the points on review and your arguments on these points, with citation only to the most critical authorities that support your arguments.

Even if the local rules do not limit your pages in this section, we would avoid going over three pages because the judges still have to read your argument section, and you do not want to wear them out with unnecessary repetition, redundancy, duplication, saying the same thing over and over again (see what we mean?).

The reader gets to the Summary first, so even if you draft it second, make it powerful and memorable. That which comes first counts more in legal writing. Judges in a hurry may read only the summary of the argument, not the whole argument section. It definitely is not a section to ignore until the day before the brief is due.

13.   Argument

We have now worked our way to the argument section. You must craft the argument with careful attention to organization, citation to authority, as well as the substance of the legal arguments you make. This topic is covered at length in section IV below.

14.   Conclusion

Fed. R. App. P. 28(a)(7) requires a short conclusion describing the precise relief sought. The usual question is whether the conclusion should include anything else. The answer typically is "no."

Be as specific as possible about the relief you want. Your request may be in the alternative. The court may deny specific relief that you fail to request. Your request for relief may need some explanation in the argument. If, for instance, you are asking for reversal and remand for the limited purpose of entering judgment in a specified amount, you will need to explain why further evidence is not needed on the question of damages. As a general rule, whenever you seek a remand only for limited purposes, you will need to explain the reasons behind your proposed limits. That explanation belongs in the argument section.

Aside from relief requested, brief writers frequently are tempted to conclude with some rhetoric that does not fit into the disciplined analysis of your argument section. Appellate courts will accept this kind of "traditional" conclusion with appropriate summary and reemphasizing of the arguments you raised. The rule does not forbid this, other than to require that the conclusion be short. If you can keep it brief, a zinger at the end does not hurt. Whether it helps is a matter of some doubt. If your brief has not been persuasive, a rhetorical closing obviously will not save it. Most last-minute points worth making are better included in the argument. You need not worry about coming up with a clever closing—if they did not get it before, they probably will not get it now in the conclusion.

15.   Appendices

Sometimes the court requires or allows you include an appendix containing a few choice items—key documents, exhibits, testimony, the full text of statutory and constitutional provisions, unpublished opinions (if the local rules allow you to cite them at all), items such as the contract or instrument sued upon, the final judgment, the notice of appeal, and other important or frequently cited materials. You should be careful about putting things other than the required items into an appendix. You do not want to make the brief twice as fat by virtue of an appendix. But a careful selection can be a great aid to the court by placing the most important documents and authorities at the judges' fingertips.

IV.   DRAFTING THE ARGUMENT

The TREAT format (discussed earlier and in <u>Appendix A</u>) applies in the argument section, and you should use your questions presented or points of error <u>Thesis</u> statements as your major headings, even if the local rules and practices require them to be excessively wordy. Use minor <u>Thesis</u> headings to guide the reader through the sub-issues that require separate TREAT.

A.   Use argumentative thesis headings.

Thesis headings should be meaningful so that they can provide a useful summary of your argument to a judge that is skimming your argument section. A good thesis heading not only reveals a conclusion but provides the "because" part—the legal principles and facts that lead up to the conclusion. For example, the following are good argumentative thesis headings:

- **Examples** of proper thesis headings in the argument

    A.   The trial court erred in its determination that Bolling provoked the dog prior to the attack because Bolling did not directly attack or threaten the dog as required under Illinois law.

    B.   The trial court erred in holding that Bolling was trespassing because Bolling was acting peacefully in a place where he had a lawful right to be when he walked on a public sidewalk at Alden Hall without causing any noisy disturbance.

    C.   The trial court erred in holding that provocation bars Bolling's recovery because the dog's attack on Bolling was vicious and disproportionate to the dusting of snow the Dog received from Bolling.

- The following are **not** good headings:

    A.   Lack of Provocation

    B.   Bolling was acting peacefully in a place where he had a lawful right to be.

    C.   The dog's attack was disproportionate.

These last three examples do not suggest enough of the facts and principles of the law to make the headings useful, and the first of these three does not even tell the author's conclusion about the topic. Do not waste a heading by writing something like these. Let your headings be a quick summary of your argument if read one right after the other.

FOOD FOR THOUGHT

Public policy plays a role in most appeals. Unlike trial court decisions, appellate court decisions are binding authority; the decisions of the court of last resort of the jurisdiction are binding on every lower court in that jurisdiction. Therefore, appellate courts and especially courts of last resort pay attention to the effect of their rulings not only on the parties before them but on society as a whole. Most courts want the rulings that they establish to be supported not only by the letter of the law but also by the public policy that underlies the law. Therefore, your role as an advocate in an appeal is to make sure you make arguments with regard and reference to how your arguments advance the public policies implicated by your appeal.

B.   Policy counts more on appeal, and precedent becomes a two-way street

In the argument, as in many of the other sections discussed above, you must bear in mind that policy plays a greater role in appellate courts' reasoning, especially in the courts of last resort. Appellate courts do not worry just about following precedent, they have to worry about making it. Appellate courts have to consider the here and now of your case plus the effect that their ruling will have on future cases. You should write briefs with that in mind. If you spend too much effort developing the arguments and equities of your client's position, you may neglect to consider the effect what you are arguing will have on future cases. You should take the time in the discussion of each major issue raised on appeal to address public policy and precedential implications of the arguments you are raising. Usually, the page limits afforded on appeals are ample enough to allow for this, and it may help you persuade more judges of the propriety of your positions even prior to oral argument when the court can drill you in the policies affected by your arguments.

In similar fashion, you might discuss how the case fits into the broader stream of relevant decisions. Fit your appeal into a broader framework of the law and the policies behind the law. Appellate judges are more comfortable applying settled principles than deciding issues of first impression. Many appeals raise something new, but it does not benefit appellant to emphasize that. The law is built on precedent. It seeks the simple and established and avoids the unfamiliar. This means that demonstrating at length the novelty or complexity of your position rarely will help. Make the novel proposition seem familiar or, at most, a natural extension of something that is clearly accepted. The more you can fit your case into established principles, the greater your chance of success.

Start at a logical beginning for the arguments you raise. The page limits generally allow you to present a discussion of the stepping stone principles, both historical steps and steps of a logical progression that lead up to the present principles of the law you are asserting. Too many briefs start in the middle of a legal analysis, rather than building from broad general principles to the specific. Do not go back to the first day or even first semester of contracts, but lay a settled backdrop down before you start throwing the colorful paint around. Put your case into a broader, established legal context first so that judges understand where you are starting. From that they will quickly grasp where you are heading.

C.   The continuing benefits of <u>explanatory synthesis</u>

Unless you have controlling precedent that exactly matches your client's case, you should emphasize **principles**, not **cases**. This is another way of looking at the benefits of <u>explanatory synthesis</u>. Individual cases may not say everything you need them to say on exactly what you need them to cover. If you find the magic, controlling, "on all fours" case, use it, but if you do not, you still can convince the court that your appeal fits the broader principles of the law that are illustrated by existing authorities. Synthesize the existing decisions to show how they fit this broader principle. Your argument should show that the cases are not the law itself, but simply illustrations of the law.

If your appeal raises a question of statutory construction, your search for broader principles focuses on what you claim is the statute's objective. Use legislative history to illustrate it. Buttress your construction with interpretations or applications by the implementing agency, and look to the commentators in treatises and law review articles. Whatever the issue, this effort is devoted to assuring the judges that you are not trying to sell them some wild new scheme, but simply that your case fits comfortably into the existing law as you have restated it in plain, straightforward terms.

D.   Be assertive rather than critical about the court below and your opponent's arguments, and remember the standard of review

Too many briefs just try to take pot-shots at the trial judge and the opponents. Even if the judge or opposing counsel have made blatant errors, you first should focus your efforts on what legal principles should apply to the case and only second on what the trial judge or your opponent did wrong. The judges on appeal are far more interested in how to reach and justify the right result. In fact, ad hominem attacks easily can turn the court against you.

You must deal fairly but convincingly with unfavorable authority. We previously have discussed the need to distinguish potentially controlling, negative authority and the decision whether (and **where**) to anticipate and handle negative persuasive authority. Add to that discussion the perception that at the appellate court level, very few dead flies in the bowl of appellate soup are going to go unnoticed. If your opponent does not find the bad case, the judges' clerks probably will. Thus, having the first word on a troublesome authority can make you look upright and truthful and gives you the chance to dull the effect of the authority before your opponent runs amok with it. That said, what is truly "adverse" can be a matter of interpretation. You really need to consider whether the authority is controlling (or just persuasive) and whether your facts are in some way distinguishable.

Finally, remember the standard of review when you are drafting your headings and the rest of the argument section. The standard of review is the keystone to court of appeals decision-making, so you must tailor your argument to it. When the standard is abuse of discretion, for example, it does no good to make arguments that apply only if the court were reviewing a question *de novo*. Define how much discretion is allowed under the law, and argue that the judge exceeded that level using authorities that actually found a violation of the applicable standard.

E.   Minimize alternative arguments

Although there is no limit to the number of good arguments you raise (within reason), alternative arguments that simply crowd the brief with imaginative possibilities choke off the best arguments and drown your better arguments in a sea of words. Such scattergun tactics rarely are effective and can dilute your major points. Your time, energy, and space is better spent bolstering your main arguments.

F.   As in other litigation documents, limit the use of footnotes, overuse of emphasis, and lengthy quotes

Limit footnotes if you can, and make sure you follow the rules of your jurisdiction. For example, sometimes the court will say that nothing **argumentative** can be in a footnote (i.e., nothing that presents part of the legal support for one of your arguments, as opposed to additional facts, statistics, or a side note of interest about something). Even if the local rules allow you to put argument in footnotes, you run the risk of the argument going unnoticed. Many judges skip footnotes completely, and others will not consider legal arguments mentioned only in footnotes.

Do not stress (underline, bold, italicize) too much in your text—you will stress out the judges! Stated otherwise: no one likes a lawyer who is constantly shouting. Overdoing your underlining or other emphasis has that same effect. Putting key words in all capitals and using exclamation points are artificial devices. Sparing use of underlining or italicizing is useful to highlight key words, but effective emphasis depends on the content and arrangement of your text.

Shorten your quotes. No one likes long quotes for at least three reasons: (1) long quotes are too boring and many readers skip over them; (2) the reader knows you are going to (and should) explain the significance of the quote anyway; and (3) readers want to hear what *you* have to say. So, distill long quotes down to their essential point and avoid long descriptions of cases.

V.   DRAFTING AN ANSWERING BRIEF

The most important point for an appellee is to make an affirmative case first before you start attacking the appellant's. This is a critical piece of advice: as the appellee, you do not want to limit yourself to the playing field that the appellant has set out. Rather, you should craft your own playing field even though you inevitably will be responding to your opponent along the way.

Accordingly, the same points made in discussing appellant's strategy (above) fit here, too: position your case into a broader framework. You want to set the playing field rather than accept the one set by your opponent. If you do a better job of that than your opponent, then when you start responding to specific arguments you can do so from a position of strength.

Storytelling in the statement of facts is as important for appellee as it is for appellant, and more so if the appellant has done a good job getting out its side of the story. If your opponent told a good story in her opening brief, you might acknowledge it, but you must immediately turn the tables around to your side: "Appellant told a good story about XYZ. Now here is the rest of the story." At best you will pull the court's attention and concern away from your opponent and on to your client. At least you should make sure the court is returned to the middle ground, neutral territory, not swayed by the sympathies of either side. This task will be difficult if your opponent was an excellent storyteller, but you must be a better one.

First, you should consider (as always) your "theory of the case," meaning that you want to tell the story of the facts in a way that most benefits your client. Do not proceed chronologically if that is not advantageous to your side. Rather, come up with a narrative of the events that benefits your side.

Second, in developing your analytical framework, it will help if you can synthesize the broad principles in a way that highlights the novelty of the appellant's position. As mentioned before, appellate judges generally take more comfort in fitting cases into established principles than in breaking new ground. If you can show that appellant is trying to turn the law on its head, you have an excellent chance of winning.

When you start responding to specific arguments, you certainly have the option to follow the sequence of issues used by appellant, and to have at them one by one. But this is *rarely* the best approach, and if you do so you very well are letting your opponent set the structural stage for the argument (rather than you). Appellant's third best point might be your best point, and appellant's best point is likely to be your worst point. It is more important to present your best point first and next best point second than it is to limit your brief to the order picked out by your opponent.

What is most important, though, is to make sure you answer all of appellant's arguments. Even if your opponent has raised an argument that obviously lacks merit, you should explain why that's so. Do not leave the court guessing whether you intended to concede something, or force the court to undertake independent research on why appellant's last two arguments should fail, simply because you failed to address them.

In addition, consider the following:

- Never assume that appellant has laid the necessary foundation for its arguments. Go through a mental checklist on each argument: Did appellant preserve this point below? Are the grounds appellant is advancing now for overturning an evidentiary ruling the same ones it offered below? Is the legal theory appellant advances now the same one presented below? If not, stress that before you even consider a response on the merits.

- If the appellant seems to have scored points by showing defects in the trial court's approach, remind the court of appeals that it is reviewing the lower court's result, not its reasoning. It can affirm on any basis supported by the law. If you have focused your brief on what should be the controlling principles, you need not worry about defending the lower court's faulty reasoning.

Appellees have an opportunity to call the court's attention to shortcomings in appellant's brief—an inference stated as a fact, an adverse case ignored, and so forth. The tendency is to overdo these comments—as if an appeal were a boxing match where you get a point for every punch you land on your opponent. Appeals do not work this way, so keep these comments to a minimum, and stress only those that are substantial. Your goal is to affirm the district court opinion in your favor, not eviscerate your opponent.

In rare instances, appellee may want to skip the jurisdictional statement, statement of the issues presented for review, statement of facts, statement of the case (or proceedings below), and the statement of the standard(s) of review (unless, of course, appellee is dissatisfied with appellant's statements of them). This can pose something of a dilemma, especially with the statements of issues or facts. You may find nothing specifically wrong with appellant's statements except their emphasis and implications. Should you accept them for fear the court of appeals will think you a nit-picker? Should you restate them in their entirety, or simply those parts you especially dislike?

You are not required to prove that appellant's statements are *wrong* before you assert that your own position is *right*. Whether you submit an entire restatement or portions of one will depend on how much needs restating. If your opponent did a decent job of telling its story in the statement of facts, you really must do your best to tell a better story or at least tell "the rest of the story" to restore equilibrium in the case. If your opponent's facts section was merely mundane, however, you need not go to great lengths to correct the record, but you should take advantage of the situation and tell your own story. Do not miss out on the chance to get the court to care about your client so that it will be happy to listen to your legal arguments that provide the means to the end of victory for your client.

VI.   DRAFTING THE REPLY BRIEF

Appellant's right to reply is a valuable right—but it is not always permitted or granted. Do not squander it by rehashing or repeating arguments already covered in your opening brief. Having the last word does not necessarily have a tremendous effect on the appeal because the judges are likely to wait until the parties have filed all their briefs and then read them all together. Appellant should use its right of reply to focus the appeal *down to its core.* You know what you said in your opening brief; you now see what appellee has said in response. Refine the issues in light of both, just as you would do in a rebuttal argument. A reply brief is the best vehicle for narrowing the true issues, so sharpen the focus. Now is your chance to tell the court what this appeal is really all about. If appellee did not answer all the issues raised in your opening brief, make the most of that. The reply is your chance to put the issues in their starkest terms that are favorable to your client.

Sometimes you also must use your reply for damage control. If appellee has hurt your position, you must do what you can to repair it. Whatever you do, do not try to interject new issues in your reply. Not only will the court likely ignore them, the judges also will be irritated that you tried to sneak something in without giving your opponent a chance to respond. If something new (a case, statute, rule, regulation, etc.) has come up that the court should know about, use the procedure for submitting supplemental authorities rather than putting it in your reply brief. That way you do not co-mingle the separate functions of replying and submitting supplemental authorities.

If under the rules you are operating, a reply brief is "optional," we cannot fathom why you would not want to submit one. Unless the local rules prohibit it, plan to file a reply (even if it is only two or three pages).

VII.   SAMPLE APPELLATE BRIEFS

The samples that follow are four student briefs. These are above average briefs that most likely would receive an "A" grade in our classes. Nevertheless, they are not perfect and we offer them not as models for you to copy or emulate, but only as samples to study and learn from. We have annotated the first two briefs with our comments and questions—the annotations appear in the electronic version of the book. The last two samples are presented without annotations or other interruptions.

Sample 1

**IN THE
SUPREME COURT OF THE STATE OF NEW YORK
APPELLATE DIVISION
FIRST DEPARTMENT**

No. 234/06

ERNO NUSSENZWEIG,

Appellant,

v.

PHILIP-LORCA DICORCIA and PACE/MACGILL, INC.

Appellees.

Appeal from the New York Supreme Court,
New York County

BRIEF FOR APPELLANT

QUESTIONS PRESENTED FOR REVIEW

1. Whether a photograph of a non-public figure
    taken <u>surreptitiously</u> by a professional
    photographer on a public street has a
    valid claim to First Amendment protection
    as artistic expression against the N.Y.
    Civ. Rights Law § 51 <u>right to privacy</u>
    <u>claim of the non-public figure</u> when the
    photograph has undergone edits and
    has been exhibited and sold by the
    photographer at a commercial art gallery?

2. Whether a professional photographer's
    nonconsensual use of a non-public
    person's photograph in a variety of
    widely disseminated materials advertising
    the display and sale of photographer's
    work is protected from the non-public
    figure's N.Y. Civ. Rights Law § 51 right
    to privacy claim as <u>an advertising use</u>
    <u>incidental or ancillary to a primary</u>
    <u>use where the primary use is considered</u>
    <u>symbolic speech?</u>

TABLE OF CONTENTS

TABLE OF AUTHORITIES

Other State and Federal Cases:

Constitutions and Statutes:

Secondary Authorities:

STATEMENT OF JURISDICTION

Appellant Nussenzweig has taken this appeal as of right from final judgment granting summary judgment to appellee diCorcia entered by the Supreme Court of the State of New York, New York County on February 16, 2006. This court has jurisdiction to hear an appeal taken of right from any final judgment of the Supreme Court of the State of New York. N.Y. C.P.L.R. 5701(a)(1) (McKinney 2006).

STANDARD OF REVIEW

The standard of review of an order granting summary judgment is a de novo standard of review. *See Sillman v. Twentieth Century Fox Film Corp.*, 144 N.E.2d 387, 392 (N.Y. 1957). A motion for summary judgment should be granted only where, "upon the papers and proofs presented, the cause of action or defense shall be established sufficiently to warrant the court as a matter of law in directing judgment in favor of any party." N.Y. C.P.L.R. 3212(b) (McKinney 2006). A motion for summary judgment should be denied upon a showing of any genuine, triable issues of fact. *S.J. Capellin Assoc., Inc. v. Globe Mfg. Corp.,* 313 N.E.2d 776, 777 (N.Y. 1974). In considering, therefore, whether summary judgment was properly granted, the question is whether or not there exists any triable or arguable issue of fact. *Sillman,* 144 N.E.2d at 392.

STATEMENT OF THE CASE

Statement of Facts

Appellant Erno Nussenzweig ("Nussenzweig") was, on an <u>unspecified day sometime between 1999 and 2001</u>, walking through Times Square in New York in conduct of his normal course of business when, without his knowledge or consent, he was photographed by appellee Philip-Lorca diCorcia ("diCorcia") (R.4-5). Unknown to Nussenzweig at the time, his picture was to become a part of a collection of photographs taken by diCorcia, a professional photographer who <u>surreptitiously</u> took the pictures of random private citizens as they walked through Times

Square in New York City (R.4). To accomplish
this, he waited to take the photograph until
the unsuspecting subject walked across the
spot on the sidewalk which he had chosen and
artificially illuminated (R.4).

Once he had enough of the photos, he
selected and edited some 17 of the pictures,
one of which was "Head No. 13," the photograph
of Nussenzweig (R.12, Exhibit 1), and published
them at the gallery of appellee Pace/MacGill,
Inc. in a collection titled "HEADS" (R.4). In
addition to taking, producing, and exhibiting
these photos, diCorcia published and
distributed a catalogue, which included "Head
No. 13," advertising the "HEADS" collection
(R.5). DiCorcia eventually sold for a price
of between $20,000 and $30,000 all ten of the
copies of "Head No. 13" which he produced
(R.6). The commercial objective and profitable
use of the "HEADS" collection is not disputed
(R.10). At no time did diCorcia seek or
obtain the permission from any of his subjects
to take or use these photos from any of his
subjects (R.4). Upon finally learning of these

activities, sometime in 2005, Nussenzweig immediately contacted diCorcia regarding the use of his photo and at which time diCorcia informed him that he intended to continue exhibiting "Head No. 13" (R.6).

Nussenzweig is an Orthodox Hasidic Jew and a member of the Klausenberg sect, a group who suffered particular persecution in Nazi-held Europe during World War II (R.6). His offense at diCorcia's use of his photograph in this manner is a product of his deeply held personal and religious convictions that such a public or commercial use of his image violates the Biblical prohibition against graven images (R.6). Having been informed that diCorcia would not withdraw "Head No. 13" from exhibit or sale in deference to his request, Nussenzweig sought to protect his right to privacy through legal means, instituting the instant action under N.Y. Civ. Rights Law § 51 (McKinney 2006) (R.6).

Proceedings Below

Nussenzweig filed his complaint in the

Supreme Court of the State of New York, New
York County (R.3). Following the filing
of the complaint, the filing of diCorcia's
answer and the filing of an amended complaint
by Nussenzweig, diCorcia moved for summary
judgment pursuant to N.Y. C.P.L.R. 3212,
seeking dismissal of the amended complaint
(R.3). The court, applying the standard that
a claim presenting only issues of law should
be resolved by the court without a trial,
Nussenzweig v. DiCorcia, No. 108446/05, slip
op. at 4 (N.Y. Sup. Ct. N.Y. County Feb. 16,
2006), granted summary judgment, holding that
Nussenzweig had failed to state a cause of
action. *Id.* at 11.

The order and opinion of the trial court
is reported as a slip opinion as *Nussenzweig
v. DiCorcia*, No. 108446/05 (N.Y. Sup. Ct. N.Y.
County Feb. 16, 2006).

SUMMARY OF THE ARGUMENT

The Appellate Division, First Department should reverse the trial court's ruling granting summary judgment for diCorcia and should remand the matter with instructions for consideration of the triable issues of fact which remain. In taking, exhibiting, and selling Nussenzweig's photo without consent and for his own benefit, diCorcia violated Nussenzweig's right to privacy. An intensely private individual whose personal and religious beliefs were violated by this public and commercial use of his image, Nussenzweig brought suit under N.Y. Civ. Rights Law § 51 (McKinney 2006) to reclaim the sanctity of his right to live quietly without having celebrity or scrutiny thrust upon him.

In 1903, the legislature enacted § 51 in response to a ruling by the New York Court of Appeals in which it ruled that a person whose privacy had been similarly violated had no common law right to privacy. *See Roberson v. Rochester Folding Box Co.*, 64 N.E. 442, 443-47 (1902). If the intent of the New

York legislature, therefore, is to be fully
effectuated it is essential that the court
afford broad protection to the legal interests
asserted by Nussenzweig.

The Appellate Division, First Department,
should reverse the trial court's ruling
granting summary judgment for diCorcia because
there remain triable issues of fact as to
whether "Head No. 13" is legally art, and,
if so, whether the diminished protection
that art, as symbolic speech, receives under
the First Amendment outweighs the interests
asserted by Nussenzweig. Categorizing any
given work as "art" is and long has been
a difficult enterprise for any court to
undertake. To help judges avoid the trap of
creating legal significance from their own
subjective tastes, courts have turned to
any number of more objective criteria for
assisting in this difficult analysis. Inasmuch
as the trail court relied largely on its own
subjective examination, the status of "Head
No. 13" as art remains a triable issue of
fact.

Even finding this photograph to be art, the trial court's automatic exemption of diCorcia under the First Amendment against Nussenzweig's right to privacy claim was premature. The United States Supreme Court's First Amendment jurisprudence regards art which is not political or in regards to a matter of public interest to be symbolic speech. The First Amendment protects symbolic speech, unlike political or newsworthy speech, only after the constitutional interests that it implicates are weighed against the interests asserted by the adverse party. The trial court here failed to recognize the diminished First Amendment status of artistic expression, and failed to conduct the necessary balancing analysis.

Finally, the Appellate Division, First Department, should reverse the trial court's granting of summary judgment because, under controlling New York case law, the incidental use exemption does not extend to protect the advertising of works of art. This exemption, created in 1919 by the First Department

in a § 51 claim, protects a party to use
without consent a person's name or image in
advertising where the advertising is found to
be "incidental" or "ancillary" to a primary
use of the name or image which is protected as
a "newsworthy" matter of public interest. The
exemption only applies to news disseminators
in the publicizing of their own products.
DiCorcia is not a news disseminator, and he has
not produced a work protected as a newsworthy
matter of public interest. DiCorcia claims
the protection of the First Amendment for his
photo as a work of art, not as a newsworthy
expression or some matter of public interest.
As such, the trial court's extension of the
incidental use exception to protect the use
of "Head No. 13" in advertising was a clear
and significant departure from binding New York
law.

ARGUMENT

I.   **NUSSENZWEIG'S INTEREST IN PROTECTING HIS RIGHT "TO BE LET ALONE" MUST BE AFFORDED BROAD PROTECTION BECAUSE <u>IT IMPLICATES PRECISELY THE POLICY CONCERNS TARGETED BY THE LEGISLATURE IN CREATING N.Y. CIV. RIGHTS LAW § 51.</u>**

The New York Law which created a civil action based on a person's right to privacy reads, in pertinent part,

> [a]ny person whose name, portrait, picture or voice is used within this state for advertising purposes or for the purposes of trade without the written consent first obtained . . . may maintain an equitable action in the supreme court of this state against the person, firm or corporation so using his name, portrait, picture or voice, to prevent and restrain the use thereof; and may also sue to recover damages for any injuries sustained by reason of such use ...

N.Y. Civ. Rights Law § 51 (McKinney 2006). This statute, along with a companion provision which makes the proscribed activities misdemeanors, N.Y. Civ. Rights Law § 50, is the sole protector in New York of an individual's right to privacy. *Flores v.*

Mosler Safe Co., 164 N.E.2d 853, 854 (N.Y. 1959).

A review of the history of the "right to privacy" in New York demonstrates that it was intended, simply, to protect "the right to be let alone." *Roberson v. Rochester Folding Box Co.,* 64 N.E. 442, 442 (N.Y. 1902). In 1890, two leading scholars suggested that the common law should recognize the right to privacy. Samuel D. Warren & Louis D. Brandeis, *The Right to Privacy,* 4 Harv. L. Rev. 193, 196 (1890). Given a chance to discern such a right in New York, the Court of Appeals declined, ruling that a private individual did not have a cause of action for emotional distress resulting from the nonconsensual use of her picture on a product package. *Roberson,* 64 N.E. at 447. In its opinion, however, the court stated that the New York legislature could protect by statute this right not protected under New York common law. *Id.* at 443. The following year, the legislature did just that, enacting N.Y. Civ. Rights Law §§ 50 and 51, the primary purpose of which was to protect the

individual's dignity. Samuel H. Hofstadter,
*The Development of the Right to Privacy
in New York* 12 (1954). In his *Roberson*
dissent, Judge Gray vividly characterized
the danger from which the legislature later
sought to protect New Yorkers as one ". .
. more formidable and more painful in its
consequences, than an actual bodily assault
might be." 64 N.E. at 450.

While New York rejected the notion of
a common law right to privacy, the majority
of jurisdictions nationally, beginning with
Georgia in 1905, *see Pavesich v. New England
Life Ins. Co.,* 50 S.E. 68, 71 (Ga. 1905),
followed the suggestion made by Warren
and Brandeis and recognized the right to
privacy as a common law tort. Restatement
(Second) of Torts § 652A cmt. a (1977). More
recently, the Supreme Court of the United
States recognized a personal right to privacy
as existing among the personal liberties
guaranteed by the Amendments to the United
States Constitution. *Griswold v. Connecticut,*
381 U.S. 479, 484-85 (1965); *Roe v. Wade,*

410 U.S. 113, 152-53 (1973). The nexus of
this array of constitutional, statutory, and
common law protections of the right to privacy
is that which they all seek to insure: "the
interest of the individual in leading, to some
reasonable extent, a secluded and private
life, free from the prying eyes, ears and
publications of others." Restatement (Second)
of Torts § 652A cmt. b (1977).

Although much of the case law considering
N.Y. Civ. Rights Law § 51 in the century since
its passage has focused on discerning when a
usage is "for purposes of trade," *see, e.g.,*
Holmes v. Underwood & Underwood, Inc., 233
N.Y.S. 153, 155 (App. Div. 1st Dep't 1929),
defining the exceptions to a use otherwise
in violation, *see, e.g., Stephano v. News*
Group Publ'n, Inc., 474 N.E.2d 580, 584-585
(N.Y. 1984), and handling claims brought by
celebrities seeking to protect the property
interest of their name or image, *see, e.g.,*
Onassis v. Christian Dior New York, Inc.,
472 N.Y.S.2d 254, 256-257 (Sup. Ct. N.Y.
County 1984), the driving purpose of the

law has remained the strict protection of
private persons from the emotional distress
and exploitation of unwanted and unsought
celebrity. *See Blumenthal v. Picture Classics,
Inc.,* 257 N.Y.S. 800, 801 (App. Div. 1st Dep't
1932) (nonconsensual use of plaintiff selling
bread on street violated § 51 where it brought
her into the public spotlight for ridicule);
Holmes, 233 N.Y.S. at 154 (violation found
where defendant photographer sold professional
photos taken during a private party at
plaintiff's home for newspaper publication);
Arrington v. New York Times Co., 434 N.E.2d
1319, 1323 (N.Y. 1982) (defendant photographer
found to have violated § 51 where he took
and sold for publication photos of plaintiff
without plaintiff's knowledge or consent).

In light of the focus of this corpus
of law on protecting non-public figures from
unwanted exposure for the benefit of others,
Nussenzweig states the prototypical N.Y. Civ.
Rights Law § 51 claim. Nussenzweig's desire,
as the *Roberson* court put it, "to be let
alone," *Roberson,* 64 N.E. at 443, is a central

and defining element of his personality. It
grows irresistibly from his identity as
an Orthodox Hasidic Jew and member of the
persecuted Klausenberg Sect and from his deeply
rooted religious belief, based on the Second
Commandment from the Book of Exodus, that no
commercial use be made of his image (R.6).
While a common law right to privacy might
afford greater protection, Nussenzweig, like
any New Yorker who holds his personal privacy
inviolate, continues to depend entirely upon §
51 to protect it from the ever-creeping reach
of those who would, as DiCorcia did here,
appropriate it for their own benefit. As his
claim implicates the particular evil which §
51 sought to remedy and as it aligns closely
with the broader conceptions of the right
to privacy, Nussenzweig's interests must be
broadly stated and vigorously protected.

**II.   THE TRIAL COURT ERRED IN FINDING "HEAD
NO. 13" TO BE EXEMPT UNDER THE FIRST
AMENDMENT AS ART BECAUSE IT FAILED TO
APPLY ANY OBJECTIVE STANDARD TO DEFINE
"ART" AND BECAUSE IT FAILED TO BALANCE
THE INTERESTS OF THE PARTIES AS REQUIRED
FOR SYMBOLIC SPEECH.**

The fundamental personal liberty of free
speech is protected in the Constitution of
the United States, where it reads, in readily
recognizable part, "Congress shall make no
law . . . abridging the freedom of speech . .
." U.S. Const. amend. I. Similarly, the New
York Constitution reads, "[e]very citizen may
freely speak . . . and no law shall be passed
to restrain or abridge the liberty of speech .
. ." N.Y. Const. art. I, § 8. In New York,
a work otherwise violating N.Y. Civ. Rights
Law § 51 can be exempt where it is found to
be protected as First Amendment speech. *See
Arrington*, 434 N.E.2d at 1322; *Stephano*,
474 N.E.2d at 585. Although there is no
controlling case on point, some lower courts
have recently begun to extend this exemption
to visual works found to be "art." *See, e.g.,
Simeonov v. Tiegs*, 602 N.Y.S.2d 1014, 1018
(Civ. Ct. N.Y. County 1993).

Conferral of First Amendment protection, however, demands that the court first determine if the work is indeed "art," a treacherous consideration against which Justice Holmes long ago warned jurists. *Bleistein v. Donaldson Lithographing Co.,* 188 U.S. 239, 251-52 (1903). Moreover, because "not all speech is of equal First Amendment importance," *Dun & Bradstreet, Inc. v. Greenmoss Builders, Inc.,* 472 U.S. 749, 758 (1985) (plurality opinion); *see also* 2 J. Thomas McCarthy, *The Rights of Publicity and Privacy* §§ 8:12-8:16 (2004), finding a work to be protected as symbolic speech requires a fact-sensitive balancing of the interests of the parties. *See United States v. O'Brien,* 391 U.S. 367, 376 (1968).

A.   The trial court erred in finding "Head No. 13" to be art because it failed to recognize that defining "art" is a problematic question of fact best considered by application of an objective test.

Courts have long struggled to define art. *See, e.g., United States v. Perry,* 146 U.S. 71, 74-75 (1892); *see generally* Christine Haight Farley, *Judging Art,* 79 Tul. L. Rev.

805, 810-819 (2005). Courts have turned to a variety of more objective tests to help mitigate this difficulty, *see, e.g., Brandir Int'l Inc. v. Cascade Pacific Lumber Co.,* 834 F.2d 1142, 1147 (2d Cir. 1987) (applying "useful articles doctrine" in copyright law); *Parks v. LaFace Records,* 329 F.3d 437, 448-49 (6th Cir. 2003) (applying "artistic relevance" test in trademark law), including copyright law's "transformative test," which sustains as art only works which are transformative of the original. *Comedy III Productions, Inc. v. Gary Saderup, Inc.,* 21 P.3d 797, 808 (Cal. 2001) (applying transformative test in a right to publicity claim); *Hoepker v. Kruger,* 200 F. Supp. 2d 340, 349 (S.D.N.Y. 2002) (applying transformative test to a New York right to privacy claim). In a First Amendment setting, the Supreme Court has held that a jury provides a constitutionally adequate means for discerning between art and obscenity. *Miller v. California,* 413 U.S. 15, 33-34 (1973).

Although it is only one of a number of potentially useful tests, the transformative

test's consideration of the interests of both
the artist and claimant makes it readily useful
in a § 51 claim setting; indeed, a survey
of the cases finding an artistic expression
exception to a § 51 claim demonstrates that
this test already has a functional role in
finding "art" in New York. *See Simeonov*,
602 N.Y.S.2d at 1015, 1018 (plaster casting
sculpture of model's face protected as art
from her § 51 claim); *Hoepker,* 200 F. Supp. 2d
at 348-50 (transformative test applied to find
composite work incorporating plaintiff's photo
to be art); *Altbach v. Kulon,* 754 N.Y.S.2d
709, 712 (App. Div. 3d Dep't 2003) (use of
local official's photo to lampoon him in
parodic caricature found to be protected art).

Applying the transformative test,
diCorcia's "Head No. 13" is not a work of
art. Upon visual examination, the photo
seems little more than a simple picture of
a man taken on a street. DiCorcia's edits
(R.9), whatever they might have been, did not
result in a work that is transformative of
the original. While it is clear, therefore,

that "Head No. 13" is not art according to the transformative test, assigning error to the trial court does not require adopting this specific test.

In light of both the array of objective criteria available to assist courts as they contemplate this difficult question and Nussenzweig's compelling interests, the court's analysis of this critical question was insufficient. Claiming to eschew a subjective determination, the court nonetheless relied on little more than the reputations of diCorcia and the gallery in ruling "Head No. 13" to be art. *Nussenzweig v. DiCorcia*, No. 108446/05, slip op. at 9-10 (N.Y. Sup. Ct. N.Y. County Feb. 16, 2006). Whether or not this court adopts the "transformative" test or one of the other, competing tests for art, testing of objective criteria must be done. In the law, art is not just whatever appeals to the eye of the beholder. *E.g.*, *Perry*, 146 U.S. at 74-75. Thus, there remains a triable issue of fact as to whether "Head No. 13" is art under New York law.

B.   Having found "Head No. 13" to be art, the trial court erred in extending automatic First Amendment protection because it failed to conduct the balancing test required for symbolic speech.

Any analysis involving a form of "speech" entitled to only limited First Amendment protection must balance the interests of the parties to determine if the expression in question will be protected under the Constitution. *O'Brien,* 391 U.S. at 376. Not all forms of "speech" receive the same degree of protection under the First Amendment. *Dun & Bradstreet,* 472 U.S. at 758 (plurality opinion). Expressions which are political or are in regard to matters of public interest receive the highest degree of protection, *New York Times Co. v. Sullivan,* 376 U.S. 254, 269-270 (1964), while "symbolic speech" receives diminished protection. *O'Brien*, 391 U.S. at 376; *Barnes v. Glen Theatre, Inc.*, 501 U.S. 560, 565-66 (1991). Visual art is considered to be symbolic speech. *See Hurley v. Irish-American Gay, Lesbian & Bisexual Group*, 515 U.S. 557, 569 (1995).

Although the First Amendment fully
protects political or newsworthy speech,
it protects symbolic speech only where the
interests implicated by the speech are
more compelling than those of the adverse
party. *Compare Arrington*, 434 N.E.2d at 1323
(newspaper's "newsworthy" use of private
citizen's photo in article defeated a N.Y.
Civ. Rights § 51 claim), *with Barnes*, 501 U.S.
at 567 (state interest reflected in public
decency law outweighed "symbolic speech" right
to nude dancing), *and Close v. Lederle*, 424
F.2d 988, 990 (1st Cir. 1970) (defendant's
interest in keeping public corridor free from
mature-content art defeated plaintiff artist's
constitutional interest in exhibiting non-
political art).

Application of this necessary balancing
analysis to the trial court's considerations
evinces the error below. Although the trial
court did take note of significant facts which
it could have utilized in such an analysis,
it failed to construct any balancing inquiry.
Nussenzweig v. DiCorcia, No. 108446/05, slip

op. at 9-10. While it accepted, for example,
the sincerity of Nussenzweig's injuries, the
court failed to consider the weight of the
legal interests, namely the compelling right
to privacy protected by New York statute and
Supreme Court jurisprudence, implicated by
those injuries. *Id.* at 11. Likewise, the
court's opinion failed to mention, let alone
analytically consider, the diminished status
of symbolic speech in the Supreme Court's
First Amendment rulings. *Id.* at 8-9. These
shortcomings in the trial court's ruling
create a clear and compelling issue of triable
fact.

III. **THE TRIAL COURT ERRED IN PROTECTING DICORCIA'S ADVERTISING UNDER THE INCIDENTAL USE EXCEPTION BECAUSE THE INCIDENTAL USE EXCEPTION APPLIES ONLY TO NEWS DISSIMENATORS WHOSE WORK IS PROTECTED AS POLITICAL OR NEWSWORTHY SPEECH.**

Nonconsensual use of a person's likeness
in advertising can be exempt from a § 51
claim as a use "incidental" or "ancillary" to
a use protected as political or newsworthy
speech. *Humiston v. Universal Film Mfg. Co.*,
178 N.Y.S. 752, 759 (App. Div. 1st Dep't

1919); *see also Velez v. VV Publ'g Corp.,* 524
N.Y.S.2d 186, 187 (App. Div. 1st Dep't 1988).
The incidental use exception allows news
disseminators to advertise their own work.
Booth v. Curtis Publ'g Co., 223 N.Y.S.2d 737,
741 (App. Div. 1st Dep't 1962). Consistent
with the United States Supreme Court's First
Amendment protection of commercial uses of
"books, newspapers, and magazines," *Burstyn v.
Wilson,* 343 U.S. 495, 501-502 (1952), a profit
motive by a news disseminator does not defeat
such an incidental use. *Velez,* 524 N.Y.S.2d
at 188.

<u>The incidental use exemption allows a
news disseminator to use a person's name or
image without consent to advertise its own
product where the advertising is ancillary to
an original newsworthy use protected as First
Amendment speech.</u> *See Humiston,* 178 N.Y.S. at
753 (defendant newsreel producer's advertising
use protected where original use was news);
Booth, 223 N.Y.S.2d at 744 (defendant
magazine's advertising of newsworthy expression
protected); *Rand v. Hearst Corp.,* 298 N.Y.S.2d

405, 412 (App. Div. 1st Dep't 1969) (same for
defendant book publisher); *Velez*, 524 N.Y.S.2d
at 186 (same for defendant newspaper publisher
against claim of political activist); *Groden
v. Random House, Inc.*, 61 F.3d 1045, 1050 (2d
Cir. 1995) (same for defendant book publisher
against claim of quoted author); *Stern v.
Delphi Internet Services Corp.*, 626 N.Y.S.2d
694,700-701 (Sup. Ct. N.Y. County 1995) (same
for defendant internet "news disseminator").
But see Hoepker, 200 F. Supp. 2d at 350
(without noting its own leap from one level of
First Amendment protection to another, court
cited only incidental use cases protecting
news disseminators, then applied the exception
to advertising ancillary to a work of art).

Considered within the confines of
controlling case law, the trial court's
extension of the incidental use exemption to
diCorcia's advertising of "Head No. 13" was
clearly in error. New York courts created this
exemption to a § 51 claim for, and without
exception have applied it only to, advertising
which is ancillary to newsworthy uses by

news disseminators. Its only application beyond this closely tailored rule was by a U.S. District Court applying New York law, an anomaly readily distinguishable as a non-binding court's misapplication of a clearly defined rule. Though ignored by the *Hoepker* court, the restriction of this important allowance to newsworthy or political speech is more than mere form; rather, it recognizes the singularly essential function of these particular expressive forms within any democracy. Non-political art, generally, and "Head No. 13" in particular, claim to serve no such function. Thus, even if "Head No. 13" were art and even if it enjoyed full First Amendment protection, the extension of the incidental use exemption to its advertising was a clear and significant departure from controlling New York case law, and was in error.

CONCLUSION

For the reasons stated above, the court should reverse the order granting summary judgment and should remand this case for

consideration of the remaining triable issues
of fact.

Sample 2

IN THE
SUPREME COURT OF THE STATE OF NEW YORK
APPELLATE DIVISION
FIRST DEPARTMENT

No. 234/06

ERNO NUSSENZWEIG,

Plaintiff-Appellant,

-against-

PHILIP-LORCA DICORCIA and PACE/MACGILL, INC.

Defendants-Appellees.

Appeal from the New York Supreme Court,
New York County
Hon. Judith J. Gische, Judge

BRIEF FOR APPELLEE DICORCIA

QUESTIONS PRESENTED FOR REVIEW

1. Whether <u>a photograph of a non-public figure taken in public by an artist-photographer</u> is considered a work of art protected by the freedom of speech and expression clauses of the United States and New York Constitutions, exempting the photographer from liability under New York's privacy law?

2. Whether the use of a photograph of a non-public figure taken in public by an artist-photographer, used in a catalog and other promotional material, is an ancillary or incidental use protected under the freedom of speech and expression clauses of the United States and New York Constitutions, exempting the photographer from liability under New York's privacy law?

TABLE OF CONTENTS

TABLE OF AUTHORITIES

United States Supreme Court Cases:

Other State Cases:

Constitutions, Statutes, and Administrative Regulations:

Treatises, Books, and Law Review Articles:

STATEMENT OF JURISDICTION

This Court has jurisdiction over the subject matter of this case because it is an appeal from the final judgment of the Supreme Court of the State of New York, New York County, entered on February 8, 2006. N.Y. C.P.L.R. 5701(a)(1) (McKinney 2006).

STANDARD OF REVIEW

The de novo standard of review applies to the review of a lower Court's decision granting summary judgment. Sillman v. Twentieth Century Fox Film Corp., 144 N.E.2d 387, 392 (N.Y. 1957). "[T]he party opposing the motion must demonstrate by admissible evidence the existence of a factual issue requiring a trial of the action or tender an acceptable excuse for his failure so to do." Zuckerman v. City of New York, 404 N.E.2d 718, 718 (N.Y. 1980). For both questions presented on review, this Court must only ensure ". . . that no material and triable issue of fact is presented." Sillman, 144 N.E.2d at 392. As this Court stated, "[i]ssue-finding, rather than issue-determination, is the key to the

procedure." <u>Esteve v. Abad</u>, 68 N.Y.S.2d 322,

324 (App. Div. 1st Dep't 1947).

STATEMENT OF THE CASE

Statement of Facts

<u>Defendant diCorcia, a professional</u>
<u>photographer for over twenty-five years with</u>
<u>a body of work which has drawn international</u>
<u>artistic acclaim</u>, has exhibited his work in fine
art museums around the world, including but
not limited to, the Museum of Modern Art (New
York), The Whitney Museum of Art (New York),
the Museo National Centrio de Arte Reina Sofia
(Madrid), and Art Space Gizo (Tokyo) (R.4).
Between 1999 and 2001, using special lighting
and editing techniques, diCorcia created
a series of photographs entitled "HEADS"
(R.4). In making those images, diCorcia took
candid un-staged photographs of people in
public, in Times Square, as they passed by
a carefully selected and specially prepared
location (R.4). He later edited and selected
the pictures to arrive at the final seventeen

photographs he included in the HEADS project
(R.4). Defendant Pace, which considers itself
one of the nation's leading art galleries
specializing in art photography, exhibits and
sells photographic art, including the HEADS
project of defendant diCorcia (R.4).

One of the photographs included in the
HEADS project is unmistakably and readily
identifiable as that of the plaintiff, Erno
Nussenzweig (R.5). Neither of the defendants
ever obtained the consent of the plaintiff
to take, use, sell, exhibit or publish his
photograph (R.4, R.5). A reproduction of the
plaintiff's photograph, entitled "Head No.
13," is included in the Appendix to this brief
(R.12). The plaintiff considers himself a
private individual not desirous of his image
being displayed publicly (R.6).

diCorcia admits to creating ten edition
prints of the photograph of Nussenzweig, plus
three artist's proofs, and claims that he
will not create any more original prints of
the photograph (R.5). The HEADS collection,
including the photograph of Nussenzweig, was

exhibited at the Pace Gallery from September 6, 2001, through October 13, 2001, and was published in a catalog to promote the exhibit (R.5, R.10). Reviews of the exhibition were printed in several local periodicals, including but not limited to, The New York Times, Time Out New York, and The Village Voice (R.5). National periodicals, including W Magazine and Art Forum International included reviews of the exhibition and reproductions of Nussenzweig's photograph (R.5). An extremely limited number of prints of the photograph were created and sold for a profit (R.5, R.6, R.10).

Proceedings Below

The plaintiff, Erno Nussenzweig, filed an amended complaint with the Supreme Court of New York, New York County, alleging that defendants diCorcia and Pace violated his rights under New York's privacy law by displaying and selling his photograph. Nussenzweig v. DiCorcia, No. 108446/05, slip op. at 3 (N.Y. Sup. Ct. N.Y. County Feb. 16, 2006). The Court below found that the

defendants had established that the contested
photograph was art and that the photograph was
therefore exempted from New York's privacy
law because it was protected speech under the
United States and New York Constitutions. Id.
at 11. The Court below further determined
that the plaintiff had not established the
possibility of the existence of any material
fact that could have an effect on the Court's
art or protected speech determinations. Id.
at 10-11. This case is on appeal from summary
judgment motions granted in the favor of the
defendants. Id. at 12.

SUMMARY OF THE ARGUMENT

This Court should affirm the Court below
because the photograph at issue is artwork
broadly protected under the United States and
New York Constitutions and exempted from the
narrow scope of liability under New York's
privacy law. Additionally, Nussenzweig has not
demonstrated the possibility of any relevant
fact being in dispute.

The United States and New York
Constitutions provide force to our society's
treasured right of free expression. U.S.
Const. amend. I; N.Y. Const. art. I, § 8.
This right stands as one of the fundamental
building blocks of the success of our great
nation and limitations placed upon this right
are few and narrow. As a historically and
traditionally important means of expression,
art is readily afforded this protection of the
United States and New York Constitutions.

It is undisputed that defendant diCorcia
is a renowned artist with over a quarter-
century of experience as a professional
photographer. The photograph which is the
subject of this litigation is a product of
diCorcia's thoughtful creativity and artistic
skill. A limited number of copies of this
work were sold, but the sale of art does not
cease to make it art. Though the appellant
contends the work is not art, he has failed
to produce any evidence which could even lead
to the inference of evidence supporting this
conclusion.

Nussenzweig bases his cause of action on New York's privacy law. N.Y. Civ. Rights Law § 51 (McKinney 2006). This statute was enacted in response to a particular evil, the unauthorized use of an individual's likeness in advertising a product (in the original case, on a bag of flour). The privacy law is not a tool which can be freely used to suppress the broad and fundamental protections enshrined within the United States and New York Constitutions regarding free expression. New York courts uniformly recognize that the privacy law is narrow in its scope and limited in its application because of the very fundamental liberty upon which it treads.

Nussenzweig argues that he has a fundamental right to privacy, however New York State only recognizes a cause of action within the limited scope of its privacy law, because of the value placed on free expression. A right to privacy can be argued to exist as a penumbra to the United States Constitution, but that implied right must yield to the expressly delineated right of free expression.

Nussenzweig's case is further weakened by
the very fact that his picture was taken in
public, demonstrating that although he is a
private person, Nussenzweig accepts that some
intrusion in his privacy is an inescapable
part of modern life.

Finally, Nussenzweig attempts to
argue that the promotion of the protected
work somehow defeats its constitutional
protections. This argument must fail if the
granted constitutional protection is to be
meaningful. Real protection would not actually
be granted by the United States and New York
Constitutions if the end effect would be to
prohibit the knowledge and dissemination of a
protected work.

Advertising is one of the few means by
which to disseminate information and express
the protected freedoms of our Constitutions.
The advertising of the protected work falls
under the same protections provided to the
work itself because the advertising is merely
ancillary or incidental to the already
protected use. If the advertising was somehow

used to promote a product or subject other than the protected work itself, Nussenzweig could have an argument. However, when the advertisements merely further the already protected message and nothing more, there can be no lessening of the advertisement's protection without seriously, if not completely, eroding the precious freedoms provided by the United States and New York Constitutions.

ARGUMENT

I.   **THE DISPLAY AND OCCASIONAL SALE OF AN ARTIST-PHOTOGRAPHER'S PHOTOGRAPH OF A SOLITARY INDIVIDUAL IN PUBLIC IS EXEMPTED FROM LIABILITY UNDER NEW YORK'S PRIVACY LAW BECAUSE OF THE WIDE SCOPE OF PROTECTIONS PROVIDED BY THE UNITED STATES AND NEW YORK CONSTITUTIONS REGARDING ARTWORK AND THE NARROW CONSTRUCTION OF NEW YORK'S PRIVACY LAW.**

The lower Court reached the only plausible decision on the facts. As is demonstrated below, the broad speech and expression protections of the United States and New York Constitutions, as well as the narrow scope of New York's privacy law, create a significant burden in any attempt to use New

York's privacy law to suppress any work that is reasonably considered artistic expression.

A.   **Any creative material purporting to be art is generally recognized as art unless it is primarily created for a commercial venture, because the United States and New York Constitutions provide far reaching protections and broad interpretations of speech and expression.**

The Constitution of the United States ensures that "Congress shall make no law . . . abridging the freedom of speech . . . ." U.S. Const. amend. I. Freedom of speech has a much broader meaning than the spoken word itself, with the Supreme Court noting that "in the area of freedom of speech and press the courts must always remain sensitive to any infringement on genuinely serious literary, artistic, political, or scientific expression." Miller v. California, 413 U.S. 15, 22-23 (1973). The First Amendment freedom of speech protection has long been incorporated against the States. Near v. State of Minnesota ex rel. Olson, 283 U.S. 697, 707 (1931). Additionally, "the degree of First Amendment protection is not diminished merely because ... speech is sold rather than given away." Lakewood v. Plain Dealer Pub. Co., 486 U.S. 750, 756 (1988).

The above First Amendment protections set the flooring upon which the New York Constitution further provides that "[e]very citizen may freely speak, write and publish his or her sentiments on all subjects, being responsible for the abuse of that right; and no law shall be passed to restrain or abridge the liberty of speech . . . ." N.Y. Const. art. I, § 8. The Court of Appeals has recognized that New York State, as a cultural and media capital of the nation, "has long provided one of the most hospitable climates for the free exchange of ideas." In re Beach v. Shanley, 465 N.E.2d 304, 312 (N.Y. 1984) (Wachtler, J., concurring). The above precedents demonstrate that the constitutional protections afforded expression are extremely broad, especially within New York State.

Art, in particular, can be "unquestionably shielded" under the First Amendment. Hurley

v. Irish-American Gay, Lesbian & Bisexual
Group of Boston, 515 U.S. 557, 569 (1995).
There is no one "rule" in New York as to what
is art, however the court below noted New
York's definition of art is a fairly broad
one. Nussenzweig v. DiCorcia, No. 108446/05,
slip op. at 12 (N.Y. Sup. Ct. N.Y. County
Feb. 16, 2006). Though it is a subjective
determination, courts readily identify
artistic creations when the overarching motive
of the creator is not primarily commercial.
Altbach v. Kulon, 754 N.Y.S.2d 709, 712
(App. Div. 3d Dep't 2003) (an oil painting
caricature of the town justice copied onto
fliers and used as advertising for an art
gallery was constitutionally protected because
it was an artistic expression); Bery v.
City of New York, 97 F.3d 689, 695 (2d Cir.
1996) (applying New York law) (the sale of
individuals' artwork on the street, including
the fact of selling on the street, was
constitutionally protected because the artwork
was an expression of the individual artists);
Simeonov v. Tiegs, 602 N.Y.S.2d 1014, 1018
(Civ. Ct. N.Y. County 1993) (the sale of an

unauthorized sculpture of an individual's
head was constitutionally protected because
it was artwork); Hoepker v. Kruger, 200 F.
Supp. 2d 340, 350 (S.D.N.Y. 2002) (applying
New York law) (a photograph used in a
composite picture was displayed and sold in
catalogs, in advertisements for the display,
on t-shirts and on various gift items without
the subject's consent was constitutionally
protected because the photographic composite
was an artistic expression); Christine Haight
Farley, Judging Art, 79 Tul. L. Rev. 805,
837-838 (2005) (noting courts have impliedly
compared the creative versus utilitarian
status of an object to distinguish "art" from
"nonart").

New York's liberal definition of art
is readily contrasted by those cases where
commercialization instead of expression is
the creator's goal and the creations are not
considered art for the purposes of broad
free speech protection. Mastrovincenzo v.
City of New York, 435 F.3d 78, 82 (2d Cir.
2006) (applying New York law) (street vendors

selling clothing painted with artwork were
not broadly protected because their t-shirt
art was primarily commercial merchandise);
Young v. Greneker Studios, 26 N.Y.S.2d
357, 359 (Sup. Ct. N.Y. County 1941) (the
unauthorized manufacture and sale of manikins
in the plaintiff's likeness was not protected
because of the exclusively commercial use of
the likeness); Comedy III Prods., Inc. v. Gary
Saderup, Inc., 21 P.3d 797, 810 (Cal. 2001)
(t-shirts and lithographic reproductions of
sketches of deceased celebrities were not
protected because without transformation
they were just a commercialization of the
celebrities' likenesses); Martin Luther King,
Jr. Ctr. for Soc. Change, Inc. v. Am. Heritage
Prods., Inc., 296 S.E.2d 697, 706 (Ga. 1982)
(an unauthorized, mass-produced bust, though
designed by a sculptor, was not protected
because it was a commercial exploitation of a
celebrity's likeness).

Both the United States and New York
Constitutions, as a direct reflection of the
freedoms so treasured by our society, provide

a wide range of protection to most forms of expression, particularly art. <u>In the instant case</u>, the photograph was taken in public using special techniques. The work was displayed in galleries and museums. The expressive nature and limited sale of the work provide clear support that it is indeed artwork because its primary purpose is to act as an expression of the artist's creativity.

In light of the fact that the photograph is artwork, it is entitled to the broadly construed protections provided by the United States and New York Constitutions regarding freedom of expression.

B. <u>Beyond the scope of protections under the United States and New York Constitutions regarding free speech, the burden of demonstrating that a photograph is not art for the purposes of New York's privacy law is very high because of the strictly limited scope of the law.</u>

The New York privacy statute allows only two specific private causes of action for violations of an individual's privacy:

> Any person whose . . . picture . . . is
> used within this state for advertising
> purposes or for the purposes of trade
> without the written consent . . . may
> maintain an equitable action . . . to
> prevent and restrain the use thereof;
> and may also sue and recover damages for
> any injuries sustained by reason of such
> use . . . .

N.Y. Civ. Rights Law § 51 (McKinney 2006).

The Court of Appeals has noted that ". . . other than in the purely commercial setting covered by sections 50 and 51, an inability to vindicate a personal predelection [sic] for greater privacy may be part of the price every person must be prepared to pay for a society in which information and opinion flow freely." Arrington v. New York Times Co., 434 N.E.2d 1319, 1323 (N.Y. 1982). Furthermore, the elements of "advertising purposes" and "purposes of trade" are construed strictly as a matter of legislative intent and constitutional values of freedom of speech. Messenger ex rel. Messenger v. Gruner + Jahr Printing and Publ'g, 727 N.E.2d 549, 552 (N.Y. 2000).

The United States Supreme Court, while applying the instant privacy statute, noted that the risk of public exposure ". . . is an essential incident of life in a society which places a primary value on freedom of speech and of press." Time, Inc. v. Hill, 385 U.S. 374, 388 (1967). In cases applying New York's privacy law to what may be considered artistic expression, it is uniformly recognized that there is no violation of the law even when there is some commercialization. Gautier v. Pro-Football, Inc., 107 N.E.2d 485, 488 (N.Y. 1952) (a television broadcast of a performance, without consent, preceded and followed by commercials was not a violation of the performer's privacy); Hoepker, 200 F. Supp. 2d at 350 (applying New York law) (a photograph used in a composite picture was displayed and sold in catalogs, in advertisements for the display, on t-shirts and on various gift items without the subject's consent was not a violation of privacy because the photographic composite was an artistic expression); Bery, 97 F.3d at 695 (applying New York law) (the sale of individuals' artwork does not remove

its constitutional protections); <u>Simeonov</u>, 602
N.Y.S.2d at 1018 (the sale of an unauthorized
sculpture of an individual's head was not
a violation of the New York's privacy law
because it was artwork).

The rule above is readily distinguished
from cases where the New York's privacy
law was violated because of a clearly non-
artistic use for advertising purposes or
purposes of trade. <u>Cohen v. Herbal Concepts,
Inc.</u>, 472 N.E.2d 307, 310 (N.Y. 1984) (a
picture of a mother and daughter used in a
magazine advertisement without consent was
a violation of their privacy); <u>Welch v. Mr.
Christmas Inc.</u>, 440 N.E.2d 1317, 1320 (N.Y.
1982) (a television commercial filmed with a
professional actor, which was aired after the
actor's consent had expired, was a violation
of the actor's privacy); <u>Cohen v. Hallmark
Cards, Inc.</u>, 382 N.E.2d 1145, 1148 (N.Y. 1978)
(posed photographs of a professional model
used for profit without her consent were a
violation of the model's privacy).

New York's privacy law was created to

provide a specific remedy for a particular problem; it is only meant to be narrowly applied, especially in light of the broad constitutional protections of free speech. Though privacy is an important value in society, it must yield to both the realities of modern life and the more important value of free expression. The photograph in question was taken in a public place. Its primary purpose was as an artistic expression and, though there were a limited number of sales of the photograph, it is not a commercialization being used for trade purposes or as an advertisement to sell a product.

   In light of the narrow construction of New York's privacy law and the artistic nature of the photograph, the photograph is exempted from liability under New York's privacy law.

**II.   AN ARTIST-PHOTOGRAPHER'S USE OF A
PUBLICLY TAKEN PHOTOGRAPH IN MATERIAL
PROMOTING THE PHOTOGRAPHER'S ARTWORK ON
DISPLAY AND FOR SALE IS EXEMPTED FROM
LIABILITY UNDER NEW YORK'S PRIVACY LAW
BECAUSE IT IS INCIDENTAL OR ANCILLARY
ADVERTISING OF ART PROTECTED UNDER THE
UNITED STATES AND NEW YORK CONSTITUTIONS.**

The United States Supreme Court held that
otherwise constitutionally protected expression
does not forfeit that protection because it is
published in the form of a paid advertisement.
See New York Times Co. v. Sullivan, 376 U.S.
254, 266 (1964). It is a natural consequence
of providing freedom of speech protections,
even in light of New York's privacy law,
that the use of the protected expression in
advertising said expression must also be
protected. See Velez v. VV Pub. Corp., 524
N.Y.S.2d 186, 187 (App. Div. 1st Dep't 1988).
If such a rule was not true, the protections
provided to the original idea would be moot.
See Humiston v. Universal Film Mfg. Co., 178
N.Y.S. 752, 759 (App. Div. 1st Dep't 1919).
Predominantly applied in media cases, it is
uniformly recognized that "incidental use . .
. in promotional materials or advertisements
is a necessary and logical extension . . . New

York courts have established [as] an exemption
to section 51 of the Civil Rights Law." Velez,
524 N.Y.S.2d at 187.

Once the work itself is deemed
protected, there is no logical basis to limit
advertisement or promotion of the work unless
the advertisement would violate the analysis
used to grant the protections in the first
place. A large body of case law supports this
idea, originating almost immediately following
the passage of New York's privacy law, and
continuing to this day. E.g., Namath v. Sports
Illustrated, 371 N.Y.S.2d 10, 11 (App. Div.
1st Dep't 1975) (the reprinting of a cover
photograph in connection with advertising is
not in contravention of the privacy statute
because it is an incidental use of a name
or likeness), aff'd, 352 N.E.2d 584 (1976);
Booth v. Curtis Publ'g Co., 223 N.Y.S.2d 737,
744 (App. Div. 1st Dep't 1962) (a photograph
of the plaintiff reprinted in advertising
for the magazine was not a violation of her
privacy because the reprinting was incidental
to the protected use), aff'd, 182 N.E.2d 812

(1962); <u>Velez</u>, 524 N.Y.S.2d at 187 (a picture
on the cover of a magazine later reprinted
in advertising is not a violation of New
York's privacy law because it is incidental
to the original protected use); <u>Humiston</u>,
178 N.Y.S. at 759 (posters used to advertise
a constitutionally protected film were not a
violation of New York's privacy law because
their use was incidental to the protected
use); <u>Altbach</u>, 754 N.Y.S.2d at 712 (an oil
painting caricature of the town justice copied
onto fliers and used as advertising for an art
gallery was constitutionally protected because
it was advertising artistic expression);
Restatement (Third) of Unfair Competition
§ 47 (1995) (noting that "'for purposes of
trade' does not ordinarily include the use of
a person's identity in . . . entertainment,
works of fiction or nonfiction, or in
advertising that is incidental to such uses").

The use of the photograph in question for
advertising and in catalogs was limited to
only promoting the already protected artistic
expression. There was no advertising beyond the

scope of the protected work. The publishing and distribution of a catalog containing only the HEADS project is readily apparent as incidental or ancillary advertising related to the original work.

As demonstrated above, materials promoting the photographer's artwork on display and for sale are exempted from liability under New York's privacy law because they are protected as incidental and ancillary uses under the United States and New York Constitutions.

CONCLUSION

For the reasons set forth above, Defendant-Appellee diCorcia respectfully requests this Court affirm the decision of the Court below.

Sample 3

IN THE UNITED STATES COURT OF APPEALS FOR THE SIXTH CIRCUIT

No. 07-234

NEWSFLASH CREATIVE MEDIA,

Appellant,

—against—

ARNOLD BLACK,

Appellee.

Appeal from the United States District Court
for the Western District of Tennessee
Hon. Shania Twain, Chief Judge

BRIEF OF APPELLANT

QUESTIONS PRESENTED FOR REVIEW

I.   Whether an active politician can enforce his right of publicity, in the face of the First Amendment, against a private company criticizing his politics and history using images of his prior career as an entertainer?

II. Whether a company using images of an active political figure in an expressive work criticizing that political figure is entitled to an affirmative parody defense, where the work significantly alters the meaning of the photographs without altering the photographs themselves?

TABLE OF CONTENTS

TABLE OF AUTHORITIES

Supreme Court Cases

Sixth Circuit Cases

Other Federal Cases

State Court Cases

Constitutions, Rules and Statutes:

Treatises, Books, and Law Review Articles:

Miscellaneous:

STATEMENT OF JURISDICTION

The Western District of Tennessee issued
a summary judgment on February 16, 2007.
Newsflash Creative Media v. Black, No. 04-C-
9345, slip op. at 8 (W.D. Tenn. Feb. 16, 2007)
(Record, R.8). Jurisdiction is proper because
this Court has "jurisdiction of appeals from
all final decisions of the district courts" of
Tennessee. 28 U.S.C. § 1291 (2007). Notice of
appeal was filed in accordance with Rule 4(b)
of the Federal Rules of Appellate Procedure.
Fed. R. App. P. 4(b).

STANDARD OF REVIEW

The appropriate standard of review in
a grant of summary judgment is a *de novo*
standard. *ETW Corp. v. Jireh Publ'g, Inc.*,
332 F.3d 915, 919 (6th Cir. 2003). Summary
judgment is granted when there is no "genuine
issue of material fact" and "the moving party
is entitled to judgment as a matter of law."
Fed. R. Civ. P. 56(c). A genuine issue of
material fact arises "if the evidence is such
that a reasonable jury could return a verdict

for the nonmoving party." *Anderson v. Liberty
Lobby, Inc.*, 477 U.S. 242, 251 (1986).

STATEMENT OF THE CASE

Statement of Facts

Appellant Newsflash Creative Media
("Newsflash") is a graphic design company run
by two Tennessee-based artists. Stipulation
of Facts ("Stip.") (Record, R.3, ¶ 1).
Appellee Arnold Black ("Black"), currently the
governor of California, is a former action
film star and bodybuilder with a pop culture
career of twenty years, and an estimated net
worth of eight hundred million dollars. *See*
Mark Matthews, *Governor Black's Tax Returns
Released*, ABC 7 News, Apr. 14, 2006, http://
abclocal.go.com/kgo/story?section=politics&id=
4085877.

On October 2, 2006, Black announced
on national television that he would visit
Tennessee to raise funds on behalf of the
Republican Party there. Stip. ¶ 5 (R.4). In
reaction to this announcement, on October 3,
2006, Newsflash introduced T-shirts bearing

various images of Black depicting him in
his violent movie roles or his bodybuilding
poses, contrasted with his current political
stance. Stip., Exhibit 1 (R.8). The shirts
also contained a pro-Democratic Party
statement urging the Tennessee reader to vote,
accompanied by Newsflash's contact details.
Stip. ¶ 6 (R.4).

Proceeds from the sale of the T-shirts
amounted to four percent of the two million
dollars that Black raised for the Tennessee
Republican party. Newsflash donated the
proceeds to the Tennessee Democratic Party,
retained no net profits, and continues to sell
the T-shirts to voice their opinion on out-of-
state political figures bringing their influence
to bear on Tennessee politics. Stip. ¶ 9
(R.5).

On October 15, 2006, Black sent a
threatening facsimile and letter via U.S. mail
in response to Newsflash's T-shirt message,
stating he would commence legal action within
eleven days if Newsflash did not comply with
his wishes to cease voicing their political

opinion by destroying any existing T-shirts containing the message and by halting production and sales of the T-shirts. Stip., Exhibit 1 (R.8).

Proceedings Below

This action was brought by both Newsflash and Black, with each filing a cross-motion for summary judgment based on the Stipulation of Facts, submitted to this court in the Record on Appeal (R.3). Both claims assumed Newsflash's use of Black's images had violated his right of publicity; argument focused on whether the use merited an affirmative defense as a form of political speech or parody.

In an order dated February 16, 2007, United States District Judge Bernice A. Donald granted summary judgment to Black, finding no exemption for the work as news or parody. *Newsflash Creative Media v. Black*, No. 04-C-9345, slip op. at 9 (W.D. Tenn. Feb. 16, 2007). Plaintiff filed a timely Notice of Appeal with the Sixth Circuit on February 16, 2007 (R.14).

The unreported opinion of the District Court is contained in the Record on Appeal before this Court (R.9).

SUMMARY OF THE ARGUMENT

Newsflash's use of Black's images to criticize his political activities is not only afforded protection as a parody, but more importantly, as political speech, which deserves the highest protection under the First Amendment. *See N.Y. Times Co. v. Sullivan*, 376 U.S. 254, 270 (1965).

Allowing a politician to censor free speech based on his celebrity violates the original principle of the First Amendment and sets a dangerous precedent. Celebrities – whether actors, astronauts or athletes – are increasingly entering the world of politics, and should not be allowed to censor any criticism of their politics simply because they had a public life prior to a life in politics.

To censor such political criticism also runs counter to the original goals of the

right of publicity, which evolved in order to
protect the economic interest of a celebrity.
Zacchini v. Scripps-Howard Broad. Co., 433
U.S. 562, 575 (1977).

A parody of a celebrity does not infringe
on the economic value of a celebrity's image,
as any work critical of a celebrity can hardly
be considered a substitute product for that
celebrity's merchandise. By adding their
political commentary, Newsflash transformed the
context and the meaning of the images such
that the shirts are unlikely to interfere with
Black's property rights in any way.

Celebrity parodies are valuable social
commentary, and as noted by the Tenth Circuit,
celebrities themselves "come to symbolize
certain ideas and values." *Cardtoons L.C. v.
Major League Baseball Players Assoc.*, 95 F.3d
959, 972 (10th Cir. 1996). Indeed, at the very
heart of Newsflash's message is a question of
which values, precisely, Black symbolizes.

Speech that criticizes a politician,
whether just or unjust, serves a function

beyond merely the commercial. Even if a significant motive of the speech is economic, this does not preclude First Amendment protection. The court below incorrectly focused on the commercial use of the T-shirts in political fundraising, dismissing any political value the speech may have. It is only necessary that the work not *solely* be an advertisement or commercially motivated. *See Cent. Hudson Gas & Elec. Corp. v. Pub. Serv. Comm'n of N.Y.*, 447 U.S. 557, 561 (1980)

That the photographs are from an earlier time does not preclude them from being a commentary on current events; these images are required to contrast Black's previous persona with his current activities, and political activity within one's home state must surely be a matter of public interest.

In order to further the principles that spawned both the right to free speech and the right to publicity, the outcome must be in opposition to the ruling of the district court.

ARGUMENT

I.   **THE JUDGMENT OF THE DISTRICT COURT SHOULD
     BE REVERSED BECAUSE NEWSFLASH'S USE OF
     BLACK'S IMAGE IS OF PUBLIC CONCERN AND
     IS PART OF A POLITICAL COMMENTARY, THE
     PROTECTION OF WHICH WAS THE ORIGINAL
     OBJECTIVE OF THE FIRST AMENDMENT FREE
     SPEECH CLAUSE.**

The First Amendment provides that
"Congress shall make no law...prohibiting
freedom of speech, or of the press; or the
right of the people to peaceably assemble,
and to petition the Government for a redress
of grievances," and is applicable to the
states through the Fourteenth Amendment. U.S.
Const. amend. I; U.S. Const. amend. XIV. The
protection of freedom of speech, and "in
particular freedom to criticize government
officials and aspirants to public office," was
the primary motivation for passage of the
First Amendment. *Douglas v. Hustler Magazine*,
769 F.2d 1128, 1141 (7th Cir. 1985).

Provided the claim is for invasion of
state-determined rights and not of specific
federal law, state law applies in right of
publicity cases. *See Landham v. Lewis Galoob*

Toys, Inc., 227 F.3d 619, 622 (6th Cir. 2000).
While this case would fall under unauthorized
use of an "individual's name, photograph,
or likeness in any medium...for purposes of
fundraising," Tenn. Code Ann. § 47-25-1105
(2006), Tennessee law will exempt particular
image uses from liability:

> (a) It is deemed a fair use and no
> violation of an individual's rights...
> if the use of a name, photograph
> or likeness is in connection with
> any news, public affairs or sports
> broadcast or account. (b) The use...
> does not constitute a use for purposes
> of advertising or solicitation solely
> because the material containing such use
> is commercially sponsored or contains
> paid advertising. Rather it shall be
> a question of fact whether or not the
> use...was so directly connected with the
> commercial sponsorship or with the paid
> advertising as to constitute a use for
> purposes of advertising or solicitation.

Tenn. Code Ann. § 47-25-1107.

Interpretation of the right of publicity
in the face of the First Amendment is still
developing, and continues to evolve through the
state and federal court systems. *See generally*
Mark S. Lee, *Agents of Chaos: Judicial*

Confusion in Defining the Right of Publicity-Free Speech Interface, 23 Loy. L.A. Ent. L. Rev. 471 (2003). While the Constitution grants a state power to statutorily give its citizens "the right to publicity value of their work," this right will be carefully balanced with the public interest in free expression. *Landham,* 227 F.3d at 626.

The following subsections will demonstrate that a proper balancing of policy objectives necessitates protection of Newsflash's speech, as its political message is exactly the type of expression the First Amendment exists to protect, and does not infringe on Black's property rights economically or otherwise.

A.   **Protecting the T-shirts as a commentary on the quality of Black as a politician in light of his past celebrity furthers the fundamental value of the First Amendment — to allow and protect criticism of political figures.**

"When the speech is of public concern and the plaintiff is a public official or public figure, the Constitution clearly requires the plaintiff to surmount a much higher barrier before recovering damages from a media defendant than is raised by the common law." *Philadelphia Newspapers, Inc. v. Hepps*, 475 U.S. 767, 775 (1986). A democracy must have open public discourse regarding its public servants, and any evaluations of First Amendment protection of political criticism will be given a wide berth. *See N.Y. Times Co. v. Sullivan*, 376 U.S. 254 (1965) (even factually inaccurate speech criticizing public official upheld); *N.Y. Magazine v. Metro. Transp. Auth.*, 136 F.3d 123, 131 (2d Cir. 1998) (criticism of mayor displayed on city transportation public advertising space upheld); *Paulsen v. Personality Posters, Inc.*, 299 N.Y.S.2d 501, 509 (Sup. Ct. 1968) (use of image of comedian who participated in mock political race upheld).

When examining celebrity property rights in relation to free speech, courts have recognized that right of publicity suits have been used to attempt to circumvent the higher standards established for libel and defamation claims. *See Hustler Magazine v. Falwell*, 485

U.S. 46, 52 (1988); *Hoffman v. Capital Cities/ ABC Inc.*, 255 F.3d 1180, 1184 (9th Cir. 2001); David S. Welkowitz, *The Terminator as Eraser: How Arnold Schwarzenegger Used the Right of Publicity to Terminate Non-Defamatory Political Speech,* 25 Santa Clara L. Rev. 651, 652-662 (2005) (discussing the use of rights of publicity "in lieu of defamation").

Black used his history as an actor and bodybuilder to win in a political arena, parlaying jokes of his past celebrity to victory against arguably lesser celebrities such as Larry Flint and Gary Coleman (Marc Sandalow, *California Political Shockwave Rocks Nation*, S.F. Chronicle, Aug. 7, 2003, at A-13) - and currently to raise funds for his political party in the state of Tennessee.

To now allow him to delineate his celebrity from his political persona when it suits him would allow celebrities to silence free speech and criticism of their political activities simply because at one time they were an entertainer or sports figure - and sets a dangerous precedent, considering the rate

of celebrities turning to politics in the
twentieth and twenty-first centuries. Because
Newsflash's speech was political criticism,
its form and use of Black's images should
be afforded wide latitude under the First
Amendment.

> B. **This speech is protected as**
>   **newsworthy in that its purpose is to**
>   **weigh in on one side of a current**
>   **political debate, which is protected**
>   **under both the First Amendment and**
>   **Tennessee law.**

Tennessee law creates an exemption for use
of celebrity images for "news, public affairs"
purposes. Tenn. Code Ann. § 47-25-1107. Use
of celebrity information and photographs in
the public domain are generally "justified by
the newsworthiness of celebrities," and does
not violate the right to publicity. *Douglas v.*
Hustler Magazine, Inc., 769 F.2d 1128, 1139
(7th Cir. 1985).

Simply because a reproduction depicts
events that took place earlier in time does
not bar First Amendment protection. *See*
Douglas, 769 F.2d at 1139 (7th Cir. 1985)
(using previously published photographs in

the public domain falls outside right of
publicity), and *Montana v. San Jose Mercury
News, Inc.*, 34 Cal. App. 4th 790, 795 (1995)
(reprinting original news publication pictures
of quarterback over a decade of Super Bowl
appearances not barred by right of publicity).

The court below interprets Newsflash's
speech too narrowly in that it sees the
pictures of Black as too dated to be of public
interest (R.11), but when the images are being
used to contrast the past and character of
a current political figure with his current
political stance, this is very much a matter
of interest to today's public. To further the
fundamental values and rights espoused in
the First Amendment requires protection of
Newsflash's commentary on the quality of Black
as a representative of his political party
as a matter of public interest in a current
political debate.

C.   **The speech does not constitute "commercial speech" because its main objective is to comment on a specific celebrity's role in politics and to urge readers to exercise their Constitutional right to vote, an activity well outside of a mere commercial interest.**

Commercial speech is afforded more limited protection than other forms of speech, but commercial speech is defined as "expression related *solely* to the economic interests of the speaker and its audience." *Cent. Hudson Gas & Elec. Corp. v. Pub. Serv. Comm'n of N.Y.*, 447 U.S. 557, 561 (1980) (emphasis added). The "core notion" of commercial speech is that it "does *no more* than propose a commercial transaction." *Bolger v. Youngs Drug Prod. Corp.*, 463 U.S. 60, 66 (1983) (quoting *Va. State Bd. of Pharmacy v. Va. Citizens Consumer Council, Inc.*, 425 U.S. 748 (1976)) (emphasis added).

That a T-shirt is used to convey this message does not lessen its suitability to bear political ideas and expressions; the message is still considered "speech" eligible for First Amendment protection. *See Cohen v.*

California, 403 U.S. 15, 18 (1971). Indeed, in
a case regarding First Amendment protection
of T-shirts sold for profit which advocated
legalizing marijuana, the T-shirts "are to the
[T-shirt vendor] what the *New York Times* is to
[its publishers] – the vehicle of her ideas
and opinions." *Ayres v. City of Chicago*, 135
F.3d 1010, 1017 (7th Cir. 1997).

Although the court below found that the
contact information on the T-shirt was merely
an advertisement for Newsflash's services
(R.10), this conclusion does not withstand
scrutiny. The speech is not "solely" for
the purposes of a commercial transaction,
and it very clearly serves an alternative
function of political criticism. On its face,
the speech does more than "merely propose a
commercial transaction"; the message on the
shirts suggests the reader "Vote Democrat"
and criticizes the Republican Party and
Black's role in Tennessee politics (R.5, ¶
6). As such, the T-shirts bear political
speech, which is afforded full First Amendment
protection, and not merely the qualified

protection given commercial speech.

II. THE JUDGMENT OF THE DISTRICT COURT SHOULD BE REVERSED BECAUSE NEWSFLASH'S USE OF BLACK'S IMAGE SERVES A CRITICAL PURPOSE BEYOND THE COMMERCIAL, TRANSFORMING THE ORIGINAL SO THAT IT DOES NOT ECONOMICALLY DETRACT FROM THE VALUE OF RESPONDENT'S PROPERTY.

The objective of the right of publicity is to protect the economic value of a celebrity's image and body of work. *Zacchini v. Scripps-Howard Broad. Co.*, 433 U.S. 562, 575 (1977). *See generally* J. Thomas McCarthy, The Rights of Publicity and Privacy § 4.23 (2d ed 2007). However, parody is a long-recognized form of social commentary and criticism protected by the First Amendment, and can serve as a defense to right of publicity claims. See *ETW Corp. v. Jireh Publ'g, Inc.*, 332 F.3d 915, 933 (6th Cir. 2003) (citing *Cardtoons L.C. v. Major League Baseball Players Assoc.*, 95 F.3d 959, 969 (10th Cir. 1996)).

In a right of publicity case, the critical analysis is whether a "derivative work" impacts the value of the estate, image or celebrity "brand", either through unjustly enriching the artist or by detracting economically from the celebrity's identity, thereby discouraging artists or celebrities from generating more creative work. *Zacchini*, 433 U.S. at 576; Restatement (Third) of Unfair Competition § 47, cmt. c (1995).

To conduct this analysis, the Sixth Circuit adopted several tests to determine the standard for whether the work will interfere with the celebrity's property right of publicity; in *ETW v. Jireh*, it used a transformative test and a separate balancing test, and in *Parks v. LaFace Records*, it applied a balancing test as used in the Second Circuit. *See ETW,* 332 F.3d at 958-60 (applying the test in *Comedy III Productions, Inc. v. Gary Saderup, Inc.,* 21 P.3d 797 (Cal. 2001), and *Cardtoons*, 95 F.3d at 970-72), *and Parks v. LaFace Records*, 329 F.3d 437, 452 (6th Cir. 2003) (citing *Rogers v. Grimaldi*, 875 F.2d 994 (2d Cir. 1989)).

The remainder of the brief will demonstrate that under any and all of the above criteria, the transformative quality and the nature of the use of Black's image entitle Newsflash's political and parodic criticism to First Amendment protection.

A. The use of the image is protected because it is transformative through its commentary and in its context.

In *ETW v. Jireh*, the Court applied the transformative test developed in *Comedy III*, which is derived from a similar test used in copyright infringement analysis. *See ETW*, 332 F.3d at 933 (referencing *Comedy III,* 21 P.3d). If the message of the work "supersedes" the original, adding a different "purpose and character," then it will be deemed transformative. *Comedy III,* 21 P.3d at page 807 (citing *Campbell v. Acuff-Rose Music, Inc.*, 510 U.S. 569, 579 (1994)). A work containing significantly transformative elements is less likely to "interfere with the economic interest protected." *ETW*, 332 F.3d at 938. If the work is sufficiently transformed to criticize its subject, then the work merits a "parody" exception and constitutes exempted use. *See Winter v. DC Comics*, 69 P.3d 473, 478 (Cal. 2003).

Contrary to the lower court's holding that the decision in *Hoffman* "did not focus solely on the text message," (R.13), whether an image or text altered the original's meaning is not relevant to the analysis. *Compare Cardtoons*, 95 F.3d at 969 (cards gave entirely new meaning to athletes' names and images through lampooning, upheld), *and Hoffman*, 255 F.3d at 1185 (altering picture and adding written message supercedes use of celebrity image, upheld), *and Hoepker v. Kruger*, 200 F. Supp. 2d 340, 349 (S.D.N.Y. 2002) (words added to otherwise unaltered photograph changed message and purpose, upheld), *with Comedy III*, 21 P.3d at 810 (literal depiction with no new message, not upheld).

The T-shirts infuse a new meaning on the photographs by contrasting through words (by adding the phrases "Governor Arnold" or "Governor Terminator" to pictures of Black's violent movie roles, for example) Black's political identity with images of his prior identity as a celebrity actor and bodybuilder (R.4, ¶ 6). The words give the images an

entirely new meaning and message, and add a
different purpose, which make it sufficiently
transformative under the *Comedy III* test.

    B.   **The use of the image is protected,
because as a parody it does not
interfere with the value of Black's
property or identity, and the First
Amendment interests therefore
sufficiently outweigh those property
interests.**

Right of publicity exists to protect "the
commercial interest of celebrities in their
identities," and a violation of the right of
publicity must impact the celebrity's ability
to gain the economic fruits of her image or
work. *See Carson v. Here's Johnny Portable
Toilets, Inc.*, 698 F.2d 831, 835 (6th Cir.
1983). To account for this, the Sixth Circuit
also applied a balancing test used by the
Tenth Circuit, which weighed the effects
of suppressing the speech as compared with
the effects of allowing the censorship. *See
ETW*, 332 F.3d at 937 (applying the test from
Cardtoons, 95 F.3d).

The right to publicity justification
is given less weight provided the parody

criticizes the celebrity at issue. *See Cardtoons*, 95 F.3d at 976. *Compare id.* (merchandise with baseball player images parodying their excessive salaries and lifestyles upheld), *and Winter,* 69 P.3d at 479 (parodic rendition of singers as slugs in comic book upheld), with *Carson*, 698 F.2d 831 at 836 (humorous use of comedian's catchphrase without lampooning him not upheld).

The primary use of the T-shirts is to criticize the image Black is currently conveying in politics compared with his prior persona. As with all parodies, these T-shirts are no substitute for a different piece of Black merchandise; no fan of Black's work interested in purchasing an item bearing his image would choose one that ridicules him.

Black's ability to exploit his identity profitably will not be impacted, and as noted by the Tenth Circuit, economic impact of the use of their image is minimal for many of today's celebrities because it is offset by their exorbitant salaries and substantial income they derive from other activities not

associated with their right of publicity.
Cardtoons, 95 F.3d at 975; *see also ETW*, 332
F.3d at 938.

Black secured nearly thirty million
dollars in his most recent starring role
in 2003 as guaranteed money, excluding all
royalties, overage, and other perks. Edward
Jay Epstein, *Concessions Are for Girlie Men:
Arnold Black's Absurdly Advantageous Contract
for Terminator 3, Slate,* May 9, 2005, http://
www.slate.com/id/2118243/. It is difficult to
assert that Black will be unable to reap the
fruits of his labor because a small number –
or any number – of T-shirts critical of his
politics remains on the market.

Because the political value of this
speech far outweighs its economic value to
Newsflash, and indeed it has no impact on the
economic value of the "brand" or body of work
Black has built, the policies that created the
right of publicity do not apply to the facts
in this case.

C. Use of the images is protected, as the shirts' derive their commercial value through their conveyance of criticism of their subject, whose images are thus integral to the work.

The remaining test applied by the Sixth Circuit is the *Rogers* test; the critical determinant is whether it is "simply a disguised commercial advertisement for the sale of commercial goods and services." *Parks*, 329 F.3d at 460 (citing *Rogers,* 875 F.2d at 1004).

Free speech will only be subsumed by the right of publicity when the work gains its commercial value through appropriating the celebrity's likeness or name without that use having "relevance" to the work. *Parks*, 329 F.3d at 453.

The T-shirts value is in their political message, which attacks Black's political stance and his presence in a Tennessee campaign, and thus the images were integral to the message that Newsflash intended to convey. The oldest images, for example, from Black's reign as a bodybuilder, depict him swarmed by adoring women in bridesmaid wear, and attempt to illustrate the hypocrisy of his representation of a pro-family values political party (R.7). Although the image is necessary for the expression, the shirts' value derives from the criticism rather than the image itself, and therefore Newsflash's speech is entitled to the parody exception to the right of publicity.

Through parody based on his prior activities as an entertainer juxtaposed with his current identity as a Republican, Newsflash sufficiently transformed Black's images without interfering with his ability to exploit his celebrity identity – and the use of those images is core to their message. It is exactly the type of speech that republican ideals set forth as protected in the First Amendment, and thus falls squarely within its scope.

CONCLUSION

For the reasons stated, Appellants respectfully request this Court to reverse the decision of the court below.

Sample 4

**IN THE
UNITED STATES COURT OF APPEALS FOR THE SIXTH
CIRCUIT**

No. 07-234

NEWSFLASH CREATIVE MEDIA,

Appellant,

v.

ARNOLD BLACK,

Appellee.

Appeal from the United States District Court
for the
Western District of Tennessee

BRIEF FOR APPELLEE

QUESTIONS PRESENTED FOR REVIEW

I.   Whether a graphic designer is exonerated
     from liability under the Tennessee
     Personal Rights Protection Act or the
     First Amendment's right to free speech
     for misappropriating a politician's image
     because the misappropriation was for news
     reporting purposes and therefore exempt
     from coverage of the Tennessee Personal
     Rights Protection Act?

II. Whether a graphic designer is exonerated
     from liability under the Tennessee
     Personal Rights Protection Act or the
     First Amendment's right to free speech
     for misappropriating a politician's image
     because the misappropriation constitutes
     a bona fide parody exempt from coverage of
     the Tennessee Personal Rights Protection
     Act?

TABLE OF CONTENTS

TABLE OF AUTHORITIES

Constitutions and Statutes:

Treatises, Books, and Law Review Articles:

STATEMENT OF JURISDICTION

The decision of the District Court for the Western District of Tennessee was entered on February 16, 2007. *See Newsflash Creative Media v. Black,* No. 04-C-9345, slip op. at 9 (W.D. Tenn. 2007) (Record on Appeal, R.13). Notice of appeal to the Sixth Circuit was filed

on February 16, 2007. R.14. This Court has
jurisdiction pursuant to 28 U.S.C. § 1291.

STANDARD OF REVIEW

As appeal was filed based on the District
Court's grant of summary judgment, and this
Court should adopt a *de novo* standard of
review. *See Landham v. Lewis Galoob Toys,
Inc.*, 227 F.3d 619, 622 (6th Cir. 2000) ("We
review a district court's grant of summary
judgment de novo.")

STATEMENT OF THE CASE

Statement of Facts:

On October 2, 2006, Arnold Black
("Black"), Governor of California, announced
on the Tonight Show with Jay Leno that
he would appear in Tennessee to support
Republican Party candidates for the November
2006 election. Stipulation of Facts ¶ 5
("Stip.") (R.4). After Black's announcement,
Newsflash Creative Media ("Newsflash"), a
graphic design business, Stip. ¶ 1 (R.3),
immediately created a line of four T-shirts

bearing Black's image with the word "Newsflash" on top and a demeaning message regarding Black at the bottom ("Robot, Statesman, Governor," "Governor Arnold," "Governor Terminator," and "Der Groppenfuhrer"). Stip. ¶ 6 (R.4). On the back of each T-shirt was a message to "Vote Democrat" and contact information for Newsflash. Stip. ¶ 6 (R.4-5).

Black's image has publicity value under Tennessee law. Stip. ¶ 8 (R.5). Black did not consent to the use of his image or likeness on the T-shirts. Stip. ¶ 7 (R.5). Newsflash sold 8,000 T-shirts with these unauthorized images for Democratic fund raising purposes. Stip. ¶¶ 7, 9 (R.5). Newsflash wishes to continue selling its T-shirts to comment on Republican politics and demean Tennessee Republican supporters like Black even though the 2006 election is over. Stip. ¶ 10 (R.5). Black requests that T-shirt sales and production cease. Stip. ¶ 11 (R.6).

Proceedings Below:

Newsflash filed suit against Black for declaratory relief under the Tennessee Personal Rights Protection Act. Newsflash and Black both moved for summary judgment based on the stipulation of facts. *Newsflash Creative Media v. Black,* No. 04-C-9345, slip op. at 9 (W.D. Tenn. 2007) (R.9). The United States District Court for the Western District of Tennessee granted Black's Motion for Summary Judgment and denied Newsflash's Motion for Summary Judgment. *Id.* at 13 (R.13). Newsflash appealed to this Court. (R.14).

SUMMARY OF THE ARGUMENT

The Court of Appeals for the Sixth Circuit should affirm the District Court's grant of summary judgment because Newsflash knowingly misappropriated Black's image without permission. The T-shirts Newsflash sold bearing Black's image directly violate the Tennessee Personal Rights Protection Act, which protects an individual's name or likeness from a knowingly unauthorized use for

advertising or fundraising purposes. Tenn.
Code Ann. § 47-25-1105(a) (2006). The only
way to avoid violation of the statute is to
assert a First Amendment defense.

The First Amendment provides that
Congress make no law "abridging the freedom of
speech[.]" U.S. Const. amend. I. Tennessee
codified a freedom of speech exemption to the
statute that permits a knowingly unauthorized
use of a name or likeness if it is in
connection with a news account or public
affairs. Tenn. Code Ann. § 47-25-1107. Black
is a newsworthy political figure and therefore
his image could be used in certain instances
without his permission. However, Newsflash's
T-shirts should not qualify for the news or
public affairs exemption. The images used by
Newsflash predate Black's entry into politics
and provide no information regarding current
events.

Newsflash cannot assert full First
Amendment protection because its T-shirts
are commercial speech, which is afforded
less First Amendment protection than other

guaranteed forms of expression and is subject
to regulations like the Tennessee Personal
Rights Protection Act. The T-shirts advertise
Newsflash, make specific reference to voting
for Democrats, and were made for fundraising
purposes. A combination of these factors
provides strong support for a commercial
speech characterization. *See Bolger v. Youngs
Drug Prod. Corp.,* 463 U.S. 60, 66 (1983).

Newsflash also lacks a First Amendment
parody defense to the Tennessee Personal
Rights Protection Act. The statute is silent
on the possibility of parody as an exemption,
but other courts have exempted parody to state
right of publicity laws. The Sixth Circuit
has given deference to other jurisdictions
regarding the right of publicity and, in
two recent decisions, adopted three outside
approaches that utilized parody analysis.
Newsflash's use of Black's image would not
qualify as parody under any of these adopted
approaches.

Newsflash did not add a transformative
element to Black's image. It simply took old

photos and reproduced them on the T-shirts. The images used provided no apparent social commentary on Black as a politician or Republican politics in general. Further, the images bear no relation to Newsflash's intent to comment on Republican politics in Tennessee.

For these reasons, the judgment of the District Court should be affirmed.

ARGUMENT

I.   **THE JUDGMENT OF THE DISTRICT COURT SHOULD BE AFFIRMED BECAUSE NEWSFLASH USED BLACK'S IMAGE IN ITS T-SHIRTS WITHOUT PERMISSION, THE T-SHIRTS DO NOT QUALIFY FOR PROTECTION UNDER THE "NEWS" EXCEPTION TO THE TENNESSEE PERSONAL RIGHTS PROTECTION ACT, AND THE T-SHIRTS ARE COMMERCIAL SPEECH SUBJECT TO GOVERNMENTAL REGULATION.**

Courts first recognized a "right of publicity" as distinct from a right of privacy over fifty years ago. *See Haelan Lab., Inc. v. Topps Chewing Gum, Inc.*, 202 F.2d 866, 868 (2d Cir. 1953). Since that recognition, a majority of states recognize some form of the right on common law or statutory grounds.

Mark S. Lee, *Agents of Chaos: Judicial Confusion in Defining the Right of Publicity-Free Speech Interface,* 23 Loy. L.A. Ent. L. Rev. 471, 479 (2003).

Tennessee codified the right in the Tennessee Personal Rights Protection Act, which protects an individual's name or likeness from a knowingly unauthorized use for purposes of "advertising . . . or for purposes of fund raising [or] solicitation of donations[.]" Tenn. Code Ann. § 47-25-1105(a (2006). Statutory protection indicates that Tennessee places a high value on the right of publicity. This value stems from an understanding that certain individuals use their names or likenesses in a commercial manner, often for endorsement purposes. *Apple Corps Ltd. v. A.D.P.R., Inc.,* 843 F. Supp. 342, 348 (M.D. Tenn. 1993) (citing legislative history of Tenn. Code. Ann. § 47-25-1105). Allowing unauthorized use of a name or likeness would thus pose a substantial threat to its economic value, *see Zacchini v. Scripps-Howard Broad. Co.,* 433 U.S. 562, 575 (1977), either through dilution from excessive use or by association with unpopular merchandise. *See* Restatement (Third) of Unfair Competition § 46 cmt. c (1995).

The First Amendment provides that Congress make no law "abridging the freedom of speech, or of the press[.]" U.S. Const. amend. I. Tennessee created an exception that permits use of a name, photograph, or likeness if it "is in connection with any news, public affairs, or sports broadcast or account." Tenn. Code Ann. § 47-25-1107. This exception lines Tennessee law up with U.S. Supreme Court jurisprudence that restricts state and federal prohibitions on public discussion. *See Burson v. Freeman,* 504 U.S. 191, 197 (1992).

Commercial speech is distinct from news and political speech in that it does "no more than propose a commercial transaction[.]" *Va. Bd. of Pharmacy v. Va. Citizens Consumer Council,* 425 U.S. 748, 762 (1976) (citing *Pittsburgh Press Co. v. Human Relations Comm'n,* 413 U.S. 376, 385 (1973)). Its First Amendment protection is less than other guaranteed expressions and can be subjected to governmental regulation. *Cent. Hudson Gas & Elec. Corp. v. Pub. Serv. Comm'n of New York,* 447 U.S. 557, 563 (1980).

In order for Newsflash to overcome a publicity right violation under Tennessee law, it must show that its violation fits into the "news" exception carved out by the Tennessee legislature or that its T-shirts are not commercial speech and therefore guaranteed full protection under the First Amendment. Each point is now addressed in turn.

A.   **Newsflash cannot assert a news or political speech exception to its violation of Black's publicity right because its T-shirts do not report a newsworthy event or provide valid political commentary.**

When determining if there is a violation of a right of publicity not protected under the First Amendment, liability seems to hinge on whether the use "serves the purpose of contributing information, which is not false or defamatory, to the public debate of political or social issues[.]" *Apple Corps,* 843 F. Supp. at 347 (citing *Estate of Elvis*

Presley v. Russen, 513 F. Supp. 1339, 1356
(D.N.J. 1981)). First Amendment protection
will not extend to the use of a name or
likeness if that use is not connected to the
dissemination of news or political discourse.
See Estate of Elvis Presley at 1358.

Exemption from a right of publicity
action will extend to duplicative use of
a name or likeness previously exempted if
the replication clearly shows no commercial
connection between the individual and the
product containing the name or likeness.
Compare Montana v. San Jose Mercury News, Inc.,
40 Cal. Rptr. 2d 639, 642-43 (Ct. App. 1995)
(reproduction of newspaper's front page as
poster, including Montana photograph, upheld
because photograph was originally protected
as newsworthy and no indication within poster
that Montana endorsed newspaper), *and Namath
v. Sports Illustrated*, 371 N.Y.S.2d 10, 11
(App. Div. 1975) (use of Namath's photograph
upheld when reproduced in an advertisement
for a periodical in which the photograph
originally appeared), *with ETW Corp. v. Jireh*

Publ'g, 332 F.3d 915, 928-38 (6th Cir. 2003) (unauthorized painting of Tiger Woods' Masters victory exempt from publicity right violation because victory was reported as newsworthy and a majority of the public would not infer a connection between Woods and painting).

Black understands that as an international movie star his political career has a national news following. Newsflash would be well within its Constitutional right to comment on Black's political activities, particularly as they relate to his newsworthy appearance in Tennessee. However, the images selected by Newsflash for its T-shirts predate Black's election and public appearance by well over a decade. By allowing use of them to stand, this Court would grant anyone the right to take any image of Black and slap it on a T-shirt under the guise of news reporting or making a political statement.

The T-shirts were created for fundraising purposes, Stip. ¶ 7 (R.5), a direct violation of Tenn. Code. Ann. § 47-25-1105(a). This was nothing more than a cost-effective way

to exploit a popular individual's image for
purposes of raising political donations and
therefore cannot enjoy a news or political
speech exception.

B.   **Newsflash cannot assert full First
      Amendment protection for its
      T-shirts because they are commercial
      speech and therefore subject to the
      Tennessee Personal Rights Protection
      Act.**

Paid advertisements, expression sold for
profit, and speech generated for purchase or
solicitation are not considered commercial
speech. *Va. Bd. of Pharmacy,* 425 U.S. at
761. However, a combination of advertisement,
reference to a specific product, and economic
motivation provides strong support for
characterization as commercial speech. *Bolger
v. Youngs Drug Prod. Corp.,* 463 U.S. 60, 66
(1983).

Commercial speech, afforded less First
Amendment protection than noncommercial
speech, can be subjected to governmental
regulation. *Central Hudson,* 447 U.S. at
563. A regulation's validity will depend on
the assertion of a substantial governmental

interest and whether the regulation advances that interest not more extensively than necessary. *Id.* at 566.

Advertising that constitutes commercial speech is not entitled to constitutional protection afforded noncommercial speech if the advertisement links a product to a current public debate. *Bolger* at 67-68.

Applying *Bolger*, Newsflash's T-shirts should be considered commercial speech. They advertise Newsflash, make specific reference to both voting Democratic and Newsflash itself, and the contribution of profits from their sale to the Tennessee Democratic Party indicates their creation was economically motivated. Stip. ¶¶ 6, 9 (R.4). The fact that Black is a political figure and hence use of his image could be considered part of the public debate on politics does not strip the T-shirts of their commercial speech status. Therefore, as commercial speech, the T-shirts are subject to regulation that does not overstep a substantial governmental interest. *Central Hudson* at 566.

The Tennessee Personal Rights Protection Act serves a substantial interest in that it protects all individuals from an unauthorized use of their name or likeness in advertisements or solicitations. Tenn. Code. Ann. §§ 47-25-1103, 47-25-1105(a). The Act only restricts use of a name or likeness without permission and is not more extensive than necessary to ensure protection from such unauthorized use. Thus, Newsflash cannot assert full First Amendment protection for its T-shirts.

The judgment of the District Court should be affirmed. Newsflash's T-shirts are commercial speech, subject to the Tennessee Personal Rights Protection Act, and cannot enjoy the statute's "news" exception.

II. **THE JUDGMENT OF THE DISTRICT COURT SHOULD BE AFFIRMED BECAUSE EVEN IF THIS COURT WERE TO ADOPT A "PARODY" EXCEPTION TO THE TENNESSEE PERSONAL RIGHTS PROTECTION ACT, THE MISAPPROPRIATION OF BLACK'S IMAGE BY NEWSFLASH WOULD NOT QUALIFY AS PARODY.**

The United States Supreme Court views parody as a valid form of fair use under copyright law. *Campbell v. Acuff-Rose Music, Inc.,* 510 U.S. 569, 579 (1994). The goals of copyright and patent law – to protect an individual's economic incentive for creating a new work – are analogous to the goals of right of publicity laws – to protect the economic value of an individual's likeness – in the states that recognize them. *See Zacchini,* 433 U.S. at 573-76; *Apple Corps.,* 843 F. Supp. at 348.

The statutory language of the Tennessee Personal Rights Protection Act is silent on the matter of parody as an additional exemption to unauthorized use of a name or likeness. However, as case law on the right of publicity is rare, this Court and others "typically give attention to the entire available body of case law [nationwide] when deciding right of publicity cases." *Landham v. Lewis Galoob Toys, Inc.,* 227 F.3d 619, 622-23 (6th Cir. 2000). Several courts have adopted a parody exemption to state publicity right laws. *See generally Cardtoons, L.C. v. MLB Players Ass'n,* 95 F.3d 959 (10th Cir. 1996); *Rogers v. Grimaldi,* 875 F.2d 994 (2d Cir. 1989); *Comedy III Prod., Inc. v. Gary Saderup, Inc.,* 21 P.3d

797 (Cal. 2001).   Recently, this Court has
adopted three of these approaches. *See ETW
Corp.*, 332 F.3d at 936 (adopting approaches
in *Comedy III* and *Cardtoons*); *Parks v. LaFace
Records*, 329 F.3d 437, 450 (6th Cir. 2003)
(adopting approach in *Rogers*).

Parody is a comedic form of artistic
expression that invokes an original,
copyrighted work by using some of its
protected elements. *See Campbell*, 510 U.S. at
580. The parodist incorporates these familiar
elements into his own original work, which in
turn serves to comment on or criticize the
copyrighted material. *Id.*

For Newsflash to assert a parody defense
for its unauthorized use of Black's image, it
must show that its use satisfies the *Comedy III*
transformative element test or the *Cardtoons*
social commentary balancing test adopted by
ETW, or the *Rogers* relatedness test adopted by
Parks. Each test is addressed in turn.

A.   Newsflash cannot assert a parody defense for misappropriating Black's image because its use lacks a transformative element.

One of the key inquiries into parody analysis is whether the new work simply replaces the protected one, or if the parody adds something transformative that distinguishes it from its target and places the target in a new light. *Campbell* at 579; *Comedy III,* 21 P.3d at 808.

Parody, as a transformative work, aligns itself with the goal of the "news" exception in right of publicity cases in that the new work that appropriates an otherwise protected image does not interfere with the commercial viability of the protected individual's identity. *Compare Winter v. DC Comics*, 69 P.3d 473, 476-80 (Cal. 2003) (depiction of celebrities in comic book significantly altered their appearance so that anyone seeking their picture would find the cartoon a poor substitute, thus preserving the economic viability of their likenesses), *and Hoffman v. Capital Cities/ABC, Inc.,* 255 F.3d

1180, 1182-89 (9th Cir. 2000) (alterations to Hoffman image were part of a magazine article using visual and verbal humor and any commercial impact to Hoffman's right of publicity was minimal), *with Comedy III* at 800-811 (sketch of Three Stooges imprinted on T-shirt contained no transformative element and thus intruded on the publicity right of the Stooges, diluting the potential market for T-shirts and other Stooges memorabilia).

The facts of this case are similar to those in *Comedy III.* Newsflash actually went one step further than the artist in *Comedy III.* Rather than imprinting an artistic representation of Black on its T-shirts, is misappropriated four photographic images of him. Stip. ¶ 6 (R.4). The new elements added to the photographs (the superimposed "Newsflash" name and the demeaning messages) would not qualify as transformative because the images themselves remain unchanged and thus could impact the market for Black photographs or endorsement opportunities.

Should this Court allow these images a

transformative parody defense, it would give
license to any company to create a poster,
T-shirt, or other item using any individual's
photograph, superimpose the company name on
the photo and thus imply the individual's
endorsement, and then assert a parody defense
when that individual seeks injunctive relief
under a right of publicity law. Therefore,
Newsflash cannot assert a parody defense
without an actual transformative element.

B.   **Newsflash cannot assert a parody
     defense for misappropriating Black's
     image because its use does not
     provide social commentary regarding
     Black.**

Celebrities symbolize certain ideas
and have become a means of expression in
our society. *ETW Corp.,* 332 F.3d at 937-
38. Therefore, a work that incorporates
a celebrity likeness and provides social
commentary can enjoy First Amendment
protection. *See Cardtoons,* 95 F.3d at 976. A
court should balance societal interest in free
expression against the celebrity's economic
interest in their right of publicity. *Id.*

Social commentary should be apparent for First Amendment protection to apply. *Compare Parks,* 329 F.3d at 452-59 (connection between Rosa Parks and rap song called "Rosa Parks" not readily apparent – no mention of Ms. Parks in lyrics or reference to the Civil Rights Movement – so remanded for finder of fact to determine if First Amendment protection should apply), *with Cardtoons* at 962-76 (parody baseball cards clearly showcased humorous commentary on major league baseball players).

Black is a prominent figure in today's political landscape and therefore subject to social commentary. Curiously, the issue open to social commentary – Black's job as governor and his appearance at a Republican fundraiser in that capacity – is not evident in any of the four photographs selected by Newsflash for use in its T-shirts. Any photograph of Black on the campaign trail, celebrating at his inauguration, or behind a podium giving a speech would have been sufficient for parodic purposes. Here, there is no way to properly distinguish what exactly Newsflash is holding

up for social commentary. Therefore, a parody
defense cannot apply.

C. Newsflash cannot assert a parody defense for misappropriating Black's image because its use is wholly unrelated to the content of the T-shirts.

Under *Rogers*, an unauthorized use of an
individual's name in a title will be protected
by the First Amendment unless the title is
wholly unrelated to the work's content or
is simply used as a means of advertisement.
Parks, 329 F.3d at 460.

Black comes from the Hollywood community
and understands the importance of parody in
creative expression. He does not dispute its
value, or that he could be parody's potential
target. However, Newsflash's use of Black's
image is wholly unrelated to its intended
message of commenting on Republican politics
in Tennessee. None of the four T-shirts even
explicitly mention that Black is a Republican.

A pertinent question - why would someone
buy a T-shirt with a celebrity's image? - is
worth asking. Russell S. Jones, Jr., *The*

Flip Side of Privacy: The Right of Publicity,
The First Amendment, and Constitutional Line
Drawing - A Presumptive Approach, 39 Creighton
L. Rev. 939, 958 (2006). If the answer
is because of the identity of the person
depicted, right of publicity should prevail
over the First Amendment. *Id*. It is hard
to see how a Democratic voter could possibly
construe the content of a Newsflash T-shirt
as Republican political commentary, and thus
sales are probably based on having Black on
a T-shirt. As Black did not authorize these
T-shirts, use of his image on them should not
be allowed to stand.

The unauthorized use of Black's image
does not qualify as parody under the
approaches adopted by this Court. Therefore,
even if this Court exempts parody from the
Tennessee Personal Rights Protection Act,
Newsflash cannot enjoy that exemption.

CONCLUSION

For the reasons stated above, this Court
should affirm the decision of the United States

District Court for the Western District of
Tennessee.

Chapter 7

Oral Advocacy at the Pretrial, Trial, and Appellate Stages

Thus far, we have concentrated on the use of *writing* for communication in the practice of law, and by now we hope you will agree that effective writing is indeed tantamount to effective advocacy. It is true, however, that any lawyer will have at least as many and sometimes more occasions to use oral communication in the practice of law. When will oral communication be necessary?

- To provide advice to a client or other attorneys in the lawyer's office

- To discuss matters or negotiate with other attorneys

- To orally communicate and argue motions, requests, objections, and other legal arguments to a decision maker, such as a judge or other arbiter of a dispute.

In fact, if we were to compare the amount of time we have spent on the telephone and talking on our feet as attorneys to the amount of time hunched before a keyboard drafting important legal documents, we are sure we would find that the former balances out and sometimes even outweighs the latter.

There is no question that clear and effective oral communication skills are a great asset for any attorney; even the best legal writers throughout their careers will doubtfully be able to rely exclusively on the magic they can produce via the written word. Even in the (seemingly) simple task of reporting your findings to a superior "on your feet," you will learn that excellent oral communication is, for a lawyer, as important as what he or she can demonstrate in writing. Indeed, very often your clients or your superiors who vote on your future in the law office will *only* have these types of verbal encounters with you—they may never have read a single thing you have written, and the only impression they will have of you as an attorney is from your speaking skills. This should be a great incentive for you to try to refine these skills.

This chapter focuses on the more particular skills of oral communication required in litigation settings. Unlike most legal method and legal writing texts, we will discuss argument in the trenches of the trial level courts before going to the mountaintop of appellate level oral argument. The skills needed in the former type of forum are slightly different and arguably more crude than the skills needed in the latter setting.

I.   BACKGROUND PRINCIPLES OF THE PRACTICE OF ORAL ARGUMENT

Lawyers often puzzle over the true meaning of oral argument. As with writing, we think it is prudent to look at oral argument from the perspective of the *audience*, the trial or appellate court judge. Judges have several ends that are achieved by oral argument:

A.   It is an efficient use of the court's time and resources

At the trial court level, complicated motions can be summarized and reported orally in capsule form to the court, which, after hearing the argument, might have an immediate answer for the parties on the merits of the motion. If the court is one in which the judge has an abundance of cases and no law clerks, oral argument enables the court to process a great number of cases in the shortest possible time. Even if the judge is forced to take a motion "under advisement" after the oral argument, the argument still may have served its purpose to educate the court enough to allow it to proceed rapidly through the briefs and memoranda filed on the motion, and ultimately lead to a quicker decision.

On appeal, the judges generally do have law clerks who can summarize the legal briefs for the judges in the form of a bench memo or draft opinion, but appellate court judges nonetheless often will take the time to personally consult the parties' briefs before the oral argument. In these instances, oral argument will assist the court in making sense of complicated issues and provide a forum to question the litigants. As discussed in sections B and C below, this Q&A ultimately is intended to assist the court in reaching its decision in a shorter period of time.

FOOD FOR THOUGHT

QUESTION: Does oral argument revolve around you, the oralist, or the court?

ANSWER: The court.

Oral argument is all about the court and its needs. No matter how carefully you design and prepare for your argument, you must expect—even hope for—the court to crash your party and upset your prepared argument with a barrage of questions. If this actually happens, rejoice! You've had a great argument! You learned what the court really was worried about, and you had the chance to address those concerns directly. This is the best possible outcome for an oral argument.

B.   It allows a judge to question the two sides about the motion or appeal

Even if the judge or judges do read and digest the motion or appellate briefs ahead of time (or their clerks do), they likely still will have questions that need to be answered before they can rule. Oral argument is just the place for this. Many advocates think of oral argument as "their time" to present their arguments, but judges quite properly think of argument as *the court's* time to clarify and explore the issues.

Thus, an advocate may spend days preparing a wonderful fifteen minute oral argument just to show up and have the court use up thirteen of those minutes peppering her with questions. This is not a failure; in fact, this is exactly what the advocate should expect and even welcome. The days spent working on and thinking hard about the case will enable an advocate to address those thirteen minutes of questions properly, and the judges will leave this argument with a much better understanding of those aspects of the case that troubled them the most.

C.   It can assist a judge in making up her mind

Trial court judges may have no idea that a motion was filed in your case until you step up to the podium and address the court on the motion. The only time you will have the judge's undivided attention on your motion is during these brief periods of argument. If the judge cannot devote long periods of time to the briefs filed by the parties (and especially if she has no law clerks to help her), the oral argument is the most important time for the judge to make up her mind about the merits of the motion.

Of the appellate court judges we have heard on this issue, most have reported that they very often make up their minds based on the *briefs* of the parties. Good news for writers. That said, arguments serve as a chance for the advocate to reconfirm this initial reaction or perhaps to offer one or two points that might push the judge a little farther in one direction or the other. Judges absolutely do allow for the possibility that from time to time the parties might explain their case orally in such a way that they actually will change their minds *solely because of the oral arguments*. This should be enough incentive for you to take the argument process seriously.

II.   ORAL ARGUMENT IN TRIAL LEVEL COURTS PRIOR TO TRIAL

An oral argument in the pretrial stage can happen several ways. The ways will depend on the local rules and local practices of the jurisdiction and occasionally on the individual judge to which your case is assigned.

A.   "No oral argument" jurisdictions

You may find yourself practicing in a jurisdiction that does not allow oral argument on motions except when it is specifically ordered by the court. This is what we characterize as a "no oral argument" jurisdiction, because the rule commonly is interpreted to mean that oral argument will be extremely rare on motions, and reserved only for the most complicated motions where the parties and the court think it will be of benefit.

The parties might request oral argument because they think it will lead to an earlier ruling on the motion. They also might think that the court will benefit from having the parties run through the motion in person, so that they can address any problems that the court might have with the facts, or the law, or the positions of the parties.

The court might go along with the request or, even more rarely, *sua sponte* order oral argument on a motion for the same reasons as stated above. Different judges have different opinions about the benefits and costs of oral argument. Some judges love to see and hear the attorneys in the case, others started their judicial career in a court where oral arguments were routinely heard, and they think of the process as a great way to clear their docket of a number of motions in a short period of time. Other judges would rather reserve their court time for trials and hearings and will not be bothered to hear motions argued.

B.   "Motion Day" or "Law Day" jurisdictions

In some courts, one or two days a month or sometimes one or two days a week are set aside for motions to be heard on oral argument pursuant to local rules. *E.g.*, Ala. R. Civ. P. 78; Ariz. R. Civ. P. 78; Ark. R. Civ. P. 78; Colo. R. Civ. P. 78; Haw. R. Civ. P. 78. These days are called "motion days" or sometimes "law days." The movant generally will have to schedule a place on the motion docket with the court, and then give notice of the date and time to all parties and the court. Occasionally, a court will allow any and all parties with pending motions simply to show up and sign up on the motion day, without prior scheduling or notice to the court. It will be necessary to notify your opponents that you are going, because if you show up by yourself, the court is unlikely to entertain an *ex parte* argument on the motion.

C.   "Open Court" Jurisdictions

Occasionally, a court will hear oral arguments on motions any day that the court is in session. A simple call to the court to confirm that they are in session on the chosen day, perhaps to sign up on the docket, too, and notice given in writing to all parties and to the court will secure your oral argument whenever it is convenient for you and the other parties.

D.   Informal matters and "show up" jurisdictions

Courts sometimes will set aside a short period of time, usually in the morning when the court first opens for business, for the hearing of informal matters and motions, and any party with such a request or motion simply can show up and present their request to the court. Prior notice to the court is not required, although it will be necessary to contact the other parties to let them know what you are up to. These sessions usually are reserved for smaller, often uncontested motions, such as requests for extensions of time to answer or to respond to discovery or to file an amended complaint, requests to file a brief with additional pages over the local page limit, for attorney admission to the court, for a minor amendment to pleadings, or other fairly simple requests. Discovery motions, such as motions to quash or motions to compel might be brought here, especially if the timing of the discovery (a deposition, for example) demands expedited attention from the court. Substantial requests, such as dispositive motions to dismiss or for summary judgment, motions for preliminary injunctions, and complicated discovery motions or motions in limine generally will not be entertained in informal matters, and the court may get angry at you for trying to bring up a complicated, contested motion in these sessions.

E.   The necessity to "notice up" motions

In many courts, other than those in category A above, the parties must call for oral argument by "noticing up a hearing" on a motion because that is the only way their motions are going to get ruled on. Notice of a hearing on a motion alerts the other parties that if they have not filed an opposition to the motion yet, do it now or before the hearing. Notice also puts the court file in the judge's hands on the day of the hearing, and gives him a strong incentive to deal with the motion then and there, rather than hear the oral argument, let the motion go under advisement, and forget about it.

F.   Style of oral argument in trial courts in the pretrial period

Oral argument at the pretrial stage differs from the appellate level oral argument in several ways. Usually, you do not get a fixed period of time to talk. You talk until the judge shuts you up, or your opponent interrupts you and cuts you off, or until you run out of things to say, or until the judge walks out and they turn the lights off in the court. You do not get just one chance to argue your position; you can go back and forth several times arguing your side then listening to your opponent argue hers, then interrupting her and trying to command the judge's attention, until she cuts you off or the judge calls it quits.

PRACTICE POINTER

Put a little P-L-A in your pretrial oral argument

If you do get the chance to make a pretrial oral argument on a motion, it often pays to follow a simple, direct structure to the argument that is less ornate and formal than the structure we will describe for appellate-level and moot court oral arguments. Long introductions and recitations of the facts are not going to cut it. Instead, follow this plan: (1) Pick as few points to argue as you can. Two to three points is best; more than three is too optimistic. (2) Roadmap your points quickly. *E.g.*, "Your Honor, the motion to dismiss must be denied, first, because the focus of this construction contract was in Idaho, not Montana, even though the parties signed the contract in Montana, so Idaho law governs the contract. Second, under Idaho law, gravesite restoration is the obligation of the builder, not the land owner, so our claim for restitution is properly asserted under Idaho law." (3) In the actual argument, make your point (thesis), followed by legal authority, followed by application to the client so that the client prevails—this is referred to as a **P-L-A structure** to the presentation. (4) Move on to the next point as soon as you are finished with the first point (if the trial judge wants to hear more about the first point, she will ask you). (5) Use any remaining time (if you haven't been interrupted yet) to rebut your opponent's points.

In the best instances, the judge will control the argument and demand an orderly presentation so that each side gets a chance to say what it wants to say. The best judges will not tolerate counsel interrupting each other and will quash such rudeness quickly. The judge may question each side so as to explore the strengths and weaknesses of their positions. The judge, not the parties, decides when she has heard enough on the motion.

At its worst, the court will not regulate the argument, and will sit by while counsel interrupt and cut each other off, and bluster and rage so as to command the most attention. In these situations, it matters much less whether or not you have a structured and logical outline, and a start and finish to the argument worked out on a pretrial motion; rather, what is important is the ability to divert the judge's attention away from your opponent and capture it long enough to say your two or three points any way that you can. Being quick of tongue, loud, blustery, and ready and willing to interrupt and cut off your opponent will help in these dismal situations.

III.   ORAL ARGUMENT DURING A TRIAL

Aside from the opening statement and the closing argument, which are directed to the jury of laypersons, not to the court, and which have nothing to do with our topic here, oral arguments to the court are not regularly scheduled during trials. However, in our experience, we have more often than not been called on to make miniature oral arguments during a trial to argue evidentiary points, to argue motions made during the trial, and to argue or defend motions for directed verdict or for judgment as a matter of law.

These arguments usually are conducted like the pretrial motions described above—you do not get a set amount of time and you get to go back and forth several times, but far fewer of the same "style" disadvantages carry over to this setting because a sense of decorum prevails during a trial that is absent in the average pretrial hearing. As a result, the arguments generally are cleaner with fewer interruptions. Nevertheless, the content of the arguments typically are no more organized, detailed, or thought-provoking than the average pretrial argument.

IV.   APPELLATE LEVEL AND MOOT COURT ORAL ARGUMENT

The rest of this chapter focuses on the more particular skills required in appellate court and moot court settings. The paradigm of oral argument for law students is appellate level oral argument. This is the model followed by most law schools in first year oral arguments and in the moot court programs and competitions in the second and third year.

Compared to oral arguments in the trial courts, appellate level argument is a "mountaintop" experience, because you get a certain amount of time to speak, no one interrupts you (except the panel of judges), and getting out your full argument does not depend on your ability and willingness to interrupt and cut off the other side.

The standard procedures for oral argument are remarkably similar from place to place and competition to competition:

- Usually there is more than one judge on the panel.

- Each side (appellant - appellee, or petitioner - respondent) gets a specific period of time in which to speak. It can be as little as ten minutes or as long as the court wants to give you, although most courts will not give each side more than forty-five minutes or an hour for any argument.

- No one except the panel can interrupt the oralist. No counsel can yell, "Objection," or "She's misstating the facts!" during the opponent's argument.

- A bailiff or clerk keeps time, and periodically will hold up a time card, light up a small light in front of you, or rap a gavel to let you know how many minutes you have left.

- Each oralist makes her arguments and answers the panel's questions and sits down.

- Generally, the appellant or petitioner oralists speak first and the appellee or respondent oralists speak second. Where there is more than one issue at stake in the appeal, some courts allow an appellant or petitioner to argue issue one followed by the appellee or respondent's argument on issue one, followed by the appellant or petitioner's argument on issue two, followed by the appellee or respondent's argument on issue two, and so on. Some moot court competitions follow this procedure, too.

- The appellant usually can reserve a few minutes for one oralist to do rebuttal, and once in a great while the rules of the court or the moot court competition will allow the appellee to reserve time for an oralist to do surrebuttal.

- If you have a partner or associate with you, your side will have to pre-determine how to split the time between the two oralists. Most of the time, an even split is the best idea. You do not want to deny the judges the opportunity to have a good look at both oralists and an equal chance to ask their questions concerning both parts of the argument.

FYI

Active, Hostile, and Hot Judges
The classic and expected practice in oral argument is for the judges to interrupt your argument with questions. Panels will vary from how **active** they are (lots of questions), how **hostile** they are (how much they show their dislike for one or both sides' arguments), or how **"hot"** they are ("hot" means they read the parties' briefs or the bench briefs carefully and are prepared to question you on the issues and authorities; "cold" means they did not read anything before hand, and will just give you a cold indifferent stare when you start). A good panel for almost any oral argumentative is an active, hot, but not hostile panel.

V.   HOW TO PREPARE FOR ORAL ARGUMENT

Appellate oral argument follows the time period allocated for the briefing of the case in which the appellant or petitioner files its opening brief, the appellee or respondent files its answering brief or opposition brief, and the appellant or petitioner files its reply brief. An argument date is set by the court. A panel of judges from the court is selected unless the matter is to be heard by the court *en banc*. As the day of the argument approaches, counsel should be doing the following things to prepare themselves for the argument:

A.   Know every case and legal authority inside and out.

You probably will be nervous before your first two or three oral arguments, but use this energy to drive you through the preparation. Channel your nervous energy into reviewing the points you will make and the points raised by your opponent in her brief. Read all of your cases and authorities again for facts, holding, rationale, and policies. Key Cite or Shepardize them one more time. Now do the same for your opponent's cases: find her bad cases.

If you have one or more partners, you should spend some time discussing all of the good and bad cases as a team when you are preparing for oral argument. Everyone on the team should have a working knowledge of the issues and the authorities in the case, both good authorities and bad. It is common in oral arguments to hear an oralist beg off a question by disclaiming "That is a question that my co-counsel will address," or worse yet, "That issue has been discussed in my co-counsel's part of the argument, and I am not able to discuss it." The only time you should be uttering these words in oral argument is if you are completely stumped by a question thrown at you by the panel, **and** it happens to be an issue that your co-counsel, who is going next, will address. If you are well up to speed on the case, you should not have to beg off. Some judges are looking to see how up to speed on the whole case you really are, and if you handle an "off your position" question well, they will be very impressed.

B.   Write an outline, not a script.

Draft an **outline** of what you want to say. You do not want to

DO IT WITH STYLE!

The Outline
You understand that you're supposed to outline your argument, not script it, but what goes into the outline? — Key words. That is all. Do not put thesis headings in the outline. Do not write complete sentences. Certainly do not put whole paragraphs into the outline because if you do, you will be tempted to read them.

write out things word for word because if you then read from a prepared text, this will not sound conversational, sincere, and from the heart. Good oral arguments sound more conversational than speeches delivered from a podium. You also are supposed to make eye contact with everyone on the panel, and you cannot do that if you are looking down at your notes. Oral arguments have the illusion of being an impromptu discussion from someone who knows and cares, and thus are more persuasive than the average lecture. If you write out your entire argument, you will have too much paper up there with you at the podium, and in trying to follow it, you may get distracted by a question and lose your place.

Your outline does not have to follow the exact order of arguments that you put in your brief. Think about ways to get to the best argument quickly and work on a transition from that to the next best argument and so on. The judges have your brief, and they can read the whole story of your case if they want to. Oral argument is the place for you to drive home your best points and make them stick in the judges' minds, so that when the judges retire to the conference that follows the arguments, they will remember these points and be more inclined to vote in your favor.

C.   Prepare an introduction : "the first forty-five"

The only exception to the rule against scripting that we encourage you to follow is for you to script the first forty-five seconds or so of your oral argument and to commit this portion to memory. But the most important thing to remember is: Do not bring the script to the podium, You must memorize it. Then destroy it.

The start of the argument has certain formal requirements expected of counsel in most jurisdictions:

- Most oralists will start their argument with the phrase, **"May it please the court."** This is a convention, not a rule in most jurisdictions, but it is a convention followed by the vast majority of oralists. If you decide to buck the convention, you should be aware that from time to time you will encounter a judge who will view your free-spirited thinking as rebellion. You will not necessarily win points for originality; instead, judges will think you started the argument incorrectly. Many oralists soften the formality by adding, **"Good morning, your honors"** or other greeting appropriate for the time of day. Oralists at the United States Supreme Court begin by stating, **"Mr. Chief Justice, may it please the court."**

- Personal introductions come next. Introduce yourself and your co-counsel, and the party you represent. Remind the court of the reason for your argument and your prayer for relief. Explain the breakdown of the points you and your co-counsel will be addressing.

Example: May it please the court. Good afternoon, your honors. My name is Walter Scott and I, together with my co-counsel, Edith Wharton, represent petitioner George Elliot. Ms. Elliot asks the court to reverse the order granting summary judgment in favor of respondent Twain issued by the United States District Court for the Western District of Tennessee. I will be addressing the issues of news

> reporting and political speech. My co-counsel will address the issues of parody and the right to comment on and criticize political figures under the First Amendment.

- The next portion should be an introduction (a **roadmap**) to your argument and your theme. Most counsel draft a short statement of the two or three major bullet points of their argument, followed by a statement of the theme of the case from your client's perspective.

Example: **{introduction}** Ms. Elliot requests that you reverse the lower court for three reasons: first, that the First Amendment protects and encourages political commentary to such a degree that respondent Twain's publicity rights must give way to Ms. Elliot's commentary. Second, that the Tennessee Personal Rights Protection Act specifically provides an exception for "news reporting" and commentary on "public affairs," and Ms. Elliot meets the requirements of this exception. Third, that Ms. Elliot's commentary is not commercial speech. **{theme}** Your honors, the protection of the right of political commentary is the core value protected by the First Amendment. The preservation of all other topics of expression is secondary to the goal of preserving an open and robust dialogue on politics in a democracy.

Some counsel will flip the theme and the introduction:

Example: **{theme}** Your honors, the protection of the right of political commentary is the core value protected by the First Amendment. The preservation of all other topics of expression is secondary to the goal of preserving an open and robust dialogue on politics in a democracy. **{introduction}** Ms. Elliot requests that you reverse the lower court for three reasons: first, that the First Amendment protects and encourages political commentary to such a degree that respondent Twain's publicity rights must give way to Ms. Elliot's commentary. Second, that the Tennessee Personal Rights Protection Act specifically provides an exception for "news reporting" and commentary on "public affairs," and Ms. Elliot meets the requirements of this exception. Third, that Ms. Elliot's commentary is not commercial speech.

Still others will combine the theme and the introduction in one statement of the case:

{thematic introduction} Ms. Elliot requests that you reverse the lower court for three reasons: first, that the First Amendment protects and encourages political commentary to such a degree that respondent Twain's publicity rights must give way to Ms. Elliot's commentary. Indeed, this is the core value protected by the First Amendment, which outweighs the protection of all other topics of speech. Second, that the Tennessee Personal Rights Protection Act specifically provides an exception for "news reporting" and commentary on "public affairs" so as to ensure an open and robust dialogue on matters of public interest in a democracy. Ms. Elliot meets the requirements of this exception. Third, that Ms. Elliot's commentary is not commercial speech and thus deserves the full protection that the First Amendment affords to political commentary.

A bullet point introduction of the two or three main points of your argument notifies the court of what you think are your most important points. The judges will appreciate the outline if it is short and manageable. An outline of five or six major points is excessive. Rarely would even the most skilled oralist be able to cover six points adequately in fifteen minutes even if the judges withheld all of their questions. The judges will be discouraged if you ask them to try to keep that many major points straight in their heads as you make the effort to cover them. It is much better to distill your argument down to two or three points. Telling the judges your two or three best points up front also allows them to direct you to address whichever of the points the judges are the most interested in, which most likely will be the points that the judges are having the most trouble with. You might be disappointed that the judges do not want to hear point one, your best point, but if they already have resolved that point in their minds, argument over this point would be a waste of your time and theirs.

Do not be misled into thinking that our recommendation of scripting your opening means that you might plan on reading from the script. Nothing could be further from the truth. The script is there for you to memorize well before you step up to the podium. After memorizing your opening, practice it several times each day leading up to the argument. Memorization and practice allows two things to happen simultaneously in your argument: first, you will be assured that you have command of the first forty-five seconds of your argument. If you are tense or nervous about the argument process, at least you will know that you can speak confidently without stumbling or getting tongue tied for the first forty-five seconds. This allows you precious time to get comfortable with the process and get into the flow of a conversation. Second, memorization allows you to make eye contact with the entire panel and to establish rapport during the opening seconds. A smooth opening relaxes the panel and draws them in. They will be happy to be listening to a competent oralist who can begin smoothly and who invites them to join the conversation by making eye contact with each member of the panel. That is why reading from your script is a cardinal sin.

If you have not had much experience memorizing passages of this length, here are two tips:

- Copy over your script by hand at least three times. The exercise of copying engages the mind in several activities at once—considering the words individually, considering how they flow one to the other, and directing your hand to write them down correctly. Actors use this technique to memorize their scripts, and on average they have a lot more lines to commit to memory than you will have.

- Practice your opening several times a day. If you stumble, go back and copy over your script three more times. Repeat this process until you have the opening committed to memory.

- Practice out loud. No matter how silly you think this is, the brain memorizes better if you speak your presentation or argument out loud.

If you still are uncomfortable with the thought of forgetting your opening, do not bring your script to the podium. Instead, outline your opening on an index card:

(1)   **May it please the court**

(2)   **Introduce yourself and your co-counsel–what are each of you arguing**

(3)   **Ask the court to reverse**

(4)   **Give your outline:**
           point one: political speech
           point two: statutory exception
           point three: not commercial speech

(5)   **Give theme: political speech and First Amendment**

At least then you will have a crutch, but you will not be encouraged to read off of the card.

D.   Themes are not just for briefs

As mentioned in the section above, you should work on a theme for your argument that fits with your facts and the majority of your written arguments. Hopefully, you already had a good theme in your brief, but if not, there still is time to come up with one. A good sound bite that sums up your arguments, that you can return to frequently in your argument and in answers to questions, can drive home your arguments faster than a long winded explanation. Try to find the best (and safest) analogy for your situation, and use it whenever you want to remind the court of the equities or legal realities that drive your arguments to their conclusions. Short and vivid themes are the best. Paint a small picture—or come up with a one panel editorial cartoon with a one line zinger that sums up you case, and build the argument around that. Do not get too wordy or complicated—think advertising copy, not a treatise discussion.

E.   Try to anticipate likely questions, and work out good answers to them

Try to think up questions your panel of judges might ask, and work out answers that are good, complete responses to the questions and which can segue you back to the points you want to raise.[1] Judges will ask about the strengths of your case and your opponent's case, and explore the weaknesses of both sides. Judges will ask about the public policy and precedential implications of the arguments you are making. They will ask questions about specific cases and authorities—What were the facts of that case? Who was the plaintiff? Did that case have anything to do with [XYZ topic]? When was that statute enacted? When did that regulation go into effect? Do not neglect your opponent's authorities and the major points of your opponent's argument; you must be prepared to discuss these, too. You can put these questions and the outline of your sample answers on a flip stack of 3X5 cards to include with the materials you will bring to the podium.

F.   Organize your materials for easy access

Ideally, your outline should fit on one or two pages. Try pasting it or stapling it to the inside of a legal size manila folder. With a manila folder, you can add a flip stack of 3X5 cards with all your important cases and authorities, your rebuttal points, and perhaps some details of the areas of law you will be discussing summarized on the cards, and a flip stack of question and answer cards described in the section above. If you think of additional points or questions, you still can stick Post-it™ notes on to the pages all the way up to the argument. We also have used three ring binders with well marked tabs leading you to your outline, your questions and answers, your rebuttal points, and your authorities information pages.

Put tabs on your brief and the opponent's brief, in case you need to look up something in these documents. If you think you might use the record, go through and tab the parts that you think might come up.

---

1   *See also* section IX <u>infra</u>, "Questions from the panel."

What you bring up to the podium matters less than your ability to use what you have brought quickly, quietly, and neatly. In most cases we will bring one binder or a legal size manila folder for our outline and our question-answer cards and authority cards, the briefs of the two sides, and whatever parts of the record we think we might absolutely have to use. We will expect to look at only ten percent of what we bring to the podium— usually only the outline. Your preparation for the argument should have instilled in your brain the information needed to answer the panel's questions and to make your argument without reference to the note cards and briefs.

At the very least, do not be the person who drags up several bulging file folders, full of papers sticking out this way and that, who takes five minutes to get set up before he can begin, and another six minutes to clean up after he is finished, while the judges stare at him with mixed feelings of ire and pity. You are trying to make an impression on the court that will cause them to vote in your favor. You do not want to lose points for sloppiness, of all things.

G.   Go and do some field research – see how this is done.

Go watch real life oral arguments and moot court arguments. Get a feeling for what goes on, and pay attention to the kinds of questions that are asked and how they are answered. Note the tone of the oralists. Very few of them will be shouting. Theatrics probably will not be evident. It will probably sound like a conversation, one in which the oralist dominates but the judges can join at any time.

If you cannot leave home or cannot pry yourself away from the law library, you can browse for dozens of oral arguments from real cases and from moot court competitions on YouTube.com—enter "oral argument" in YouTube's search box. In addition, you can take advantage of the work of Prof. Jerry Goldman at Northwestern University Law School, who has prepared Real Audio® files of hundreds of oral arguments of U.S. Supreme Court cases that you can access and listen to at the Oyez Project web site, www.oyez.org (last visited April 27, 2009). The U.S. Supreme Court typically is a very active and hot panel, so you can listen to how the oralists handle intense questioning in their arguments. A Google.com search of "oral arguments" most likely will lead you to appellate court websites where videos of recent oral arguments at the court are available for viewing.

H.   How do you get to the Supreme Court? – practice, practice, practice.

Practice arguing in front of a camcorder or mirror; then practice in front of your friends and teammates. You do not necessarily have to give a legal argument in order to get the feeling of standing at a podium; present any kind of argument for some position, and answer questions from your "judges." Whatever topic you choose, take the process seriously, because you will not learn much from a session that breaks down into kidding and laughing. Just getting the feeling of talking and answering questions on your feet can make you more comfortable with the process.

After this, hold regular moot court practice sessions with your classmates or teammates—at least two or three a week in the weeks that precede the arguments. You and your teammates should grill each other as best as you can on the weaknesses and trouble spots of the case. It may seem foolish and tiresome the fourth or fifth time you do it, but practice rounds of oral argument are like batting practice or shooting free throws: the more you drill yourself to respond cooly and competently to hard questions, the more likely it will be that you will respond cooly and competently to these same questions when you are at your oral argument and the pressure is on. Have someone videotape these practice sessions. Watching yourself on tape will reveal all kinds of amazing things you never imagined yourself doing.

VI.   MOOT COURT JUDGES

Whether you are facing an oral argument as part of your first year curriculum or you are facing it in the context of an upper division moot court competition, you are likely to face the same kinds of judges. The common pool for intramural and interscholastic competitions are alumnae of the school where the competition is being held, whether they be private practitioners, government lawyers, public defenders and prosecutors, in-house counsel, or actual judges. Even a regional moot court competition is going to be housed by local lawyers and judges.

The sponsors of a national competition may draw in a number of judges from out of town (the Jessup International Law Moot Court competition coordinates their international final rounds with the yearly convention of the American Society of International Law, so they have a bunch of conventioneers to choose from). You are more likely to get high powered judges who are actually judges at a regional or national competition finals.

Almost all judges you will face had a strong interest in moot court in law school, and most will have had several years of experience in litigation and oral advocacy. Most will know that they should ask questions, and many of them even will know how to ask short, cogent questions without droning on for a minute or more. (Just kidding, judges!). Judges will try to test your arguments with worst case scenarios, parades of horrors, and the edge of the slippery slope.[2] They may try to test your composure by interrupting you frequently and trying to quarrel with you about the law or the facts. Do not take the bait; they are testing you to see if you will get angry and fire back at them, but they are expecting you not to.

Actual judges are not necessarily the best oral argument judges. Actual members of the judiciary have a habit of listening to arguments rather than spicing them up with a lot of questions. This carries over from actual courtroom practices. Something about wearing a black choir robe every day makes a person more dignified and ready to listen, rather than fostering a desire to stir things up and test the knowledge and abilities of the advocates before them. Do not expect real judges to behave like television's "Judge Judy" and give you a good tongue lashing. A panel of actual judges can get all riled up in moot court as well as in real court, but in our experience, practitioners ask more and harder questions on average than actual judges.

VII.   DECORUM, APPEARANCE, AND DELIVERY

Strict rules of decorum apply in appellate level oral argument. You must show respect for the panel at every turn. You always should address a judge as **"Your honor,"** or two judges as **"Your honors,"** and the whole panel as **"the Court."**

---

2 *See also* section IX <u>infra</u>, "Questions from the panel."

Disagree with a judge or judges gracefully and respectfully. When you want to say "no" to a judge, say **"I respectfully disagree"** or **"Your honor, the answer is not [XYZ]"** or **"With all due respect, your Honor, the cases in [PDQ jurisdiction] do not support the argument that . . ."** Avoid saying "No" or "No, your honor" directly to a judge unless the judge asked you a "yes-no" question that demands a "yes-no" answer. This is a matter of decorum and politeness, not substance. The judges expect you to disagree with them when they try to undo part of your case, but you should explain your disagreement with grace and respect.

Polite attention and eye contact is expected and is effective in oral argument. Staring or glaring at a judge for minutes at a time is not. Grinning, laughing, or otherwise goofing or joking at oral argument is not acceptable. If a judge makes a joke, you should politely laugh (not bust a gut and slap your knee), and smile and move on with your answer or with your argument. Resist the temptation to make a follow-up joke. Oral argument is serious business, not open-mike night at the local comedy club.

There is no "backstage" in the courtroom, so behave yourself at the counsel table. Sit patiently and listen attentively and respectfully or quietly take notes during your opponent's oral argument. Do not roll your eyes or snort or slam your pen down; these theatrics cost you much more than they will ever gain you. If you have a partner, pay close attention to the back of her head and give her focus in this way when she is arguing. Resist the urge to nod vigorously or pump your fist in the air when she makes a good point. You do not want to draw focus away from her and to yourself by nodding, fidgeting, picking your fingernails, slouching on the table, leaning way back in your chair, spinning your chair back and forth, or other such distracting conduct. Do not try these things on your opponents, either; it is very unprofessional and detrimental to the judges' opinion of you. Beaming happily at the back of your partner's head is permitted.

In every oral argument, whether it be in a real appellate court or in moot court, your appearance must be professional and appropriate. Wear your best job interview suit for an interview at a stodgy law firm. Wear your hair in a conservative lawyerly way. Jewelry and accessories (men's ties, women's scarves, chains, and earrings) should be somewhat subdued and preferably conservative. Do not wear a watch or jewelry that is loose and clunky that you might bang the podium with in the middle of your argument.

You should stand fairly still at the podium with your hands gently placed on the edge near you or gently intertwined at your stomach; the latter is especially good if you have no podium and have to argue in front of a table or desk. The reason for this is to keep your hands where you need them and not where you do not want them—it gives your hands something to hold on to in a tidy way. Often the panel will not be able to see your hands in these positions because of the podium. In these positions, your hands can rise up to make a gesture of emphasis, or flip pages, or lift a note card smoothly, quickly, and quietly.

If you can stand and comfortably deliver your argument with your hands at your sides, that can look very impressive. The trouble is that few people can do this for a long enough period of time, and wind up letting their hands go somewhere they do not want them to go; they snake into a pocket, or one or both hands wind up on your hips, or your hands start swinging back and forth, which are inappropriate places for them to be during the argument.

Do not sway back and forth or from side to side at the podium. You will make the panel seasick. Do not wander from your spot—this is not a closing argument before a jury where you may want to walk the rail and make eye contact with all of the jurors. Do not grip the podium like a dying man or lean your full weight on it or slouch with your elbows on it as if you are exhausted or lazy.

Arms crossed are hostile. Arms forced behind the back or nailed to your sides will look peculiar and should be avoided unless you were in the military or other occupation where you were asked to stand in a rigid, formal posture and you are the most comfortable standing that way. Putting one or both hands in your pockets looks cavalier or disrespectful; it is too casual for this situation. Hands on the hips look impatient or disapproving.

Small gestures used sparingly for emphasis can be effective, but do not point or shake a finger directly at a judge or take any other subliminally hostile action. Arm waving or fist shaking is beyond the pale. Any arm gesture that puts your hands above the level of your shoulders is suspect. Think friendly counselor, not fire-and-brimstone preacher. Never pound the pulpit no matter how worked up you get. It is too comical and theatrical for a serious situation like oral argument.

A conversational tone may come naturally to you, or you may have to work at it. Tape yourself and listen to what you sound like. Ask your friends and associates to listen to you and evaluate your tone. Does it sound like a normal tone of voice for speaking? Does it sound like the start of a conversation that a person would feel comfortable joining? Or does it sound like preaching, shouting, addressing a large crowd from a stage, or other public speaking style that no one would characterize as conversational.

High speed is your enemy. It is hard enough to be understood when explaining something orally, speeding up just a little can lose your audience a lot. If your normal conversational tone is rushed, consciously slow yourself down a little bit. But — do — not — talk — abnormally — slowly — because — this — does — not — allow — your — argument — to — sound — conversational. Ask your co-counsel to evaluate how well you are doing.

Never try to rush to squeeze in one more point in the last minute or two of the argument when you see the time card or the light indicating one or two minutes remaining. A rushed end to the argument will leave a bad taste in the judges' mouths. They will lose track of the argument if they cannot understand it because of your hyper-speed. The best practice is to continue at the same pace. Perhaps, at the one or two minute mark, you could announce and summarize an additional point; if a judge is intrigued, she may ask a question or grant you additional time to make the final point.

Above all, try to consciously eliminate verbal fillers such as "uhhh," "ahhh," "ummm," and lackluster vernacular phrases such as "uh-huh," "ya-know," "like" (as in "It's like so illegal," or "The Constitution like bans this conduct."). These phrases are distracting and can make a judge tune you out. Worse yet, the judge might start a score card with how many "uhhh's" and "ummm's" you say in the argument; take it from us—that judge is not paying proper attention to the substance of your argument any more.

VIII.   CONSTRUCTING THE ARGUMENT

A.   The First Oralist's Argument

As mentioned above, when designing your oral argument's structure you do not have to rigidly follow the outline of your brief. Truly consider what is your best argument, and find a way to get to that argument quickly and logically. Then plan the transition to the next best argument and so on.

Certainly do not plan to argue using just the table of contents from your brief as your outline. Presume that the judges have read that much. Instead, focus on planning a route to your best issue so that you have a shot of getting that out before the questions start firing.

It is customary in some courts for the first person who argues to ask if the court requires a **recitation of the facts** (note that this is ***not*** expected of the second, third, or fourth person to argue in the session). If you are lucky, they will turn you down and not waste five to ten minutes of your allotted time on background facts. Of course, if you want to talk about the facts, just launch into them; this applies whether you are arguing first or last in the session. If the judges really do not want to hear about the facts, they will tell you to move on. If you absolutely do not want to present a summary of the facts, ask the court for permission to **dispense with a recitation of the facts**. State: **"With the court's permission, may I dispense with a recitation of the facts?"** This should help to remind the panel that you do not have enough time to dwell on facts.

As mentioned above, you should write a **theme** for your argument and interject it whenever the point you are arguing or the question you are answering touches on the theme. It helps you drive home points and tie things together in a memorable way. Your theme must fit the case and your facts, of course.

Be prepared to be interrupted and distracted with questions from the panel, so make sure you have in mind the few points you absolutely want to make in the argument, so that you can fight to return to them each time you are sidetracked. You always have the option to make your own points in response to the questions posed by the court; the court will be asking about many of the same issues of the case that your own points are intended to address. When the court is straying from your best points in its questions, you can use the technique of **transitioning** to fully the answer the question posed by the court but using your answer to bring the discussion back to an issue that is more helpful to your client's position.

B.   The Second Oralist's Argument in Opposition

The oralist going second, in response and opposition to the "first oralist(s)" described in the section above, has the choice to proceed with a structure that is exactly the same as a first oralist: outline your best points and proceed through the outline point by point, trying hard to get through or transition back to your two or three best points before you sit down. The planning of the points and the presentation of your theme are the same as if you were going first in the argument.

Alternatively, oralists going second may try to use an open-ended **rebuttal structure** to the argument. What this requires is that you listen carefully to your opponent's argument and then stand up and deliver a point-by-point rebuttal of the opponent's argument addressing the exact same points in the exact same order that your opponent delivered them. This is not the easiest thing to accomplish, and you definitely should practice the technique several times before airing it live in court or in the actual moot court competition. (Practicing it properly will require you to have a first oralist deliver a serious argument for you to follow and rebut, and it would be best if the practice opponent herself mixes up her version of the first argument in different ways forcing you to respond to a different structure each time).

The rebuttal structure is impressive for several reasons: it looks harder than the straightforward method of preparing your own argument and sticking to a preset outline. It also has the potential to help the court sort out the issues if you meet the issues of the opponent (usually the appellant or petitioner) head on and make your case against them directly. Lastly, it assists the court with its own questions because the same points are taken up in a now familiar order and the same troubles the court had with the appellant can be explored with the appellee.

Although the rebuttal structure is challenging, it is not a magic act. There are several concrete things you can and should do to prepare for this type of argument: first, you have your opponent's brief already;

you know what she is going to argue. There rarely are going to be any surprises on the points she will take up. Similarly, you can see the cases and authorities your opponent is relying on and how she is using them. You can plan an attack on the strongest of these cases and authorities to distinguish them or dampen their effect. With these two sources in your hands, you can make a rough outline—perhaps on half sheets of paper— that you can shuffle to reflect the actual order chosen by your opponent for her argument.

Second, you should listen not only to the opponent's argument but also to the court's questions posed to your opponent. When you hear the opponent strike a clanging note, you can replay the exact note word for word to remind the court of the problem: "Your Honors, my opponent stood here and argued this afternoon that, 'Religious freedom is inconsequential in balancing free expression concerns and privacy concerns.' Inconsequential. Appellee Jones must respectfully disagree with every part of that statement." If you hear a judge's concern about the strengths or limits of an opponent's argument expressed in a question directed to the opponent, you can reinforce that concern: "As Judge Judy noted in my opponent's argument, allowing a right to arm bears will result in a lot of armed bears roaming though campsites and national parks."

Third, you should listen for the cases and authorities your opponent is trying to make the most of in her argument so that you can stand up and distinguish those very cases and dampen the effect of any other authorities she has tried to lean on. Thus, you not only are addressing and rebutting your opponent's argument point by point, but also her legal authorities one by one.

C.   The First Oralist's Rebuttal

Rebuttal is an exciting two or three minutes for the first oralist to use to try to roll back her opponent's entire argument, but the opportunities to make a difference for your client in rebuttal do not match the adrenaline rush you might experience when you stand up to deliver the rebuttal. Two to five minutes isn't enough time to rebut a fifteen or twenty minute argument (and, as noted above, you cannot speed-talk your way through any part of your argument, trying to turn three minutes into six; no one will be persuaded by that kind of babble). You open yourself up to a distressing attack from the judges when you stand up to deliver a rebuttal; the judges have heard your entire argument and your opponent's argument and they now are well up to speed on all the weak points and shortcomings of your side. Your carefully conceived, devastating, three part attack on your opponent's position may dissolve into a panicked, defensive, three minutes of duck and cover while the court pummels you with the hardest questions of the argument. Not that this is the worst outcome; if you can answer all of the court's questions, so the much the better for your client—questions are good, whether they are hard or easy—but you will not have the satisfaction of pulling apart the opponent's case point by point as you planned.

Before we forget, remember that in every court that we have heard of, you must reserve your time for rebuttal on the day of your oral argument either before your argument begins (often by consultation with the bailiff or court clerk at the argument) or at the start of your argument. *E.g.*, "May it please the court. My name is . . . I am representing . . . The lower court's decision should be reversed because . . . **With the court's permission I would like to reserve three minutes for rebuttal**."

That said, the process of preparing for rebuttal is exactly the same for the first oralist as it was for a second oralist using the rebuttal structure for her argument. You can use the opponent's brief to plan a rough outline for the rebuttal; you then must listen carefully to the opponent's argument and the court's questions to the opponent to find specific ammunition for the rebuttal. Then you must sort out your notes in a matter of seconds to set the order for your rebuttal—best rebuttal point first, next best second, and so on.

How much time should you reserve for rebuttal? Certainly no more than 20% of the time allocated for your argument in chief. If you have as much as 25-30 minutes for your argument, you might consider reserving five minutes for rebuttal. Two or three minutes is a better choice to reserve for a fifteen minute argument. Note, too, that in some jurisdictions, if you reserve time for rebuttal and then wind up asking the court's permission to finish part of your argument after time has expired, the borrowed time you take to finish up is deducted from your reserved time for rebuttal. Thus, if you reserve three minutes, and then in your principle argument you ask for grace time to finish an answer to a question and you ramble on for two more minutes, you may find you only have one minute left for your rebuttal.

How many points should you plan to rebut? Given the time considerations above, you really should plan no more than two or three points of rebuttal. If you get one important point across in two minutes you will have done a good job. Remember that the judges may use your rebuttal time to rain questions down on you, so you will have to make the effort to cover the rebuttal points in your answers to questions or transition to the rebuttal points in the course of answering questions.

IX.   QUESTIONS FROM THE PANEL

Aside from showing up and being respectful in your argument, the most important part of oral argument is effectively dealing with and responding to the questions from the panel. These questions are your friends—in real life and in moot court. In real life, they represent the issues that the judges are sticking on and need to be resolved by you before they are willing to vote for your side. This is information you want to have, so you should be happy to get questions. In moot court, the ability to answer questions well and still transition back to your argument and make points along the way is what you are being graded on. At the very least, questions indicate that the judges are listening to your argument. Welcome the questions; pray that your argument does not end without a single question being asked.

You must never show annoyance or frustration over being interrupted by a question. Do not ever snort or roll your eyes or fume when you are repeatedly interrupted. It is much more important to answer all the panel's questions than it is to get through your outline.

Decorum and respect require you to stop talking the instant a judge on the panel starts talking. Literally stop in mid-sentence—in mid-syllable if necessary.

If your time runs out during a question or during your answer to a question, the proper thing to do is to politely point out to the panel that your time is up and ask permission to complete your answer to the question. 99% of the time permission will be granted, but do not take this as an opportunity to drone on for five more minutes. Answer the question completely and correctly, but as succinctly as you can. Never bring up a new argument or issue in this "grace" period.

There is great value in answering questions quickly and succinctly, but do not leave out important information in the process. Complete answers are better than quick answers. Impress the judges with your candor.

If you can, during your answer (thinking on your feet, remember), try to plan a **transition** from the answer you are giving back to a point of your own that you want to make. For example:

- Question: What about the appellee's Internet cases? Do they answer this issue and go against you?

  Answer: Your Honor, the Internet cases relied on by my opponent do not cover the situation of transaction of business via the Internet. This is an issue of first impression in this jurisdiction and, I might add, in this country, and there is no controlling authority on this point. **{transition}** However, the analogous area of law covered in the controlling law of this jurisdiction is business conducted over telephone wires and electronically by facsimile and telephone and email. The cases on this point, including *Scullin*, definitively support my argument, because they hold . . .

Try once, and perhaps twice not to concede an important point even if it is clear that the judges are not buying your argument. It is especially important not to concede the ultimate issue of the case (are we liable or not, for instance)—never give in on the ultimate issue. But if one section of your argument definitely annoys the panel and you cannot convince them that you are right the first two times, **and** you have alternative arguments to rely on if you give in on that sticking point, then concede the point and move on. Do not keep beating the dead horse three and four times. If you do not concede, the panel may tell you to move on, and at that point you had better do what they tell you.

Oral argument judges tend to gravitate to certain types of questions, so we have prepared a chart of the most common questions and what you should try to do when answering them:

Form of Question	Why are they Asking it?	What you should do to Answer it
The Information Seeking Question – What is the holding of that case? When did the statute go into effect? Did your client telephone the authorities that night or not?	These are fairly mundane questions designed to illicit information about the record or the authorities. Usually, the court is seeking the information for a simple reason: they want to know the answer. Occasionally, a judge will ask this type of question to test your knowledge of the record or the authorities.	Be prepared to discuss the facts from the record and the authorities on the law. Re-read your own authorities and your opponent's authorities. Study the most important documents and testimony from the record. Make sure when you do your practice rounds that your "judges" quiz you on details such as these so that you will not be thrown when you get your first question of this kind.
The Slippery Slope Question - Aren't you opening the floodgates to ...? Aren't you asking the Court to set a dangerous precedent for ...? Aren't you asking the Court to plunge into uncharted and dangerous territory?	Appellate courts in general, and courts of last resort in particular, must be cognizant of the fact that they are not just deciding the single case before them but also are setting a rule and precedent for all future cases in that jurisdiction. They do not want to issue an overly broad opinion. They do not want to create a rule that might work fine in the case before them, but it might be applied to other situations to produce unintended negative results.	Be aware of the impact of your arguments on future cases. Take a long view and a broad view when you are drafting your brief and preparing for oral argument. Think of the ways your arguments might affect future cases, related and analogous areas of the law, and other kinds of parties (plaintiffs and defendants) than are in the case at hand. Be prepared to discuss how your arguments can and should be limited to the parties in the case at hand and other future parties just like them. Show how the impact of your arguments is limited to the case at hand, and only will control future situations just like the one at hand. Alternatively, if you think a broader precedent should be set, be prepared to discuss the parameters of the new rule you would have the court set and the public policies that are furthered by the new rule.

Form of Question	Why are they Asking it?	What you should do to Answer it
The Drawing the Line Question - How do we draw the line? Where do we need to draw the line?	Related to the above type, drawing the line here does not refer to an aggressive act to defy someone (i.e., drawing a line in the sand), but rather to finding the place where the strength and logic of the arguments you are making ends. The court wants to know where your arguments should be cut off so that they can articulate reasons in their opinion why the precedent they will create will be limited to certain types of situations, such as the situation involving the parties in the case before them, and not to other situations. The court is searching for a way to write a more limited rule and precedent.	Once again, you should be prepared to discuss the reasonable, logical, and lawful boundaries of your arguments. How and why should your arguments be limited to the parties in the case at hand and other future parties just like them? Show how the impact of your public policy arguments is limited to the case at hand, and why the precedent to be set by the court need only control future situations just like the one at hand. Show how the logic of your arguments easily answers the issues in the case at hand but does not need to be extended further. Try to articulate standards for drawing the line that you have derived from the authorities, rather than simply describing individual factual situations from cases that are "good" and cutting off the situations of cases that are "bad." Alternatively, if you think a broader precedent should be set, be prepared to discuss the parameters of the new rule you would have the court set and the public policies that are furthered by the new rule.
The Roving Hypothetical – What if the plaintiff were a ...? What if a defendant came along and tried to ...? What if the next case involves a ...?	Law students probably are familiar with this kind of question because it is part and parcel of the Socratic method. Yet, sometimes they are surprised to find Socrates wearing a black *(Continued)*	Because the purpose of these questions is to try to test your ability to think on your feet, you might think it is hard to prepare for them. But, as with the categories of questions *(Continued)*

Form of Question	Why are they Asking it?	What you should do to Answer it
	robe and bearing down on them in an oral argument. The purpose of these questions is twofold: first, the judges are testing you to see how well you are able to think on your feet; second, they may indeed be trying to find the limits of your argument—the future situations you think will be controlled by their decision and which will not be—which relates to the category of questions discussed above.	discussed above, you should prepare ahead of time by thinking through the impact of your arguments on future cases. Think of the ways your arguments might affect future cases, related and analogous areas of the law, and other kinds of parties (plaintiffs and defendants) than are in the case at hand.

The first answer to these questions should not be, "Well, your honor, that is not our case." After wrestling with a hypothetical or two, you may wind up having to bring the court back to the case at hand somewhat more skillfully—"Your honor, that might be true if the plaintiff were to . . . but in our case, plaintiff did not do X-Y-Z and so . . ." Do not get lost in a sea of hypotheticals. If the court is marching into stranger and stranger territory, calmly bring them back to reality and drive home that your arguments easily answer the issues raised by the case at hand. As with all of these question types, when you hold your practice sessions, have your 'judges' drill you on hypotheticals. Have them force you to think on your feet so that you can become comfortable addressing strange and troubling hypotheticals while standing at the podium. |

Form of Question	Why are they Asking it?	What you should do to Answer it
The "If we do X-Y-Z, do you lose?" Question – If we do not buy your argument that . . . do you lose? If we do not accept your position on . . ., can you still win? If we rule against you on this claim, is your case finished?	This question is testing you on your knowledge of the law and your knowledge of the issues of the case and the arguments needed to answer them. The judges are looking to see if you have the ability to recognize alternative arguments that are alternative pathways to victory; or they want to see if you understand that in order to prevail, you must convince the court of at least some parts of your argument. This type of question also is used as a test to see how strongly you feel about some of the alternative arguments you are raising, and whether you are willing or able to abandon some claim or alternative argument you are raising.	In order to address this type of question, you must be well versed in the law and the necessary steps in the pathway to victory. Very often there are multiple pathways to victory, but some paths are harder to get through than others. Most of this book is devoted to getting you to think through your strongest arguments and present them first and foremost in your brief and oral argument. In preparing for oral argument, you must be certain of the necessary steps that the court must pass on in order for you to win. As for the alternative steps, you should be aware of those that can be abandoned with little or no impact on the rest of your arguments, and those whose abandonment might have a negative impact on your legal or public policy arguments elsewhere in the case. Do not concede an argument just because you have others—if you have raised it in your brief or oral argument, the judges will expect you to be able to defend it as far as it goes—but you must know the distance you are willing to go on alternative arguments, and do not dig in your heels past the necessary and logical end of your arguments when the panel is trying hard to knock you off your posi- *(Continued)*

Form of Question	Why are they Asking it?	What you should do to Answer it
		tion. Defending your positions is expected, but being flexible about the pathway to victory when you can be flexible also is a virtue. Of course, you never should concede a necessary step on the pathway to victory.
The "What would you have this Court do?" Question – What would you like our opinion to say? What precedent would you have this court set? What is the rule of law that you think we should write on this issue? What cases are you arguing that we should overrule? What relief are you seeking here?	This type of question is asking you to clarify what you want the court to do. As an aid to drafting their opinion, the court may want to know what you think their opinion should hold, what prior cases should the court reconsider or overturn, and what new law should the court write as a precedent for future cases. At a minimum, the court is testing you to see if you understand the relief you are seeking, but more often, the court is testing you to see if you really understand what the court needs to do in order to rule in your favor.	Strangely enough, this type of question can be a real stumper in moot court. Having been alerted to it, you should prepare for oral argument by writing a page or an index card that lays out exactly what you would like the court to do. Do not just focus on the obvious—e.g., please reverse the decision of the court of appeals—but also lay out the essentials of the opinion you think the court should write, and the precedent to be set, which discusses the factual situations that should be covered by the rule that you are stating should be applied, and the cases and other authorities that should be clarified or overruled by the court's decision. This type of inquiry really is not intended to be a trick question, and it will not be one if you have prepared for it ahead of time. Your response to the question may prompt the court to inquire further—why do you think the Smith case should be overruled?—but that is true of any solid response to a question.

X.   OTHER CONSIDERATIONS

A.   Winning points

You win points by proper argument and proper answers to questions. It is proper and customary to address points raised by your opponent in her brief, and to respond to things she said in her oral argument if you are going second. Do so in a professional way, countering the legal or factual points of your opponent's position. You do not win points by beating up and ridiculing your opponent or your opponent's brief or her argument, or by beating up the lower court.

B.   Candor toward the court

Do not pretend to know things you do not really know. If you are asked about a case or a law review article that you never have heard of, confess that you are not familiar with it and ask for more details. If it is a major case that you should have found, you may be marked down for failing to uncover it in you research, but you cannot take the chance of being shown to be a liar and a cheat as well as a poor researcher by pretending that you are familiar with the case and that you are ready to discuss it.

If the panel asks about facts and details that are not in the record, it is appropriate to state that they are not in the record. If you are wrong, so much the worse for your score, but in most cases, the judge is trying to see if you know the limits of the facts that are in the record. Often a judge will not be as up to speed on the facts as she needs to be, and your job is not to assume that the judge knows something about the facts that you have forgotten.

If the question really is addressed to an inference from the facts, and you think it is a proper and logical inference, go ahead and address it as an inference—you actually might say, **"That is logical to infer from the facts"**—but be prepared to stop and remind the panel that the record does not expressly indicate that a fact exists. Inserting facts into the record is fraught with peril. The panel might call you on it, and your opponent might beat you up about it when they get up to argue second or on rebuttal. In most instances, the court will know when the record is silent on a certain topic, and they will expect you to respect this situation.

C.　Finishing your argument

If you finish your outline and still have a minute or two left in your allotted time, the safest practice in moot court and even in real court is to simply conclude by reciting the relief you request (*e.g.*, **"For these reasons, appellant respectfully requests the court to reverse the decision of the district court and remand this case for a new trial"**). Then say, **"Thank you, your Honors,"** and move to sit down. If the panel is not through with you, they will jump in with more questions. They might do this even if your time has expired. Asking the panel if they have any additional questions before you sit down is a risky business. This invitation usually prompts a mean old question or two, usually the ones the judges were holding onto for a while, just waiting for a chance to dump them on you.

D.　Pay attention to the stop sign.

As discussed above, if you still are talking when time runs out, ask for permission to finish your sentence or the point you were making (*e.g.*, **"I see that my time is up. May I finish what I was saying?"**), or simply ask for permission to conclude, which generally means stating your request for relief, as shown in the example in the paragraph above. If you were in the middle of answering a question, ask permission to finish your answer (**"I see that my time is up. May I finish answering your question, your Honor?"**). Do not ignore the stop sign, and never use the permission granted by the court as an opportunity to continue your argument for a minute or more. It is especially bad to try to use the grace period to make a new point. The panel may decide to cut you off altogether, and that can be embarrassing.

E.　Wait and listen to the whole question.

Wait and listen to the whole question that is being asked. Do not start answering before the judge gets the whole question out just because you are sure you know where the question is going. Judges can give amazingly long and rambling questions, and sometimes they change their minds midstream and the question takes a turn at the end that you were not expecting. If at the end of the question you realize you have no idea what the judge wants you to answer, do not just launch into something; explain that you do not understand and politely ask the judge if he might clarify or restate the question.

Note well that you only should ask for clarification when you ab solutely need it. It is a cheap and shoddy trick to ask for clarification every time you get a question that you want to think over for a few minutes before answering, so you attempt to buy the "mull over" time by asking for clarification. The court will recognize this tactic right away and will not be pleased by your tactical behavior.

F.   Give a direct "yes-no" answer to a "yes-no" question; then explain.

Counsel sometimes react to yes-no questions as if they were Superman and the court had handed them a box full of kryptonite. Not every yes-no question is a trap; many times the court just wants the answer, nothing more. So, give a direct answer to a "yes-no" question first (*i.e.*, answer "Yes" or "No"), then immediately proceed to explain your answer. Above all, do not attempt to dodge the substance of the question because you are uncomfortable with it or because you are not quite sure what answer the judge wants you to give. If you try to avoid answering, the judge simply will point out that you did not answer her question, and she will ask it again.

G.   Unexpected events

Do not be worried if you sneeze or cough or if you lose your train of thought in mid-sentence. The judges know you are human. Pick up where you can and move on. If you completely lose your entire train of thought, take a moment to try to get back on track, but if the thought is gone forever, simply confess to the court: "I'm sorry, I have completely forgotten what I was about to say." If you think a question was asked, but you do not remember what it was, ask: "Is there a question pending?" or "May I hear the question again?" or if you simply do not know what end is up, say "May I proceed with my next point?", and jump back into the argument wherever you can. A charley-horse of the brain sometimes happens, and these are appropriate ways to massage it out.

If a cellular phone or pager goes off in the room, it is best to ignore it. Let the judges comment on it if they choose. Your own cellular phone or pager never will go off because you **never** should have an activated telephone or pager with you in any courtroom or moot court room.

H.   Poker face

A good poker face is an asset for an oralist. If your opponent makes a great point, do not blanch and furiously start looking up things in your materials in a panic. Stare forward as if nothing has happened. If you realize that your argument is coming apart at the seams during questioning, keep a stiff upper lip and remain calm. Judges may not immediately know that your opponent has made a great point or that the panel has hit on the lynch pin of your case which, if removed, will pull the whole thing apart. But if your face reveals it, they will know it immediately.

Chapter 8

Strategies for Moot Court and Beyond

I. MOOT COURT COMPETITIONS

Moot court very well may be your first foray into a simulated litigation experience. Some law schools allow you the chance to experience this in your first year. Most law schools run intramural competitions and sponsor interscholastic moot court teams for second and third year students. Sometimes, you will be asked to pair with another student for a moot court competition. Below, we discuss tips for moot court success in partnerships or teams in intramural or interscholastic competitions.

A. A taste of practice

Moot Court competitions typically simulate appellate practice, but some competitions include other types of adversarial situations (such as negotiation, client counseling, or arguing a dispositive motion in a trial court). By briefing your side and arguing it in person, you will learn important skills in advocacy that will carry on into your practice *regardless of what type of practice you do.* Certainly, moot court skills translate directly to litigation both at the trial and appellate levels. If you do wind up becoming a litigator, we are sure that you will be reminded of your moot court experience; in fact, many litigators will tell you that they "caught the litigation bug" by participating in a moot court competition in law school. But even if you never litigate a case or argue a motion in court, you will find that the skills you can hone in a moot court competition— researching, writing, and the ability to present complex information orally and answer tough questions on your feet—translate well to the basic practice of being a lawyer in any area of specialization. In short, moot court is not just a good experience for future appellate litigators.

Much of your time in practice will involve researching and writing your analysis of legal issues, explaining your analysis orally, and defending it before your colleagues, clients, and the courts. Your first "oral arguments" in practice likely will not be in front of an appellate panel, but rather in an armchair in front of your boss's desk, as you explain your research to her, and she probes the strengths, weaknesses, and troubling spots of your analysis with questions. Corporate attorneys, banking and real estate attorneys, even trusts and estates attorneys all have to face this kind of probing and explain themselves to senior colleagues in their office when these colleagues want to explore their research and legal conclusions. Being able to calmly and competently think on your feet—even if you actually are sitting in an armchair—and address your colleagues' concerns will further your professional career at the firm.

Some of your toughest audiences will be your clients. One of the authors recalls that his toughest, most unpleasant oral arguments were before an in-house counsel at one of his firm's clients. She would drag him back and forth on his findings and recommendations, working him over like an old punching bag. He would welcome a chance to be vetted by the state supreme court before going back to her "court" again. Then, there were the oral arguments with clients over legal bills. Try explaining why it cost $10,000 to produce a 10 page research memorandum to an irate client some time. You will long for the patient attention of a moot court panel after going through that exercise once or twice. An experience in moot court will help you prepare for these and other real practice encounters.

Certainly, a moot court simulation cannot exactly duplicate actual practice. For one thing, the record in moot court typically is extremely limited. You likely will only be working with documents that are absolutely necessary for the problem, whereas as an actual practitioner, you inevitably will have many more files and documents—even a multi-volume record—to plow through before engaging in oral argument. For example, in real appellate practice, you will have to sort through the entire court file as it has been complied to date—with all of the pre-trial motions and orders in it, all the documents and things produced in discovery, deposition transcripts, trial preparation materials, a complete trial transcript along with all the exhibits entered into evidence and any that were refused, and any post-trial motions. Although some legal writing and moot court directors tell us that they have at times gone so far as to pair up with a prosecutorial appellate department or other organization (from which they have obtained actual files and complete "records" for their students to use in moot court classes—including, for example, little glassine pouches containing the actual bullets that killed the actual person whose homicide prompted the prosecution), most moot court records consist of only a few documents. You might get a stipulation of facts, an exhibit or two, and the orders and opinions of the lower courts. This can be frustrating—you might really *want* to see the actual complaint in a case, for example. Always remember, though, that you will be given everything you really need to work with, which may be just a bare bones snapshot of only the most necessary items, or parts of them.

Whatever documents you have to work with in a simulated competition, moot court forces you to engage in a process of in depth review of a client's case, to research and analyze that case as thoroughly as possible given the materials, and to think about how to present your findings both in writing and orally. You will be required to write a significant document laying out your arguments, and stand on your feet and defend your client's position against an onslaught of questions. Rarely in law school do you get to work up a single case as thoroughly as you will in moot court. You will know your client's facts and the law that governs the case intimately. In the several weeks or months that you work on your moot court problem, you will become an expert on the particular issues implicated by this client's case. This is truly what litigation practice is like.

B.   Devil's advocacy skills

There are some twists and turns in moot court that are atypical of real practice. For starters, you very well may be called upon to switch sides or argue "off brief"—argue the position you did not initially brief—during one or more of the oral argument rounds. This requirement will force you to look at the case as a whole, to evaluate the strengths and weaknesses of your brief position and the opposite side's position, and to make a convincing argument for either side.

Though unlikely to happen precisely like this in practice, this exercise is not just a trick invented by law professors to amuse themselves and befuddle their students. To the contrary, having to argue both sides of a case promotes a certain degree of objectivity in your perception of your own client's case, and objectivity is an asset to any litigator. Too often lawyers get caught up in their clients' cases and fail to see the weaknesses and shortcomings until their opponents shove them in their faces at some inevitably critical juncture in the litigation. Being a good *devil's advocate* is an excellent skill to develop, and moot court often forces you to work on that skill.

WHAT'S THAT?

Off Brief = Lawyers speaking out of both sides of their mouths?

Moot court competitions do not ask you to argue "off brief" in favor of the other side's position just to perpetuate the perception that lawyers can speak out of both sides of their mouths at the same time; *i.e.*, that the truth or matters of justice and principle matter not to lawyers, only the interests of whomever is paying the bill. Instead, the "off brief" assignment is intended to drive home the message that lawyers in general and litigators in particular must remain objective about their case. They must study, understand, and be able to explain the strengths of the other side's position as well as the weaknesses of their own client's position. Thus, arguing "off brief" is not just an academic exercise, it is a requirement to force you to think long, hard, and objectively about the case as a whole to reach the point where you can marshal the other side's best points against your own client and defend the other side's position in an oral argument presentation with questioning from the judges.

If you are confident and skilled enough to present a coherent and credible argument for either side of the case, you have excellent skills for law practice. But it takes a lot of thought (flexible thought), an in depth examination of all of the issues and all of the authorities, and sufficient attention to the policies and themes of the area of law to pull off this task in a coherent and credible manner. If you can be so objective in each of your cases, then you will be much sought after as a lawyer, even if the devil never pays you a retainer.

II.   INTERPRETING MOOT COURT RULES

More than a few tears of frustration are shed trying to figure out some of the rules that arise in intramural and interscholastic moot court competitions. The following is our take on some of the more common and troublesome rules we have seen. Be aware that this is *only* our interpretation—the final arbiter of any competition's rules is the organization or committee that sponsors and runs the competition and writes the rules. Our interpretation is based on our own experience as litigators, but also as moot court coaches in reading rules, trying to comply with rules, and seeing the kinds of penalties that are levied for non-compliance.

A. Read the rules!

The first advice we can give you is to read the rules. In fact, do not just read them, parse them thoroughly. Pour over them. Outline and summarize them. Discuss them with your partner or teammates. It is too easy to neglect your compliance with detailed, persnickety rules, and as a result, this is where many easy points are lost in moot court competitions.

There is a hidden educational aspect of moot court competitions: they can teach you the importance of reading and interpreting rules. Litigation in the real world is chock full of rules—local rules, administrative orders of the court, rules of procedure, standing orders, and more. Failing to follow these rules may lead to dismissal of your case for purely procedural reasons, and that can be rather difficult to explain to your client (even where it is not out-and-out malpractice).

Similarly, failing to follow moot court rules will cause you to incur penalties, and when you lose points that way, you really are taking yourself out of contention in the competition. As recently as November 2000, the last time one of the author's law school hosted the regional of the Association of the Bar of the City of New York's National Moot Court competition, he observed that a Best Brief contender was edged out of the title by a competitor who scored lower on the substance of the brief, but had fewer penalty points than the contender. This happens frequently in competitions across the country each year.

B. What rules to follow?

It all depends on the rules that the competition has adopted. Some moot court competitions will create their own "local rules." Others will choose to adopt the <u>Rules of the Supreme Court of the United States</u>, or the rules for a particular circuit court. Even where that's true, however, you may find variations in competition rules and the specific, technical formatting rules of the selected jurisdiction. Always keep in mind—and understand precisely—what the rules call for in the following categories:

1.   Rules on typesetting and printing

The Supreme Court rules require briefs to follow strict typesetting and printing rules, to be permanently and professionally bound, and to use a reduced paper size of 6 X 9¼ inches (more like a "Monarch" sized stationery page than a standard 8½ X 11 inch page). *See* U.S. Supreme Court Rule 33.1(a, d). Most competitions have recognized the impracticality of these printing rules, and have opted out of them. But if your competition has adopted the Supreme Court rules whole cloth, then you should be aware of what they entail. And even if you need not get your briefs professionally bound, you certainly will need to comply with the formatting and printing requirements that the rules set forth. We have known moot court judges to get out their rulers and measure the margins and line spacing, so do be sure to follow the specific formatting requirements specified.

2.   Brief covers; binding

The brief cover rules for the U.S. Supreme Court are complicated only because there are a lot of colors to choose from. To make things simple, many moot court competitions simply adopt the "standard" circuit court rules for brief covers. Typically, this means that the Appellant (Petitioner's) brief on the merits is light blue, and the appellee (Respondent's) brief on the merits is red. *See* U.S. Supreme Court Rule 33.3(e, f). (The rules say "light red," but no one really knows what light red is (so neither will the guy at Kinkos®).

DO IT WITH STYLE!

Appellees are red, appellants are blue . . .
What color is that brief color? The rules may say "light red," but that does not mean pink, and likewise you should not interpret it to mean deep crimson. Red or light red should be red enough to not look pink, but not so dark that you hardly can read the black text printed on it.

Where do you find colored card stock? Copy shops, office supply stores, often major retailers like Wal-Mart will have some choices. But do spring for the actual colored card stock. Once, one of the authors received a moot court brief with a white cover page that was *colored in* with a blue magic marker. The other author once received a brief with a cover that was white but the student had written "Blue" on it with arrows pointing right and left, up and down. Try not to do that with your briefs.

The requirements for binding briefs also typically will be specified in the rules of the competition. Sometimes a specific binding is identified, such as "three staples on the left margin." Other times, it will be more cryptic, such as "bound in a volume." We read "bound in a volume" to mean some kind of nonremovable binding that creates a booklet, such as tape binding. Velo-binding might satisfy this requirement, as might spiral or comb binding. In any event, if there is a certain kind of binding that is identified as acceptable in the rules, go with that kind of binding rather than taking a chance of being wrong, even if that means using three staples.

3.   Brief length; page limits; typeface rules

This is a critical component of the rules. There are a number of ways to express page limitations. The idea is to make sure everyone has a level playing field and turns in a brief with no more than a certain number of words. You can imagine the chaos if everyone could decide their line spacing, text size, characters per inch, and so on.

Look at the word and/or page limits. Page limits are very straightforward. There most often will be a limit on the number of pages you can devote to the argument section, and sometimes a limit on the number of pages for the other parts of the brief, or a limit on the total length of the brief overall. Somewhat trickier to comply with are rules specifying the number of "characters per inch" (such as "type at no more than 12 characters per inch," or "type size not capable of producing more than 12 characters per inch"). Competitors that trip up on this rule usually do so because they use a non-uniformly spaced font to exceed the page limit.

A quick tip: `Courier` is a uniformly spaced font; Times Roman and CG Times are proportionally spaced fonts.[1]

Some competitions avoid all of this font measuring by setting a limit on the number of words that the brief can contain (or possibly that the Argument section can contain). If you have a choice to follow one or the other, you may find that following the word limit rules get you more pages overall. You may have to submit a separate certification specifying your word count, which is easily calculated through a function in most word processing formats.

Line spacing also most likely will be regulated. Many competitions use double spacing as the rule; others use a limit of so many lines of text per vertical inch, or so many lines of text per page, which usually comes out to mean double-spacing. We can tell you from experience in grading papers that when you cheat and try to use 1.9 or 1.8 spacing or anything less than 2.0 spacing, it is painfully obvious to the grader, and you will get penalized for it.

FYI

Shrunk to Fit Briefs?!

The "shrink to fit" function on many word processing programs—used to "shrink to fit" your argument into the 30 pages allocated for such—merely compresses the line spacing, font size, and kerning (spacing between characters) so that the text will fit the number of pages you tell it to fit. All of this tweaking stands out like a sore thumb when the brief grader reads several correctly formatted briefs in a row, and then gets to the "shrunken to fit" brief.

---

1 In Courier font, every character and space between characters is the same width. If you set the type size of 10 or 12, you can measure how many characters you will get per inch on your printout. In Times Roman and CG Times, certain characters are narrower than others; t's and f's and i's and l's are especially narrow. If you use Times Roman or CG Times, you will not know how many characters per inch you will get when you use 12 point font. More particularly, 12 point font size in Times Roman or CG Times is capable of producing more than 12 characters per inch. Brief graders are attuned to this fact, and they probably will assess a penalty if they see Times Roman or CG Times anywhere in your document, even if you increase the font size to try to compensate for the uneven spacing. If the rules of your competition have a limit on the characters per inch your font can generate, use Courier to be on the safe side, not Times Roman or CG Times.

C.   Outside assistance

The rules of moot court competitions typically limit the kind of help you can get when writing the brief, and sometimes even when preparing for oral argument. There are at least three ways of going about this: first is the absolute prohibition on assistance; second is the prohibition of "direct" or "specific" assistance; and third is the allowance of assistance on specific topics, such as allowing assistance on issues, organization, and strategy, but prohibiting assistance on research, brief writing, editing and proofreading (or allowing assistance on oral argument preparation but not at all on brief preparation).

In the absence of a rule limiting outside assistance, presumably, you can talk to anyone about anything, and use any material you find, as long as you do not plagiarize. That said, we have never seen an interscholastic competition that did not put some limit on outside assistance.

Of course, on the other end of the spectrum, an absolute prohibition is easy to understand—do not look for assistance from anyone, and do not take any.

But "no direct assistance" or "no specific assistance" can be fuzzy. We take it to mean direct or specific assistance in researching, writing, editing, and proofreading the brief, and direct assistance in answering or organizing a response to the very issues presented by the problem; *i.e.*, you cannot have a faculty member review your draft of the brief and offer advice on how to revise it, nor can you ask her how to complete your research to pump up your brief with better authorities. But this rule should not prohibit general questions about the subject matter of the problem, or questions about the area of law in which the problem arises, or general advice and assistance about brief writing in the area of law in which the problem arises. This does allow a significant gray area to tread in, and it might be easy to stray from the gray into the black (or red, as it were).

> • *Example:*   If the problem involved the effect of the 1999 OPRAH amendments to ERISA regarding Medicare disclosure requirements for home health care workers who follow the teachings of television's Dr. Phil (we made up these amendments—do not get excited), we would find it a violation of the

"no specific assistance" rule to approach an ERISA expert (faculty member or practitioner) and ask, "In general, in what ways are home health care workers affected by the new Medicare disclosure requirements in the 1999 OPRAH amendments to ERISA." However, we would find it acceptable to ask about the OPRAH amendments in general, or the process of Medicare disclosure in general, but not the process as currently applied to home health care workers.

In contrast, other competitions liberally allow outside assistance. For example, the Jessup International Law Moot Court Competition states in its rules:

> Each Team must research, write, edit, and develop its own legal and factual arguments without the assistance of persons who are not members of the Team.
>
> . . .
>
> As a general principle, a Team shall have no greater number of Team Advisors than is necessary to adequately prepare the Team for fair competition. . . . Team Advisors may provide advice to a Team, provided such advice is limited to:
>
> (a)   general instruction on the basic principles of international law;
>
> (b)   general advice on research sources and methods;
>
> (c)   general advice on memorial writing techniques;
>
> (d)   general advice on oral advocacy techniques;

(e)   general advice on the organization and structure of arguments in the Team's written and
oral pleadings;

(f)   general commentary on the quality of the
Team's legal and factual arguments;

(g)   advice on the interpretation and enforcement
of these Rules; and

(h)   advice as to pleading option or similar strategy.

Philip C. Jessup International Law Moot Court Competition, 2009 Official Rules, Rules 2.4.1, 2.4.3. So, no one can draft and edit your brief (the
"memorial," as it is called in Jessup) for you, or tell you how they would
answer the problem, but they can help you with almost anything else.

Some competitions, such as the National Health Law Moot Court
Competition, have a rule that states, **"no participants shall procure a
copy of any pleadings or papers actually filed in any trial or appeal
of any case upon which the record is founded. Contact with the actual litigants or their attorneys is prohibited . . ."** 2007-2008 National
Health Law Moot Court Competition, Official Rules, Rule 8(a). This
seems like a dead giveaway that the sponsors of the competition use an
actual lawsuit as the basis of their problem. The rule creates an interesting
"Catch 22" situation—the rule does not prohibit the procurement of materials from a case that the problem is not based on, but how do you know
if the materials you procured from an actual case are from the actual case
the problem is based on unless you procure the materials and read them?
That's a tough one. The bottom line rule-of-thumb should be: when in
doubt, do not seek assistance.

III.   ANALYZING A MOOT COURT PROBLEM

A.   Careful reading

The best advice anyone can give you about your moot court problem is to read it carefully. Yes, this should go without saying, but we have read enough briefs and seen enough oral arguments to know that students do not always get the facts right, whether they are the historical facts that led up to the lawsuit, or the procedural facts about how the case wound its way through the court system to get to the court where the problem is set. Summarizing and synthesizing the facts should force you to come to grips with them, and the process of writing often reveals gaps or areas that you glossed over on your earlier readings. All of this is time well spent in the process of getting ready to research and analyze the problem.

FOOD FOR THOUGHT

The Value of First Impressions

There is something to be said for "first impressions" with regard to the facts of a case. We find it useful to review a moot court problem (and this advice extends to "real" practice) and document in some way—immediately upon reading the problem—your reactions and impressions. You very well may come back to this present tense moment to formulate your theory of the case.

B.   Handling the facts

Once you have read through the problem a few times, it is time to get serious with the facts. The facts determine what you can argue, how you can argue it, and the strength of the various arguments you can make. Of course, facts dictate the law that determines the case—is it a contracts problem, a torts problem, a tax problem, or a combination of several areas?—the way the law is going to be applied to the case, and the play of the public policies around the area of law you are briefing. But to succeed at moot court, you must be adept at organizing and marshaling the facts that support your client, and at explaining, defusing, and otherwise handling the facts that hurt your client.

1.   Put the facts in chronological order

To begin the process of mastering the facts of the problem, you first should put all of the facts in chronological order. The problem may not present the facts in this kind of sequence. As lawyers, we often look at facts in chronological order, and getting the facts down in date sequence probably will help you make sense of the case. In addition, the significance of certain facts may jump out at you more readily when you put them next to other facts that happened at the same time. Gaps in the factual information provided to you may become obvious when you lay out the facts in date sequence. At the very least, putting the facts in chronological order will produce an orderly version of the facts to refer to in later stages of the process.

2.   Separate good facts from bad facts

The next step is to separate the good facts from the bad. You may not be able to complete this task your first time through because your research and analysis into the law will often help reveal those answers. You can start with your gut feeling about the facts, and then return to the facts again and again as you are researching the law to make sure you have the good and the bad facts straight. The point of this exercise is to compile those facts that you will want to emphasize in the statement of the facts and throughout the brief, and those that you will want to downplay or put your best spin on.

PRACTICE POINTER

Moot court writing is adversarial writing, and you should never be satisfied with a complete chronological approach to the facts in your writing and argument unless you are in that rarest of situations where all the facts—or at least the A to Z chronology of them—seem to go your client's way.

3.   Draw reasonable and logical inferences from the facts

It is appropriate to draw reasonable and logical inferences from known facts. What you must avoid is drawing inferences that are too extreme and are unsupported by the facts. This is the equivalent of inventing facts that are not in the record. The judges certainly will mark you down for inventing facts, and your standing similarly will be discounted if you try to stretch the facts to the breaking point.

Be conservative and draw only the most reasonable and logical inferences from the facts:

- *Example:*   If the facts indicate that the Maryland Board of Healing Arts describes two hours as the average time for a surgical procedure, and a certain doctor did the procedure in one hour, it would be a logical inference to state that the doctor operated "quickly." It is completely safe (and obvious) to point out that the doctor did the procedure "in half the time provided by the Maryland Board of Healing Arts."

    What would not be reasonable is to infer that the doctor "rushed" the procedure. "Rushing" implies a state of mind, and nothing in the facts we have revealed shows the doctor's state of mind. Performing the procedure in half the time is not automatically rushing; you do not have enough facts to make that inference. Perhaps the doctor is the most skilled surgeon in the state, and twenty experts would testify that she ought to take half as much time to do the procedure because of her expertise.

    You also cannot draw the inference that the doctor was "negligent" or "reckless." Aside from the problem that these are legal conclusions, you do not have enough facts about the doctor, her state of mind, her expertise, and a host of other factual information that would affect that inference. All you can say is that she performed the operation "quickly" and "in half the time provided by the Maryland Board of Healing Arts."

Missing information from the record necessarily will limit the kind of inferences you logically can draw (alternatively, it may leave you some room for argument). As stated above, in moot court competitions, your record will be more limited than in a typical, real life litigation. Do not get caught up in a spirit of advocacy and fill in details that affect the logical limits of the facts in the record.

- *Example:*   If the record states that the defendant had five alcoholic drinks in a two hour period, you should not automatically draw the inference that the defendant became intoxicated. Intoxication depends on a host of factors (such as the defendant's weight, percentage of fatty tissue to lean tissue in the body, whether the alcohol was consumed with other food or beverages that might limit its rate of absorption into the body). The concept of intoxication also depends on the context; do you mean too intoxicated to drive, or too intoxicated to sit in a chair and watch television? You can state exactly what the facts state: "the defendant drank five alcoholic drinks in two hours."

    If you know the blood alcohol content of the defendant, you then can combine this with other facts to make further inferences. For example, if the record indicates that the defendant had a blood alcohol content of 0.12, you can perform research that might indicate that "defendant's blood alcohol level was above the legal limit for operating a motor vehicle in all fifty states of the United States."

4.   Group the facts by topic and subject matter and look for themes

The next step is to group the facts by topic and subject matter so that you can evaluate what the potential themes (or theories) of the case will be. The theme of the case is different from the legal issues raised by a case and the subject matter of the applicable law that governs these legal issues. You cannot have a theme that lacks one of the essential elements of facts, law, and public policy. The facts you are studying will reveal potential, viable themes. You cannot superimpose a popular theme onto your case if the facts will not support the theme.

MAJOR THEMES

Themes are a rhetorical device, designed to reinforce your arguments and persuade the reader to accept your position and vote in favor of your client. A theme—also called the "theory of the case" when viewed holistically—should be used in the brief and in oral argument as a focal point to tie together the facts of the case, the legal arguments you will make, and the policy issues you will argue.

- *Example:* One potential theme in a business dispute over the performance of a contract is that the larger company took advantage of the smaller company, and exerted improper pressure and used abusive tactics rather than performing the contract in good faith. When you begin to group the facts by topic, you notice that the two companies had a long working relationship, and the relationship was punctuated by fairness and equity at every point discussed in the record. Your theme is doomed—there is no point to asserting a factually unsupportable theme to the case, because sooner or later your theme is going to be shot down by your opponent, and the brief grader and oral argument judges will mark you down for this.

  On the other hand, if the problem throws you some bones that make it look like your company was trying to do business with a Wal-Mart-like behemoth or a Microsoft-type giant or other functional monopolizer, it would behoove you to pursue a theme that the reason the court should accept your legal interpretation of the contract and your argument that the contract was breached is because your opponent is an arrogant giant that uses its superior size and market position to wrest improper demands from its contractual partners. This argument uses the facts to bring the public policy against monopolizers and unfair competitors into view, and thus to cast a favorable light on your legal arguments regarding the contract and its performance.

Themes are the sunshine and pleasant breeze of legal rhetoric that make the brief graders and oral argument judges want to hang out in the backyard of your argument. Cheap window dressing that is not held up by solid facts in the record will crash down on your head, and cause these same brief graders and judges to walk out on your party early, leaving low scores behind. Thus, a careful review of the facts that are available for various topics and themes is essential.

5.   Return to the facts again and again

You must return to the facts at every stage of the moot court process: spotting the issues, researching the issues, analyzing the case, drafting and revising the brief, and preparing for oral argument. The facts determine the issues, and if you think that an issue might be present, you must confirm that the facts exist to create an appropriate question for appellate review, as discussed further in the section that follows. At the research and analysis stage, certain facts that you reviewed in your initial run-through will take on new meaning and new importance to your case. At the drafting stage, you must return to the facts again for crafting the statement of facts or statement of the case, and to confirm and provide citations to details that you are using in your argument section. At the oral argument stage, you must determine which facts and themes you will present first and will return to in answers to questions and transitions from answering questions back to your argument.

All of this means that your initial review of the facts is only an initial review. The facts are too important to the moot court process to allow you to visit them once and learn them wrong. You should be reciting the facts in your sleep before the moot court competition is over.

C.   Issue spotting

Issue spotting is the next important task in the moot court process. In some competitions, it can be a relatively straightforward process. The problem might set out the issues as "questions presented" as part of the packet. In other competitions, the notice of appeal or petition for (or order granting) certiorari in the packet might set out the issues in clear and straightforward language. In these instances, there is no guesswork involved. The authors of moot court problems for intramural or inter-scholastic competitions often do not want you to guess at the issues or brief irrelevant ones, so they often will take great pains to write a problem that makes the issues obvious.

On occasion—and perhaps too often for comfort's sake—the author intentionally or unintentionally obscures the issues, or intentionally or unintentionally allows issues into the record that can be spotted and briefed. The record may leave the door open for a jurisdictional argument, or a preservation of issues argument, or it may reveal a constitutional defect in the proceedings. The material that follows will help you to spot these issues and to determine whether and to what extent they present questions that should be briefed and argued on review.

1.   Harmless error, appealable error, preservation, and clear error

This subsection covers—in brief—some of the errors that a court may have made to generate the moot court problem as you find it. What we cover here dovetails with the "standard of review" information we have provided previously and what you undoubtedly will be learning about that important concept in other classes.

Not every error or mistake that occurred in the trial court presents a proper issue for review. No one is guaranteed a perfect trial or perfect handling of their case in the trial court. The doctrine of **harmless error** provides that if an error caused no harm to your client, you cannot raise it on appeal. If a jury instruction was requested and not given, the instruction that was given in its place must be more favorable to the party that prevailed on that issue; if the instruction given was less favorable, or your client actually prevailed on this particular claim or defense, you cannot appeal from this error. If a witness was barred from testifying, but the substance of the witness's testimony presented in an offer of proof obviously duplicates testimony from other witnesses that were allowed to testify, then the barring of this one witness may be harmless error.

In general, an issue must have been raised and preserved in order for it to be an **appealable error**. If you never asked the trial court to do something, and the court winds up not doing it, you cannot later raise the court's failure as an error. Thus, if you did not request a continuance to allow a witness to appear, or did not ask for leave to amend a petition to insert a new claim, you cannot later complain on appeal that a continuance was not granted to you and the witness did not appear, or that your additional claim was not heard. In general, an issue must have been raised and the trial court must have had the opportunity to address the issue and correct the mistake in order for the error to be raised on appeal. As we have noted, often these issues are already resolved for you in that the problem tells you what is in dispute.

Preservation is a trickier concept. Some errors require a formal procedure to preserve the issue, such as a defect in venue or personal jurisdiction, which must be raised through the timely assertion of a motion to dismiss, and not later abandoned by a general appearance in the case without preserving the error in the pleadings. Evidentiary issues raised in motions in limine or during trial generally must be preserved by the aggrieved party through a formal statement on the record and sometimes with an offer of proof that is received into the record but not presented to the jury. In many jurisdictions, the rules of procedure require a litigant to raise all points of error in a post-trial motion for new trial in order for them to be preserved for appeal.

If the record presented in your moot court problem is complete enough to make a determination whether the issues have been preserved or not, you should use the record to prove that each issue you will argue was properly raised and preserved. However, your moot court problem may prevent you from resolving these questions because it may not give you any indication whether or not an issue was properly preserved at or before trial. Some moot court problems consist of a trial level opinion (and/or an appellate level opinion), with nothing before or in between. One or both of the opinions may make a catch all saving phrase to the effect that "This issue was properly raised at trial and preserved for appeal," in which case the author of the problem wants you to forget about objection and preservation as issues in the case. But the problem might be silent. Unless the issue is one of venue or personal jurisdiction (discussed in the next section), if the issue is discussed by both courts, you should presume that the issue is preserved for review even if there are no facts in the problem that expressly spell this out.

An exception to the objection and preservation requirements is the doctrine of **clear error** or **plain error**. If an error is so egregious that it should have been taken up by the court *sua sponte* and a mistrial ordered, the fact that no party raised the issue in the trial court does not bar it from being raised on appeal for the first time. A potential clear error is not subtle. It should leap out at you from the record, and cry out for justice. Even if you think you have found one, research the applicable law of your jurisdiction to make sure that this type of error has been identified as clear error or plain error before. Appellate court judges and moot court judges will not readily accept an issue as clear error or plain error if you do not have the goods to prove to them that it is one.

2.   Jurisdictional errors in the trial court

You should always review the jurisdiction and venue of the trial court over the subject matter of the action and the parties to the action, because improper jurisdiction can present an appealable issue. You will recall from legal research and writing and civil procedure that a court must have three kinds of power in a case:

- **subject matter jurisdiction over the claims raised in the action;**

- **personal jurisdiction over the parties to the action effectuated by proper service of process; and**

- **venue over the place where the action occurred or arose, or over the parties or the subject matter of (the *res* or property involved in) the suit.**

A clever author of a moot court problem may sneak a jurisdictional issue into the problem. A not-so-clever author might let one in without knowing it, in which case it will most likely be a problem with the subject matter jurisdiction of the trial court. That is because questions regarding personal jurisdiction and venue must be raised and properly preserved or they are waived, and if the author has gone to the trouble of putting enough information into the record to indicate that a personal jurisdiction or venue issue is preserved, then it should be obvious to you that the issue is present and appealable.

3.   Appellate court jurisdictional issues

You also should verify that the appellate courts that heard the case had proper jurisdiction over the case. Appellate courts can only take jurisdiction over an action by three means:

- **extraordinary writ,**

- **interlocutory appeal, or**

- **appeal after final judgment.**

A petition for an extraordinary writ may be filed at any time, and if the record indicates that an extraordinary writ was issued and the lower court was required to answer, then there is little else to stick up the works in the form of appellate procedural error. Your moot court problem may or may not include the petition for a writ, the response of the opponent, and any orders requiring an answer or issuing a preliminary writ. The problem may simply state that the petition for a writ is granted, in which case there is little to question in the way of appellate jurisdiction.

Interlocutory appeals also may be filed at any time. In federal court, 28 U.S.C. § 1292(b) provides that the trial court may certify one or more issues for immediate review, and the appellate court may accept review of the certified issues under Fed. R. App. P. 5. This is a popular way for the author of a moot court problem to get two discreet issues of law sent up for review.

If your problem involves an interlocutory appeal, you should look to see that the requirements of 28 U.S.C. § 1292(b) and Fed. R. App. P. 5 have been met. At a minimum, the district court opinion should have stated that the court's "order involves a controlling question of law as to which there is substantial ground for difference of opinion and that an immediate appeal from the order may materially advance the ultimate termination of the litigation." 28 U.S.C. § 1292(b). However, the author of the moot court problem may not have given you enough information to resolve the question. If the problem indicates that an intermediate level appellate court took up and resolved an issue arising from an interlocutory order of the trial court, it probably is safe to presume that the requirements of the rule and statute were met.

An appeal after final judgment must be initiated by a timely filed notice of appeal, as per the requirements of <u>Fed. R. App. P. 3</u> and <u>4</u>, or their state rule equivalents. The author of your moot court problem may inadvertently have allowed an untimely appeal to have been filed by not being careful with the dates in the record. This almost assuredly was unintentional, because the issue of timeliness is jurisdictional, and if the appeal is untimely, there is nothing the appellate court can do to help the parties out. Your moot court argument would end right then and there. If you figure out that the dates in the problem indicate that an appeal was not timely, contact the sponsor of the moot court program and request a clarification of the dates.

A shrewd author might allow an issue as to whether a judgment was final or not when the notice of appeal was filed. If this was inadvertent, then the record probably will be corrected rather than allowing this defect to destroy the entire appeal. If you suspect that a claim or defense of a party was not resolved by the order and judgment of the trial court, you should request clarification, and if none is given, you should research the definition of finality in your jurisdiction to see if your author has created a dispositive issue for briefing and argument.

In addition, check the record to see that the steps required for the filing and docketing of the appeal appear to have been followed in the case, but do not be surprised if the record is silent on these facts. Authors of moot court problems rarely attempt to confound law students by inserting an issue regarding the filing or docketing of the appeal, so if the record says nothing, assume that this means the problem intends no issue regarding filing or docketing. Only worry about these factors if the author inserts facts into the record that affirmatively indicate that a filing or docketing was botched.

There may be a subject matter jurisdiction issue in the appellate court. An appellate court's subject matter jurisdiction is governed by the applicable constitution, statutes, or court rules of the jurisdiction. An example of this is the rule set out in <u>28 U.S.C. § 1295</u> that provides that all appeals from patent cases litigated in the U.S. District Courts are to be heard by the U.S. Court of Appeals for the Federal Circuit, rather than the court of appeals that would normally entertain appeals from the district court in question. If you stumble on an appeal from a patent case that is filed in the U.S. Court of Appeals for the Eighth Circuit, you have a bona fide appellate court subject matter issue to research and brief.

The courts of last resort most often have limited jurisdiction whereby parties seeking to have a case heard in these courts must **request a transfer** to the court or **petition** the court for the issuance of a **writ of certiorari**, or **writ of mandamus**, or other writ, to allow the case to be heard by the court. If the record does not indicate that one of these procedures was used to get to the court, but the problem indicates that the current appeal is pending in the court of last resort, it is probably attributable to poor attention to detail on the part of the writer of the problem. You can point it out in your brief and oral argument, but the record probably will not contain enough information to actually argue the effect of the omission.

4.   Constitutional defects of justiciability

There are several constitutional law doctrines regarding the justiciability of actions:

> **Case or Controversy**: In federal court, <u>Article III of the U.S. Constitution</u> provides that the courts shall only hear cases or controversies, which means that if a party has yet to be injured by the conduct of the opponent, the case should not be heard. Federal courts are not to issue advisory opinions. There are some kinds of cases that present a clear enough picture of the type and amount of injury that will occur that they can be heard prior to the actual injury's occurrence, such as an imminent breach of a contract or licensing agreement, and there are some procedures, such as temporary restraining orders and preliminary injunctions, that might stop the impending injury in its tracks. But if someone has jumped the gun and gone to court before an injury has taken place, it is worth researching the issue to see if a case or controversy is present. The same defense might apply in a state court, but you should research the constitutional and procedural law of the jurisdiction to be certain (if the problem identified an actual state, as opposed to the "State of Apex" or other fictional jurisdiction).

> **Ripeness**: Ripeness is related to the concept of case or controversy.

If the injury complained of in the action is speculative, and has not occurred and may not occur, a ripeness issue may exist.

Mootness: Although moot court is the name of the game, if the cause of action and the injury, and the position of the parties in the underlying action cannot be affected or resolved by the order of the court, then the problem is moot and should not be litigated. There are some exceptions, such as an injury that is capable of repetition yet evading review. See Roe v. Wade, 410 U.S. 113 (1973). If it looks like the court's handling of the case might be futile no matter who prevails in the case, then you should research the mootness issue for possible inclusion in your brief and argument.

Standing: The standing of the plaintiff to bring the action has got to be the sleeper issue of the century for moot court oral argument judges. No competitor ever thinks it is an issue, because those old Supreme Court cases on standing—Baker v. Carr, 369 U.S. 186, 204 (1962); Flast v. Cohen, 392 U.S. 83, 101 (1968); Sierra Club v. Morton, 405 U.S. 727, 732 (1972); and others—do not make any impact on you when you cover them in two or three class periods in your first year civil procedure or constitutional law courses. Nevertheless, in real life, judges get very agitated when they suspect that someone is trying to stand as a private attorney general, or assert the rights of others by assignment or by some other actual or implied legal relationship, or is trying to sue as a third party beneficiary of an agreement. You should spend some time thinking about standing, and if there is any indication in the problem that the plaintiff was not the person directly and personally harmed by the action of the defendant, you should research and resolve the issue in your brief and oral argument.

D.   Appellant's determination of which issues to raise

After your issue-spotting and research is complete, you are charged with weeding out the specific issues you want to brief. This is particularly necessary if you think you have found five or more main issues to argue. Moot court is supposed to simulate actual appellate practice, and in actual appellate practice, when you are evaluating the possible errors committed by the lower court, quality is far more important than quantity.

The authors of moot court problems typically intend to present two significant issues to brief—often identified by upper-case Roman numerals I and II in the court opinions found in the record—and most authors probably hope that there are no other issues suggested by the facts. Although two main issues is the norm, occasionally, a moot court problem will present three or more main issues. We discussed above how an author may intentionally or inadvertently insert a jurisdictional or constitutional issue into the problem. When additional issues are suggested by the facts of the problem that are not part of or related to the issues that were discussed in the problem in the sections under the big Roman numerals, then you will have to decide if these side issues are worth briefing. If you have undertaken the analysis described in this chapter, and you have determined that the issue is an appealable error (*e.g.*, it was raised and preserved), and is not harmless error, then the issue probably should be briefed.

If, however, you are in a situation where it appears obvious that the author only intended for there to be two issues, and you are stuck on a third, an appellant safely can jettison a side issue as long as it has absolutely no bearing on the main issues that are presented in the problem. We say this because every appellate court judge and every worthy appellate practitioner will tell an appellant that *less is more*. It is better not to go fishing for issues or sub-issues to write about. In moot court, as in actual appellate practice, you will do much better if you find and argue the two horrible, unforgivable errors that are set out in the record, rather than digging for and briefing a dozen somewhat troublesome errors that arguably might be raised. In real life, certain litigators will throw up as many assertions of error as they can think of, hoping that one will stick and cause the case to be overturned. This is a tactic of desperation, not of effective advocacy. Moot court judges are sensitive to this tactic, and they will not want you to develop such bad habits, so they will punish you on your score if you let a quantity of "also ran" errors drown out the effectiveness of your arguments on the main issues of the case.

However, an appellant should make sure that any "side issue" he is thinking about discarding really does not have an impact on the analysis of the other, main issues in the case. The validity of a signature on a contract in a licensing case, or inconsistent testimony about the road conditions in a car accident case may not stand alone as separately appealable issues, but they also might have an impact on the main issues of liability and defenses to liability in the case. If the side issue has a direct bearing on the "main" issues, it should not be discarded. You may wind up briefing it as a sub-issue or threshold issue that leads up to one or more of the ultimate issues in the case.

If you find three or more issues to be in play, and the problem does not indicate how to split them up, you may have to figure out how to divide them with your partner. There is no magic to this, and the decision is not so critical under our plan for drafting and revising the argument section because all teammates will wind up looking at the brief as a whole when the first complete draft of the brief is written.

E.   Appellee's determination of which issues to rebut

An appellee or respondent must analyze the problem in a similar way as the appellant in order to anticipate what issues the appellant is likely to raise. One of the serious ("unreal") limitations in moot court as it is practiced today is that the appellee typically does not have the opportunity to see and respond directly to the appellant's brief and the issues the appellant chooses to raise. Instead, appellees most likely will be required to turn in their brief at the same time as appellants. Most moot court problems fail even to provide the notice of appeal filed by the appellant, which also would give a strong indication what the questions presented will be. (This is intentional, and it has more to do with testing the appellants to see if they can spot appealable issues than with punishing appellees by not giving them enough information.) Unfortunately, you may have to make an educated guess as to what issues are going to be raised by your opponent.

As discussed above, however, authors of moot court problems usually do not want you or the appellant to have to guess about the issues. They usually will go to great lengths to point out that there are two main issues that they want both sides to address. But sometimes your review of the record will uncover a potential appealable issue that is not one of the two main "Roman numeral" issues presented by the problem. You may have identified an issue regarding the subject matter jurisdiction of the trial court or the appellate court, or one regarding ripeness or mootness, or the standing of the plaintiff—who might be you—to have brought the action in the first place. Appellees do not have as much discretion to jettison issues as appellants have. Even if you think an issue is tenuous, not likely to produce a reversal, and easily refuted, it most likely is in your best interest to raise it and rebut it as quickly and competently as you can. (Spend about a page or less on a straightforward issue that is resolved by controlling authority; spend more time on a more complicated error that requires analysis of the facts, controlling and persuasive authority, and public policy.)

As a general matter, you will not be penalized for discussing actual appealable issues found outside the main "Roman numeral" issues. In fact, it may separate your brief from the pack and boost your score if your keen analysis reveals a thorn that almost everyone else overlooked. On the other hand, chasing after hobgoblins that are not reversible errors, or raising straw men issues just so you can tear them down in your brief, will not be a credit to your analytical skills. You also must be cognizant of not spending too much time and too many pages on tertiary issues that crowd out more important analysis and discussion of the main issues. Being able to budget your space is one of the skills on which you will be graded in moot court.

V.   THE COLLABORATIVE WRITING PROCESS

This section is directed toward those of you that are writing collaboratively in a moot court competition. If you are charged with writing your own brief as part of your legal writing class, or if the particular moot court competition in which you are engaged requires you to write alone, then you can ignore this subsection.

Moot court may be your first foray into the collaborative process of legal writing, the style of writing which is used most often in actual legal practice. Through this process, each team member edits, comments on, and redrafts the work of the other member or members of the team to produce the best possible final product. You should take advantage of this opportunity, not only to get a very accurate taste of what real law practice is all about, but also to employ the premise that two or three heads are better than one. If done properly, following the advice given below, your moot court brief will be a much better product than if you follow the less demanding method of splitting your writing between team members who do not comment on each other's work, and merely agree to meet the evening before the brief is due to try to cram the individual work of each team member into one somewhat coherent brief.

The advice below is hard, demanding, and time-consuming, and it will sound extraordinary in comparison to what you have done for other writing assignments in law school and elsewhere. That is the great thing about advice—you can take it or leave it. If you cannot devote the time to do it all, do as much as you can.

A.   Write a complete first draft of the brief as early as you can

Out first advice is to write a complete first draft of the brief as early as you can, preferably three weeks before the final brief is due. Note that we said a **complete** first draft—we mean everything but the table of contents and table of authorities. Draft the questions presented, statement of jurisdiction, statement of the case or statement of facts, and summary of the argument, as well as a complete draft of the argument section. The purpose of this is to allow yourself the time properly to review the problem and evaluate the brief. You should leave yourself the time to make mistakes, to change your mind, to add new issues and to drop others. You must leave the time for your teammates to edit and critique the brief. This amount of time is generous, but not overly generous when you think about how busy you will be in the middle of a semester with your other classes and responsibilities.

If you have a teaching assistant or advisor who, under the rules of the competition, can comment on the drafting of the brief itself, producing a complete product for her to look at and evaluate is much better than an outline and a few notes about things you promise to fill in. No one knows what to say about notes you write in the draft such as: "Add section on preemption," "Find cases," or "Here I'm going to argue that the award is unconstitutional under <u>Perry</u>."

B.   Write multiple drafts

This advice holds for writing a brief collaboratively or on your own. Do not just do one complete draft and then the final. You should know from experience that the first two or three drafts take a lot of time to write and revise, but the next two or three will take a lot less time, and each draft after that will take even less time to turn around. When you get to the level of fine tuning each sentence and paragraph, you may be able to turn around drafts in a matter of one or two hours.

C.   Meet frequently with your teammates and let them comment on each draft

We mentioned choosing people who can give constructive criticism on legal writing, and that you should leave your ego at the door on a team project such as this. The sessions you spend hashing over the brief and discussing its contents will be some of the most valuable time you will spend in your legal education if you have top notch teammates who all can contribute to the effort. Rarely in private practice did we ever get to sit down for several hours and hash through a brief that we were working on with other lawyers; you simply do not get the time to do it, or the client will not pay for these consultation sessions. When this did occur on major projects, we savored the experience. We invite you to have a taste of it while you still are in law school. Do not cut yourself short in these sessions. Anything less than two hours is a rush. You should try to schedule *several* two-hour sessions with your teammate(s).

D.   Talk about each section the first week, each paragraph the second and third weeks, and each sentence and word the last week

Start big in your evaluations of the brief by looking hard at each major section of the brief and the Argument section. Ask yourself: Is this section coherent? Is there enough authority here? Does this argument ring true? Are these facts sufficient, or are they too detailed? Is this Summary of the Argument strong and punchy enough? Does the whole section flow easily and read quickly without having to go back and reread it one or more times? Am I transitioning to the next section adequately?

Next, look at each paragraph: Does it have a good topic sentence? Is the idea stated in the paragraph clear enough? Is it coherent? Is it short enough, or is it too wordy? Does it flow easily? Can you easily understand it without having to read it two or three times?

Remember that three sentences can be an excellent paragraph, and even two sentences will work when you want to be extremely direct and punchy. We have not met any brief judge who will criticize you for having a paragraph that is too short, but many will comment on a paragraph that is too long. Readers will get lost in a long paragraph, and will start to ask themselves questions—"Why did I get into this discussion? How did this start? Are we still talking about the same topic?" Our rule of thumb is that no paragraph should be more then five sentences or more than one third of a page in length. Use the editing process to cut every paragraph down to size.

The last effort should be word-smithing; going sentence by sentence and word by word, and making the language as tight and convincing as possible. Do we need this word? Why do we say "immediately" instead of "quickly"? Let's rephrase this sentence and make it shorter. This part of the process usually is where we get into the most trouble with our cohorts—we like a certain word or phrase, and they do not. Try to get along, but remember, your ego should not matter and the end result should be a team effort. If you have three or more people, vote on final changes if you need to.

E.   Thoroughly discuss each authority

When you are working through each draft, discuss each authority that you citing: Why are we citing this case? What does it mean? What are the facts? Does this authority stand for this exact proposition? Can we rephrase the sentence so that we do not have to say *See* or *See also* or *Cf.* when we cite the authority? Isn't there a stronger case for this point? Are there any negatives associated with using this case? Are we opening ourselves up to a counterattack because we are using this case?

The value of this exercise to your brief should be apparent, but you also will be doing yourself a favor when it comes time for oral argument. All this discussion and review will help you learn everything you need to know about the authorities for oral argument. You will be a walking, talking expert on this little area of the law before you are through, and that will make you a deadly force in oral argument.

F.   Use another team or persons briefing the opposite position if the rules allow it

If you are in a situation where the rules of the competition allow you to consult with another team or persons that are briefing the opposite position on the problem (usually a team from the same school), take the opportunity to consult with them. You will learn a lot from the fresh and contrary perspective of an opponent. They can try to poke holes in your argument, question your sources, present their take on the issues, and discuss how the authorities support or do not support certain positions. Of course, you can help them with their brief, too.

G.   Use all the outside help the rules allow

Outside assistance typically will be limited by the moot court competition's rules. Where it is permitted, you should plan to take advantage of it, and scheduling a date and time with one or more faculty members and practitioners will help you to stay on track and get your act together before these meeting dates arrive. Unless you really are struggling with the issues or the research, you should wait until your research is fairly complete and your brief is well on the way to completion before inviting a law professor or practitioner to comment on it. Every legal professional values her time, and law professors are no exception. Law professors also tend to be a very critical audience, so you should strive to have a strong product in place before you fly it past them. We never felt comfortable in law school dogging our professors to ask them advice on moot court briefs until we were good and prepared on the law, and had specific questions to ask.

Remember, too, that even if you ask for help, you may not get very good outside assistance regarding a moot court problem because the issues chosen for moot court treatment usually are cutting edge issues for which people do not have a good answer. You can get direction, and a sense of what track is right and which tracks are wrong, but the answer will be up to you and your team. At the end of the process, your team will be better experts on this narrowly focused area of the law than anyone else who has not handled an actual case with the same issues. That is what actual litigation practice in the real world is like, too.

VI.   IDEAL TRAITS FOR A MOOT COURT PARTNER

If you are wondering how you might select a teammate (when permitted or required to do so), consider the following tips. An ideal teammate should have the following traits:

> ### MAKE THE CONNECTION!
>
> The power of a good team effort really can make a huge difference in moot court. Try to imagine the Lone Ranger without a Tonto; Batman without a Robin; George W. Bush without a Dick Cheney. A moot court partner should not be a silent partner. Both partners, or as many partners as are on the team, should plan to take on the same amount of work and the same amount of responsibility. It will do no good if one person on the team winds up doing 90% of the work. This will require careful selection of your teammates, if you are able to choose. It will not help you to figure out that you made a bad choice when you are several weeks into the drafting of the brief.

A.   Dedicated and hardworking

Find teammates who are as driven and devoted to excellence as you are. Ask the following questions about any prospective partner: Have you and your prospective partner ever worked or studied well together on legal matters? Does she study as much as you do, or is she always several rounds ahead of you when you run into her at the local hangout after the library has closed? Even a hard worker may not be a good match. Ask whether your work styles are compatible—do you like late nights and weekends and she likes early days and ruthless scheduling between classes? Such considerations can affect your success as a team.

B.   Available

The hardest working student in the law school is not an ideal partner if she never is available to discuss the brief or do a practice oral argument. Many of the best students are over-committed. If you are equally over-committed, and will have to carve out the time to edit and revise the brief through ruthless time management, then a workaholic partner may be ideal for you. But consider the downside if you have put moot court as your number one priority for the semester, and your partner is on a journal and has a part-time job and has several other high priority time commitments. That said, note that being on a journal, participating in a moot court competition, and carrying a full load of classes is not an impossible task for an upper level law student. The point is to pick a partner who you can work with. So, if you plan to spend twenty hours each week working on moot court, and there is no way your prospective partner can do that in her schedule, face up to that fact, discuss it, and figure out whether you can work with it. It is the unspoken resentment building up over time that destroys most moot court partnerships.

C.   Balanced

Moot court competitions grade heavily on *both* brief writing and oral argument. Neither skill can be counted out when forming your team. If you have the luxury of having three or more team members, and only two need to argue, then you can cherry pick a team with a brief writing specialist and two oral argument specialists. Add to that an editing and proofreading specialist, and you will have a juggernaut that cannot be stopped. But in most intramural competitions and some interscholastic competitions, you only will have two members on the team, so each one must be adept at brief writing, editing, proofreading, and oral argument. A team with one good brief writer may do fine in the brief portion of the competition, but oral argument scores always are based on the scores of both oralists, so you will trip up in that portion of the competition if your team lacks two strong oralists.

Conversely, you may be attracted to a partner because you have witnessed his dazzling oral argument skills. Some people's gifts in that area are very obvious. It is harder to evaluate someone's writing and editing skills. Experience on a journal or law review may indicate something, as will disclosure of someone's first year legal writing grade. But the most important thing to do is ask: "Are you comfortable at brief writing, editing, and proofreading?" You may be a great brief writer, editor and proofreader, but unless you plan to carry the bulk of the writing load, and the responsibility for that part of the grade, be wary of persons who disclaim that they really are only in it for the oral argument experience.

D.   Good match for your strengths and weaknesses

A good partner should complement your team, not throw it out of kilter. If you are a better oralist than a brief writer, you should try to find someone who is a great brief writer, and at least a decent oralist. Two great oralists with no brief writing and editing skills may fare well at the arguments, but rarely will they progress to advanced rounds. The same goes for two excellent brief writers and editors who cannot perform well on their feet.

There certainly is room for different styles of oral argument. You can match two oralists who have very different argument styles, as long as each style is effective and will score well based on the applicable judging criteria. But two brief writers with very different writing styles may present a real problem. If you are a flamboyant writer and your partner is low key, you may have to decide whose style will give way when you get around to the editing process and are striving to make a single coherent document out of the two parts of the brief each of you has drafted. Are you willing to go toe to toe over whether that paragraph will remain in section II(B) on page 18 of the brief and still walk away friends?

Having someone on the team who is a meticulous editor, proofreader, Bluebook checker, and grammarian will be a great asset to a moot court team—as long as everyone knows their work will be ruthlessly edited and corrected. Being able to take criticism also is a must in this process. As a potential partner on a moot court team, you must ask yourself whether you can you give and receive constructive criticism on writing and oral argument in a way that will not drive you and your partners apart forever. This should be a team effort to produce a team brief that maximizes the team's oral argument performance. It is not about you, it is about the team (and there is no "I" and no "U" in "Team").

Appendix

The TREAT Method of Organization and Explanatory Synthesis

The practice of advocacy and rhetoric (i.e., persuasion) requires close attention to the needs and expectations of your audience. In the case of adversarial legal writing, we are talking about judges as the primary audience. Judges are law-trained readers who, in general, are very demanding when it comes to matters of the style, substance, and convenience of the legal writing that is put before them. Most judges think they have more than enough work to do, and more than enough writing to review in any given week, so a careful and effective advocate will make their writing as acceptable and attractive to this audience as possible.

The TREAT paradigm and the doctrine of explanatory synthesis discussed in this appendix are both organizational methodologies and substantive theories designed to improve the substance of legal writing. The TREAT paradigm doctrine holds that the presentation of legal discourse in a carefully constructed order not only promotes clarity and satisfies audience expectations but also maximizes the communicative potential and persuasiveness of the material. The explanatory synthesis doctrine casts aside the prior methodology of "explanation" of governing legal standards in legal writing and instead combines the substantive doctrine of precedent and stare decisis that underlies the Anglo-American common law tradition and the doctrine of analogical reasoning that supports the presentation of common law and positive rules. Explanatory synthesis accomplishes these objectives by illustrating the effect of the precedent where the rules were applied. It improves the substance of legal writing by combining precedents in a process of inductive reasoning within a deductive reasoning structural paradigm and reveals the factors and policies that determine the outcome of precedent.

This appendix discusses both of these methods. It will take you and your writing beyond the simple IRAC structure and advance your ability to persuade your most difficult and demanding audiences. We will discuss the handling of issues (legal questions) in all types of legal writing. In other words, the methodology discussed herein works in objective-predictive legal writing as well as in adversarial-persuasive legal writing. In your adversarial works of advocacy, you will be answering legal issues with a certain perspective in mind---your client's---and the Thesis headings we discuss will be argumentative thesis headings that summarize the points of your argument on behalf of your client in the section of text that follows the thesis heading. Your Application sections will advocate your client's position by working through the application pf the law to the client's facts to demonstrate why the client wins. The objectives of a work of advocacy are different from that of an objective, predictive office memoranda, but the methodologies of the TREAT paradigm and explanatory synthesis work the same in both forms of legal writing.

I.　　MOVING FROM ISSUES TO ANSWERS AND *IRAC* TO *TREAT*

A.　　Simple IRAC

As you know, a legal issue is a question for a lawyer to answer. Some legal issues are very simple, having only one question to answer, and the question can be answered by looking at one rule and applying it to the facts without having to explain the rule to the reader.

> Question: What is the statute of limitations for a tort in New Mexico?
>
> The statute of limitations for a tort in New Mexico is governed by N.M. Stat. § 23-45-8 (2005), which states: "The following causes of action have a five year

---

1　Rule-Based Reasoning Syllogism: The answer is X because the authorities establish the rule that governs this situation, and the rule requires certain facts to be present, and these facts are present, so the application of the rule to the facts produces X result.

> limitations period: . . . all actions of . . . tort . . . ."
>
> Client was involved in an automobile accident from which her cause of action for negligence arose. Client's negligence action is a tort action that will be governed by New Mexico's five year statute of limitations for tort actions.

This is short, and certainly not complicated, but it does reflect all the steps of your analysis of this simple issue. You presented the issue and the rule that answers the issue, you applied the rule to the client's facts, and you reached a conclusion. This example follows the rule-based reasoning syllogism[1] by stating the general rule, applying the specific facts, and drawing the conclusion that follows. This is **IRAC** formulation in its simplest form: state the **I**ssue, state the **R**ule that answers the issue, **A**pply the rule to the facts, and draw your **C**onclusion from this process.

B. Moving from IRAC to TREAT

Most of life and law practice is not that simple. As the issues you are resolving grow in number and complexity, you have got to raise your game to meet the challenge. Raising your game in this context means presenting your writing in a format that anticipates and addresses the needs of your law-trained readers better than simple IRAC does. The particular method we discuss in this book— TREAT —is designed to improve IRAC by giving answers to issues up front, by explaining the rule to readers, and by reinforcing the rule and the explanation of the rule using inductive reasoning and analogical reasoning within the rule-based reasoning syllogism. The following chart shows our movement from IRAC to TREAT and we have highlighted our improvements to the simple IRAC method:

---

2   A good lawyer using IRAC will explain the rule, too, but our method uses a rigorous explanation formulation called explanatory synthesis that employs inductive and analogical reasoning to illustrate how the rule works. This is above and beyond any simple IRAC explanation of rules and it is much more useful to a busy, law-trained reader who does not have the time to synthesize multiple cases and other authorities in order to fully understand the operation of a typical, complicated legal rule.

IRAC terminology		TREAT terminology	
Issue	Identifies the issue for the reader	**Thesis**	**Identifies the issue for the reader and states your conclusion — your answer to the issue — up front where it helps the reader the most**
Rule	States the legal principles that govern the issue	Rule	States the legal principles that govern the issue
		Explanation	**Explains and illustrates how the rule works in actual situations[2]**
Application	Applies the rule to the facts of the case at hand	Application	Applies the rule to the facts of the case at hand
Conclusion	States your conclusion on the issue	**Thesis restated as conclusion**	**Restates your conclusion on the issue to reinforce your answer and to bring closure to the discussion**

IRAC is simpler than TREAT, but in this business, simple is not the highest priority. Helping the reader to understand and appreciate your legal analysis is the highest priority, and in that task, TREAT is head and shoulders better than IRAC.

FYI

Where did we get TREAT?
We often are asked, "why do you use TREAT rather than IRAC"? The simple answer to this question is: TREAT is simply a more sophisticated version of IRAC. When we analyzed countless briefs and office memos that law firm partners and judges considered excellent samples of what they were looking for, we discovered that "IRAC" was a little simplistic. At their core, all of the odd-sounding acronyms that mark the stages of legal analysis — TREAT, CREAC (Conclusion, Rule, Explanation, Application, Conclusion), CRAC (Conclusion, Rule, Application, Conclusion), CIRAC (Conclusion, Issue, Rule, Application, Conclusion), etc. — share one thing in common: they are progeny of IRAC. You cannot get away from these IRAC derivatives in legal writing. Why? Because all of them are derived from the rule-based reasoning syllogism — or stated more simply: all of them mark steps in the process of deductive

> reasoning (which is what you are doing when you are asked to find a governing rule and to apply it to a new set of facts). TREAT picks up where IRAC stops and anticipates that readers are going to need and appreciate the answers to the issues up front and would benefit from a thorough explanation of how the applicable rules work that is derived from concrete examples of situations where the rules worked to produce a definite outcome — namely the cases you will synthesize in a process of inductive reasoning. TREAT makes your writing stronger than IRAC can do on its own.

TREAT is the format for the discussion of a single issue. Most legal problems contain a number of issues and many of the rules that will answer your issues will have multiple parts that each might raise separate questions (issues) to answer. Each issue gets its own TREAT — if it is one of two separate questions (*e.g.,* Will the homeowner be liable to the scout for dog bite liability, and will the homeowner be liable to the scout for negligence?), then each issue will be resolved in a separate presentation of <u>T</u>hesis on the issue—<u>R</u>ule that answers the issue—<u>E</u>xplanation of the rule—<u>A</u>pplication of the rule—and <u>T</u>hesis Restated on that issue. But if the rule that answers the issue itself raises questions (*e.g.,* To answer the question, is the homeowner liable for negligence, you must answer at least two questions raised by the rule: Did the homeowner owe the scout a duty of care, and did the homeowner breach this duty of care?), then each of the questions raised by the rule will be resolved in it own TREAT internal to the discussion of the main issue; we will call these internal discussions "sub-TREATs." Every main question or subsidiary question in a legal discussion will be resolved one way (main TREAT) or the other (sub-TREAT) in a presentation of <u>T</u>hesis-<u>R</u>ule-<u>E</u>xplanation-<u>A</u>pplication- and <u>T</u>hesis Restated on that question.

II.   THESIS HEADING

As a quick reminder: your involvement with the TREAT paradigm begins when you have done all of the research and analysis of an issue and are ready to report your conclusions. In advocacy, this process begins in the Argument section of a brief or litigation memoranda when you begin to argue your client's position on the issue. Your discussion of an issue should begin with **your position on the issue**, which we are calling your thesis. The thesis almost always is written in one sentence; it should articulate what the issue is and how the issue should come out based on your analysis. In advocacy, you will use argumentative thesis headings which summarize your argument in the section that follows the heading.

Presenting your thesis on the issue first brings to the front the most important part of the discussion: your answer to the legal question posed by the issue. In addition, putting your thesis in a heading that precedes the discussion of the issue further highlights this critical information for the benefit of the reader. When you consider that most of the writing you will do will discuss a number of issues in the same document, you can begin to understand that separating and highlighting your conclusions by use of thesis headings will help even the busiest reader to pick up the most important parts of your discussion quickly and efficiently.

FOOD FOR THOUGHT

Helping busy readers, highlighting information for the benefit of the reader . . . what is this all about? We are emphasizing that TREAT is designed to make it easy for a busy law-trained reader to access your writing, and thereby appreciate it all the more because you aren't wasting her time. When you consider how many lawyers and judges are busy, you can start to appreciate the benefits of the TREAT format. It is an audience-friendly writing format.

In this appendix, we will examine the legal situation of a client who owns a Doberman Pinscher. Your client's dog encountered a girl as she was selling Girl Scout cookies, and the dog became agitated when the girl swung her bag of cookies at the dog's head. The dog apparently thought the girl was threatening it and it reacted by clamping its jaws onto her arm. Unfortunately, the girl and her mother got into it with the dog, and in the skirmish, the girl received several deep cuts on her arm. The case was analyzed under the mythical law of Apex, but for the purposes of this appendix, we will present the law as if you had done the research in Texas.

Imagine that after completing your research and analyzing your client's situation under the Texas rule, your conclusion is that your client, the dog owner, will be liable for the injuries inflicted on the girl's arm by the dog. When you write up your analysis, your thesis might be, "The dog owner will be liable for plaintiff's dog bite injuries."

At a minimum, the Thesis statement must reveal the issue (*e.g.*, Will Client be liable for dog bite injuries?) and the answer (*e.g.*, Yes, Client will be liable for dog bite injuries) in the same statement. One additional part to consider adding is an explanation of *why* — why is the answer yes and not no. One of the authors recommends using a "because clause" in the thesis that says in a nutshell what the position you are taking is based on (*e.g.*, "Client will be liable for Scout's dog bite injuries because Scout did not provoke the dog."). This accomplishes three things that help the reader: it tells the reader the issue, the answer to the issue, and a brief explanation of the answer.

DO IT WITH STYLE!

THESIS HEADING DRAFTING TIPS

1. Should the Thesis use the parties' names or is "plaintiff" and "defendant" sufficient?
As a general matter, legal readers prefer when you use the parties' names rather than titles. We occasionally might have used a title (plaintiff or defendant) in an example or two just for simplicity's sake, but you are better off using names unless you have thought it through and consciously decide otherwise (for example, some litigators prefer calling the opposing party by title rather than proper name in order to "depersonalize" their opponent).

2. Should the thesis use "sentence case" or "title case" capitalization?
There are many right answers here; you should defer to your instructor's preference for font, formatting, and capitalization rules. In the future, you should check the formatting preferences for your place of employment or the local rules for the court and jurisdiction in which you are filing.

You want to be careful not to include *too much* information here, or else your thesis will become unwieldy (*e.g.*,"Client will be liable for Scout's injuries because there are three elements to dog bite liability in Texas and one of them is lack of provocation and Scout's actions in swinging a bag of cookies at the dog's head does not constitute provocation under the rule in Texas.") However, *if you can* boil the explanation down to the most important nugget, it is effective to include that information (*e.g.*, "Client will be liable for Scout's dog bite injuries because Scout did not provoke the dog.").

When drafting the discussion of an issue, the thesis is stated as the heading of a section, and the paragraph that immediately follows the heading will state the rule, as in the following example:

1.   <u>**Client will be liable for Scout's dog bite injuries because Scout did not provoke the dog.**</u>

Client will be liable for Scout's dog bite injuries because Scout did not provoke the dog. In Texas, a dog owner is liable for all injuries caused by his dog unless the dog is provoked by the victim. Smithy v. Jonesy, 123 S.W.2d 345, 347 (Tex. 1965); Johnson v. Anderson, 789 S.W.2d 234, 237 (Tex. App. 1989). The elements of a cause of action for dog-bite liability are therefore: (1) defendant's ownership of the dog, (2) injuries caused by the dog, and (3) lack of provocation of the dog by the plaintiff. See Smithy, 123 S.W.2d at 347.

POINT-COUNTERPOINT

Should you repeat the Thesis heading as the first line of the text that follows the heading?

The authors differ on this point. Author DeSanctis favors repeating or rephrasing the Thesis as the first line of text following the heading, while author Murray does not favor this practice. Rephrasing the Thesis headings allows you to write slightly shorter headings, saving some of the important information about your thesis for the first line of text. It also preserves the thesis for those readers who skip over reading the headings in documents. If you do not repeat or rephrase the heading, you will have to put all of the important information about the thesis into the heading (the issue, the most important facts, and the "because clause" that explains why the thesis comes out the way it does), but this also provides a more useful summary for those readers who skim the discussion section reading only the Thesis headings. This is a style point on which reasonable law-trained writers will differ, and you should employ the technique that best suits your writing.

III. RULE SECTION

A. Statement of legal principles and requirements that govern the issue

The rule section follows the thesis, and states the rule or rules that govern the legal issue. You will recall that a rule of law is a statement of the legal principles and requirements that govern the analysis of a legal issue. Sometimes there is one rule that is followed by all the authorities in your jurisdiction. However, in many instances different authorities will state the rule differently, perhaps just using different language, but sometimes illuminating or adding a new factor to the rule.

There are three basic scenarios for the kind of rule section you should draft based on what you find in the authorities. The simplest is the rule that comes from a single source (more often a statute or administrative rule than anything else), that is free of additional modification or interpretation in later authorities:

> The statute of limitations for a tort in New Mexico is governed by N.M. Stat. § 23-45-8 (2005), which states: "The following causes of action have a five year limitations period: . . . all actions of . . . tort . . . ."

In this example, this might be the entire rule section. But more often than that, the rule in the jurisdiction will have undergone some development over time. Perhaps the rule started with a statute and then was interpreted and modified by cases:

> The Illinois statute pertaining to liability of an owner of a dog attacking or injuring persons provides:
>
> > If a dog or other animal without provocation, attacks or injures any person who is peacefully conducting himself in any place where he may lawfully be, the owner of such dog or other animal is liable in damages to such person for the full amount of the injury sustained.
>
> Ill. Rev. Stat. ch. 8, par. 366 (1973).

Under this statute, Illinois courts have found that there are four elements that must be proved: injury caused by a dog owned or harbored by the defendant; lack of provocation; peaceable conduct of the person injured; and the presence of the person injured in a place where he has a legal right to be. Siewerth v. Charleston, 231 N.E.2d 644, 646 (Ill. App. Ct. 1967); Messa v. Sullivan, 209 N.E.2d 872, 873 (Ill. App. Ct. 1965); Beckert v. Risberg, 199 N.E.2d 811, 815 (Ill. App. Ct. 1964), *rev'd on other grounds,* 210 N.E.2d 207 (Ill. 1965).

Most common of all is a rule that has developed over time with modifications to the rule itself and with further interpretations and constructions in later authorities which affect the meaning of the rule:

Under U.S. copyright law, a work using copyrighted material of another author may be protected from copyright infringement prosecution if it is found to be a "fair use." The U.S. Copyright Act reads, in pertinent part,

The fair use of a copyrighted work . . . for purposes such as criticism [and] comment . . . is not an infringement of copyright. In determining whether the use made of a work in any particular case is a fair use the factors to be considered shall include—(1) the purpose and character of the use, including whether such use is of a commercial nature; . . . (2) the nature of the copyrighted work; (3) the amount and substantiality of the portion used in relation to the copyrighted work as a whole; and (4) the effect of the use upon the potential market for or value of the copyrighted work . . . .

17 U.S.C. § 107. In applying this law, courts have rejected the use of bright line rules, calling instead for a case-by-case analysis which weighs together a consideration of all four of the included factors. Campbell, 473 U.S. at 577-78. Significantly for the issue in the principal case, parody may be considered a fair use, qualifying as such under the first factor, "purpose and character of the use." Id. at 579.

Parody, qualifying as fair use, is a work that (1) targets the borrowed original work and, at least in part, makes comment on it, and (2) is transformative of the original work, rather than simply superseding it. <u>Id.</u> at 579-80. It has additionally been

FORMULATING THE RULE (RULE SYNTHESIS)	
Start with the highest and most recent controlling authority	If you have a statute (or regulation), start with the statute
	If you have a watershed case that is controlling, start with that
	If your best authority is from the court of last resort, take the most recent opinion from that court, and start with that
	If these first three criteria do not apply, start with the most recent actual controlling authority that is on point
	Only if none of the above applies would you consider turning to non-controlling authority—primary or secondary
	Don't expect to use all of your authorities
Reconcile differing statements or phrasings of the rule from controlling authorities, and attempt to synthesize the material into one coherent statement of the legal principles that govern the issue	DON'T change the wording of or paraphrase rules from statutes, administrative rules and regulations, and watershed cases
	Unless an applied rule can be written smoothly and effectively in one sentence or phrase, write the rule first with modifications second
Write the rule first, interpretative rules second, and exceptions to the rule third	Write interpretive sub-rules on elements of the rule in the section or sub-section of the discussion that discusses that element of the rule. Write exceptions to the sub-rules after you lay out the sub-rules themselves
Do not write a rule with inherent contradictions	Check for ambiguity in the terms you have used to formulate the rule (even if some of these terms came from the authorities)
Do accept the <u>remote</u> possibility that two competing rules on the same issue might exist in the same jurisdiction	When this happens, you may have to analyze the facts under both competing sets of rules. You will have to present two rule sections and work through the analysis of the problem under both rules, noting any differences in the outcome caused by the differing rules

DO IT WITH STYLE!

RULE SECTION DRAFTING TIPS

1. What do you mean by rule "section"?

We mean simply the space that it takes to articulate the rule in writing. You likely will have multiple rule "sections" in a single document because your problem will present multiple questions to answer, each of which will have a rule section presenting the rules that apply to answer the question. Note that we are making a fine distinction for now between the "R" and the "E" in the TREAT paradigm: the Rule section is for the rules that apply to answer the issue, and the Explanation section is used to illustrate how the rules in the Rule section work in actual situations.

2. In general, how long should the Rule section be?

Again, the answers here vary depending, of course, on the rule itself. Occasionally, it might be a single paragraph, or, for rules with several modifications and interpretations, it may take several paragraphs or even several pages to present. If, for example, there are multiple accounts of the rule (as in the case where your jurisdiction has not answered the question posed and other jurisdictions follow different approaches), then you may have multiple paragraphs presenting it. As with most legal writing, there is some discretion involved here, and you will develop a better sense of what your reader will need or might want to know as you become more familiar with an area of law and even with different readers. But do not ignore the guidance of simple logic: if there is a settled, straightforward rule in your jurisdiction, then you probably need not include the entire history of how that jurisdiction arrived at the rule or the policy underlying it. In contrast, if the rule is in question in your jurisdiction, then you are going to need some additional support for your interpretation or approach.

3. To what extent should I cite or discuss authorities in the rule section?

Certainly, you are going to want to cite primary authorities (statutes, regulations, or cases) in the rule section. Without citations, your reader will not understand where you are getting the rule from. Whether you actually quote authorities depends on the type of rule you are working with; rules from statutes or regulations or watershed cases should be quoted, but rules derived or synthesized from a line of cases might not be. As for discussing cases (such as presenting the facts of particular cases), you are going to have plenty of room to do that in the course of explaining and applying the rule, discussed in more detail below. For now, we are really only talking about stating what the rule is.

found to be immaterial whether the alleged parody is in good or bad taste, id. at 582, whether the work is labeled as a parody, id. at 583, or whether the copyright owner would endorse or prohibit the work. Leibovitz, 980 F.2d at 115.

The following chart should refresh your recollection about how to go about "synthesizing" a rule section from multiple authorities:

B. Interpretive rules

We have hinted at something above that we must now make explicit: rule sections contain two different kinds of rules that both apply to answer and resolve the issue. Most of our discussion so far has been about the rules that define the legal standards that govern the issue. We might call these **definitional rules** or more simply, the **main rules** presented in the rule section. But the rule section also will present **interpretive rules** from primary and secondary authorities. Interpretive rules are statements from legal authorities that instruct lawyers and judges how to interpret or apply the rule on the issue at hand. They are not elements or factors of the rule (rather, those are part of the rule itself), and they are not the same as the principles of interpretation that you will derive from your synthesis of the authorities (discussed below). Instead, interpretative rules are individual statements about the rule that come from authorities that have discussed and applied the rule in question. They are, in fact, rules about how to interpret and apply other rules. But interpretive rules are crafted by the authors of legal authorities to give guidance on the interpretation and application of specific, individual rules, not all legal rules in general.

> For example, in the hypothetical problem we have been using, assume that one case from your jurisdiction characterizes the rule on dog bite liability as a "disfavored cause of action," and states that "in order to prove liability for a dog bite, the plaintiff must prove each element of the claim with clear and convincing evidence." Next, assume that a second case discusses relatively recent developments in the law on this issue and explains that dog bite liability has moved from a point where "every dog was entitled to one unprovoked bite," to a point where "each attack by a dog, even the first, may give rise to a valid claim against the dog owner." These interpretative rules belong in the same section as the actual statement of the rule and its elements, but you should save this information for after you have laid out the elements of the actual rule.

One of the examples above shows the use of Interpretive Rules in the context of a more complicated rule section:

> **[Definitional Rule:]** Under U.S. copyright law, a work using copyrighted material of another author may be protected from copyright infringement prosecution if it is found to be a "fair use." The U.S. Copyright Act reads, in pertinent part,
>
> > The fair use of a copyrighted work . . . for purposes such as criticism [and] comment . . . is not an infringement of copyright. In determining whether the use made of a work in any particular case is a fair use the factors to be considered shall include—(1) the purpose and character of the use, including whether such use is of a commercial nature; . . . (2) the nature of the copyrighted work; (3) the amount and substantiality of the portion used in relation to the copyrighted work as a whole; and (4) the effect of the use upon the potential market for or value of the copyrighted work . . . .
>
> 17 U.S.C. § 107. **[Interpretive Rules:]** In applying this law, courts have rejected the use of bright line rules, calling instead for a case-by-case analysis which weighs together a consideration of all four of the included factors. Campbell, 473 U.S. at 577-78. Significantly for the issue in the principal case, parody may be considered a fair use, qualifying as such under the first factor, "purpose and character of the use." Id. at 579.
>
> **[Definitional Rule:]** Parody, qualifying as fair use, is a work that (1) targets the borrowed original work and, at least in part, makes comment on it, and (2) is transformative of the original work, rather than simply superseding it. Id. at 579-80. **[Interpretive Rule:]** It has additionally been found to be immaterial whether the alleged parody is in good or bad taste, id. at 582, whether the work is labeled as a parody, id. at 583, or whether the copyright owner would endorse or prohibit the work. Leibovitz, 980 F.2d at 115.

In the example quoted in section I above, the rule on liability for dog attacks in Texas was stated the same way in each of the authorities we used. If we had also found the interpretive rules just mentioned, the rule section instead might read as follows:

THESIS HEADING AND RULE SECTION:

1. <u>The Dog Owner will be liable for Scout's dog bite injuries.</u>

[**Definitional Rules:**] In Texas, a dog owner is liable for all injuries caused by his dog unless the dog is provoked by the victim. <u>Smithy v. Jonesy</u>, 123 S.W.2d 345, 347 (Tex. 1965); <u>Johnson v. Anderson</u>, 789 S.W.2d 234, 237 (Tex. App. 1989). The elements of a cause of action for dog-bite liability are therefore: (1) defendant's ownership of the dog, (2) injuries caused by the dog, and (3) lack of provocation of the dog by the plaintiff. <u>See</u> <u>Smithy</u>, 123 S.W.2d at 347. [**Interpretive Rules:**] The rule on dog bite liability has moved from a point where "every dog was entitled to one unprovoked bite," to a point where "each attack by a dog, even the first, may give rise to a valid claim against the dog owner." Hawthorne v. Melville, 999 S.W.2d 17, 20 (Tex. App. 1998). That said, a claim seeking to impose liability for a dog bite is a "disfavored cause of action" in Texas; as such, "the plaintiff must prove each element of the claim with clear and convincing evidence." <u>Roberts v. Thomas</u>, 676 S.W.2d 34, 37 (Tex. 1979).

IV.   EXPLANATION SECTION AND EXPLANATORY SYNTHESIS

The "E" section is critically important; however, it is a step that many writers omit, confuse with application, or approach in an unsynthesized (and therefore less helpful) manner.

A.   Purpose of the explanation section

In the explanation section, you will use some or all of the legal authorities you have found in your research to explain the rule and to show how the rule operates in various situations. The goal of this section is to teach the reader the principles learned from earlier authorities that show lawyers **how to interpret** (and then later apply) the rule.

How is this different from the rule section, just discussed? In the rule section, you spell out the actual legal standards that govern the issue. A law-trained reader may be able to review those standards and make an educated guess as to how these standards will operate in factual situa-

THE GOAL OF THE EXPLANATION SECTION	
The goal is to illustrate how the rule is to be interpreted and applied based on how the authorities have applied it in actual concrete factual settings, and on how commentators have interpreted the rule.	You are going beyond what the courts already have said about the rule in interpretive rules found in cases. Specifically, you are presenting principles of interpretation that are supported by a careful reading of the cases. You are doing the work of digesting and synthesizing the cases so the reader doesn't have to.
Case by case presentations make the reader do most of the work and they are wasteful of space and time (i.e., the reader's attention span).	Avoid case-by-case presentations even though they are easy to write and even though courts sometimes use them. The only time to resort to a case by case presentation is when you have one or two cases that are so close to the facts that you want to cover them in great detail through analogical reasoning, or if you want to distinguish one or two troublesome cases in enough detail to make your point through converse analogical reasoning.

tions, but this will only be a guess. You can greatly facilitate the reader's understanding of how the rule does (or should) operate by **illustrating and explaining** how the rules worked in actual situations, which requires referring to the cases that have applied those rules. However, your explanation should be something more than just a laundry list of cases.

Consider the following:

FYI

What is the difference between showing and telling?
The Rule section **tells** the reader **what** the rules are that answer the issue. The Explanation section **shows** the reader **how** these rules are supposed to work basing this illustration on actual, concrete situations (cases) where the rule has worked to produce a fixed outcome. What is the difference between showing and telling? Consider this:

Your father has bought a new German Shepherd puppy. Several of your father's buddies have told him about a county ordinance that states, in its entirety, "All owners of dangerous dogs must register the dog and obtain a permit to keep the dog at the owner's residence in the county." Your father turns to you to determine whether he needs to register and obtain a permit for the puppy. You can **tell** your father the words of the statute and further tell him that other legal sources have said the following about the rule:

> "Dangerous dogs present more than the average risk of injury to persons than ordinary dogs present." "Dangerous dogs are brutal and short-tempered." "Dangerous dogs have a propensity to cause injury beyond the normal propensity of common, domestic dogs."

All of these could be characterized as **Interpretive Rules**, and they may or may not give your father a better idea about how the rule is interpreted and applied. But if you research and read all of the dangerous dog cases in the county and find that the dangerous dog cases have certain things in common, you can **show** your father how the rule works in a way that plainly communicates how the rule is to be interpreted and applied:

> The breed of dog matters greatly in dangerous dog cases. The only breeds that courts have found to be dangerous are: Pit Bull Terriers, Doberman Pinschers, and German Shepherds. Dangerous dogs are those who have been trained to fight and defend persons and property, as well as those who actually have attacked intruders perceived to threaten the same. No case involving a German Shepherd has found the dog to be dangerous unless it had been trained to guard persons and property and attack intruders; absent that special training, German Shepherds are not considered dangerous.

Your father would probably take your word for it, but a law-trained reader would want you to cite all of the cases you looked at and write brief illustrations (in parentheticals) of how and why the cases support these additional principles of interpretation and application that you have derived from a careful reading of the cases. This is the process of **explanatory synthesis**: you read the cases as examples of situations where the rule produced a certain outcome, you carefully induce the truths from these examples about how the rule is supposed to be interpreted and applied, and you write up the results of this inductive reasoning with illustrations from the cases that concentrate on **showing how** the rules work and not just repeating the main rules and interpretive rules that you found in the cases.

The explanation section does not exist simply to provide titillating details from a number of cases to entertain the reader, and it does not exist to fill up the space from the end of your rule or to the beginning of your application section. Details from cases can be exciting, but the facts and details themselves do not teach the reader how the rule actually works. The explanation section exists to present principles of interpretation derived from cases and secondary authorities that will show the reader how a rule or sub-rule works.

Lawyers and judges have a number of ways to approach this task. The common ***unsynthesized*** way used by many junior attorneys is to write a series of sentences and paragraphs describing the facts and holding of several cases. Typically, the author discusses one case at a time, devoting an entire paragraph to each case. At the end of it, the author hopes the reader has learned something from this list of factual details and holdings. In fact, the author hopes the reader has learned what the author probably already knows but hasn't put into writing. As a consequence, it is entirely up to the reader to make the connections between cases that otherwise are factually different. In effect, the typical author simply is saying to the reader: "Here are a number of cases where the rule was applied and here is the outcome of those cases. You make sense out of it."

For example, a case-by-case explanation section might look like this (but we mercifully have dropped out most of the details that the author could have droned on about):

In <u>Nelson</u>, a two-year old girl was playing crack the whip near a Dalmatian when she accidentally was thrown on top of the dog. Her actions were inadvertent and unintentional. The dog reacted by scratching the girl on her right eye. The dog did not bite the girl; however, the girl did suffer an injury to the tear duct of her eye . . . .

In <u>Siewerth</u>, two boys, age six and seven, were playing with a Collie dog on the seven-year old's front porch. The six-year old began hitting the dog on the head with a plastic toy truck. He persisted in hitting the dog on the head until the dog nipped him on the hand. The boy then started punching the dog in the dog's side with his two fists, and the dog reacted by biting the boy on the arm . . . .

In <u>Messa</u>, a five year boy accidentally pushed open the wrong door to an apartment on the same floor of the apartment building where he lived, and encountered a German Shepherd. At first the dog only barked at the boy while he tried to back away from the doorway, but after the boy started to run away, the dog pursued him down the hallway. The dog eventually caught up to the boy and . . . .

In <u>Beckert</u>, a postal carrier was going house to house delivering the mail. At Beckert's house, the mail carrier opened the outer, screen door to put the mail inside the door, when he found himself face to face with Beckert's Boxer dog. The mail carrier tried to back away from the dog, but the dog followed him. The mail carrier picked up his pace slightly, trying to get away from the dog, and the dog chased him to the sidewalk. The dog then bit the mail carrier on his leg . . . .

These might have gone on and on. The point is not about length or wordiness (or *not all* about length and wordiness); it is about something more important: your reader. If you take a leisurely stroll through the cases and pile on the details as thick as you can, you will find your reader stopping you in the hall instead of reading the memorandum, and asking you, "Just tell me what these cases mean. How do they affect the client's claim?"

Explanatory synthesis anticipates these questions and addresses them. It focuses on the principles that can be induced from the cases not on the cases themselves. Consider the following, and notice the principles that are extracted:

> The age of the dog bite victim is not determinative of the dog owner's liability. <u>See</u> <u>Nelson</u>, 344 N.E.2d at 270 (denying recovery where two-year old provoked the dog); <u>Siewerth</u>, 231 N.E.2d at 647 (denying recovery where six-year old provoked the dog); <u>Messa</u>, 209 N.E.2d at 875 (determining that five-year old was entitled to recover in the absence of provocation); <u>Beckert</u>, 199 N.E.2d at 813 (determining that thirty-seven year old postal worker was entitled to recover in the absence of provocation). Even small children acting intentionally or unintentionally can provoke dogs into attacking and forfeit the chance to recover. <u>See</u> <u>Nelson</u>, 344 N.E.2d at 269 (finding provocation where two-year old girl unintentionally fell on dog); <u>Siewerth</u>, 231 N.E.2d at 647 (finding provocation where six-year old boy hit dog on head). Rather, the cases turn on whether the dog bite victim made hostile physical contact with the dog; those that did were held to have provoked the dog, while those that did not were held not to have provoked the dog. <u>See</u> <u>Siewerth</u>, 231 N.E.2d at 647 (finding provocation where victim repeatedly hit dog); <u>Messa</u>, 209 N.E.2d at

875 (finding no provocation where victim escaped dog and never touched dog); <u>Beckert</u>, 199 N.E.2d at 813 (same). The physical contact need not have been intentional; even accidental contact may give rise to a finding of provocation if sufficiently threatening to the dog. <u>See</u> <u>Nelson</u>, 344 N.E.2d at 270-71 (finding provocation where victim was thrown on top of dog).

We do not mean to suggest that specific cases are not important; to the contrary, notice how we incorporated the facts both in constructing the principles (or themes) themselves and, as well, in parenthetical information when certain details were illuminating.

In addition, an *in text* discussion may well be prudent and necessary when you want to fully illustrate one or more cases that are exactly on point to show how completely they should control your client's situation. If you are representing a toddler who was shoved and landed on a dog that bit her, your reader certainly will want more detail about the <u>Nelson</u> case.

Similarly, an in text discussion of one or more cases may be necessary when you need to explain an analogy you are drawing or to fully distinguish a potentially controlling authority that goes against your thesis. The process of distinguishing certain authorities especially may require a detailed discussion of the facts, issues, and holdings of the cases in order to separate them from your case. If you are representing a postal mail carrier who opened a screen door and encountered a dog who menaced the carrier, but the carrier took the opportunity to clobber the dog with her mail bag before being bit, you had better be ready with a detailed explanation of why the <u>Beckert</u> case does not guaranty victory for the client.

In most instances, however, you will not have any positive or negative case that is this much "on all fours" with your case. You will have a number of helpful cases that establish a landscape from which you can predict an outcome to your client's situation, and some that are not helpful, but none that is spot-on. In these situations, a synthesis of the authorities will aid the reader more than a recitation of one case after another. If, instead, you write an unsynthesized explanation section, you will not have presented sufficient guiding principles for the reader to determine how the rule really works. For example, how do you know what "breaking" (an element of burglary) means? If you found one case in which a defendant broke a window and the court found that this was a breaking, and you merely describe the factual circumstances of that case, your "explanation" of the element will be deficient. It might lead the reader to believe that breaking means breaking a window. This conclusion is logical, but inaccurate because it is incomplete.

For additional guidance on incorporating cases into your analysis, click on our "Good Use of Cases" Tip Sheet.

B.   Explanatory synthesis

Inductive reasoning is the backbone of the scientific method. We do not spring from the womb knowing general principles about mitosis in cells or the nature of light waves any more than we know how to interpret and apply the four factors that determine a successful fair use in copyright law or the seven elements of common law fraud. With each pursuit, however, we can take examples (experiments on the one hand, cases on the other) and study them to induce truths about the subject matter. Explanatory synthesis uses induction to find principles of interpretation and application of legal rules from a sample of cases. Therefore, you should proceed with explanatory synthesis in a scientific manner:

THE PROCESS OF EXPLANATORY SYNTHESIS	
Read cases and look for common facts and common outcomes	Group cases by facts Divide groups of cases by outcome
Review the groups to find the factors or public policies that make the difference in the outcome	Reconcile cases that have different outcomes; what policy or theme or factor determined the outcome in these cases Reconcile cases that have the same outcome on different facts; what common policy or theme or factors brought about the same outcome on different facts

THE PROCESS OF EXPLANATORY SYNTHESIS	
Write principles of interpretation that explain your findings	Phrase your principles of interpretation in rule language; your principles should sound like new interpretive rules for the main rules Often you can use interpretive rules as principles that tie together multiple authorities. The authors of existing interpretive rules no doubt wrote them after carefully examining the cases and inducing general principles from the cases. There is no requirement that you always have to come up with brand new principles
Cite the cases that support your principles of interpretation with parentheticals that provide facts or other information about each case	Parentheticals should contain enough information to illustrate how the individual case supports the general principle you have laid out **Parentheticals allow you to use shorthands and abbreviated phrases to save space,** *e.g.*, *Haley*, 12 W.2d at 23 (hitting dog was provocation; claim denied); *Bijou*, 11 W.2d at 787 (same)
When you draft the Application section, apply the principles of interpretation to your own facts; as a general rule, do not apply individual cases to your facts	Applying principles to facts will make your analysis more convincing; you have spelled out the connections to be made between the authorities and then followed through and showed how the principles learned from a study of the authorities determines the outcome of the case at hand **The exception to this rule is when you have one or two fabulous cases that are worthy of individual attention in the Explanation section; these should be discussed individually in the Application section, whether as support or to distinguish them**

You should think of explanatory synthesis as your "value-added" to the rule. It is where you digest the relevant authorities and derive from them one or more principles of interpretation for application of the rule. These principles are derived from common factual elements, policies, or themes found in the cases and other authorities that are relevant to the interpretation.

Optimally, however, you should strive to identify a policy or theme that underlies the earlier authorities and that resonates with and defines the applicable rule and the particular area of law in which the rule is found.

A principle of interpretation that is derived from the central meaning, common ground, public policy, or theme behind a group of earlier cases where the rule was applied is probative of how the rule properly is to be interpreted and applied in cases in the present and future, such as your own. Furthermore, when you apply this principle to the facts of your client's case in the application section, the results will be more reliable than if you simply were to compare one at a time the earlier case to the facts of the client's case.

For example, if all the dog injury cases in your jurisdiction can be tied together with the theme that "the law provides a remedy for injuries suffered when the victim is acting peaceably and the dog is not," then use this as your explanation of the rule, followed by indicative reference to examples of how this theme is played out in the earlier authorities. (Note that no case may have said this precise phrase; rather, this is your synthesis of the relevant authorities). This technique tells the reader how the rule has worked in your jurisdiction in the past, and how it should work again in the future. This is much more useful to the reader than simply writing a paragraph on each case, even if you conclude each paragraph with: "Once again, plaintiff recovered because the victim was acting peaceably, and the dog was not."

It is this kind of digested analysis of the cases that is missing from the average lawyer's explanation section, yet this is what is important to an understanding of how the rule works.

TAKE NOTE!

Do not be fooled by the fact that judges do not always synthesize the cases they discuss in judicial opinions when they attempt to explain how the rules work. This is not an indication that unsynthesized explanation sections are superior; on the contrary, it is an indication that the purpose of judicial opinions is to adjudicate cases not to educate readers about how the law works. Judges want to explain their opinion, not educate readers about the law. Any education that seeps out, just like any rule-making that occurs in a judicial opinion, is a by-product of the actual purpose which is to resolve and adjudicate a problem in a lawsuit.

The writers of treatises, on the other hand, do have the primary goal of educating readers about how the rules work. Thus, as you will see when you read treatises in the course of your research, the authors do synthesize the cases to induce from them truths about the area and topic of law that the authors are writing about. You may only need to write a micro-treatise on the small bit of law that governs the liability of a dog owner for his dog's bites, but your job is to educate your reader as to how that law works, so follow the path of the treatise writer and synthesize the cases.

Secondary authorities may state principles of interpretation and application directly — the authors of treatises, hornbooks, restatements, and law reviews go to great lengths to digest and make sense of the law for the reader — but judicial opinions often do not. The factual details and holdings from a group of individual cases do not in and of themselves define the category of situations that will satisfy the standards of the rule or a particular element or factor of the rule and what categories of situations will not. The factual details of cases often are exciting to write about, but presenting a laundry list of these details is not much better than presenting photocopies of the cases themselves to your reader. This approach may prove that you have read the cases, but your reader is looking for something more from you: some ***analysis***, or the reasons why certain kinds of cases have satisfied the rule in the past and will again in the future, while others did not and will not.

Hopefully, it is becoming clear that the goal of the explanation section is to explain how the law works in several relevant indicative situations without making it appear that each case you cite or discuss is a law unto itself. A case is not a rule; it is an example of a situation where a rule applied and produced a specific outcome. A line of precedent should not look like an obstacle course to get through before victory can be won. The cases to use in the explanation section are those that are most indicative of how the courts have applied the rule to facts that are relevant to the case at hand. The questions to ask yourself when drafting this section are: "Does this case add something new to my explanation of the rule?" and "Will my explanation be weaker if the reader does not know about this case?" If the answer to both questions is "no," leave the case out.

Where the individual facts of the authorities you are using are important, ***case parentheticals*** are the primary option that you can use to present some key facts. Consider, for example, our use of parentheticals several pages ago when we discussed the <u>Nelson</u>, <u>Siewerth</u>, <u>Messa</u>, and <u>Beckert</u> cases. In addition, consider using the "<u>compare</u> . . . <u>and</u> . . . <u>with</u> . . . <u>and</u>" format of citation to make the kind of connections you need to make to further reinforce how the rule works in various situations. (For more information, consider the information on parentheticals in our Good Use of Cases <u>Tip Sheet</u>.)

When you explain how the rule works in the various situations represented by your cases, you should bring to the forefront the facts and circumstances that make the ***positive cases*** (the cases where the result is the same as what you predict your client's result will be in your thesis) sound more like your client's case than the ***negative cases*** (the cases where the result goes the other way from what you predict in your thesis). This technique is called ***analogizing*** to the positive cases and ***distinguishing*** the negative cases, and it is a technique you also will use in the application section. Synthesis aids this process because you can link together a number of positive authorities that stand for a proposition that supports your thesis, and you also can link together a number of negative authorities that do not support your thesis and show a common reason (facts, law, or policy) why each of them should not control the outcome of the instant case. If you do a good job of it, the reader is more likely to agree with your thesis.

C.   Comparing unsynthesized and synthesized explanation sections

You may already know what ***unsynthesized*** explanation sections look like, because you can find them in many of the legal opinions you have been reading. An unsynthesized explanation section takes the reader on a historical walking tour of the cases that have interpreted the rule. We will attempt to show the difference between an unsynthesized explanation section and a synthesized section in the following examples.

Example 1:

One element of adverse possession is "exclusive possession" of the disputed land. Assume that you have already stated the rule for adverse possession, and now you are proceeding to address this particular element (sub-rule) of "exclusive possession," which is at issue in your case.

UNSYNTHESIZED EXPLANATION

In <u>Flowers</u>, the claimant cleared a road and cut down trees and used the land for his own purposes for ten years. He even built a fence, but the neighbors who owned the land pulled down the fence. The court held that the possession was exclusive anyway because the neighbors did not move back onto the land to use it after taking down the fence. <u>Flowers</u>, 979 S.W.2d at 470.

In <u>Conaway</u>, the claimant had no fence. He used the disputed land to build a shed and a horseshoe pit, and he put a little fountain on the land. He cut the grass and maintained the land and the improvement he had put on the land. His neighbor, who actually owned the land, came over and pitched horseshoes from time to time, and may have cut the grass once or twice in ten years, but these visits were sporadic. The claimant was the only one to make use of the land for ten years. The court held this to be exclusive. <u>Conaway</u>, 972 S.W.2d at 445.

In <u>Witt</u>, the claimant had a fence around the disputed land. Although the true owner of the land testified that he thought he could use the disputed land any time he wanted, the evidence revealed that the claimant was the only person who used the land. <u>Witt</u>, 845 S.W.2d at 667. Therefore, the claimant proved that his possession was "exclusive." <u>Id</u>.

Instead, this is how you could present the same information using a ***synthesized*** explanation section:

SYNTHESIZED EXPLANATION

Exclusive possession in Tennessee refers to situations where the claimant is the exclusive user of the land rather than to situations where the claimant has taken action to exclude other people from coming on the land. See Flowers, 979 S.W.2d at 470 (finding exclusive possession where claimants were only ones to use land for ten year period); Witt, 845 S.W.2d at 667 (same); Conaway, 972 S.W.2d at 445 (finding that claimants were principal users of land because true owner only made sporadic visits). Exclusive is used as an adjective to mean that the claimant is the principal user, rather than as a verb meaning to exclude. See generally Flowers, 979 S.W.2d at 470; Witt, 845 S.W.2d at 667; Conaway, 972 S.W.2d at 445. Actions that might exclude others, such as fence building, do not determine whether a possession is exclusive. Compare Witt, 845 S.W.2d at 667 (claimant had fence), with Conaway, 972 S.W.2d at 445 (claimant had no fence), and Flowers, 979 S.W.2d at 470 (claimant built fence, but owners removed it). Total exclusion is not necessary, because the true owner can make sporadic visits to the land without defeating an adverse possession claim. See Conaway, 972 S.W.2d at 445 (sporadic visits by true owner to play horseshoes and cut grass did not defeat exclusive possession of claimant); Flowers, 979 S.W.2d at 470 (owners' tearing down of claimant's fence did not defeat exclusive possession because true owners did not take over parcel for own use).

The difference between the two methods is that in the unsynthesized explanation section the reader learns a lot of interesting details from the cases but never hears about the underlying principles of interpretation that would help the law-trained reader apply this element to all future situations. The focus of the unsynthesized explanation section is on the cases, not on the principles or themes of interpretation that the cases support. A devoted law-trained reader may be able to ponder your history of the cases and draw her own conclusions about the categories of situations that will satisfy the rule, and those that will not, but most readers would prefer you to take the time to think this through and present a complete analysis of how this element of the rule works.

The synthesized explanation section, in contrast, focuses the reader's attention on the principles of interpretation and application that can be discerned from the cases. This section resembles a small scale treatise on this particular element of the adverse possession rule. Factual details are presented when they are necessary to draw connections between cases and to distinguish positive cases from negative cases. (In our example, we have used parentheticals to communicate factual details; however, if a case is particularly relevant, you might include the same information in text and still produce a synthesized explanation.) A law-trained reader that reads this section will not have to wonder about the categories of situations that satisfy this element of the rule.

Example 2:

In Connecticut, the elements of money had and received are: (1) Receipt of money; (2) by mistake; (3) under circumstances that render the retention of the money unjust. Again, assume that you have already stated this rule and have focused attention on the third element, whether retention of the money was unjust:

UNSYNTHESIZED EXPLANATION

In <u>First Federal Bank</u>, defendant Stevens received an unexpected wire transfer from the plaintiff Bank. 678 N.E.2d at 237. The court granted summary judgment to Stevens, allowing him to retain the funds, because Stevens was entitled to the mistakenly transferred sum as an offset of a judgment he had obtained against the Bank in an earlier lawsuit. The court held that the prior debt gave just cause for Stevens to retain the funds. <u>Id.</u>

In ATI, 778 N.E.2d at 44-45, defendant Adams had a potential claim against ATI, but no action had been filed and no judgment entered. Through a fortuitous mistake, Adams received a wire transfer from ATI that was intended for Adams's replacement on a construction project. ATI immediately informed Adams of the mistake, but Adams refused to relinquish the funds. The court held that there was no justification for this retention. <u>Id.</u>

Blue Cross, 688 N.E.2d at 566-68, shows the effect of time and laches on the unjust enrichment evaluation. Defendant Carson was a regular beneficiary of payments from Blue Cross for medical expenses. The case arose from a mistaken quarterly payment by Blue Cross of three *years* of benefits to Carson instead of three months. Blue Cross did not notice the mistake until a year later; by then, Carson had spent the money on his medical care and nursing home expenses. The court refused to order Carson to reimburse Blue Cross, because Carson had a valid expectation of indefinite quarterly payments from Blue Cross, and had changed his position drastically in reliance on his good faith belief that he was entitled to whatever payments he received from Blue Cross, no matter if they may have been larger or smaller than the average quarterly payment.

A *synthesized* approach to this explanation section might look like the following:

SYNTHESIZED EXPLANATION

Connecticut case law has demonstrated the importance of a present obligation from the transferor to the transferee in determining whether the transferee's retention of the funds is unjust. See First Federal Bank, 678 N.E.2d at 237 (finding no unjust enrichment where transferor had present obligation); Blue Cross, 688 N.E.2d at 566-68 (same); ATI, 778 N.E.2d at 44-45 (finding unjust enrichment where transferor had no present obligation). If there is an outstanding debt due between the transferor and the transferee, the fact that the transferor did not intend to pay the debt at the time of the transfer does not prevent the transferee from justly retaining the funds it fortuitously received. See First Federal Bank, 678 N.E.2d at 237; ATI, 778 N.E.2d at 44-45. Even if the funds were not all due at the time of transfer, the expectation of receipt of funds through an existing account or payment scheme can render the retention just. See Blue Cross, 688 N.E.2d at 566-67 (finding of unjust enrichment was buttressed by transferor's laches).

As in example 1, the unsynthesized explanation section focuses on the cases themselves while the synthesized explanation section focuses on the principles of interpretation and application that can be derived from the cases. You may notice that many of the individual facts from the cases are left out of the synthesized explanation section. Facts such as the horseshoe pit and shed in one adverse possession case and the wire transfers in two of the money had and received cases are only relevant if they tell the reader something about how the rule properly is applied and how the facts affected the outcome produced by the application. Because these facts did not affect the application of the rule and the outcome of this application, they were omitted from the synthesized account entirely. The facts about fences in the three adverse possession cases and the facts about debts and current obligations in the three money had and received cases were relevant to an understanding of how the rule works, so these facts were included in parentheticals in the synthesized version. Arguably, that information could have been included in the text, and that may be a valid choice when your own facts are particularly analogous to (or distinguishable from) the factual scenarios raised in the cases.

A synthesized method is shorter in terms of using up fewer pages out of your page limit than the unsynthesized method. But this result only is one reason to use explanatory synthesis, not the best reason. It is not just a time and space-saving device; it makes the reader's comprehension of the situation clearer and your analysis and conclusions stronger.

Explanatory synthesis also has a positive effect on the application section, discussed in section IV, below. If the facts and policies of the cases are synthesized in this way, it makes it easier to compare the client's situation to the category of prior situations that satisfy the rule that are defined by the authorities. You will not write an application section that says,

> "As in Flowers, our claimant had a partial fence . . . . Unlike in Witt, the fence did not go all the way around the disputed parcel; rather . . . ."

which make it seem like the cases are the rule, rather than the cases standing as individual examples of situations where the rule was applied to produce a certain outcome. Your application section instead might state that,

> "Claimant and her predecessor in interest were the only persons to use the disputed parcel for fourteen years. Therefore, they will

satisfy the exclusive possession requirement."

Using the above example on money had and received, it would be simple to write an application section that states,

"In the instant case, there was no outstanding debt or payment scheme to justify the defendant's retention of the funds,"

and thus to apply the rule to the client's facts in a short, straightforward manner.

What you are doing in the process of explanatory synthesis is setting up your Application section so that you can apply the principles induced from the cases and to the client's facts, and not applying cases — thus, you avoid perpetuating the myth that cases are rules unto themselves instead of the truth that cases are simply examples of situations where the actual rules applied to produce a concrete outcome. The cases you would consider citing and discussing in the Application section only should be ones that are so close to your client's facts that you must spend time analogizing to them or distinguishing them. On average, you may not have cases of this nature to discuss and you will not need to cite any cases in the Application section (*see* <u>section IV</u> below).

PRACTICE POINTER

Increasing the *n* of your samples
Scientists and statisticians rejoice: One huge advantage to explanatory synthesis over the other forms of explanation is that you are able to drastically increase the *n* (the number) of your examples, namely cases, when you are inducing principles of interpretation and application from the sample group. Case-by-case presentation tests the patience of your readers — your busy, stressed out, law-trained readers — such that it is inadvisable to present more than three or four cases in any given explanation section. That is a very small statistical sample, especially when you consider that an established rule of law may have been applied in scores of cases all of which are available to you in the sample pool. Explanatory synthesis is very economical in its use of words both in the statement of the principle and in the use of parentheticals to provide illustrative details, and you can drastically up the number of cases from which you derive your principles of interpretation and application.

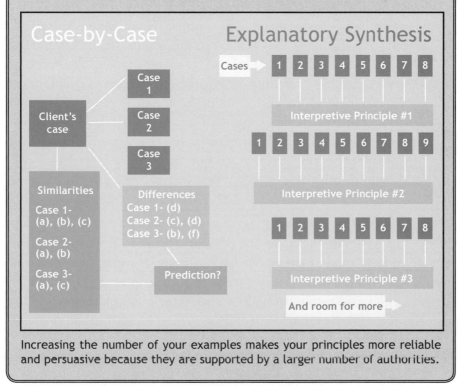

Increasing the number of your examples makes your principles more reliable and persuasive because they are supported by a larger number of authorities.

D.   Use of secondary authorities

The explanation section also might include discussion of secondary authorities —scholarly works that interpret or explain the law. These authorities cannot control the outcome of your case but they can be used to help persuade the reader that you are on the right track with your thesis. In other words, secondary authorities can be used as support for a principle that you are deriving from the cases in your jurisdiction. If you are joined by one or more scholars in drawing the conclusion that there is a relevant underlying theme that ties together most if not all of the prior cases, then reference to the work of these scholars will make your explanation section more persuasive than if you were to write your own personal thoughts on the same topic and present these thoughts by themselves.

An example of the use of secondary sources to explain a rule is demonstrated in the following paragraph:

> The underlying public policy behind the Texas rule is that persons "attacked by a domesticated animal when the person is acting peaceably and not directly threatening the animal" shall recover from the owner of the animals. See Chester A. Arthur, Texas Animal Laws 234 (1953). Although Professor Arthur was referring to the Roaming Livestock Damage Act, Tex. Agric. Code Ann. § 222.1234 (Vernon 1944), there is no practical difference between livestock that are roaming loose on the property and domestic animals, such as dogs, that are encountered on the property. See Arthur at 235. The law provides a remedy for injuries suffered when "the victim is acting peaceably and the dog is not." Mary M. McDermott, When a Best Friend Bites: Dog Bite Liability in Texas, 45 Tex. L. Rev. 122-23 (1979).

This paragraph discusses the policies at work in the situation that mitigate in favor of your thesis. We made a point of using secondary authorities that discuss these policies rather than just spinning them out of our own mind and recollection. It is important to support every statement about the law by referring to authority, even if you are talking about public policy.

Given the priority of primary controlling authority in legal analysis, in legal writing, you should discuss the cases from the applicable jurisdiction in your explanation section **before** you present secondary authorities that further support the principles of interpretation you have derived from these cases. The secondary authorities should be used to buttress the principles found in the controlling case law, not to supersede them.

E.   Explanation of rules not found in cases

Thus far, we have been focusing on rules found in cases. Of course, you also will be writing about legal rules that come from constitutions, statutes, and administrative rules and regulations. The same process applies, because to explain the rule that is found in a constitution or statute or regulation, you still will use cases as examples of specific situations where that rule was applied and secondary authorities that explain how the rule should be interpreted. If the statute or regulation is fairly new and there are no reported cases where that statute or regulation was applied and no secondary sources explaining the rule, you will use the principles of statutory interpretation discussed in Chapter 4 and your own powers of legal rhetoric.

Consider the following two examples dealing with the fictional 1999 Nevada Pit Bull Control Law and its effect on your client's case. Assume that your client owns a Pit Bull Terrier, but this dog was not the dog that caused the injury to the victim (you will recall from prior examples that client's Doberman Pinscher was involved in the incident). The statute provides in pertinent part:

> Pit bull terriers pose a significantly greater risk of danger to the public than other dogs . . . . There is no way to insure the safety of persons coming into contact with a pit bull whether or not the person provokes the dog. Therefore, an owner of a pit bull shall be strictly liable for all personal injuries caused to humans by his dog(s) regardless of whether the victim provoked the dog(s) or not.

In the absence of interpretive authorities, you might write a rule, explanation, and application section that would look like something like this:

Rule, Explanation, and Application sections when there are no authorities interpreting the statute	In 1999, the Nevada Legislature passed the Pit Bull Control Law, Nev. Rev. Stat. § 222.5678 (1999), which provides in pertinent part that:

> Pit bull terriers pose a significantly greater risk of danger to the public than other dogs . . . . There is no way to insure the safety of persons coming into contact with a pit bull whether or not the person provokes the dog. Therefore, an owner of a pit bull shall be strictly liable for all personal injuries caused to humans by his dog(s) regardless of whether the victim provoked the dog(s) or not.

No case or commentator has interpreted this section, and nothing in the legislative history sheds light on the meaning of this section of the statute. Although on its face this section contains an ambiguity as to whether the owner of a Pit Bull is strictly liable for injuries caused by any of his dogs, Pit Bulls or others, the statute otherwise is clear that the purpose of the provision is to protect the public from the special dangers presented by Pit Bulls. It defies the meaning of this text and the logic of the statute to assert that the provision imposes strict liability on a dog owner simply because he owns a Pit Bull who had nothing to do with the injuries inflicted in the case at hand. Because the plaintiff was injured by defendant's Doberman, not his Pit Bull, this statute will have no effect on this case and will not cause defendant to be strictly liable for plaintiff's injuries.

If there are authorities that have addressed the interpretation and application of the statute in ways that are relevant to your analysis, you would discuss these authorities in the following manner:

Rule, Explanation, and Application sections when there are authorities interpreting the statute	In 1999, the Nevada Legislature passed the Pit Bull Control Law, Nev. Rev. Stat. § 222.5678 (1999), which provides in pertinent part that: Pit bull terriers pose a significantly greater risk of danger to the public than other dogs. . . . There is no way to insure the safety of persons coming into contact with a pit bull whether or not the person provokes the dog. Therefore, an owner of a pit bull shall be strictly liable for all personal injuries caused to humans by his dog(s) regardless of whether the victim provoked the dog(s) or not. Although on its face the statute contains an ambiguity as to whether the owner of a Pit Bull is strictly liable for injuries caused by any of his dogs, Pit Bulls or others, the statute has been limited to attacks by Pit Bulls on humans. See Chuy v. Taylor, 887 P.2d 246, 248 (Nev. 2000). A dog owner will not be strictly liable for an attack by one of his other dogs, a non-Pit Bull, simply because he owns a Pit Bull who had nothing to do with the injuries inflicted in the case at hand. See id.; see also Carlos R. Rivera, Current Developments in Nevada Law, 66 UNLV L. Rev. 322-23 (2000). Therefore, this statute will have no effect on this case and will not cause defendant to be strictly liable for plaintiff's injuries.

V.   APPLICATION SECTION

The Application section is where you actually apply the rule to your client's facts and show how the rule will work in your client's situation. If you are writing an informative objective work such as an office memorandum, you will explain how you think the client will fare based on your analysis of the law. If you are writing a persuasive piece of advocacy, you will use this section to argue exactly why your client wins when the law is applied to the facts.

In the Application section, you must make or reject the connection between your client's situation and the situations in the authorities you are relying on in support of your thesis. This section presents the second half of the logical reasoning process that you began in the explanation section; it takes the general principles derived from cases and applies them to a new set of facts, your client's. Thus, it connects the fruits of inductive reasoning back into the deductive rule-based reasoning paradigm. The Application section also continues the process of analogical reasoning when you have found one or more cases that are so close to the client's facts that you must spend some time analogizing to or distinguishing them from your client's facts in order to drive home your thesis.

A typical case-by-case, **unsynthesized** Explanation section will produce a typical case-by-case Application section that looks like this:

APPLICATION SECTION FOLLOWING AN *UNSYNTHESIZED* EXPLANATION SECTION

In the instant case, there is no dispute that the defendant's dog attacked and caused injury to Mrs. Robinson, his neighbor, when she walked out of her apartment and bumped into the dog with her shopping bag. Thus, the first two elements of this cause of action are established. In reference to the third element, lack of provocation, Mrs. Robinson did nothing to present a serious threat to the dog, let alone strike the dog, in contrast to the plaintiff in Smithy. Mrs. Robinson may have swung her shopping bag near the dog in a careless manner, but this is a far cry from the beating that the dog in Smithy received before it attacked the victim in that case. Like the plaintiff in Johnson, Mrs. Robinson was using a public hallway that led to the front door of the apartment building. See Johnson, 789 S.W.2d at 237. According to Johnson, walking in a hallway is not a provocative action, id., and it certainly is no more provocative than mistakenly opening the wrong door of an apartment where the dog is found, as was the case in Russell. See 797 S.W.2d at 44.

Although the postman in Johnson was acting in the ordinary course of his daily employment duties, whereas Mrs. Robinson was doing something outside of her ordinary employment activities, this should not be viewed as a legally significant difference precluding plaintiff from recovery. A decision in favor of Mrs. Robinson, moreover, furthers the policy of allowing recovery where the victim was acting peaceably and the dog was not. See Merriweather, 90 Apex L. Rev. at 666.

If, however, you used explanatory synthesis to combine authorities in the Explanation, the Application section will apply the principles of interpretation derived from the common facts or themes of the earlier cases, rather than simply comparing the facts of the instant case first to one earlier case, then the next, then the next, and so on. You will explain how the common underlying theme is furthered by your interpretation of how the rule will apply in your case, or you will distinguish the earlier cases because of their common facts or policies that are not present in the instant case.

Consider the following modified application section that follows a **synthesized** Explanation section:

APPLICATION SECTION FOLLOWING A *SYNTHE-SIZED* EXPLANATION SECTION

Here, there is no dispute that defendant's dog attacked and caused injury to Mrs. Robinson, his neighbor, when she walked out of her apartment and bumped into the dog with her shopping bag. Thus, the first two elements of this cause of action are established. As for the third element, lack of provocation, the underlying theme of the Texas cases is that a plaintiff who is peaceably going about her business and is attacked by an aggressive dog will recover, while a plaintiff who picked a fight with the dog and caused injury to the dog first will not recover. Mrs. Robinson did not pick a fight with defendant's dog. She did nothing to present a serious threat to the dog, let alone intentionally strike the dog. Mrs. Robinson may have been careless in swinging her shopping bag near the dog, but that is a far cry from beating the dog. A decision in favor of Mrs. Robinson, moreover, furthers the policy of allowing recovery where the victim was acting peaceably and the dog was not.

This explanatory synthesis and application of synthesized principles only works if it is fair to link all of the prior cases together under the theme of "a plaintiff recovers when the plaintiff was acting peaceably and the dog was not." You cannot invent a common theme that is not present in the earlier cases, nor can you assume common facts that are not discussed in the cases. However, if you can discern a common set of facts and theme or policy that is important to the understanding of how the rule should work, it is helpful to your reader to point this out.

There is no bar on referencing or citing cases in the Application section. In fact if you are going to use analogical reasoning to link your case to an earlier case that is on all fours with yours, or use converse analogical reasoning to distinguish an earlier case that is very close to yours, then you will have to refer to (or cite to) the earlier cases, as shown here:

APPLICATION SECTION USING ANALOGICAL AND CONVERSE ANALOGICAL REASONING

The two leading cases in Texas addressing dog bites suffered by mail carriers, Johnson and Beckert, provide guidance for the resolution of this action. Plaintiff Newman's case is like Beckert, in which the mail carrier opened the outer screen door of the dog owner's home and encountered the dog. The dog gave chase and bit the mail carrier while he was trying to escape. Similarly, Newman, a mail carrier, opened the outer storm door of the home to place a parcel inside, out of the rain. Defendant Wiley's dog approached Newman and chased her from the front steps of the house to the sidewalk. While Newman was attempting to evade the dog, it bit her on the leg. As in Beckert, Newman did not provoke the dog and thus should be allowed to recover. See 199 N.E.2d at 815.

Johnson does not control this case. There, the mail carrier first used her mail bag as a shield, but then used it to hit the dog several times. Despite being hit by the heavy mail bag, the dog was not deterred and responded by biting the mail carrier. Johnson was denied recovery because the mail carrier initiated this physical attack on the dog, and only thereafter did the dog bite. See 789 S.W.2d at 237 (determining that initiating physical contact with a dog constitutes provocation). Because Newman did not make any contact with the dog, unwelcome or otherwise, before the bite, she should recover from Wiley for the injuries inflicted by his dog.

While referencing or citing cases in the Application section is acceptable where it is necessary or prudent to do so, the point here is that is it may be ***unnecessary*** to refer or cite to cases ***unless*** you are engaging in the direct kind of one-on-one analogical reasoning shown above. When you are drafting the Explanation section, the explanatory synthesis methodology requires you to cite the cases from which you are inducing principles relating to the proper interpretation and application of the rule. It is those principles that should be applied to the client's facts in the Application section, not the individual case samples from which the principles were induced. Analogical reasoning is an exception to this basic principle, and a useful exception when you have one or two cases that are close enough to the client's facts to warrant special attention. In addition, if you want to draw your reader's attention to a specific legal authority that supports your thesis, then you should cite to it, whether or not you refer to the authority in the text of your analysis.

VI.   THESIS RESTATED AS A CONCLUSION

Finally, as a general matter you should complete your discussion of an issue by restating your thesis as a conclusion. This is not the most critical part of the discussion, but we find that it makes a difference to the reader of legal writing to have that one sentence at the end that brings closure to the discussion.

The conclusion you make can be one sentence, and it can come at the very end of the last paragraph of your application section. As an example, the thesis as conclusion line of the example we have been working with might be:

Therefore, defendant Wiley will be required to compensate Client for her dog bite injuries in this case.

We do not intend to imply that the thesis restated as conclusion is a throwaway. It often is a single sentence, simply there to say this section is completed. But you can spend more time with a conclusion and use it to advance your argument one more step, or to make a smooth transition to the next topic. This one is up to you, and you are limited only by your own creativity.

VII.   IDENTIFYING MULTIPLE ISSUES

So far in this appendix, we have been discussing the treatment of an individual issue in your client's case. The dog bite example with which we have been working boils down to one issue — whether the plaintiff provoked the dog. We mentioned in the Rule and Application sections the other two elements, but only so far as to point out that they are not in dispute. If that is the case, then there is no need to have a separate discussion of each element. Yet, we did not ignore them, because you must include in your writing some discussion of each required element or factor of the rule that applies to the case. But a single sentence is all the treatment these undisputed elements required.

In practice, this is an unusual position in which to be. More often than not, you will have many more than one issue (or element) to write about. In the real world, a client or supervisor will come into your office with a problem, and you will have to identify exactly what issues are implicated by the facts of the situation as you know them. Each problem that reaches your desk likely will raise more than one issue, and each issue will have at least one rule that applies to it. In addition, each rule that applies can and often will have multiple elements or factors, each of which can present other sub-issues for discussion. An element or factor of a rule can have a sub-rule that has elements or factors, some of which will require separate treatment.

It can get fairly complicated, but the TREAT format is flexible enough to accommodate that much complexity.

In order to determine the number of issues you have to treat, consider the following:

A.   What are the separate legal questions you have to answer?

Most problems your client will bring to you will present more than one legal question to answer. If the client literally asks two questions, or one question that will involve the discussion of two unrelated legal issues — such as what separate causes of action might the plaintiff bring against the client based on the facts — then each question presents a major issue in your discussion. In an outline, the answers (your theses, or conclusions) to these questions will appear as the major headings. In other words, you should plan to state a thesis on each major issue (or element) as a heading of the discussion on that issue.

In the single issue discussion above, the major issue was: "Is the dog owner liable for Client's injuries?" We translated this into the thesis heading: "The dog owner will be liable for Client's dog bite injuries because Client did not provoke the dog." If there were two or more possible claims that your client might bring against the dog owner, your writing would have two or more major issues and major theses on these issues. For example, Roman I might be: "The dog owner will be liable to Client under common law dog bite liability standards," Roman II might be: "The dog owner will be liable to Client under a theory of negligence," and Roman III might be: "The dog owner will not be strictly liable to Client under the Nevada Pit Bull Control Law." Each major issue must be handled in a separate TREAT discussion.

B.   Which elements or factors of the rules and sub-rules of the rules are at issue?

A separate "TREAT" discussion is necessary to address each legal question (issue or sub-issue). This means that each part of the problem — each legal issue raised or element in dispute — is really its *own* issue. If the rule that governs the issue at hand has one basic requirement, and thus one element, it may be handled in a single discussion of Thesis, Rule, Explanation, Application and Thesis as conclusion. Similarly, if the rule has multiple elements or factors, but only one is in dispute, you also may discuss the entire rule in one TREAT discussion, as in our dog bite example above, where provocation was the only element of the rule that was in dispute. But, as is more likely, if the rule itself presents multiple legal questions to answer, it will require more than one TREAT discussion. For present purposes, where the separate legal questions that must be answered are all based on elements or sub-parts of a **single rule**, we will refer to yourt analyses as "**sub-TREATs.**" This becomes important when you consider how to organize your thoughts and research findings in writing.

For example, if there was a serious question whether the defendant "owned" this Doberman Pinscher within the meaning of the law — maybe it was a stray, and the defendant had just been feeding it each day — then you would have to include some analysis of this element of the tort in addition to addressing whether the plaintiff provoked the dog or not.

What we are emphasizing here is that you **must cover every element or factor of a rule in your discussion.** That said, if the element or factor is established without question in your case because you are told that by the person assigning the project or because your opponent specifically admits it, the discussion of that element or factor does not require a full-blown TREAT analysis. One sentence (which we call a *roadmap sentence*) can convey the required information: for example, you might simply state in conjunction with stating the rule itself that: "Defendant concedes that he is the owner of the dog that injured the plaintiff and, thus, this element is not in dispute."

When multiple elements of a rule are in dispute and present separate issues for sub-"treatment," you should consider how you want to present your analysis. Consider which elements are the most important to your analysis — these should be discussed first even if they don't come first in a court's articulation of the rule. Also consider whether and how many sub-rules must come into play.

For present purposes, we are grouping issues under the main rules that spawned them, meaning that we are attempting to get you to think about each specific question you need to address, whether it is a main legal issue (such as "dog bite liability") or a sub-issue (such as "lack of provocation"). **Each of these matters will necessitate a separate "TREAT" analysis** — in the one case, a main TREAT and in the other a sub-TREAT.

VIII. STRUCTURING THE DISCUSSION OF MULTIPLE ISSUES

An obvious question should flow from the above: how do you organize a section of a memo or brief when multiple issues or elements are in question? If you have multiple elements or factors at issue and sub-rules that present multiple issues to answer, you must organize your writing so that each part of the major rule or sub-rule is discussed in a TREAT-like format. In the case of a rule with multiple elements, a "**sub-TREAT**" on a single element will contain your <u>T</u>hesis on how that element will work in your client's case, any sub-<u>R</u>ule of law concerning that element, an <u>E</u>xplanation of what that element means and how that element works in various situations, an <u>A</u>pplication of that element or the rule concerning that element to your client's situation, and your <u>T</u>hesis on that element restated as a conclusion. Within a sub-TREAT, if a sub-Rule on an element itself presents multiple issues, these issues must be resolved in their own TREAT, too, which we call a **sub-sub-TREAT**. **For example**, a dog bite liability issue might raises two issues for sub-TREATS: (1) ownership, and (2) provocation of the dog; and the issue of provocation itself might raise two additional issues for sub-sub-TREATs: whether the victim (a) presented a physical threat to the dog, (b) in a manner likely to provoke the average dog to attack.

Take a moment to consider the structure of the following outline of a discussion where the rule on the major issue has two elements, and the rules governing the two elements of the rule on the major issue also have multiple elements — a scenario that is all too likely. We have highlighted the Thesis heading, sub-Thesis headings, and sub-sub-Thesis headings that answer all of the issues raised by this scenario:

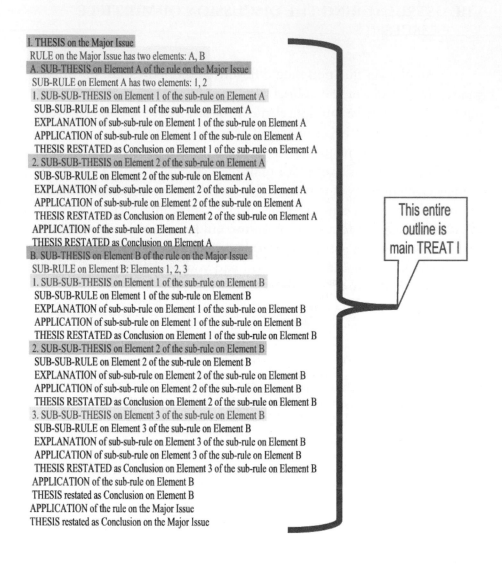

The chart that follows shows the structure of the sub-TREATs. Two sub-TREATs are necessary to address the issues raised by the two elements of the rule on the major issue:

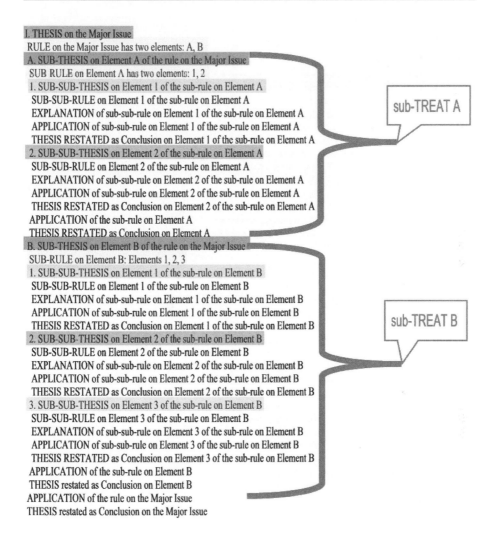

I. THESIS on the Major Issue
RULE on the Major Issue has two elements: A, B
A. SUB-THESIS on Element A of the rule on the Major Issue
SUB RULE on Element A has two elements: 1, 2
1. SUB-SUB-THESIS on Element 1 of the sub-rule on Element A
SUB-SUB-RULE on Element 1 of the sub-rule on Element A
EXPLANATION of sub-sub-rule on Element 1 of the sub-rule on Element A
APPLICATION of sub-sub-rule on Element 1 of the sub-rule on Element A
THESIS RESTATED as Conclusion on Element 1 of the sub-rule on Element A
2. SUB-SUB-THESIS on Element 2 of the sub-rule on Element A
SUB-SUB-RULE on Element 2 of the sub-rule on Element A
EXPLANATION of sub-sub-rule on Element 2 of the sub-rule on Element A
APPLICATION of sub-sub-rule on Element 2 of the sub-rule on Element A
THESIS RESTATED as Conclusion on Element 2 of the sub-rule on Element A
APPLICATION of the sub-rule on Element A
THESIS RESTATED as Conclusion on Element A
B. SUB-THESIS on Element B of the rule on the Major Issue
SUB-RULE on Element B: Elements 1, 2, 3
1. SUB-SUB-THESIS on Element 1 of the sub-rule on Element B
SUB-SUB-RULE on Element 1 of the sub-rule on Element B
EXPLANATION of sub-sub-rule on Element 1 of the sub-rule on Element B
APPLICATION of sub-sub-rule on Element 1 of the sub-rule on Element B
THESIS RESTATED as Conclusion on Element 1 of the sub-rule on Element B
2. SUB-SUB-THESIS on Element 2 of the sub-rule on Element B
SUB-SUB-RULE on Element 2 of the sub-rule on Element B
EXPLANATION of sub-sub-rule on Element 2 of the sub-rule on Element B
APPLICATION of sub-sub-rule on Element 2 of the sub-rule on Element B
THESIS RESTATED as Conclusion on Element 2 of the sub-rule on Element B
3. SUB-SUB-THESIS on Element 3 of the sub-rule on Element B
SUB-SUB-RULE on Element 3 of the sub-rule on Element B
EXPLANATION of sub-sub-rule on Element 3 of the sub-rule on Element B
APPLICATION of sub-sub-rule on Element 3 of the sub-rule on Element B
THESIS RESTATED as Conclusion on Element 3 of the sub-rule on Element B
APPLICATION of the sub-rule on Element B
THESIS restated as Conclusion on Element B
APPLICATION of the rule on the Major Issue
THESIS restated as Conclusion on the Major Issue

sub-TREAT A

sub-TREAT B

Finally, this last chart shows the structure of the sub-sub-TREATs. These were necessary because the rule that answers the issues raised by the sub-TREATs itself had elements that presented issues that needed to be resolved. To resolve issues raised by a sub-Rule you need sub-sub-TREATs:

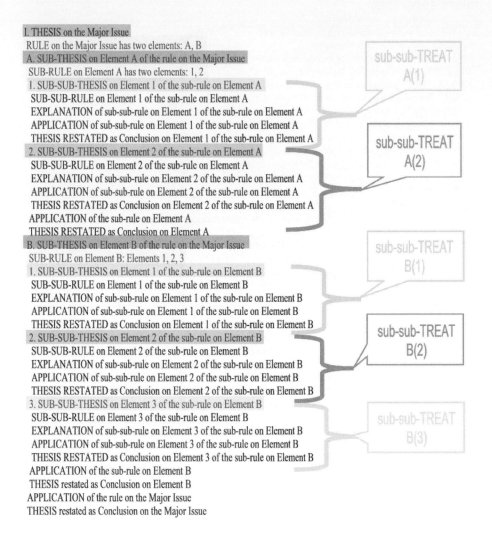

You will note that when a rule presents multiple issues, the sub-TREATment of those issues really takes the place of the "explanation" of the major rule. In other words, the sub-TREATs themselves explain the Rule on the major issue. The same goes for a sub-sub-TREATment of a sub-Rule on an element of a major rule — the sub-sub-TREATs themselves explain the sub-Rule on an element of the main Rule. You write the sub-sub-TREATment as the explanation of the sub-Rule and return to the sub-Rule's TREATment in the Application section.

INDEX

References are to Pages

†